Module F

ESTABLISHING AND SUSTAINING A CONTINUUM OF BEHAVIOR SUPPORT

Module 6 of 6 in *Foundations: A Proactive and Positive Behavior Support System* (3rd ed.)

Randy Sprick
Mike Booher
Paula Rich

© 2014 PACIFIC NORTHWEST PUBLISHING, INC.

The purchaser is granted permission to use, reproduce, and distribute the materials on the CD solely for the purpose of implementing a *Safe & Civil Schools* schoolwide improvement plan. Except as expressly permitted above and under the United States Copyright Act of 1976, no materials in this book may be used, reproduced, or distributed in any form or by any means, electronic or mechanical, without the prior written permission of the publisher.

Published in the United States by
Pacific Northwest Publishing
21 West 6th Ave.
Eugene, Oregon 97401
www.pacificnwpublish.com

ISBN: 978-1-59909-074-0

Part of *Foundations: A Proactive and Positive Behavior Support System* (3rd ed.)
ISBN: 978-1-59909-068-9

Cover by Aaron Graham
Book design and layout by Natalie Conaway

TRENDS is a registered trademark of Pacific Northwest Publishing
in the United States.

Pacific
Northwest
Publishing

Eugene, Oregon | www.pacificnwpublish.com

Any resources and website addresses are provided for reader convenience and were current at the time of publication. Report any broken links to info@pacificnwpublish.com.

CONTENTS

CONTENTS

ABOUT THE AUTHORS

Randy Sprick, Ph.D.

Randy Sprick, Ph.D., has worked as a paraprofessional, teacher, and teacher trainer at the elementary and secondary levels. Author of a number of widely read books on behavior and classroom management, Dr. Sprick is director of *Safe & Civil Schools*, a consulting company that provides inservice programs throughout the country. He and his trainers work with numerous large and small school districts on longitudinal projects to improve student behavior and motivation. Efficacy of that work is documented in peer-reviewed research, and *Safe & Civil Schools* materials are listed on the National Registry of Evidence-Based Programs and Practices (NREPP). Dr. Sprick was the recipient of the 2007 Council for Exceptional Children (CEC) Wallin Lifetime Achievement Award.

Mike Booher, M.Ed.

Mike Booher, M.Ed., worked as a school psychologist and supervisor of psychological services in the Guilford County Schools (North Carolina) for 33 years. While in Guilford, he served for 8 years as a project coordinator, trainer, and coach for Guilford's implementation of the *Safe & Civil Schools* Foundations and CHAMPS programs. He coordinated the district's school-based intervention teams who responded to teacher referrals of students having academic and/or behavioral challenges, and provided training and coordination for the district's intervention services for a school in crisis or a student in a suicidal crisis. From 2000 to 2005, Mr. Booher served as a clinical instructor in School Psychology at UNC–Chapel Hill. He has worked as a national trainer and consultant for *Safe & Civil Schools* since 2005.

ABOUT THE AUTHORS

Paula Rich, B.Mus.Ed., M.Mus.

Paula Rich, B.Mus.Ed., M.Mus., has been a substitute teacher in public schools and was a freelance musician and taught private music lessons for many years in the Boston, Massachusetts, area. Since joining Pacific Northwest Publishing in 2006, she has contributed original stories and poems to the *Read Well* curriculum for second-grade readers and has edited several of Randy Sprick's staff development and behavior management books and papers. She was instrumental in developing TRENDS, Pacific Northwest Publishing's online behavioral data management system, as well as Connections, an online check-and-connect program.

SAFE & CIVIL SCHOOLS

THE SAFE & CIVIL SCHOOLS SERIES is a comprehensive, integrated set of resources designed to help educators improve student behavior and school climate at every level—districtwide, schoolwide, within the classroom, and at the individual intervention level. The findings of decades of research literature have been refined into step-by-step actions that teachers and staff can take to help all students behave responsibly and respectfully.

The hallmark of the *Safe & Civil Schools* model is its emphasis on proactive, positive, and instructional behavior management—addressing behavior before it necessitates correction, collecting data before embarking on interventions, implementing simple corrections before moving to progressively more intensive and time-intrusive ones, and setting a climate of respect for all. As a practical matter, tending to schoolwide and classwide policies, procedures, and interventions is far easier than resorting to more costly, time-intrusive, and individualized approaches.

Foundations and PBIS

Positive Behavioral Interventions and Supports (PBIS) is not a program. According to the U.S. Department of Education, PBIS is simply a framework to help provide "assistance to schools, districts, and states to establish a preventative, positive, multi-tiered continuum of evidence-based behavioral interventions that support the behavioral competence of students" (A. Posny, personal communication, September 7, 2010). That framework perfectly describes *Foundations*. *Foundations* provides instructions for implementing such an approach—with detailed processes and hundreds of examples of specific applications from successful schools. Furthermore, *Foundations* provides step-by-step guidance for involving and unifying an entire district staff to develop behavior support procedures that will prevent misbehavior and increase student connectedness and motivation. *Foundations* moves well beyond a simple matrix into how to guide and inspire staff to take ownership of managing and motivating all students, all the time, every day.

SAFE & CIVIL SCHOOLS

Resources in the series do not take a punitive approach to discipline. Instead, *Safe & Civil Schools* addresses the sources of teachers' greatest power to motivate: through structuring for student success, teaching expectations, observing and monitoring student behavior, and, above all, interacting positively. Because experience directly affects behavior, it makes little sense to pursue only the undesired behavior (by relying on reprimands, for example) and not the conditions (in behavioral theory, the antecedent) that precipitate experience and subsequent behavior.

The *Safe & Civil Schools* Positive Behavioral Interventions and Supports (PBIS) Model is listed in the National Registry of Evidence-based Programs and Practices (NREPP) after review by the Substance Abuse and Mental Health Services Administration (SAMHSA).

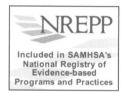

Inclusion in NREPP means that independent reviewers found that the philosophy and procedures behind *Foundations, CHAMPS, Discipline in the Secondary Classroom, Interventions,* and other *Safe & Civil Schools* books and DVDs have been thoroughly researched, that the research is of high quality, and that the outcomes achieved include:

- Higher levels of academic achievement
- Reductions in school suspensions
- Fewer classroom disruptions
- Increases in teacher professional self-efficacy
- Improvement in school discipline procedures

For more information, visit www.nrepp.samhsa.gov.

The most recent evidence of the efficacy of the *Safe & Civil Schools* PBIS Model appeared in the October 2013 issue of *School Psychology Review.* "A Randomized Evaluation of the *Safe and Civil Schools* Model for Positive Behavioral Interventions and Supports at Elementary Schools in a Large Urban School District," by Bryce Ward and Russell Gersten, shows how the *Safe & Civil Schools* PBIS Model improves student behavior and school climate. Thirty-two elementary schools in a large urban school district were randomly assigned to an initial training cohort or a wait-list control group. Results show reduced suspension rates, decreases in problem behavior, and evidence of positive academic gains for the schools in the training cohort.

Observed improvements persisted through the second year of trainings, and once the wait-list control schools commenced *Safe & Civil Schools* training, they experienced similar improvements in school policies and student behavior.

 Download and read the full article at:
www.nasponline.org/publications/spr/index.aspx?vol=42&issue=3

Safe & Civil Schools acknowledges the real power educators have—not in controlling students but in shaping their behavior through affecting every aspect of their experience while they are in school: the physical layout, the way time is structured, arrivals and departures, teaching expected behavior, meaningful relationships with adults, and more. These changes in what adults do can create dramatic and lifelong changes in the behavior and motivation of students.

ACKNOWLEDGMENTS

As lead author, I owe a huge debt to many people who have guided the development and revision of *Foundations* over the past three decades. Betsy Norton, Mickey Garrison, and Marilyn Sprick were instrumental in the development and implementation of *Foundations* long before the publication of the first edition in 1992. Dr. Jan Reinhardtsen received the very first federal grant on the topic of positive behavior support and, with Mickey, implemented the first edition of *Foundations* as the basis for Project CREST in the early and mid-1990s. Jan also came up with *Safe & Civil Schools*, which became the name of our staff development services. Dr. Laura McCullough implemented a brilliant state-level Model School project in Kentucky, followed by the Kentucky Instructional Discipline System (KIDS) project that taught me so much about the importance of training and coaching to assist schools with implementation of both schoolwide and classroom behavior support.

I want to thank my coauthors of the different modules within this edition. Susan Isaacs, Mike Booher, and Jessica Sprick are outstanding trainers of *Foundations*, and their respective expertise has added depth to the content that makes this edition more practical, rich, and fun than previous editions. Paula Rich has provided both organizational skill and writing expertise to weave together a vast amount of content with many school- and district-level examples to create a highly accessible and user-friendly resource.

Thanks to the awesome staff of Pacific Northwest Publishing: Aaron Graham and Natalie Conaway with design, Sara Ferris and K Daniels with editing, Matt Sprick for directing both video and print development, Sam Gehrke for video editing, Robert Consentino and Jake Clifton for camera and sound, and the rest of the Pacific Northwest Publishing and *Safe & Civil Schools* staff—Jackie Hefner, Karen Schell, Sarah Romero, Kimberly Irving, Brandt Schram, Caroline DeVorss, and Marilyn Sprick—for their great work.

Implementation of *Foundations*, *CHAMPS*, and *Interventions* would not have thrived without the skill and dedication of great staff developers and trainers: Tricia Berg, Mike Booher, Phyllis Gamas, Laura Hamilton, Andrea Hanford, Jane Harris, Susan Isaacs, Debbie Jackson, Kim Marcum, Bob McLaughlin, Donna Meers, Carolyn Novelly, Robbie Rowan, Susan Schilt, Tricia Skyles, Pat Somers, Karl Schleich, Jessica Sprick, and Elizabeth Winford as Director of Professional Development.

ACKNOWLEDGMENTS

Fresno Unified School District and Long Beach Unified School District in California allowed us to visit with the Pacific Northwest Publishing video crew to capture the excitement, professionalism, and commitment of school and district personnel. These districts have taught us so much about the importance of common language and district support in creating a sustainable implementation.

Lastly, I want to the thank the schools and districts that have implemented *Foundations* over the years and graciously shared their lessons, posters, staff development activities, forms, and policies that you will find as examples throughout the print and video presentations. These real-world examples will help your implementation process by illustrating how other schools and districts have successfully implemented and sustained *Foundations*.

—R.S.

HOW TO USE FOUNDATIONS

This third edition of *Foundations* is constructed as six modules to accommodate schools that are just beginning their implementation of multi-tiered systems of behavior support (MTSS) as well as schools that already have some, but not all, pieces of behavior support firmly in place. For example, a school may have done great work on improving behavior in the common areas of the school but very little work on intentionally constructing a positive, inviting climate or addressing conflict and bullying in a comprehensive way. This school could go directly to Module C: *Conscious Construction of an Inviting Climate*, and after implementing those strategies, move to Module E: *Improving Safety, Managing Conflict, and Reducing Bullying*.

Each module incorporates multiple resources to assist you: video presentations on DVD, the book you are reading now, and a CD with forms and samples. The videos can guide a building-based leadership team through implementing *Foundations*. The same content is available in print format; we provide eight copies of this book for each module, one for each member of the leadership team. Teams can decide which content delivery form works best for them—video or print.

Each book comes with a CD that contains reproducible forms, examples of policies and procedures from real schools that have implemented *Foundations*, and other implementation resources. The CD also includes PowerPoint presentations that correspond directly to the video and print content. Your leadership team can use these presentations to deliver the most relevant *Foundations* information to the entire staff.

Beginning Behavior Support

For schools and districts that are just beginning with behavior support or are unsure where to begin, we suggest starting with Module A: *Foundations of Behavior Support—A Continuous Improvement Process*. This module is the foundation of *Foundations*. It describes the importance of a well-designed leadership team, a formalized continuous improvement cycle, how to use multiple data sources to drive that cycle, and how to involve and unify the staff in implementation. Without laying this groundwork, any specific work on procedures, such as improving the cafeteria, is unlikely to be effective or sustainable.

Once your team is collecting and analyzing data, you will probably move through Modules B–F (described below) in order. You'll work on the common areas of the school, then positive climate, and so on. Once a module has been implemented, you are not done with that module. For example, after implementing the procedures in Module B for a couple of common areas and a couple of schoolwide policies, such as dress code, you may move on to Module C to work on improving school climate. However, you will concurrently continue to implement Module B procedures for additional common areas and schoolwide policies. Working through all six modules will take about two to five years of development and implementation.

MTSS in Progress

Schools and districts that have been effectively implementing other approaches to PBIS should follow these guidelines when implementing *Foundations*.

You may be able to use the modules in a nonlinear fashion if your school has a highly functional team, uses multiple data sources to involve the entire staff in continuous improvement of behavior support, and has worked to improve several common areas or schoolwide policies. To self-assess where to begin, a resource called the Foundations Implementation Rubric and Summary is included in Appendix A of the book and on the CD for each module. The rubric can help your leadership team assess which modules have information useful to your school at this time and help you make judgments about where to begin. Print the rubric, work through it as a team, and summarize your findings, and you will see patterns emerge. (Instructions are included with the rubric.)

For example, if all the conditions described at the beginning of this paragraph are in place, you will probably find that you are already implementing many of the procedures delineated in Modules A and B. One school may have an urgent need to go directly to Module E because the school has no programs or policies to address conflict and bullying, whereas another school may go directly to Module D because staff are very inconsistent about when and how to use disciplinary referral to the office. Another school may go directly to Module F because their schoolwide structures are relatively well established, but they have yet to address classroom management or the integration of universal, targeted, and intensive interventions.

HOW TO USE FOUNDATIONS

Appendix B of each module presents an Implementation Checklist for that module. The Implementation Checklist details the summarized items on the rubric. You will use this tool as you near completion on any module to ensure that you have fully implemented it, and it's also useful for reviewing the implementation every three years or so. The checklist can identify strengths to celebrate and catch gaps in your implementation that you may be able to fill before a major problem emerges.

OVERVIEW OF MODULES

The modules in *Foundations* are designed to be used sequentially by a school or district that is just getting started with behavior support. However, if a school or district is already implementing a team-based, data-driven approach to continuous improvement of climate, safety, discipline, and motivation, the modules can be used in any order.

This module—**Module F: *Establishing and Sustaining a Continuum of Behavior Support***—outlines how the Foundations Team can analyze and guide an integration of universal prevention, targeted support, and intensive support for students. This process includes adopting and supporting a schoolwide or district approach to classroom management that creates a common language and ensures that teachers, administrators, and support staff are on the same page about classroom organization and management. For students who need individual support, this module provides staff training in early-stage interventions and a variety of problem-solving structures that match the intensity of student need to the intensity of school- and district-based resources. Finally, Module F provides guidance in sustaining *Foundations* at the building and district level so that effective procedures are maintained and improvement continues, even when school administration changes.

- Presentation 1: The Vision of a Continuum of Behavior Support
- Presentation 2: Supporting Classroom Behavior—The Three-Legged Stool
- Presentation 3: Articulating Staff Beliefs and Solidifying Universal Procedures
- Presentation 4: Early-Stage Interventions for General Education Classrooms
- Presentation 5: Matching the Intensity of Your Resources to the Intensity of Student Needs
- Presentation 6: Problem-Solving Processes and Intervention Design
- Presentation 7: Sustainability and District Support
- Appendix A: Foundations Implementation Rubric and Summary
- Appendix B: Module F Implementation Checklist
- Appendix C: Guide to Module F Reproducible Forms and Samples

Other modules in *Foundations: A Proactive and Positive Behavior Support System* are:

Module A: *Foundations of Behavior Support—A Continuous Improvement Process* covers the essential processes for involving the entire staff in developing, implementing, and sustaining positive behavior support. It includes detailed information about establishing a building-based leadership team (Foundations Team) to represent the entire staff. This module advises the team on how to collect and analyze data, identify and rank a manageable number of priorities for improvement, and guide the staff in revising, adopting, and implementing new policies and procedures for each priority. This process creates a cycle of continuous improvement that empowers and unifies the entire staff.

- Presentation 1: Foundations: A Multi-Tiered System of Behavior Support
- Presentation 2: Team Processes
- Presentation 3: The Improvement Cycle
- Presentation 4: Data-Driven Processes
- Presentation 5: Developing Staff Engagement and Unity
- Appendix A: Foundations Implementation Rubric and Summary
- Appendix B: Module A Implementation Checklist
- Appendix C: Guide to Module A Reproducible Forms and Samples

Module B: *Managing Behavior in Common Areas and With Schoolwide Policies* delineates processes for ensuring that common areas (arrival, cafeteria, hallways, and so on) and schoolwide policies (dress code, electronics use, public displays of affection, and so on) are structured for success and that expectations for behavior are directly taught with clarity and repetition to students. In addition, this module includes detailed information for all staff about how to provide positive and systematic supervision and how to correct misbehavior calmly, consistently, and respectfully.

- Presentation 1: Laying the Groundwork for Consistency in All School Settings
- Presentation 2: Structuring Common Areas and Schoolwide Policies for Success
- Presentation 3: Teaching Expectations to Students
- Presentation 4: Effective Supervision, Part 1—Protect, Expect, and Connect
- Presentation 5: Effective Supervision, Part 2—Correct and Reflect
- Presentation 6: Supervising Common Areas and Schoolwide Policies—for All Staff
- Presentation 7: Adopting, Implementing, and Monitoring Improvements to Common Areas and Schoolwide Policies
- Appendix A: Foundations Implementation Rubric and Summary
- Appendix B: Module B Implementation Checklist
- Appendix C: Guide to Module B Reproducible Forms and Samples

Module C: *Conscious Construction of an Inviting School Climate* guides the entire staff in creating and sustaining a school environment that makes all students feel welcomed and valued. This process includes developing Guidelines for Success, a set of behaviors and traits that provides a common language and common values among staff, students, and parents. This module explains how and why to maintain at least 3:1 ratios of positive interactions and covers the importance of regular attendance and strategies for improving attendance. Strategies for meeting the basic human needs of all students are also discussed. Finally, the module outlines how to welcome and orient staff, students, and families who are new to the school in a way that connects them to the school community.

- Presentation 1: Constructing and Maintaining a Positive Climate
- Presentation 2: Guidelines for Success
- Presentation 3: Ratios of Positive Interactions
- Presentation 4: Improving Attendance
- Presentation 5: School Connectedness—Meeting Basic Human Needs
- Presentation 6: Programs and Strategies for Meeting Needs
- Presentation 7: Making a Good First Impression—Welcoming New Staff, Students, and Families
- Appendix A: Foundations Implementation Rubric and Summary
- Appendix B: Module C Implementation Checklist
- Appendix C: Guide to Module C Reproducible Forms and Samples

Module D: *Responding to Misbehavior—An Instructional Approach* focuses on the vital importance of an instructional approach to correction in reducing future occurrences of the misbehavior. It provides information on training and inspiring all staff to correct all misbehavior by giving students information about how to behave successfully and by using the mildest consequences that reasonably fit the infractions. Module D describes how to get consensus among staff about when (and when not) to use office discipline referral. It provides menus of corrective techniques for mild and moderate misbehavior, from gentle verbal correction to time owed after class to restorative justice. All staff learn strategies for de-escalating emotional situations, and administrators are introduced to a comprehensive game plan for dealing with office referrals and implementing alternatives to out-of-school suspension. This module includes sample lessons for students on how to interact with people in authority.

- Presentation 1: The Relationship Between Proactive Procedures, Corrective Procedures, and Individual Student Behavior Improvement Plans
- Presentation 2: Developing Three Levels of Misbehavior
- Presentation 3: Staff Responsibilities for Responding to Misbehavior
- Presentation 4: Administrator Responsibilities for Responding to Misbehavior
- Presentation 5: Preventing the Misbehavior That Leads to Referrals and Suspensions
- Appendix A: Foundations Implementation Rubric and Summary
- Appendix B: Module D Implementation Checklist
- Appendix C: Guide to Module D Reproducible Forms and Samples

Module E: *Improving Safety, Managing Conflict, and Reducing Bullying* guides the Foundations Team in assessing school strengths and weaknesses related to safety, conflict, and bullying. The module begins by examining the attributes of safe and unsafe schools and offers suggestions for moving your school toward the evidence-based attributes that contribute to safety. One potential risk to safety is poor conflict management, so this module includes a simple conflict resolution strategy that students can use to manage conflict in peaceful and mutually beneficial ways. Bullying is another serious risk to safety. Module E provides a step-by-step process for analyzing strengths and gaps in your school's bullying policies and procedures as well as suggestions and examples for turning gaps into strengths. This module includes lessons for students on safety, conflict, and bullying prevention and intervention.

- Presentation 1: Keeping Students Safe From Physical and Emotional Harm
- Presentation 2: Attributes of Safe and Unsafe Schools
- Presentation 3: Teaching Conflict Resolution
- Presentation 4: Analyzing Bullying Behavior, Policies, and School Needs
- Presentation 5: Schoolwide Bullying Prevention and Intervention
- Appendix A: Foundations Implementation Rubric and Summary
- Appendix B: Module E Implementation Checklist
- Appendix C: Guide to Module E Reproducible Forms and Samples

The Vision of a Continuum of Behavior Support

CONTENTS

Introduction to Module F

INTRODUCTION TO MODULE F

In this presentation, we describe a game plan for using the other presentations in this module. **Presentations 2, 3, and 4** provide information on supporting a schoolwide classroom management model, solidifying your universal schoolwide procedures, and implementing early-stage interventions for the classroom. In **Presentations 5 and 6** we examine Tier 2 and Tier 3 intervention support for individual students. And in **Presentation 7** we discuss the importance of sustainability—that is, ensuring that all the programs and policies you worked so hard to develop continue to be vital components of your school culture long term.

Let's review the terms Multi-Tiered Systems of Support (MTSS) and Response to Intervention (RTI). These terms are used differently in different states; some states emphasize MTSS, while others emphasize RTI. The language of the concept continues to evolve, but both MTSS and RTI are characterized by layers of support that schools can use to ensure that no student falls through the cracks. In this book, we use the term MTSS.

Whatever service delivery is called in your state or district—MTSS, RTI, or something else— there's probably a behavior side and an academic side to the work, although the two are really not opposites in any way. Behavior affects academics, and academics affect behavior. The behavior side of service delivery may be called Positive Behavioral Interventions and Supports (PBIS) or something else; that is the framework for ensuring that work on the behavior side is proactive, positive, and evidence based. *Foundations* focuses on the behavior (or PBIS) side of MTSS.

Work on universal procedures first.

The first five modules of *Foundations* emphasize the schoolwide aspects of a multi-tiered system of support for behavior: continually improving climate, safety, and motivation to reduce misbehaviors such as dress code violations, conflict between students, bullying, and so on. In the *Foundations* continuum in Figure 1a, you can see that almost all of the work suggested in Modules A through E fits into the base of the continuum, the section labeled *schoolwide*. At this universal level, schools do everything they can to reduce the number of students who need individual support, not because they don't *want* to provide support, but because most schools have very limited resources for individual interventions.

But what about the two sections of the triangle supported by the base of positive climate, safety, and continuous improvement? The *classroom* and *individual* sections

Figure 1a   *Foundations continuum of behavior support*

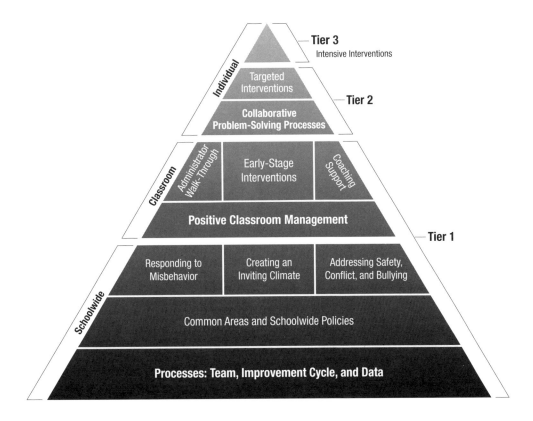

complete the continuum. Module F is about ensuring that you create and sustain a continuum of behavior support that includes all three tiers so that every student receives support commensurate with his or her needs. The goal is that no student falls through the cracks, meaning that your continuum should truly be a seamless set of universal (schoolwide and in every classroom), targeted, and intensive support procedures that ensure that every student gets what he or she needs when he or she needs it.

If your resources were unlimited, every student could work one-on-one with a teacher, a counselor, a social worker, and a school psychologist. But of course that scenario is unnecessary and absurdly costly. So, given that you have significantly less than unlimited funding, you have to use your limited resources wisely.

You probably have a few students who have very little need for support. They would be fine even if they were attending a chaotic and disorderly school with lots of bullying. But because you are educators, you know that to be successful in school and in life, all students—even those who don't need support—can benefit from a school that's safe, positive, consistent, and inviting.

You also know that what happens in the *classroom* is vitally important to students' success. Students spend most of their time in school in the classroom, so they benefit from—and many desperately need—great teachers in orderly, fast-paced, well-managed, academically challenging, and encouraging classrooms. The level of need for most students can be characterized as including the schoolwide section and classroom behavior support (Figure 1b). That's why **Presentation 2** is about extending behavior support to the classroom level.

Figure 1b *The level of need for most students (Student A) includes the schoolwide section and classroom behavior support.*

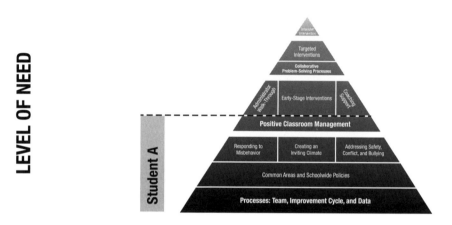

Presentation 3 is about solidifying your universal practices at both the schoolwide and classroom levels by having your staff (or, in a small district, all district personnel) define their beliefs about the principles of behavior support that can create a longitudinal, value-driven process for continuous improvement. One major objective of defining staff beliefs is to ensure that you maintain and extend positive universal practices while you explore and extend your resources for meeting the needs of students with greater behavioral challenges.

No matter how well you implement schoolwide practices and no matter how great a teacher is at managing his or her classroom, some students will exhibit behavioral or motivational problems that interfere with their success. Some students need a bit more support from their classroom teachers. Therefore, teachers need to be equipped with a protocol of early-stage interventions that they can implement during the earliest stages of a problem (Figure 1c). These strategies should have a reasonable track record of making a difference.

Presentation 4 is about early-stage interventions and how to implement a district protocol for them. In the simplest terms, the protocol is this: Try this intervention first, and if it doesn't work, try the next. One of the benefits of such a protocol is that

__Figure 1c__   Some students (Student B) need a bit more support from their classroom teachers, so teachers need to be equipped with a protocol of early-stage interventions.

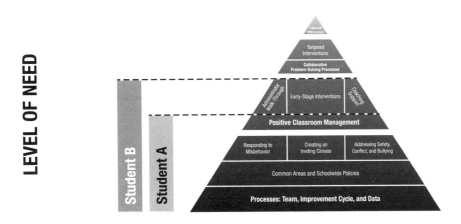

all teachers become active problem-solvers with a common language about those early-stage interventions.

An analogy from the field of medicine helps to explain what a protocol is. Let's say you're beginning to have chronic headaches. You've taken aspirin and other over-the-counter medications, but they don't reduce the pain or frequency of the headaches. Your next step is to see your doctor. The doctor, because of her education and experience, knows that she should follow a standard protocol. Depending on your specific symptoms, she orders tests and prescribes certain treatments. Any other doctor you might see for this problem would probably follow the same standard protocol.

If initial treatments don't work, the doctor will have you consult a neurologist, a doctor with more specialized education and experience. The neurologist will also follow a standard protocol. He'll review tests and treatments you've had so far, examine you, and probably prescribe additional tests and treatments based on his findings. So a standard protocol of interventions is a set of common steps that professional practitioners implement.

For most students, universal procedures, including early-stage intervention protocols, are all they need to be successful. That's why we include early-stage interventions as part of universal procedures in *Foundations*. Standard practice should be that for any student who demonstrates chronic misbehavior or motivational problems in the classroom, the teacher first tries certain basic interventions. In our medical analogy, early-stage interventions are the equivalent of remedies you would try before seeing a doctor: aspirin, getting more rest, acetaminophen, eliminating alcohol, and so on. If none of those early-stage strategies works, you then consult your doctor.

Note: We consider early-stage interventions to be a bridge between universal prevention and targeted (Tier 2) support. When districts adopt a formal protocol for the use of early-stage interventions and train all teachers to implement that protocol in the early stages of a problem (as we recommend), the use of early-stage interventions becomes universal practice. As teachers progress through our suggested protocol, the interventions become more data driven and analytical about function, two hallmarks of Tier 2 support.

Imagine a long bridge over a river—for example, the four-mile-long Astoria-Megler Bridge that spans the Columbia River, linking the states of Oregon and Washington. There is an exact spot on that bridge that marks the official border between Oregon and Washington, but for all practical purposes, the entire four-mile bridge is the border and connector between the two states. Early-stage interventions can arguably be called either universal or targeted, but the key point is that they constitute the bridge that links the two tiers.

Work on Tier 2 and Tier 3 interventions when universal procedures don't work.

You will have students who need more than early-stage interventions, no matter how well they are implemented (Figure 1d). The need might be temporary, as in the case of a student who is having a tough time adjusting to a new school, or it might be long term, as in the case of a student with severe attention deficit disorder challenges. These students need additional support and resources from your established Tier 2 programs and from interventionists—administrators, nurses, counselors, school psychologists, social workers, behavior specialists, and so on—who can design and implement Tier 2 targeted supports.

For clarity, we refer to the people in Tier 2 and Tier 3 problem-solving roles as *interventionists*. People in positions such as school psychologist, behavior specialist, social worker, school resource officer, counselor, nurse, dean, and administrator typically fill the role of interventionist.

And, of course, there are a few students whose needs are so great they need intensive support from programs and personnel (Figure 1e). **Presentations 5 and 6** are about integrating Tier 2 and Tier 3 interventions for individual students to ensure that all students get the intensity of services and support they need, when they need it.

Presentation 5 is about using universal screening to identify students with externalizing disorders (students who act out a lot) and internalizing disorders (students who may be at risk for depression or anxiety). Red flags are problems that data analysis

Figure 1d   Some students (Student C) need more than early-stage interventions. Additional support and resources are provided by your established Tier 2 programs and from interventionists who can design and implement Tier 2 targeted supports.

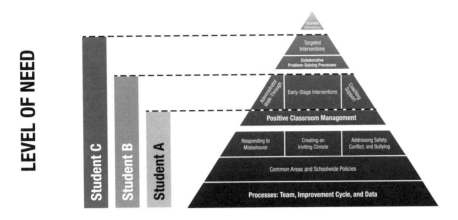

Figure 1e   A few students (Student D) need intensive, targeted support from programs and personnel.

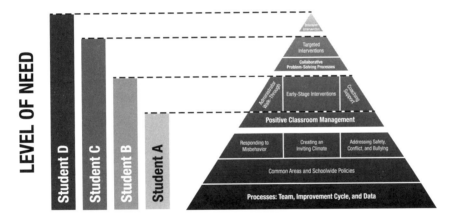

can reveal, such as chronic absenteeism, past retentions, chronic discipline problems, and other factors known to be associated with school failure and dropping out of school. The information from universal screening and red flags can be used to ensure that the system strategically and economically rallies to match the intensity of support needed to ensure that the student can be successful. We also discuss personnel (advocates and interventionists) who can help students get the support they need through ready-to-use Tier 2 interventions and problem-solving processes.

Presentation 6 explains three processes for efficient problem solving and intervention design. The first is called the 25-Minute Planning Process. This process can be used by grade-level teams or by a representative group of teachers for a teacher-to-teacher level of problem analysis and intervention design.

The second process is called Intervention Decision Guide: Teacher Interview (IDG:TI). It can be used by lead teachers, counselors, behavior specialists, school psychologists, and other staff members who assist classroom teachers with assessing the possible function of the behavior for the student—what the student is gaining from the behavior. The IDG:TI is *not* a complete functional behavior assessment (FBA). It is a teacher interview process that prompts the teacher to develop some hypotheses about function and to use that information to design an intervention to address the function.

The third process, Intervention Decision Guide: Multidisciplinary Team (IDG:MDT), can be used for problems that have been resistant to Tier 1 and Tier 2 problem solving and intervention. A multidisciplinary team structure probably already exists within your system—we mean a team of many different staff members with many levels of expertise, such as counselors, nurses, mental health professionals, school psychologists, who work with teachers to help individual students.

The multidisciplinary team approach is comprehensive, but expensive. Given your limited resources, you cannot go directly to a multidisciplinary team for every behavioral and motivational problem unless that problem has not been solved by simpler solutions. You just don't have the resources.

Our slightly facetious definition of Multi-Tiered System of Support (MTSS) is this: Try the easiest, cheapest thing first, and hope it works. If it works— great! The behavior is no longer a problem. If it doesn't work, you need to dig a little deeper into your menu of interventions and problem-solving processes.

Who should work on the Tier 2 and Tier 3 levels?

As we move up the continuum of behavior support to problem solving and intervention design for students with greater needs, one reasonable question is this: Is the Foundations Team the logical group to work on the Tier 2 and Tier 3 levels?

First, we should clarify that the Foundations Team should never work on helping a *specific* student. That's not the purpose of the Foundations Team or the MTSS Team. Your staff-student support team, care team, teacher assistance team, or similar team should work with individual students. The Foundations Team should be monitoring all of your programs and processes to ensure seamless implementation. The team should have a deep understanding of how your schoolwide and classroom universal supports are *integrated* with your Tier 2 and Tier 3 processes for individual students.

So to implement this module, we suggest that the Foundations Team is the logical group to examine how behavior support is working at the classroom level. The team should continuously strive to answer the question: Are students and teachers getting the level of support they need? We encourage the Foundations Team to work through **Presentations 2, 3, and 4**—the team should be deeply involved in those processes.

For **Presentations 5 and 6,** we encourage the Foundations Team to work with your current problem-solving teams (such as a staff-student support team) and interventionists, such as counselors, behavior specialists, school psychologists, and school social workers. Together, you can assess what is already in place in your school, any gaps that might exist, and who should be responsible for closing those gaps.

Envision your effective continuum of behavior support.

Envision how a truly effective tiered system of support will work in your school.

- All staff continuously strive to improve universal practices at the schoolwide and classroom levels.

- For a student who does not respond to universal practices, the teacher implements a standard protocol of early-stage interventions and documents the effort and outcome.

- If early-stage interventions are not successful, the teacher asks for assistance. Universal screening and red flags in the data may also identify a student who needs help (red flags might be chronic discipline referrals or chronic absenteeism, for example). The student is assigned to a school-based advocate (a counselor, administrator, or nurse, for example) who will be responsible for monitoring processes for meeting the student's needs (described in the next four bullet points) to ensure that the needs are met.

- The school-based advocate may link the student to a ready-to-use Tier 2 support such as a mentor or a meaningful school-based job.

- A teacher-to-teacher problem-solving process is implemented in which general education teachers share and brainstorm ideas for helping the student.

- If the teacher-to-teacher problem-solving team is not successful in helping the student, the teacher and the school-based advocate may choose to bring in an interventionist—a lead teacher, school psychologist, school social worker, or counselor, for example—to work with the teacher and the student. This person conducts an IDG:TI and uses information from the teacher to design and implement another intervention. This process could be repeated a couple of times across weeks or months.

- If the intervention is not successful, a multidisciplinary team of interventionists works on designing, implementing, and monitoring fidelity of a much more intensive intervention.

Figure 1f illustrates this continuum of behavior support in a flowchart. This flow-chart is provided on the Module F CD (Sample F-36).

Figure 1f   Flowchart for Tier 2 and Tier 3 behavioral interventions protocol (F-36)

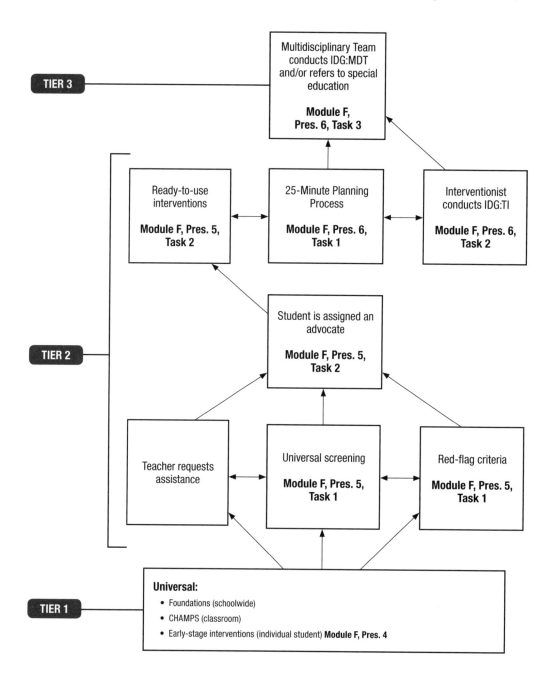

Eliminate the gaps.

In most schools, however, the system is not as seamless as the ideal system above. Following are three gaps that we typically find in school and district systems of support.

Potential Gap 1: It's not my job! In many districts, there's a gap between classroom procedures and Tier 2 and Tier 3 supports. Some teachers' behavior management plans consist only of correcting misbehavior. They do not consider function or proactive strategies to help the student learn and be motivated to behave appropriately. Their attitude is "I do what I do, and if that doesn't work with a student, get him out of my room and fix him." All teachers need to become active problem-solvers and implement evidence-based practices. Rather than expecting someone else to "fix" a student with a chronic problem, teachers should try an intervention. If it doesn't work, they should think about why and then try another intervention.

Potential Gap 2: Hurry up and wait. Most highly skilled professionals—school psychologists, behavior specialists, and so on—have long waiting lists of students who have been referred to them. Some of those students don't need complex interventions. For example, a student who needs only more adult attention can benefit greatly from a relatively simple intervention such as Meaningful Work. That student should not have to wait for help. Systems should be in place that allow teachers and school-based advocates to connect students with simple, established proactive programs *before* the student is placed on a waiting list for more intense interventions.

Potential Gap 3: Where's the data? Frequently, the first question an interventionist asks the teacher of a referred student is, "Do you have any data?" And all too often the answer is no, or the teacher offers a stack of anecdotal notes. (By the way, more than five anecdotal notes are not data; they are a story.) But interventionists need objective data, such as frequency counts, duration measures, latency measures, and ratings of magnitude or quality of behavior—that is, something that can be charted. When no data are available, the interventionist has to say, "Well, the first step is to collect data," prompting the teacher to think, "Great. Another hoop I have to jump through to try and get this kid the services he needs." The interventionist becomes the bad guy, a roadblock, rather than a partner in the problem-solving process. Data collection needs to be part of the standard protocol and needs to occur early in the process.

Those three gaps must be eliminated. All staff members need to recognize their roles in supporting students, understand and follow the steps in the protocol, and collect and use data. The continuum of behavior support has to be seamless. So we recommend that the Foundations Team work through **Presentations 5 and 6** with your interventionists and problem-solving teams.

And finally, **Presentation 7** is all about sustainability at the building and district levels. If you have worked through some or all of the other *Foundations* modules, you know that implementing the concepts well is neither easy nor simple. It is time consuming, and sometimes great creativity is required to adapt our suggestions to fit the unique needs and nature of your building. The policies and procedures you worked so hard to put into place also require effort and planning to keep them going, or they will deteriorate over time.

Homeowners among you will appreciate this analogy: Moving into a new house or finishing a massive remodel on an existing house is very exciting. However, by your second or third day of occupancy, you have to think about vacuuming the rugs and cleaning the floors. By the end of the first week, you need a regimen for cleaning the bathrooms and kitchen and dusting all the rooms. And months or years later, you'll think about repainting certain rooms, adding a deck, landscaping the yard, or building an addition. A home requires constant maintenance and periodic improvement. Constructing or remodeling your behavior support practices at all levels—schoolwide, classroom, and individual student—is what *Foundations* is all about. **Presentation 7** guides you through some considerations for ensuring that the programs and processes you create do not deteriorate, but instead continue to get better every year.

Supporting Classroom Behavior: The Three-Legged Stool

CONTENTS

Introduction

Task 1: Adopt a Schoolwide Classroom Management Model

For the Foundations Team

Task 2: Administrators—Clarify Expectations for Outcomes of the Classroom Management Model

For the Foundations Team, especially the administrator

Task 3: Provide Coaching and Support, and Facilitate Continuous Improvement

For the Foundations Team, instructional coaches, and other teacher-support personnel

DOCUMENTS*

- CHAMPS Implementation Requirements, Grades K–8 (F-03)
- Discipline in the Secondary Classroom Implementation Requirements, Grades 9–12 (F-04)

* All documents listed are available on the CD.

INTRODUCTION

In previous *Foundations* modules, we focused on the school as a whole by addressing topics such as common areas, schoolwide policies, responding to misbehavior, positive climate, safety, conflict, and bullying. These areas are all vitally important, but students spend most of their time in school in the classroom. Ensuring that every classroom is a well-organized, positive setting that prompts responsible and motivated behavior from students must be a major part of your universal behavior support practices.

This presentation focuses on classroom-level prevention. However, we do not train you in classroom management. Rather, we explain how the Foundations Team can integrate classroom management into the continuum of behavior support that you're constructing. We help you answer this question: How can the school honor each teacher's unique style and organization while ensuring that all students benefit from a safe, well-organized classroom that fosters academic progress?

 How can the school honor each teacher's unique style and organization while ensuring that all students benefit from a safe, well-organized classroom that fosters academic progress?"

The first part of this question acknowledges that teachers need significant autonomy of style and organization. A kindergarten classroom will be different in organization than a seventh-grade PE class, which will be different from an 11th-grade lab-based physics class. Two teachers who use the same sixth-grade language arts standards will organize their respective classrooms differently. One might emphasize cooperative group activities while the other prefers brief, turn-to-your-partner tasks.

In addition, teachers are different from each other stylistically. Some teachers are very theatrical, while others frequently use social stories. Some are businesslike and straightforward, and some teach like motivational coaches, continually pumping the classroom up. All of those teachers can be masterful teachers.

*E*xample From the Field

An assistant superintendent in an urban district asked me to help with setting up an implementation for eighth-grade students who were way below grade level in reading. The goal was to develop a districtwide approach, but we realized that the best way to begin would be to identify three really great teachers and spend a year training them in implementing this approach. Then those three teachers could train and coach other teachers.

We used a program called *Corrective Reading—Decoding B*, a direct instruction program. Our plan was to train the teachers, then return periodically during that first year to observe them in the classroom and do some demonstration and side-by-side teaching with them.

When I first met these teachers—Brett, Margaret, and Nan—I thought they were all very bright and motivated, but I honestly had some concerns about their styles. Brett was businesslike and almost cold. He spoke with little inflection in his voice, and when we practiced teaching skills, he moved and spoke woodenly.

Margaret was 68 years old at the time. She came across as a classic Texas schoolmarm: braided buns on the sides of her head, wire glasses slightly askew, floral print dress, and matronly figure. She was excited and delighted about everything and very loving toward her students.

In contrast, Nan was a very petite, quiet, almost shy teacher.

The initial training took place before the start of the school year, and I had a great time working with these teachers. But because they would be teaching some of the toughest, lowest achieving eighth-grade students in an impoverished inner city, I was concerned about the success of the program. Then we found out that the class size had been increased from 15 to 30! I became seriously concerned because I thought that, with their styles, the teachers wouldn't be able to handle the behavioral challenges of the students.

Two weeks later, I returned to the school to observe the three teachers. Brett was first. Even though he was still stiff and unsmiling, within that style he was a masterfully motivational teacher. The students responded very well to him. I thought of many positive comments to give him and only a few minor ideas for improvement. In fact, I thought that my teaching skills would pale compared with his—I was scheduled to demonstrate teach his class later that day.

As I walked to Margaret's room to observe her second-period class, I thought about how the eighth graders would behave with a 68-year-old loving, motherly woman. They'll probably walk all over her, I thought. But Margaret, like Brett, turned out to be a masterful teacher both instructionally and motivationally. All the students were riveted to her presentations and directions.

And it turned out that Nan, in her quiet, almost shy, businesslike way, was an equally effective teacher.

I had the privilege of working with these three teachers for 10 days spread throughout the year—teaching side by side, observing them, and giving them feedback. They also observed me teaching, and we discussed our strengths and weaknesses. It was a fabulous experience.

Before that year, I, as a teacher trainer and coach, made the error of trying to train teachers to teach as I teach—as though they should all use my style of teaching. Those three master teachers taught me that teachers can be radically different in their styles and still be wildly effective. —R.S.

Although you need schoolwide consistency in dress code, hallway expectations, arrival procedures, and so on, you do *not* need a schoolwide pencil-sharpening policy or a schoolwide policy on how and when students hand in their classwork. Those policies should be at the discretion of each classroom teacher. There is nothing in the research that says, "This is exactly how you organize a sixth-grade language arts classroom" or "This is exactly how you interact with eighth-grade students who are below grade level." So within the approach that we propose, teachers' professional judgment needs to be honored.

However, autonomy always has some limits. For example, you can drive your car anywhere you want when you leave the school, but there are limits you must follow—you must drive on the right side of the road, obey the posted speed limits, come to a complete stop at stop signs, and so on. To explore the limits on autonomy, let's go back to the original question: *How can the school honor each teacher's style and organization while ensuring that all students benefit from a safe, well-organized classroom that fosters academic progress?*

The second part of the question refers to limits on teachers' autonomy. Within an individual teacher's unique classroom, students need to be safe and in an environment that promotes learning. One teacher cannot have so much autonomy that other classrooms are negatively affected. For example, a teacher might have a very high tolerance for noise in the classroom and be able to teach effectively in that environment, but if that noise affects the ability of nearby colleagues to teach, limits need to be drawn on that teacher's autonomy regarding noise level.

Likewise, a teacher cannot have so much autonomy that she can choose not to require students to learn math concepts during math class. And a teacher cannot decide that student behavior is not his problem. If he thinks that it doesn't matter whether students are on task, whether they're mean to each other, or whether they follow his directions—that is, he thinks his job is to teach content, not behavior—that is too much autonomy.

The tasks in this presentation are designed to help you honor autonomy while ensuring that all teachers are managing their classrooms in a way that promotes responsible and motivated student behavior. We use the metaphor of a three-legged stool, with these legs:

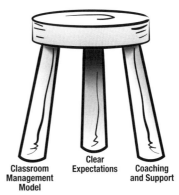

1. An adopted *classroom management model* that all teachers are trained in

2. *Clear expectations* from administrators for behavioral outcomes of the classroom management model

3. *Coaching and support* to facilitate continuous improvement

A stool cannot stand on one leg, nor can it stand on two, but with three legs a stool is stable and strong. Each task in this presentation represents a leg of the stool.

Task 1: Adopt a Schoolwide Classroom Management Model provides information about training staff in an adopted classroom management model to create a common language and common approach.

Task 2: Administrators—Clarify Expectations for Outcomes of the Classroom Management Model assists school leaders with providing very clear expectations to staff about behavioral outcomes for students. Training by itself (Task 1) is very weak, so Task 2 is the essential second step to supporting classroom behavior management. Are students behaving the way they need to behave?

Task 3: Provide Coaching and Support to Facilitate Continuous Improvement provides the information you need to ensure that the training and expectations are continually reviewed and emphasized so teachers can strengthen and solidify their classroom management plans. This third leg of the stool ensures that the other two legs are and continue to be effective.

TASK 1

Adopt a schoolwide classroom management model

In this task, we discuss the benefits of adopting a classroom management model for your school or—even better—your district and training all teachers in this model. You may be familiar with CHAMPS, Randy Sprick's classroom management model. We use examples from CHAMPS in this presentation, but feel free to adopt whatever model fits the behavior goals of your school. It does not have to be CHAMPS. Everything we suggest in this presentation can be adapted to work with any good classroom management model.

> *CHAMPS: A Proactive and Positive Approach to Classroom Management* (2nd ed.) is written for grades K–8. Another resource, *Discipline in the Secondary Classroom* (3rd ed.), applies the CHAMPS principles to grades 9–12. Both books are available from Pacific Northwest Publishing (www.pacificnwpublish.com).

Why do you need a schoolwide or district classroom management model?

A classroom management model common to the school or district can provide the following benefits.

Everyone who supports new teachers will use the same reference point. One benefit of an adopted model is that everyone who supports teachers who are new to your building, whether they're first-year teachers or experienced new hires, will use the same base level of procedural recommendations.

In a large urban district where we have been training for several years, we moved into classroom-level work in about the second year of implementation. The first-year teachers reported to us that they were a bit overwhelmed by the well-meaning advice on classroom management they were receiving from other staff members, such as their principals and assistant principals, mentors, and district first-year support personnel. Every adult who was trying to help these struggling teachers suggested a different approach to behavior management. For example, the principal suggested Harry Wong's procedures, the assistant principal recommended *Safe & Civil Schools* materials, and the mentor suggested Carolyn Evertson's COMP program. New teachers said, "I've been told to consider seven different approaches, but I don't even know what to do tomorrow, let alone how to learn seven different approaches." Having just one approach to learn and rely on will significantly improve those first-year teachers' likelihood of success.

The model can serve as a framework that matches the school and teacher effectiveness literature. As you shop for a classroom management model, we encourage you to consider the following resources that we think are great summaries of the research literature:

- Epstein, M., Atkins, M., Cullinan, D., Kutash, K., & Weaver, R. (2008). *Reducing Behavior Problems in the Elementary School Classroom: A Practice Guide* (NCEE #2008-012). Washington, DC: National Center for Education Evaluation and Regional Assistance, Institute of Education Sciences, U.S. Department of Education. Retrieved from http://ies.ed.gov/ncee/wwc/publications/practiceguides

- Hattie, J. (2008). *Visible learning: A synthesis of over 800 meta-analyses relating to achievement.* New York, NY: Routledge.

- Hattie, J. (2011). *Visible learning for teachers: Maximizing impact on learning.* New York, NY: Routledge.

- Marzano, R. J., Marzano, J. S., & Pickering, D. J. (2003). *Classroom Management That Works: Research-Based Strategies for Every Teacher.* Alexandria, VA: Association for Supervision & Curriculum Development.

Hattie's approach is much broader than just classroom management. It includes identifying all of the variables that have been demonstrated through multiple studies to make a difference in learning. It also summarizes a number of classroom management variables.

Two classroom management models provide frameworks that best tie in to the research literature. One is CHAMPS, which we mentioned earlier and use as our main example throughout this presentation. The other is Classroom Organization and Management Program (COMP) by Dr. Carolyn Evertson of Vanderbilt University. Both approaches are detailed frameworks that guide teachers in making decisions about organizing their classroom and interacting with students in ways that prompt responsible behavior. Both approaches fit the research but allow for adaptation to individual teaching styles. More information about COMP is available at http://www.comp.org/AboutCOMP.html.

A good classroom management model creates a common language. When teachers, administrators, and support personnel such as counselors, coaches, psychologists, social workers, and behavior specialists speak a common language, communication and understanding are greatly enhanced. For example, CHAMPS implementations are so widespread that the acronym CHAMPS has become a verb. Teachers ask, "Have you CHAMPed that activity?" And everyone knows they mean, "Have you clarified your behavioral expectations for students for **Conversation**, how to get **Help**, the particular **Activity, Movement** during the activity, and how to **Participate**?" STOIC (Structure, Teach, Observe, Interact positively, and Correct fluently), which represents how the CHAMPS model is organized, has become a common language in many districts. *Ratios of positive interactions* is a phrase that is shorthand for the concept of delivering more positive than corrective attention to students among CHAMPS teachers. It also includes the ideas of constant monitoring and continuous improvement.

The model guides decision making about classroom management—it is not a canned program. The model you adopt should be a *guide* for making decisions about classroom management rather than a set of canned procedures. A procedure is canned when, for example, every teacher is expected to implement a certain point system in their classroom or use "marbles in a jar" as a reinforcement strategy and positive feedback mechanism. Or every teacher must correct misbehavior by using a wall chart of student names with red, yellow, and green sections and a clip that moves up or down through the colored sections. All of those procedures can work well under the right circumstances, when they match the needs of the students and the style of the teacher. But if all teachers are expected to use a canned procedure, the procedure inevitably won't match every teacher's style.

In contrast, a framework for making decisions will clarify, for example, that the research supports the usefulness of posted classroom rules, but the framework won't tell a teacher exactly what the rules need to be. It provides guidance in how to develop the rules, gives examples of ways that different teachers have approached developing rules, and provides guidance for how to incorporate the rules into the classroom.

A districtwide model makes it easier for students to transfer from one building to another. In one large urban district that we work with, all of the teachers have been trained in the CHAMPS approach and are required to post expectations for every activity. So when the activity is cooperative group, for example, students can look at a poster, a section of interactive whiteboard, or some other visual created by the teacher that uses the CHAMPS acronym—Conversation, Help, Activity, Movement, and Participation—and quickly know how they are expected to behave during the activity. Figure 2a shows a sample CHAMPS poster.

This district has reported that when students transfer from one building to another, they know how to learn and understand the expectations in their new schools because the CHAMPS visuals are in every classroom, just like they were in the students' previous schools. The common language and structure across the entire district make learning the expectations relatively easy and quick.

Substitute teachers can use the model to improve their consistency in implementing teachers' plans. When substitute teachers are trained in the model, they can function with more confidence and consistency knowing that, although each classroom has its own style and organization, there is an overarching framework that all teachers use and all students expect. In addition, substitutes can use the teachers'

Figure 2a   *CHAMPS expectations poster for science stations*

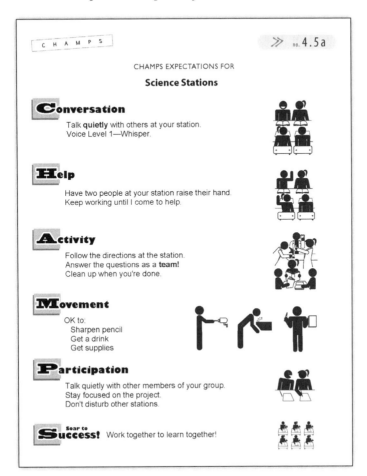

written management plans that incorporate common elements and structure from the model.

A model can create an empowered sense of problem solving. Problem solving is a much better strategy than helpless problem admiring (*Isn't this awful?*) or problem wallowing (*What could anybody do in this situation?*). Teachers trained in a classroom management model feel empowered to *take charge*—whenever a student or group is not behaving the way the teacher expects, the teacher knows how to analyze the problem and pick some procedures that are likely to work. If they don't work, she tries other procedures. In other words, she manipulates variables to find solutions to problems. A good framework empowers people with more and more variables to experiment with.

A model can create a mindset toward continuous improvement. Master teachers know that teaching, including both the instructional and behavior management elements, is a lifelong learning task. No matter how much you know, you can always learn more about teaching students effectively.

Once a model has been adopted, train your staff.

The standard approach to training staff in an adopted classroom management model is to conduct one-day workshops or seminars. Time spent on staff development is very worthwhile, and we certainly recommend that course of action. But we also encourage you to go deeper. Consider establishing voluntary study groups of teachers during the initial stages of adoption so that teachers can learn from one another and bounce ideas around. Later, when the model is truly in place schoolwide, you might conduct book studies on your model for the whole faculty so that teachers work through it across at least 1 and possibly even 2 school years.

As part of training, you will also need to ensure that teachers who are new to the district or the building are trained. Every year you will have some new teachers, so every year you need to have a plan for training those teachers.

Also consider something like an online collaboration site (such as SharePoint) or discussion group so that teachers can pose questions to and discuss issues with their colleagues. This site can also be used to share resources, such as visual displays. The more staff discuss and communicate about the classroom management model, the more the common language and structure of the model will get ingrained into the school culture.

Examples of success with CHAMPS

The CHAMPS model, paired with the other legs of the stool, has been used in districts as diverse as Bellevue, Washington, which includes communities with a range of socioeconomic strata, some with high percentages of college-bound students; Chicago, Illinois, which of course includes a vast range of communities; and Northwest Arctic Borough School District in Alaska, which includes many small schools spread very far apart, some in villages so remote that the children may have never seen, let alone ridden in, a car. Other large cities that have implemented CHAMPS with great success are Fresno, California, and Wichita, Kansas.

Duval County Public Schools in Jacksonville, Florida, and Alief Independent School District outside of Houston, Texas, have been implementing the CHAMPS model for over 12 years as of this writing. Ventura County Office of Education serves multiple school districts, and they have done a fabulous job of using the CHAMPS model to create an effective framework in districts of wildly different socioeconomic levels, including a school that serves children on the severe end of the autism spectrum and a school for children who have had struggles with the law.

Task 1 Conclusion

Adopting a model is only one leg of the three-legged stool, but it's an important leg. You need a powerful and sustainable model that creates a common language. Once you've decided on a model and trained all staff, you need to support that training with clear expectations from administrators (the topic of Task 2) and nonevaluative help from coaches and colleagues (the topic of Task 3) so that everybody is working together to create and sustain the best, most effective teaching staff possible.

Task 1 Action Steps & Evidence of Implementation

Action Steps	Evidence of Implementation
1. Discuss whether the school or district has adopted a classroom management model. If so: • Do all teachers new to the school or district receive training? • Do all returning staff members get a refresher course? • Do staff discuss model strategies when problem solving? • Are there multiple opportunities for reviewing, applying, and extending the model? If the answer to any of the above questions is No, discuss actions and goals. 2. If you don't have a classroom management model, discuss whether the school could benefit from adopting and using a model. If so, discuss the actions the team might take to move your school or district toward adopting a model.	Foundations Process: Meeting Minutes Information about the adopted model can be filed in: • Foundations Archive: Classroom Management Model • Staff Handbook: Classroom Management Model

TASK 2

Administrators: Clarify expectations for outcomes of the classroom management model

This task is about the second leg of the three-legged stool: administrator expectations for outcomes of a good classroom management model. As a result of effective classroom management, students should be on task and engaged with learning, be respectful to students and adults, and follow the teacher's directions and procedures.

Evaluate the efficacy of teachers by examining student behavior rather than teacher behavior.

A large suburban district of over 40,000 students asked me (Randy) to help them implement the CHAMPS model (and *Discipline in the Secondary Classroom* for high school) districtwide. This was a great opportunity to positively affect many students and teachers, and I worked with the district to schedule several training sessions and create a cadre of district-based trainers.

Then they asked me to help with developing a checklist that administrators could use to evaluate whether teachers were implementing CHAMPS correctly. I struggled with that request because I realized that some teachers might do everything on the checklist but still have a chaotic classroom. In that case, the completed checklist would imply that the model was implemented correctly but did not work. Conversely, a great teacher might not do some items on the checklist but still elicit on-task, respectful, and cooperative behavior from potentially very difficult students. In that case, the completed checklist would imply that the teacher did *not* do a good job implementing the model, when in fact he did.

As we explained in the previous task, CHAMPS is not a program. It's a framework for making decisions about classroom management. A teacher is never really done implementing it. If a particular procedure does not result in the student behavior you want, you need to manipulate some other variables. You don't just check off the procedure as implemented, then let students continue to misbehave if the procedure doesn't work.

Here's what we mean by *manipulate variables:* Any teacher can experience a class in which it is challenging to keep students engaged in independent work. Remember Brett, Margaret, and Nan, the three teachers we mentioned in the introduction to this presentation? Brett might reflect that he has not been providing enough guided practice before having students work independently. Margaret might realize that she is not circulating enough throughout the entire classroom because she spends too much time with the first couple of students who have questions. Nan might question whether she needs some kind of structured reward system to motivate students to stay focused. In each case, the goal is to increase on-task behavior; in each case, the needs of the class and the style of the teacher are different. Each teacher tries to manipulate a different variable (strategy) to see if the change increases on-task behavior.

Brett, Margaret, and Nan might not do one or two things on a checklist. They might teach in a different style than a checklist suggests, but their students' behavior is engaged, respectful, and cooperative from the start of the class period to the end. They are great teachers.

A flexible approach to classroom management can include the axiom, "If it ain't broke, don't try to fix it." With a checklist, you might think you need to fix things that aren't broken. A flexible approach to classroom management can also include the principle, "If it *is* broken, don't keep trying to fix it in the same way." There are an almost endless number of variables to experiment with until you find something that works.

As you might imagine, I did not develop a checklist for this district. It just didn't seem like a viable approach. Instead, I emphasized to administrators that the way to evaluate teachers and assist them in implementing evidence-based behavior support at the classroom level is to provide *clear expectations* on the outcomes of good classroom management. In other words, what are teachers ultimately accountable for? Good behavior from their students.

What are reasonable expectations for good student behavior?

Expectations can be summarized into three groups: academic engagement, respectful interactions, and following classroom expectations.

Academic engagement. At least 90% of the students in class are actively engaged in instruction, regardless of the nature of the instructional activity. During a walk-through, administrators should note how many students are on task. Whether the activity is cooperative group, pair practice, or teacher-directed instruction, at least nine out of ten students should be on task.

In addition, every student should be engaged at least 90% of the time. For example, let's say that during every walk-through of a particular classroom, the administrator observes that almost all the students are on task—except Jeremy. The administrator should tell the teacher, "Your on-task behavior for the whole class is wonderful, but every time I come into your room, Jeremy is not engaged. What variables can you manipulate to engage Jeremy?"

Respectful interactions. Students are respectful toward other students and adults, and adults are respectful to students. Students cannot thrive unless they feel connected to their schools; research suggests that school connectedness is directly related to success in school. But students are unlikely to connect with schools where they are treated cruelly or disrespectfully by other students or where some students are overtly disrespectful to adults. And students are extremely unlikely to build connections to a school where adults are disrespectful to students. So respectful interactions are expected. If disrespect occurs in the classroom, the teacher needs to address it.

Following classroom expectations. Students follow their teacher's unique classroom expectations. Given that teachers have great autonomy in how they organize routines and procedures in the classroom, they need to clarify their policies and procedures and post their expectations so that all students can easily see and follow them.

An example of the power of posting expectations comes from a principal in Florida who was opening a brand-new high school. In his previous high school, he had done a great job of implementing *Foundations* and *Discipline in the Secondary Classroom* (the CHAMPS model for high school). He said to me, "Randy, I've heard you say that it doesn't matter whether we post classroom expectations—the important thing is to have and teach expectations. But I have decided to require my teachers to display four different sets of expectations in academic classrooms. The visuals might be posters, on an interactive whiteboard, in a PowerPoint presentation, or something similar, but they have to be highly visible to every student in the room." The four sets of expectations that he wanted all teachers to create were for these activities:

- Teacher-directed instruction
- Independent seatwork tasks
- Cooperative groups
- Tests

I asked the principal about his rationale for requiring that expectations be posted. He said, "Think how difficult it is for kids to go to six different classrooms every day, where each teacher has his or her own rituals and routines. We want teachers to keep their unique rituals and routines, but kids should never have to *guess* what teachers expect of them."

When that new school opened, the overwhelming positive feedback from students, parents, and teachers about the clarity of expectations changed my thinking. I began to recommend that teachers be required to post their expectations and instruct students to follow the posted classroom expectations.

Conduct walk-throughs and, when necessary, clarify expectations.

During walk-throughs, if the administrator finds that all three categories of behavior are good—students are engaged and respectful, and they follow classroom expectations—the administrator can just provide positive feedback to the teacher later in the day. Then the remaining minutes of the walk-through can be devoted to observing instructional variables.

But if any of the three behavioral variables are not in place—less than 90% of students are engaged or students are engaged less than 90% of the time, disrespectful interactions occur, and students are not following the teacher's procedures—the administrator should create an expectation for improvement. If the teacher responds, "But my expectations are posted," the administrator would say, "That's great, but what else are you going to do to get kids on task?"

Figure 2b shows Form F-03, CHAMPS Implementation Requirements (Grades K–8), and Figure 2c shows Form F-04, Discipline in the Secondary Classroom Implementation Requirements (Grades 9–12). These documents are also available on the Module F CD. They are examples of how an administrator or administrative team can clarify for teachers the expectations for implementing a classroom management model—they are essentially memos to the staff. Although our examples are based on the CHAMPS approach, you can easily adapt them for other classroom management models.

Task 2 Conclusion

Adopting a model and training all staff in the model is the first leg of the three-legged stool. Clarity from administrators on the expected outcomes—good student behavior—creates accountability and is the second leg of the stool. But these two legs by themselves cannot support anything. A third leg is necessary, and that leg consists of supportive, collaborative coaching and peer facilitation for teachers. That's the topic of the next task.

Foundations: A Proactive and Positive Behavior Support System

REPRODUCIBLE
FORM
F-03

CHAMPS Implementation Requirements, Grades K–8

What you need to do • What I hope to see

I. **Structure** your classroom for success (CHAMPS, 2nd ed., Chapters 1 and 2).

   ▶ Complete a classroom management plan (Chapter 3 and Chapter 5, Task 1).

II. **Teach** your expectations—clarify and communicate them to students (Chapters 4 and 5).

   A. Post expectations for each major instructional activity as it occurs, including teacher-directed instruction, independent seatwork, cooperative groups, and tests.

   B. Reinforce your expectations in a variety of ways:

      ▶ Posters on permanent display

      ▶ CHAMPS worksheet on projector

      ▶ CHAMPS wall chart

      ▶ Flip chart

      ▶ Other

III. **Observe** and monitor student behavior (Chapter 6).

   A. Physically circulate.

   B. Visually scan.

   C. Collect and analyze data.

IV. **Interact** positively by providing praise and noncontingent attention (Chapters 7 and 8).

   A. Strive to create a positive classroom climate and positive relationships with students.

   B. Supply positive feedback, intermittent celebrations of success, and (as needed) structured reward systems.

   C. Maintain at least a 3:1 ratio of positive to corrective interactions. (Note that this is an average; there is nothing inherently wrong with a short interval in which the ratio is skewed to the corrective side.)

V. **Correct** misbehavior fluently (Chapter 9).

   A. Get back to instruction as quickly and as seamlessly as possible.

   B. Be calm, consistent, brief, and immediate.

Note: The goal is positive student behavior. As long as students are respectful and actively engaged in your instructional activities, you are implementing the CHAMPS approach successfully.

© 2014 Pacific Northwest Publishing

 Forms can be printed from the Module F CD.

Figure 2c *Discipline in the Secondary Classroom Implementation Requirements, Grades 9–12 (F-04)*

Foundations: A Proactive and Positive Behavior Support System

REPRODUCIBLE FORM

F-04

Discipline in the Secondary Classroom Implementation Requirements, Grades 9–12

What you need to do • What I hope to see

I. **Structure** your classroom for success (*Discipline in the Secondary Classroom*, 3rd ed., Chapters 1–3).

 ▶ Complete a classroom management plan (Chapter 4 and Chapter 6, Task 1).

II. **Teach** your expectations—clarify and communicate them to students (Chapters 5 and 6).

 A. Post expectations for each major instructional activity as it occurs, including teacher-directed instruction, independent seatwork, cooperative groups, and tests.

 B. Reinforce your expectations in a variety of ways:

 ▶ Posters on permanent display

 ▶ CHAMPS or ACHIEVE worksheet on projector

 ▶ CHAMPS or ACHIEVE wall chart

 ▶ Flip chart

 ▶ Other

III. **Observe** and monitor student behavior (Chapter 7).

 A. Physically circulate.

 B. Visually scan.

 C. Collect and analyze data (appendixes and chapter self-assessments).

IV. **Interact** positively by providing praise and noncontingent attention (Chapter 8).

 A. Strive to create a positive classroom climate and positive relationships with students.

 B. Supply positive feedback, intermittent celebrations of success, and (as needed) structured reward systems.

 C. Maintain at least a 3:1 ratio of positive to corrective interactions. (Note that this is an average; there is nothing inherently wrong with a short interval in which the ratio is skewed to the corrective side.)

V. **Correct** misbehavior fluently (Chapter 9).

 A. Get back to instruction as quickly and seamlessly as possible.

 B. Be calm, consistent, brief, and immediate.

Note: The goal is positive student behavior. As long as students are respectful and actively engaged in your instructional activities, you are implementing the CHAMPS approach successfully.

© 2014 Pacific Northwest Publishing

Task 2 Action Steps & Evidence of Implementation

Action Steps	Evidence of Implementation
1. *Administrators:* Consider whether observing for the three student behaviors described in Task 2 fits within your school or district's relationship with teacher evaluation and your own leadership style. Be prepared to talk with the team about whether to use the three suggested behaviors or others that relate to your adopted classroom management approach.	
2. *Foundations Team:* Discuss whether and how clarifying expectations will become part of administrative classroom walk-throughs and staff feedback. If applicable, share that decision and information with the staff.	Foundations Process: Meeting Minutes Foundations Archive: Classroom Management Model Staff Handbook: Classroom Management Model

TASK 3

Provide coaching and support to facilitate continuous improvement

If teachers are to be held accountable for the behavior of students, as discussed in the previous task, the system must create supportive and collaborative structures to ensure that teachers are successful. In this task, we suggest some ideas and questions for your team to consider regarding the level of expert and peer support you might provide for teachers who are dealing with difficult student behavior. We've broken down the task into three topics:

- Designated coaching
- Peer coaching
- Building-based facilitation of continuous improvement and problem solving related to student behavior

Offer designated coaching.

Your district might already have instructional coaches, and those coaches can probably assist teachers with classroom management as well as instructional techniques. But anyone whose position allows them to be in teachers' rooms in a supportive capacity can be a coach. In some high schools, departmental chairs may have time to visit other teachers' rooms. Some schools and districts employ teachers on special assignment to function solely as support personnel. In some elementary schools, counselors can support teachers and visit classrooms. So in this task, our definition of coach includes anyone who can help teachers with classroom management in a collaborative, nonevaluative, confidential capacity. We include people who formally have the role of coach as well as people who may assist teachers less formally.

Notice that we used the terms *nonevaluative* and *confidential* to describe designated coaching. These concepts need to be very clear to administrators, coaches, and teachers. We recommend that administrators be informed whenever coaches and teachers work together, but they should never require coaches to share details about the coaching process. Teachers need to know that their work with a coach will never be part of a formal evaluation. Coaches must be able to build trust with teachers so that teachers never have to worry about what the coach is saying to the administrator or their colleagues about them and their abilities.

Coaches need to be trained in the adopted model alongside teachers so that both coaches and teachers use the same language. Initially, coaches do not have to be experts—they need not know everything about classroom management. They just need the time, willingness, and motivation to visit classrooms, collaborate, and explore options with teachers. They may help teachers by, for example, collecting data on student behavior and discussing options for problem solving. Over time, they will develop a level of expertise and will increasingly be able to provide teachers with suggestions for effective strategies.

For more information about coaching, we recommend the book *Coaching Classroom Management: Strategies and Tools for Administrators and Coaches* (2nd ed., Sprick, Knight, Reinke, Skyles, & Barnes, 2010). This book provides detailed guidance for adopting a schoolwide classroom management model, training all teachers in using the model, and clarifying expectations for behavioral outcomes—the first two legs of the three-legged stool. The first three chapters are about the administrative support aspect of coaching, and the rest of the book covers the coach's role—how to function as a nonevaluative support to classroom teachers for classroom management.

More information about coaching is available in: Sprick, R., Knight, J., Reinke, W., Skyles, T. M., & Barnes, L. (2010). *Coaching classroom management: Strategies and tools for administrators and coaches* (2nd ed.). Eugene, OR: Pacific Northwest Publishing.

Provide peer coaching.

Peer coaching—teachers observing and supporting other teachers—is another valuable tool. Be sure to clarify that peer coaching is entirely nonevaluative and that teachers have a great deal of discretion about who observes them. You might set a minimum requirement for coaching. For example, each teacher should arrange to be coached for at least one 15- to 30-minute observation period per semester, followed by a debriefing period of the same length. Teachers can ask any other teacher to coach.

Teachers should also be able to specify what they want the coach to observe. Following are some examples of how teachers might approach fellow teachers and ask them to observe and coach.

Transition times. "I am really struggling with transitions with this group. Would you observe at 1:00 and 1:20? That's when students transition into cooperative groups and then from groups back to teacher-directed instruction. Could you time the length of those transitions? And then I'd like to talk with you about ideas for making those two transitions more efficient."

Ratios of positive interactions. "Ann, I've gotten really grumpy lately, and I would love to have you count my ratios of positive interactions. In other words, count my attention to positive behavior and the corrective comments that I give."

Two-column scripting on a particular student. "I want you to observe and collect data on Jonathan. I'm really struggling with him, so what I would like you to do is try two-column scripting. Identify a time, and then write what am I doing at that moment in one column and what Jonathan is doing in the other column. When an activity changes or Jonathan's behavior changes, write what Jonathan and I are doing. If you can script 20 minutes of class time, I think it would help me think about what I can do to adapt and help Jonathan be more successful."

Opportunities to respond. "Jack, would you please count my opportunities to respond? Am I just lecturing too much for these ninth-grade students? What can I do to create questions and activities to keep them engaged?"

On-task behavior. "Would you please observe and take data on on-task behavior between 9:30 and 9:50? I would really like to know the approximate percentage of on-task behavior during different activity structures during this 20-minute period."

Instructional strategies. "Janet, I've been watching the *Explicit Instruction* video to get some ideas on how to improve my delivery. Would you be able to observe me teaching and then discuss this technique with me?"

Peer coaches do not evaluate. Their job is to simply observe and give feedback. Even though the strategy is relatively easy, there are many benefits.

The people who were observed get useful data, and they also get a chance to put their best foot forward. That is, they know a colleague will be visiting the class, so they are motivated to prepare the best possible lesson and use the best possible management and instructional strategies. An analogy we've used previously in *Foundations* is that most people's homes are cleanest right before company arrives. The prospect of having a guest observer in the classroom can motivate a teacher to clean house—clear away the cobwebs of tired routines, uncover fresh ideas, and scrub away bad habits that might have crept into teaching and behavior management practices.

Observers also benefit. They get to see how other teachers' classrooms work, a learning opportunity that is not often available for teachers. They observe different procedures. Some are better than their own, so they might adapt them to improve their own classrooms. Some are not as good as their own, prompting an analysis of the advantages and disadvantages of both procedures. Observers get to see common problems and possibly come to new understandings about how *all* staff struggle with kids who are off task or disruptive.

When you create systems for peer observation and peer support, you break down the doors and walls between classrooms a bit, and the entire staff becomes less isolated and defensive as well as more collaborative and supportive about practices.

Facilitate building-based continuous improvement and problem solving related to student behavior.

Facilitation is the third concept related to this idea of support for teachers. Identify someone in the building to be responsible for keeping classroom behavior on everyone's radar. This person could be a classroom teacher, a counselor, an administrator, or someone else, but it should be someone with a lot of credibility with the vast majority of the staff. This facilitator won't be a stand-and-deliver trainer; he or she doesn't need to formally present to staff. The facilitator just needs to be passionate about the model and motivated to keep the dialogue going about classroom management as a lifelong learning task. If the person is on the Foundations Team, that's great, but it's not required. You might even assemble a small task force to act as facilitator.

Following is an example of facilitation as a long-term process:

Year 1: If you haven't adopted a classroom management model, the facilitator might organize a small group of staff members who are motivated to explore different models. If you have adopted a model, the facilitator might organize a whole-staff yearlong book study. CHAMPS and DSC each have nine chapters that include self-reflection exercises and topics for peer discussion. The staff could devote one month to each chapter for book study. You can apply this idea of book study to any other classroom management model, too.

The facilitator might organize grade-level or departmental teams and have each team take responsibility for preparing and leading the review and study of one chapter—first-grade teachers lead the September sessions on Chapter 1, second-grade teachers lead the October sessions on Chapter 2, and so on. In a secondary school, the chapter assignments might be given to different departments or professional learning communities so that eight or nine separate groups are formed. The facilitator doesn't do all the work. He or she organizes the teams, schedules the study sessions, and ensures that staff are engaged in both presenting and sharing knowledge and ideas and conducting discussions and spirited debates about classroom management procedures.

Year 2: In Year Two, the facilitator might have grade-level or departmental teams prepare 15-minute refreshers on each chapter. The teams might compete for prizes for the most fun refresher, the most insightful refresher, and so on. Each group should also be responsible for preparing and leading a repeat of last year's book study activities for staff who are new to the building.

Year 3: The facilitator might arrange for groups of three to four teachers from different grade levels or departments who collaborate to use tools for both self-assessment and peer coaching. Both CHAMPS and DSC provide specific data collection tools for those purposes. It's important to debrief with all staff by holding "What did we learn?" discussions.

Year 4: During the fourth year, the grade-level or departmental teams could prepare in-service presentations, each focusing on a different problem. Topics could include the challenges of getting students to remember their homework, chronic absenteeism, dealing with students who refuse to follow directions, and issues related to the reporting of bullying. Each team would use your classroom management framework as the common language for how you might approach and try to solve those problems.

Task 3 Action Steps & Evidence of Implementation

Action Steps	Evidence of Implementation
1. Discuss and plan to present to the faculty the concept of designated coaching. (Whether to offer coaching is probably a district-level staffing decision, but how the coaches are used for classroom management purposes should be shared with the staff.) • Who can be designated a coach? • How will coaches get training, if needed? (Options include book study, district inservice, personal study.) • How will the coaching service be advertised? (How will you tell teachers about the people available to visit their classrooms to talk about behavioral and instructional issues?) *(continued)*	Foundations Process: Meeting Minutes, Classroom Management Model Foundations Archive: Support Available to Staff

Action Steps	Evidence of Implementation
2. Discuss and plan to present to the faculty the concept of peer coaching. • Would peer coaching benefit teachers? • Should it be optional or required? • How can we structure a peer-coaching program? • How will the program be evaluated and the results reported? (For example, conduct a brief survey at the end of the year: Was the coaching beneficial? Should we continue it next year?)	Foundations Process: Meeting Minutes, Classroom Management Model Foundations Archive: Support Available to Staff
3. Discuss and plan to present to the faculty the concept of facilitating continuous improvement. • Would a facilitator in your building be beneficial? • How will that person be designated? • Will the facilitator be one person or a small task force? • What actions will be required to put a facilitator into place?	Foundations Process: Meeting Minutes, Classroom Management Model Foundations Archive: Support Available to Staff

Articulating Staff Beliefs and Solidifying Universal Procedures

DOCUMENTS*

- Statement of Beliefs from Four Schools (F-37)
- Creating a Statement of Beliefs About Behavior Support: Authors' Responses to Question 1 (F-05)
- Creating a Statement of Beliefs About Behavior Support: Authors' Responses to Question 2 (F-06)
- Creating a Statement of Beliefs About Behavior Support: Authors' Responses to Question 3 (F-07)
- Staff Beliefs Nomination Form (F-09)

* All documents listed are available on the CD.

INTRODUCTION

The process of defining, documenting, and actively using staff beliefs is an important element of *Foundations*. In this process, school personnel identify key behavior management and discipline principles that will guide the school, and they incorporate those principles into a written statement of staff beliefs. This guiding statement can help the school in two important ways:

- It helps ensure that staff behaviors, as well as school policies and procedures, are *goal directed*.

- It helps prevent school behavior management practices from deteriorating over time—drifting away from the preventive, positive model and toward an ineffective, reactive approach.

Lucius Annaeus Seneca, the Roman Stoic philosopher, wrote, "If one does not know to which port one is sailing, no wind is favorable." In other words, without an end goal, you might have difficulty formulating and consistently enforcing policies and procedures, and the staff could have difficulty working together. The statement of staff beliefs, along with your school mission statement, is the goal. All staff should be on one ship, moving in unity toward that goal by using positive, effective behavior management practices. Figure 3a shows a sample statement of staff beliefs.

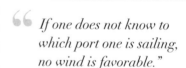

If one does not know to which port one is sailing, no wind is favorable."

LUCIUS ANNAEUS SENECA
(c. 4 BC–AD 65), Roman Stoic philosopher

This concept can be extended to the district level—district personnel can formulate a statement of beliefs to guide all schools in the district. This process may be driven or supported by school board policy. A district-level belief statement is valuable because it can create commonality across schools, something that can be particularly important in districts with lots of students who move from school to school. Like any mission or belief statement, however, there is a risk that the statement will be forgotten as soon as it is written. It will take effort by district personnel to keep the beliefs visible and alive—staff should refer to them often.

Following are suggestions for ways to incorporate district-level beliefs:

- When all schools in the district have adopted *Foundations* and the staff beliefs of individual schools have more similarities than differences, an overarching set of district-level beliefs can unite the schools and emphasize the common purpose of all staff in the district. District-level beliefs might be difficult to develop if the school staff beliefs are too different from each other.

Figure 3a *Excerpt from Statements of Staff Beliefs from Four Schools (F-37); Lincoln Elementary School Statement of Beliefs (composite of beliefs from several schools)*

SCHOOL SAMPLE

Lincoln Elementary School
Statement of Beliefs
(composite beliefs from several schools)

All staff members contribute to LES's friendly, inviting environment. We set the tone through our actions and attitudes. We demonstrate our continuous support and encouragement for all students in four important ways:

1. We teach students the expectations for responsible behavior in all school settings. Our schoolwide Guidelines for Success are:
   - Be responsible.
   - Always try.
   - Cooperate with others.
   - Treat everyone with respect.

2. We provide positive feedback to students when they are meeting expectations and following the Guidelines for Success.

3. We view minor misbehavior as a teaching opportunity, and we respond calmly and consistently with consequences and corrections.

4. We work collaboratively to solve chronic and severe behavior problems.

- The district, using suggestions from school staff, could develop a set of beliefs that serves as a starting point for the schools. Each school can embellish and customize the beliefs to fit their staff.

- The district (with suggestions from school staff) can develop a set of beliefs that all schools will adopt. This can be a good strategy with small districts that comprise, for example, two elementary schools, one middle school, and one high school.

- A large district may be able to develop beliefs by devoting some personnel to investigate and summarize the research literature and best practices on behavior. To browse a range of ideas on how districts incorporate positive behavior support, conduct an online search for "district behavior support policies."

If you have district or board policies that emphasize prevention, teaching of expectations, and positive interactions and recognition, along with a traditional code of conduct, you may not need to work through the tasks in this presentation. Instead, you might just review your current school and district policies with staff to reenergize and refresh their commitment to them. However, if your district policies are mainly a delineation of misbehaviors and corresponding consequences, this task can benefit your entire school community.

*E*xample From the Field: The Power of Staff Beliefs

An exceptional, wonderful principal and her staff developed a core set of beliefs similar to the examples we give later in this presentation. They diligently built behavior management procedures that fit within the beliefs. Discipline problems decreased dramatically, staff relationships with students improved greatly, and the teachers' sense of satisfaction and their empowerment to deal with children whose lives are difficult increased tremendously. These improvements occurred within the first 3 years of working with the *Foundations* program.

At the end of about 3 years of behavior improvement work by this school, the district announced that it needed a school that could house two special programs. One program was for students who were in crisis or in transit—homeless kids who needed a school for a month or so until they found a home and kids who lived with their mothers in battered women's shelters, for example. The other program was for severely emotionally disturbed students who could be mainstreamed into general education classrooms. Because the staff had been operating from staff beliefs about meeting the needs of all students and because they felt empowered to deal with children whose lives were in crisis, they said to the principal, "Tell the district that we want both of those programs here in our school because we are the best school in the district for those children."

This principal decided to retire a year or so later. She told her superintendent how proud she was of her staff, who, through *Foundations*, had developed a strong culture of unity, clarity, consistency, and positive discipline. She gave the school's statement of staff beliefs to the superintendent and said, "Would you please use this statement of staff beliefs as you interview for my replacement? If you hire an administrator who has a different philosophy, such as a my way or the highway attitude, you would tear my staff apart."

The superintendent replied, "Not only will I use your staff beliefs for selecting your replacement, but I'm also going to suggest to your replacement that he or she use it for selecting new staff members for your school."   —Authors

This presentation provides information about the process of defining and documenting the shared beliefs that underlie a school or district's behavior management and discipline practices.

Task 1: Understand Staff Beliefs provides and explains some sample statements of staff beliefs, describes the benefits of this improvement priority, and gives an overview of how to develop, document, and use the statement.

Task 2: Clarify Staff Beliefs describes an effective process that involves the entire staff in developing a statement of staff beliefs.

Task 3: Implement Staff Beliefs provides suggestions for ensuring that agreed-upon staff beliefs regarding behavior management and discipline are used and do not become simply words on paper.

Why Staff Beliefs Now?

You may wonder why this presentation about staff beliefs appears near the end of *Foundations*. In earlier editions of *Foundations*, information about staff beliefs was placed near the beginning. We realized, however, that it's best for staff to define what they believe in after hands-on work with the positive and proactive concepts and strategies of the *Foundations* approach. If staff begin committing their beliefs to paper too early, before they know what works and what doesn't work in their school, they might become divided as they debate the merits and drawbacks of teaching expectations, expecting teachers to maintain high ratios of positive interactions with students, using three levels of misbehavior, and so on.

On the other hand, when staff have worked on improving common areas and schoolwide policies by manipulating the STOIC variables (Structure, Teach expectations, Observe, Interact positively, and Correct fluently) and have seen the resulting improvements in student behavior, they are more likely to be unified in their beliefs. Although you can work through this presentation at any point in *Foundations*, we recommend you do so after many of the basic procedures for managing student behavior are aligned. Then the process of developing a written set of staff beliefs becomes a culminating celebratory activity of defining who you are as a staff.

TASK 1

Understand staff beliefs

In this task, we provide and explain some sample statements of staff beliefs, describe the benefits of this improvement priority, and give an overview of how to develop, document, and use your statement of staff beliefs.

What are staff beliefs?

A statement of staff beliefs is a written description of principles related to behavior management and discipline, as developed and agreed on by the faculty. Typically, only professional teaching staff are involved in developing the beliefs—students, parents, and other school personnel are not available for staff meetings or to participate in professional learning activities. But consider including representative paraprofessionals and students in the development process. If parents or community groups are influential partners in working with the school, consider including representatives of those groups as well.

The staff beliefs guide staff actions—their behavior and interactions with students— as well as the development and implementation of school policies and procedures.

Staff beliefs should support the school's mission statement.

The principles spelled out in the statement of staff beliefs should relate directly to the school's mission. Think about your school's mission statement. Do you refer to it frequently? Does it represent the culture of your school? Many schools have mission statements that they don't use and that have become empty words filed away in a drawer.

Here are two examples of good mission statements:

- *The staff of Franklin Middle School are committed to helping every child develop a love of learning and motivating every child to reach his or her full potential.*

- *Every day, every child in every classroom learns, grows, and feels respected.*

When I ask school leaders during training how many staff members, students, and parents can describe the mission of their school, the answer from most schools is: probably none. Actively use your mission statement. Talk with people about it. Celebrate it. And as you develop your staff beliefs, ensure that you are constantly asking yourself and other staff: Will these beliefs and principles achieve the mission of the school?

Decide when to develop a statement of staff beliefs and who will develop it.

As we explained in the introduction, we recommend working on staff beliefs after staff members have had time to work on some of the more action-oriented improvement priorities, such as developing Guidelines for Success and improving common areas. You will develop more staff buy-in and reduce resistance to improvement efforts when staff experience some early successes; then they might be better able to work together to develop staff beliefs. So a good time to work on staff beliefs is when you are in the middle or toward the end of working through the other *Foundations* modules.

Decide who will guide the development and implementation of a statement of staff beliefs—this will probably be either the Foundations Team or a dedicated task force. The team or task force should seek suggestions and opinions from the staff.

Document the staff beliefs.

Document the finalized statement of staff beliefs in writing and include it in the Foundations Archive and the Staff Handbook. Figure 3b shows samples adapted from staff beliefs developed by *Foundations* schools that went through the process we explain in the next task. These samples nicely summarize all the principles of *Foundations*. They are available as Sample F-37 on the Module F CD. You may use them as templates for your own statement, but your school staff must develop their own beliefs. It is critical that staff members believe in and *own* their staff beliefs.

Actively use the statement of staff beliefs.

Your statement of staff beliefs can be used in many ways:

- It can guide staff development. Whenever you are working on improving or developing policies and procedures, ask, Does this policy or procedure fit with our staff beliefs?

- It can solidify the culture of the school, even across changes in administration.

- It can create a sense of unity, belonging, and pride among staff members.

- Use it as part of the interview process when hiring new staff members. Some schools give a copy of their staff beliefs to potential staff members before job interviews, explain that the statement defines the culture of the school, and ask the interviewees to be ready to discuss how the staff beliefs fit with their own teaching style.

- Use it as part of the orientation process for new staff members. Staff beliefs can give a powerful, positive first impression of your school.

***Figure 3b**   Sample Statements of Staff Beliefs from Four Schools (F-37); thanks to Duncan U. Fletcher High School, Arlington Middle School, and Duval County Public Schools in Florida*

SCHOOL SAMPLE

Statements of Staff Beliefs from Four Schools

Fletcher High School
Staff Beliefs About Behavior Support

1. We believe that staff, parents, and students are responsible for managing student behavior. However, the adults in the building have the greatest responsibility.

2. We believe that the purpose of our behavior management efforts is to provide a safe, civil, and productive school where mutual respect is apparent.

3. We believe that our behavior management goals can best be achieved by providing a positive, respectful environment and ensuring that the Guidelines for Success are embraced throughout our school.

4. We believe that minor misbehavior should be regarded as a teaching opportunity.

5. We believe that all staff members should apply consistent, clear student expectations and respond to misbehavior consistently.

Arlington Middle School
Staff Beliefs

The faculty and staff will promote a friendly and inviting learning environment at Arlington Middle School through positive attitudes and actions. We will demonstrate our support and encouragement for all students by doing the following:

- Teach, model, and practice the 3 R's: Respect, Responsibility, and Restraint.
- Treat everyone with respect.
- Work collaboratively to solve chronic and severe behavior problems.
- Hold faculty, staff, and students accountable for their own behavior.

 This sample can be printed from the Module F CD.

Figure 3b (continued)

SCHOOL SAMPLE

Lincoln Elementary School
Statement of Beliefs

(composite beliefs from several schools)

All staff members contribute to LES's friendly, inviting environment. We set the tone through our actions and attitudes. We demonstrate our continuous support and encouragement for all students in four important ways:

1. We teach students the expectations for responsible behavior in all school settings. Our schoolwide Guidelines for Success are:

   - Be responsible.
   - Always try.
   - Cooperate with others.
   - Treat everyone with respect.

2. We provide positive feedback to students when they are meeting expectations and following the Guidelines for Success.

3. We view minor misbehavior as a teaching opportunity, and we respond calmly and consistently with consequences and corrections.

4. We work collaboratively to solve chronic and severe behavior problems.

Adams School District
Districtwide Beliefs About Behavor Support

(composite beliefs from several small districts)

The staff of Adams School District are committed to providing welcoming and supportive educational settings where all students can thrive. We believe that:

- Staff behavior creates the climate of the school, and a positive, welcoming, and inviting climate should be intentionally created and continuously maintained.

- All student behaviors necessary for success need to be overtly and directly articulated and taught to mastery. "If you want it, teach it!"

- All students should have equal access to good instruction and behavior support, regardless of their skills or backgrounds.

- Clarity of expectations and consistency of enforcement are essential for all common areas and schoolwide policies.

- Punitive and corrective techniques are necessary, but have significant limitations. Misbehavior presents teaching opportunities.

- Everyone (even students who make poor choices) should be treated with respect.

Task 1 Action Steps & Evidence of Implementation

Action Steps	Evidence of Implementation

1. Preview Tasks 2 and 3 of this presentation.
 	
2. Decide *when*—before, in conjunction with, or after other priorities—to develop the statement of staff beliefs.
 	
3. Decide *who* will guide the development and implementation of a statement of staff beliefs.
 	
   • Foundations Team: Have team members review Tasks 2 and 3 of this presentation and do the Action Steps for those tasks.
   • Dedicated task force: Establish the task force. Then have the task force members watch this entire presentation (Module F, Presentation 3) and do the Action Steps for Tasks 2 and 3.
 	
4. Have all professional staff and everyone who will be involved in the meeting to define staff beliefs view or read this task.
	Foundations Process: Meeting Minutes, Staff Beliefs

TASK 2

Clarify staff beliefs

The first step in the process of defining staff beliefs is to design an effective development plan. Remember that all faculty need to be included in the process guided by the Foundations Team. And don't expect to hammer out the staff beliefs during one faculty meeting—schedule a period of about 90 minutes on an early-release or professional development day. The sample plan presented below is for a 90-minute meeting. You may implement it as is, modify it, or just use it to prompt ideas for creating another development plan.

If you cannot arrange a 90-minute block, you can accomplish the same work with a series of brief discussions over a period of several weeks. A detailed plan for this alternative development process is available as Form F-08 on the Module F CD.

Consider reviewing the school's mission statement before the 90-minute meeting. This review will set the stage for articulating staff beliefs about behavior and discipline. You might choose to include the entire staff in this review. This is a great opportunity to reenergize the staff. Emphasize that the mission is not just words on a website—it is the reason you all come to school and work so hard every day. Following are some common features of effective mission statements:

- They emphasize *all* or *every* student. The school should not cater only to certain groups, such as high achievers. It should serve everyone.
- Staff members, students, parents, and families know the mission statement.
- Staff members use the mission statement.

Prepare for and conduct the staff beliefs meeting.

Determine who should be involved in the meeting to articulate staff beliefs. The entire professional staff should attend. Consider inviting nonprofessional staff and parent and community groups. In secondary schools, consider inviting student leaders (leaders from different social groups, not just elected leaders).

Before the meeting, prepare copies of the following three Creating a Statement of Staff Beliefs About Behavior Support documents (see the Module F CD) for each person who will attend the meeting.

- Authors' Response to Question 1 (F-05; Figure 3c)
- Authors' Response to Question 2 (F-06; Figure 3d)
- Authors' Response to Question 3 (F-07; Figure 3e)

You will distribute these documents separately, so don't staple them together.

You'll also need a timer to ensure that the self-reflection and discussion periods stay on schedule.

Figure 3c ~~tatement~~ *of Beliefs About Behavior Support: Authors' Response to Question 1 (I~~-~~*

Creating a Statement of Staff Beliefs About Behavior Support: Authors' Response to Question 1

QUESTION 1: Who is responsible for managing student behavior in a school?

The adults in a school (the staff) must assume ultimate responsibility for managing student behavior. The responsibility must be shared by all staff members, both certified and classified, with classroom teachers taking the lead.

Rationale for Authors' Response to Question 1

The adults in a school (the staff) must assume ultimate responsibility for managing student behavior.

In schools where students are expected to behave responsibly and be actively engaged and highly motivated, staff members are required to be:

- PROACTIVE: They must structure settings to maximize student success.

- POSITIVE: They must interact with students in friendly and optimistic ways.

- INSTRUCTIONAL: They must teach expectations, provide descriptive positive feedback, and use calm, consistent, and informational corrections.

The focus on adult responsibility does not mean that students are not held accountable or taught to take responsibility for their own actions. It simply means that staff members realize that the first steps—being proactive, positive, and instructional, and responding calmly and consistently to misbehavior (especially chronic or severe misbehavior)—are theirs.

Administrators, no matter how competent, cannot cure misbehavior by themselves. The only way students will learn to behave responsibly is if every staff member thoughtfully and consistently implements all adopted behavior management policies and procedures. All staff members should assume responsibility for managing student behavior in common areas: They should correct misbehavior when they see it (running in the hall, for example) and provide attention and positive feedback for responsible behavior. Classroom teachers should assume the primary responsibility for managing student behavior in their own rooms. The building administrator should help the staff deal with severe and chronic misbehavior. Specialists (counselors, social workers, school psychologists, district behavior specialists) should be available to all staff members for help with establishing individualized management plans.

 Forms can be printed from the Module F CD.

Creating a Statement of Staff Beliefs About Behavior Support:
Authors' Response to Question 2 (p. 1 of 2)

QUESTION 2: What should the goals of a school's behavior management efforts be?

Two major goals of a school's behavior management efforts should be:

a) *Create a productive school environment for students and staff.*
b) *Create a physically and emotionally safe environment for students and staff.*

Rationale for Authors' Response to Question 2

The ultimate goal of behavior management policies and procedures is that more learning (and more joy in learning) takes place when those policies and procedures are implemented than when they are not implemented. If the result of a staff's behavior management efforts is only a quieter and more orderly school with no additional learning taking place, the efforts are largely a waste of time. We believe that it is important to help students learn to behave responsibly and be highly motivated while engaged in meaningful activities. This does not mean that we believe misbehaving students should be removed from their classrooms. Students who are repeatedly removed from their classrooms do not have a chance to learn. The best behavior management policies and procedures reduce the negative impact of one student's misbehavior on the learning of other students. At the same time, they help the misbehaving student learn how to behave more responsibly in the future.

When students do not feel physically safe, learning will not take place. In his hierarchy of needs, Abraham Maslow* suggests that a person who is afraid of physical injury will not be motivated to engage in higher-order or noble purposes—for example, satisfying the need to know and learn. The student who has been stuffed into a locker by bullies, the student who has been sexually molested in a restroom, and the student who has been shoved around at recess all have one thing in common—their major focus during the school day is figuring out how to keep physically safe. They cannot focus on learning, belonging, or growing.

This focus on physical safety may be difficult for staff members to understand, particularly if they themselves feel safe. Staff members may assume that because they feel physically safe, students must as well. Unfortunately, there is increasing evidence that a distressing number of students do not feel physically safe while at school.

Just as people are not motivated to higher purposes when they fear for their physical safety, they are also not motivated when they fear emotional trauma. A student who has been publicly ridiculed by a teacher is not likely to try to excel in that teacher's classroom. At best, the student might attempt to keep a low profile so he won't be ridiculed again. At worst, the student might seek revenge against the teacher by setting up

---

* Abraham Maslow (1908–1970) was a psychologist and one of the founders and driving forces behind humanistic psychology, a school of thought that became popular in the 1950s. At a time when most psychologists were focusing on abnormal behavior, Maslow sought to understand the positive aspects of mental health. His 1954 book (the third edition was published in 1987), *Motivation and Personality*, lays out his theory of human motivation and the hierarchy of needs.

Creating a Statement of Staff Beliefs About Behavior Support:
Authors' Response to Question 2 (p. 2 of 2)

an ongoing battle of wills or even resorting to violence. It is critical that staff members understand that ridiculing, humiliating, or belittling students in any way is not appropriate and cannot be tolerated.

Students also need to be safe from emotional victimization by other students. Although it may not be possible to completely eliminate teasing, cliques, put-downs, ganging up, and so on, a school staff can and should make every effort to minimize the likelihood of any student being victimized, verbally or nonverbally, by other students.

 Forms can be printed from the Module F CD.

Figure 3e *Creating a Statement of Beliefs About Behavior Support: Authors'*
Response to Question 3 (F-07)

Creating a Statement of Staff Beliefs About Behavior Support: Authors' Response to Question 3 (p. 1 of 2)

QUESTION 3: How can a school's behavior management goals best be achieved?

Note: The answer to this question obviously depends on what the school's goals are. This model answer assumes that the goal is to have a safe, civil, and productive school.

> *A school's behavior management policies and procedures should be:*
>
> * *Designed to meet students' basic needs*
> * *Proactive*
> * *Positive*
> * *Instructional*

Rationale for Authors' Response to Question 3

Students, like all people, have basic needs. Meeting students' basic needs is not only fundamentally humane, but it is also practical. Students who are not getting their needs met sometimes engage in misbehavior to get them met. For example, a student who is not getting the attention she needs might misbehave because she has discovered that adults pay attention to students who break the rules. A student who is not having his needs for belonging and purpose met might be tempted to join a destructive clique or gang.

One of the most effective means of ensuring a safe, civil, and productive school is to establish expectations and structure that increase the likelihood that students behave responsibly. A school might:

* Teach students explicitly how they are expected to behave.

* Ensure that the structural and organizational features of the various school settings prompt responsible rather than irresponsible student behavior.

* Ensure adequate adult supervision for all school settings.

* Give staff members sufficient information and support regarding the behavior management policies and procedures they are expected to implement.

Students will behave more responsibly at a smoothly run school where the adults know their roles, feel competent and supported, and are upbeat and encouraging than they will at a disorganized school where staff members don't know what other staff members are doing and are generally depressed and negative.

All staff members should interact with each other, with students, and with parents in positive, respectful, and optimistic ways. Positive interactions and attitudes breed positive behaviors and attitudes in others, and it is the responsibility of staff to set this tone in the school. Staff also need to understand that there is tremendous power in interacting frequently with individual students when the students are not engaged in misbehavior. Interactions include acknowledging students when they behave responsibly, giving students noncontingent attention (simply greeting and showing an interest in them, for example), and providing highly interactive forms of instruction. Frequent and positive interactions with staff when they are behaving

Creating a Statement of Staff Beliefs About Behavior Support: Authors' Response to Question 3 (p. 2 of 2)

responsibly show students that staff are genuinely interested in them as people and in their success as students. On the other hand, students who have predominantly negative interactions with staff will most likely learn that staff members simply want to control their behavior and that it is easier to get attention by misbehaving than by behaving responsibly.

Students should not have to guess about the behavior that is expected of them. If staff expect students to behave responsibly, they must teach the students what responsible behavior is—in each school setting. If staff expect students to be motivated and engaged in meaningful activities, they have to create meaningful activities, communicate the value of those activities to students, and directly teach students how to be engaged and motivated.

Staff members also need to give frequent positive feedback when students are meeting the expectations. First, the feedback lets students know when they are doing things right. This is not as silly as it sounds. Some students actually do not realize they are behaving responsibly unless they are "caught" and given information that communicates the importance of what they are doing. This kind of feedback eventually leads to self-motivated individuals who know what it takes to be responsible.

Second, positive feedback lets students know that staff members notice and are pleased when the students try to meet the positive expectations. If staff want and expect students to behave responsibly and be actively engaged, they must take the time and make the effort to communicate to students that they are aware of and appreciate the students' efforts.

Finally, staff members need to remember that their main purpose when responding to student misbehavior should be to teach students how to behave more responsibly. When a misbehaving student does not know the behavioral expectations or how to meet the expectations, a staff member's response should give the student information and/or have the student practice the appropriate behavior. When a student misbehaves despite knowing what is expected, a staff member's response should be the unemotional implementation of an appropriate correction to help the student learn that actions have logical costs.

 Forms can be printed from the Module F CD.

INTRODUCTION. Before beginning the discussion portion of the meeting, explain and define staff beliefs as the guiding principles for schoolwide behavior management and discipline. Also explain the purpose and benefits of developing them. You may skip this step if the entire staff read or viewed Task 1 of this presentation. (5 minutes)

STEP 1. Display Question 1 and read it aloud.

> *Question 1: Who is responsible for managing student behavior in a school?*

For 1 minute, have all staff members silently reflect on this question and make notes about their initial answers. Note that the question refers to schools in general, not your school specifically. Be sure to emphasize the no-talking rule! (1 minute)

STEP 2. Have staff gather in small groups (table groups of three to five people, for example) to discuss the similarities and differences in their answers. (5 minutes)

STEP 3. Distribute the Authors' Response to Question 1 document (Form F-05) to each staff member. Have everyone read the document and then discuss the authors' perspective compared with the answers of people in the group. Each group should also prepare a brief summary of their discussion. (5 minutes)

STEP 4. Have each small group give a brief report on their discussion of Question 1. Then have the entire staff have a general discussion about the similarities and differences in the groups' answers and how they compared with the authors' response. (5 minutes)

STEP 5. Repeat Steps 1–4 with Question 2 and Question 3.

> *Question 2: What should the goals of a school's behavior management efforts be?*
> *Question 3: How can a school's behavior management goals best be achieved?*

STEP 6. When staff are finished discussing Question 3, distribute Sample F-37. Have participants read the samples and discuss them in their small groups. (5 minutes)

STEP 7. Bring everyone back together and encourage open discussion about the words and phrases that describe the staff's goals and beliefs about their work in your school. What words or phrases define the identity of the staff as a whole and represent the positive school culture you are trying to develop? (17 minutes)

STEP 8. If you've adhered to our suggested time limits for each step, you will have about 15 minutes remaining for this last step of the 90-minute meeting. Lead the whole group in an effort to achieve consensus on a written statement of staff beliefs.

If the group agrees on a set of beliefs by the end of 15 minutes, you can formally adopt your statement of staff beliefs and briefly celebrate. Be sure to schedule a lengthier and more elaborate celebration later. Staff should be excited about their accomplishment and feel a greater sense of unity—they have defined who they are as a staff.

If staff don't reach consensus during that last 15 minutes, consider doing this: Identify specific areas of disagreement and inform the participants that the Foundations Team or staff beliefs task force will develop alternative statements for staff consideration at a subsequent meeting. Encourage attendees to write their ideas and opinions on their sample staff beliefs handouts before they leave the meeting. What did they like about the proposed staff beliefs or the samples? What didn't they like? Have them sign their names so the team can ask them questions later. The team can use this input from staff to develop some new proposals.

> More information about the Adopt step of the Improvement Cycle, including voting criteria, is in Module A, Presentation 3, Task 3.

Continue this development process until you reach consensus. Subsequent discussions about proposed statements of staff beliefs should take no more than 10 minutes of a staff meeting. If the statement is adopted, celebrate! If not, the team will work on a revised proposal. We suggest you limit the revisions to two; that is, the staff will vote three times—the initial vote during the 90-minute meeting and two more votes on revisions. If a statement is not adopted after the third voting cycle, the administrator should put together a statement that best represents the staff's overall ideas and opinions.

> If you cannot arrange a 90-minute block of time, you can accomplish the same work with a series of brief discussions over a period of several weeks. A detailed plan for this alternative development process is available on the Module F CD as Form F-08.

Task 2 Action Steps & Evidence of Implementation

Action Steps	Evidence of Implementation
Design and implement a development plan for creating a statement of staff beliefs for your school. Begin with a review of your school's mission statement.	Foundations Process: Meeting Minutes, Staff Beliefs Final adopted statement of staff beliefs should be included in: • Foundations Archive: Mission Statement/Staff Beliefs/ Team Purpose • Staff Handbook: Staff Beliefs • Student and Parent Handbook: Staff Beliefs

TASK 3

Implement staff beliefs

You've developed and formally adopted a statement of staff beliefs. Now it's time to introduce your statement to others and establish it as an affirmation of your school culture.

Launch your statement of staff beliefs.

Consider the following suggestions for launching your statement of staff beliefs.

Celebrate the completion of the statement with something as simple as an announcement during a staff meeting or as elaborate as a staff party or a parent/community reception. Whatever you do, use the occasion to communicate pride in the cooperation that staff displayed and emphasize that the statement of staff beliefs is more than just words.

- For staff members, it provides key information about what they believe in and are committed to.

- For district-level administration, it is a reflection of the staff's unanimity of focus.

- For the community, it is an affirmation of the staff's commitment and dedication to a student-centered approach to education.

Make the statement of staff beliefs highly visible. Formally add the statement of staff beliefs to your Staff Handbook. Share the statement of staff beliefs with students, parents, families, district administration, and the community.

Ensure continued and effective use of the statement of staff beliefs.

You should also take steps to ensure the continued and effective use of the statement of staff beliefs. The staff put a lot of time and effort into creating it, so it would be a shame to let it fall by the wayside. Following are some suggestions for keeping the statement of staff beliefs embedded in your school culture.

Review the statement of staff beliefs at least once a year. Use the review to encourage staff self-reflection. For example, say to everyone at a staff meeting, "Between now and our next staff meeting, think about which of our staff beliefs you operate from daily. Which beliefs do you tend to forget during times of stress? When you feel stressed, how will you remind yourself to base your actions on the beliefs?"

Also use the review to identify staff development and training needs. If staff members seem to be drifting into reactive forms of discipline, for example, perhaps an inservice is needed to remind them about the importance of proactive and positive discipline.

Include the statement of staff beliefs (and mission statement) in administrative reviews and coaching. The statements can guide goal setting, for example. Staff members can be encouraged to set goals that demonstrate that they are working toward achieving the mission of the school and following the staff beliefs daily.

Share the statement of staff beliefs when hiring and welcoming new staff members. This action communicates that the staff places a high value on the beliefs and sets clear expectations that new staff should value the beliefs as well.

Incorporate the statement of staff beliefs into school rituals and traditions.

- Create a ritual to use when a staff member retires or moves away. For example, give an award or certificate that celebrates how the person exemplified the staff beliefs.

- Develop a program in which awards based on the principles reflected in the statement of staff beliefs are presented to individual staff members throughout the school year. The Foundations Team can periodically ask staff members to nominate a staff member who exemplifies one of the beliefs—for example, "We apply behavioral expectations for common areas and schoolwide policies, as well as consequences for not meeting those expectations, consistently throughout the school." The nominations are entered into a drawing for a prize, such as the principal covering their class for a half hour. Figure 3f on the next page shows a sample nomination form. Form F-09 is provided on the CD as a Word document that you can customizer for use in your school.

Figure 3f   *Staff Beliefs Nomination Form (F-09)*

Staff Beliefs Nomination Form

Nominated Staff Member: _____   Nominated by: _____

How did the nominated staff member exemplify the staff beliefs checked in the box below?

☐ We understand that staff behavior creates the climate of the school. A positive climate needs to be intentionally created and continuously maintained.

☐ We believe that all students and their families should feel welcome and included in our community.

☐ We teach students the expectations for responsible behavior in all school settings by relating student actions to our Guidelines for Success. That is, we encourage students to be responsible, always try, do their best, cooperate with others, and treat everyone with dignity and respect.

☐ We provide positive feedback to students when they are meeting expectations and following the Guidelines for Success.

☐ We understand that punitive and corrective techniques have limitations and that misbehavior is a teaching opportunity.

☐ We apply behavioral expectations for common areas and schoolwide policies, as well as consequences for not meeting those expectations, consistently throughout the school.

☐ We work collaboratively to solve chronic and severe behavior problems.

☐ We believe that all students should have equal access to good instruction and behavior support, regardless of their skills and background.

☐ We understand that if we want it, we have to teach it. (We explicitly teach expectations to students.)

☐ We endeavor to treat everyone with respect every day.

 This form can be printed from the Module F CD.

Task 3 Action Steps & Evidence of Implementation

Action Steps	Evidence of Implementation
1. Develop and implement a plan for celebrating the completion of your school's statement of staff beliefs. 2. Develop and implement a plan for making your school's statement of staff beliefs visible.	Foundations Process: Staff Beliefs
3. Schedule an annual review of your school's statement of staff beliefs.	Foundations Process: Planning Calendar
4. With the administrator, identify ideas for using your school's statement of staff beliefs in administrative reviews and coaching. Make a plan for at least one of the identified ideas to be implemented. 5. Identify ideas for school rituals and traditions that incorporate your school's statement of staff beliefs. Make a plan to implement at least one of the identified ideas.	Foundations Process: Staff Beliefs

Early-Stage Interventions for General Education Classrooms

CONTENTS

DOCUMENTS*

- Discussion Record (F-10)
- Student Status Report, Version 1 (F-11a)
- Academic Assistance, Version 1 (One-page form; F-12a)
- Goal Setting, Version 1 (F-14a)
- Long-Range Goal Setting (F-13)
- Misbehavior Recording Sheet, Daily by Student Name (F-16)
- Misbehavior Recording Sheet, Weekly by Student Name (F-17)
- Behavior Counting Form (F-15)
- Countoon Behavior Counting Form (F-18)
- Interval Chart/Scatterplot, Version 1 (F-19a)
- Interval Chart/Scatterplot, Version 2 (F-19b)
- Rating Scale (F-20)
- Participation Evaluation Record (F-21)
- Plan for Connecting and Motivating (F-22a)
- STOIC Intervention Planning Form (F-24)

* All documents listed are available on the CD. Other documents not shown in this presentation are also available on the CD (see Appendix C for a complete list).

INTRODUCTION

In this presentation, we cover a set of early-stage interventions that classroom teachers can implement before they rally more intensive support for students with behavior problems. These interventions are part of a Multi-Tiered System of Support (MTSS) or Response to Intervention (RTI) for behavior.

In many districts, there is a gap between general education and special education. Classroom teachers work very hard to implement effective instruction and classroom management, especially when they are supported by schoolwide behavior initiatives such as *Foundations* and CHAMPS. But when an individual student exhibits chronic misbehavior, such as disruption, off-task behavior, or disrespect, that is resistant to the teacher's management procedures, the teacher sometimes believes that the student needs to be placed elsewhere. However, because most districts have very limited resources, there are very few *elsewheres* available. In addition, the elsewheres that special educators *have* created often do not benefit students with behavior problems.

We do not mean to be critical of special education or general education. We are simply saying that our national educational system has evolved in a way that fostered a vast gap between general education and special education.

The move toward MTSS is an effort to reduce that divide between general and special education and to ensure that school resources are matched to students' needs. However, unless bridges are built between universal procedures (what you do with all students) and targeted and intensive procedures (what you do with students with greater needs), even MTSS can fail to create what schools need: a seamless provision of services and a professional mindset that all school staff need to be active problem-solvers.

You can build part of that bridge between universal and targeted procedures by empowering general education teachers with a building-based or—even better—district-based protocol of early-stage interventions. In this protocol, teachers try the simplest strategy that is likely to work. If it doesn't work, they try another. And if that doesn't work, they try another. You might think that a protocol is limiting to professional practice. But doctors, nurses, architects, engineers, and pilots all have protocols of professional practices. When they are presented with a particular circumstance, the protocol tells them to try x first, then y, then z.

Here's an example of a nonprofessional medical protocol that many of you can relate to. Let's say you awake one morning with a mild headache. You have no long-term history of headaches, so you have never consulted a doctor about them and have no established course of action to treat them. You would probably not call an ambulance or even your doctor for this mild headache. You would probably follow a common early-stage standard protocol for headaches—take a couple of aspirin and hope they work. If the aspirin relieves the headache, you'll probably follow that same protocol 6 months or a year later when you have another mild headache.

But if the headaches become chronic and aspirin doesn't reduce the frequency of the problem, you would probably try some over-the-counter medications. If they are not effective, you will begin to think about other possible contributing factors. You might consider stress levels, the amount of rest you get every night, your diet, and allergies.

If you had frequent headaches for several weeks, you would probably see your doctor, who would follow a protocol to determine the cause and best treatment for your problem. She would take your history and prescribe a medication. If the medication didn't work, she would try another. She would probably want data and ask you to keep a log: when the headaches occur, their intensity on a scale of 1 to 10, what you were doing before you got the headache, and so on. If the headaches continued, she would probably conduct tests to search for and rule out possible causes. She would examine your stress level, blood pressure, respiration, blood oxygen levels, diet, allergies, and so on.

We suggest that your school or district develop a similar protocol for the behavior and motivation problems of individual students. All staff should be trained in that protocol. Teachers will then speak a common language and be empowered with an intervention plan that does not have to be reinvented for each new problem. They will not have to spend time creating unique interventions or waste time being indecisive— the protocol allows them to operate on semiautomatic pilot.

The adoption of a standard protocol also creates accountability to actually implement these interventions. Sometimes teachers think, "I just know this student needs more help than I can provide. Why do I have to go through the protocol?"

Well, let's return to the headache example. Let's say your over-the-counter remedies don't work and you go to the doctor, a general practitioner. The doctor immediately refers you to a neurosurgeon, telling the surgeon, "I just know that this patient needs brain surgery right away." The neurosurgeon would of course work through the protocol of early-stage nonintrusive medical interventions and tests before even thinking about an expensive CAT scan, much less surgery. If any of those early-stage interventions work, the problem is solved. If none of them work, the neurosurgeon has learned more about your problem, and that information guides all subsequent intervention efforts. But the neurosurgeon's time and expertise is much better spent on patients with life-threatening illnesses. The time he spends treating your minor headaches is time taken away from much sicker patients.

The protocol can't be a rigid set of hoops that one has to jump through, however. If you awoke with an extremely intense headache, you would call a doctor immediately.

And that doctor would, under the circumstances, launch a different protocol. Because your symptoms suggest a stroke, which needs immediate attention, she would send an ambulance and tell you what to do while you wait and what to expect when you arrive at the hospital.

So how does this example translate to education? MTSS must be flexible. For example, let's say a student with no records from previous schools moves into your district. The child is obviously visually impaired. No one should say, just to follow the MTSS structure and protocol, "Let's move through a tiered system of support for this child for several weeks before we investigate special education." You would investigate special education immediately. Likewise, in the event of truly extreme behavior deficits or excesses—if a student threatens to hurt himself or others, for example—you would involve other players immediately and forget about the early-stage protocol.

We advocate that all general education and special education teachers be trained in a standard protocol of early interventions for students who exhibit behavioral and motivational problems. Each task in this presentation describes a different intervention within this protocol:

- Task 1: Use Planned Discussion
- Task 2: Use Academic Assessment and Assistance
- Task 3: Have Students Set Goals
- Task 4: Collect Data and Debrief
- Task 5: Maintain High Ratios of Positive to Corrective Interactions
- Task 6: Use a STOIC Function-Based Analysis and Intervention.

These early-stage interventions can become part of your standard protocol. If you choose to adopt them as such, the tasks in video, book, or PowerPoint format can be used in professional development settings such as after-school inservices and study groups.

We have not included Action Steps after each task in this presentation, as we do in most of the other presentations in *Foundations*. Rather, we include some Action Steps below for you (the Foundations Team) to consider as you decide whether and how to use the concept of early-stage interventions as an adopted protocol that all teachers learn and follow.

Action Steps & Evidence of Implementation

Action Steps	Evidence of Implementation
1. Discuss whether your school should adopt a protocol for early-stage interventions and whether to recommend that your district do so. 2. If so, discuss when and how to train teachers in the protocol. Options include: • Develop your own protocol of interventions and provide training. • Use the *Foundations* books and videos to introduce the staff to each of the early-stage interventions. • Use the book *Interventions: Evidence-Based Behavioral Strategies for Individual Students* (2nd ed.) by Randy Sprick and Mickey Garrison (2008). Section 2 provides an in-depth study of the six early-stage interventions and includes tools for whole-staff book study. 3. Discuss whether to require teachers to document their implementation of each intervention. Part of MTSS involves documenting each attempted intervention and its outcome.	Foundations Process: Meeting Minutes Final protocol, training plan and materials, and expectations for documentation should be filed in the following: • Foundations Archive: Interventions for Individual Students • Staff Handbook: Early-Stage Interventions

TASK 1

Use Planned Discussion

Planned Discussion has the potential to positively affect just about any behavior and should be an integral part of the intervention plan for any child whose language skills are sufficient. This intervention may work by itself for a minor concern or in the early stages of a moderate problem. Even when a problem requires more intensive intervention, engaging in discussion is usually worth the time. It will almost certainly improve the results of other interventions you try.

The purpose of Planned Discussion is to demonstrate your concern so that the student truly understands it, to involve the student in brainstorming solutions toward her own success, and to let that student know with certainty that you are there to help her learn and grow. Low in structure and high in potential, Planned Discussion should be one of your first steps in designing an intervention.

For more information about Planned Discussion, see Sprick, R., & Garrison, M. (2008*). Interventions: Evidence-Based Behavioral Strategies for Individual Students* (2nd ed.; pp. 71–92). Eugene, OR: Pacific Northwest Publishing. This task corresponds to Intervention A in the *Interventions* book.

STEP 1. Prepare to meet with the student.

A. Identify the central concern.

Before meeting with the student, go through a mental list of behavioral concerns about the student and define for yourself the primary concern. How pervasive is the problem? What other factors should be considered? Where, when, and how often does the behavior occur? Is the problem more likely to occur in particular situations or with certain people? Keep this information in mind as you go through the planning steps.

B. Establish a focus.

Isolating your target concern may be relatively simple—off-task behavior, work completion, interactions with other students, problems with authority, and similar issues. Sometimes, however, a student presents an interrelated set of misbehaviors. In this case, narrow the focus of your discussion to just one or two problems. Introducing too many concerns at once may increase the student's sense of inadequacy and reduce the likelihood of success. Also, addressing just one issue often produces a ripple effect—other behavioral problems improve even though they weren't addressed specifically.

Be sure to identify some of the student's strengths. When you talk with the student, you want to be able to begin and end the discussion with valid information about the student's positive behaviors. Doing so demonstrates interest, perceptiveness, and authentic concern. When a student hears positive attributes from a voice of authority, the comments often register more deeply than even the student is aware of. As time goes on and you discuss progress or lack of progress with the behavior of concern, plan to keep coming back to the student's strengths as a way to maintain a positive and encouraging tone.

C. Determine who should participate in the discussion.

Inform the student's parents that you will be meeting with their child to discuss a concern and invite them to participate. If the issue is relatively mild, however, you can meet only with the student. For more serious concerns, consider asking the school counselor, an interventionist, or even the administrator to attend. In any case, be sure that the student feels like a partner in the discussion rather than the focus of an inquisition.

D. Schedule the discussion for a neutral time.

Planned Discussion should not take place in the immediate aftermath of an incident. An interaction at that time tends to take the form of a reprimand rather than a productive discussion. Emotions may be high, and the conversation is more likely to be defensive and argumentative. A better strategy is to put enough distance between yourself and the incident for emotions to cool, but schedule the meeting close enough in time for the concern to still be relevant. For minor or infrequent concerns, this might be 20 minutes or 1 hour after the incident. For a major issue, wait until the next day. Create an agenda for the discussion, and keep the time free from distractions and interruptions.

E. Make an appointment with the student to discuss the concern.

Let the student know who will be present and why you will be meeting. Invite the student to think about the concern in advance. By arranging the discussion for a neutral time, you are clarifying that the discussion is not just a response to an immediate concern, but also a time to work on a plan.

F. Plan to keep a written record of the discussion.

We recommend that you use a form such as the Discussion Record shown in Figure 4a on the next page (available as Form F-10 on the Module F CD) to document your Planned Discussion. The Discussion Record prompts you to write a

Figure 4a   *Discussion Record (F-10) with sample notes*

Discussion Record

Student __Joey__   Teacher __Mr. Anderson__   Date __10/1__

Participants __Mr. Anderson, Joey, Mrs. Burke__   Grade/Class __3__

Describe the problem. __Joey has trouble getting his work done. The problem seems to be__ __motivation. He goofs around instead of working about half the time. He has a hard time__ __sitting still.__

Establish a goal. __Help Joey learn how to stay on task during independent work time.__

Brainstorm. _____

✓   Move Joey's desk to the side of the room so he can sometimes stand up while he works

✓   Sharpen two pencils before class.

✓   Give Joey a checklist so he can keep track of the work he finishes each day.

✓   Talk to other kids only at recess.

✓   Go to the restroom after recess.

    Mr. Anderson could give a signal when Joey is off task.

    Send home a daily report card.

✓   Joey's mother goes through Joey's papers with him & starts a scrapbook of his best work.

Select actions.

- Check selected actions from the list of brainstormed ideas.
- Identify who will be responsible for taking each action.

Mr. Anderson will move Joey's desk, give him a checklist each day, and precorrect Joey for sharpening pencils, limiting his talking with others, and going to the restroom after recess. Mrs. Geske (counselor) will talk with Joey's mother.

Set up next meeting.

Date __10/7__   Time __10:30__   Other participants _____

 This form can be printed from the Module F CD.

brief anecdotal summary of the discussion. You describe the problem, establish a goal, brainstorm solutions, select an action, and set up the next meeting.

One advantage of documenting the discussion is that you create a record that can guide future intervention efforts. In addition, when a student sees you writing notes during the discussion, she is more likely to take the situation seriously.

STEP 2. Meet with the student.

A. Work with the student to define your concerns.

Throughout the meeting, orient your discussion to the future. When you refer to past problems, clarify that you are not attaching blame. Rather, you are looking for better ways to handle situations in the future. Use the as-if treatment—treat the student *as if* she is responsible and sensible and *as if* the misbehavior is just a momentary interruption or mistake.

Outline your concerns and encourage the student to share her perspective. Communicate your concerns positively and with high expectations, rather than with frustration at the student's behavior. The student should understand that this is a joint problem-solving session, not a lecture about what she must do differently. State the concern from your perspective. Starting with "I have a concern . . ." tends to work better than "You have a problem . . ." When you avoid statements that might appear to lay blame, the student will be less defensive and it will be easier to engage in a productive discussion.

> *Treat people as if they were what they ought to be, and you help them to become what they are capable of being."*
>
> JOHANN WOLFGANG VON GOETHE (1749–1832), German author, scientist, and statesman

B. Brainstorm actions that each participant in the discussion can take to help the student resolve the concern.

Brainstorming can help a student understand that many things can be done to help her become more successful, and it's a great way to open a dialogue. Clarify that the goal at this stage is to develop ideas, not to finalize a plan.

C. Set up an informal action plan.

Select a few actions from the brainstormed list that seem manageable and likely to increase the student's success. At this level of intervention, the best actions generally do not require an exorbitant amount of time on anyone's part. Simply helping the student find strategies to focus her attention is a good place to start.

D. Schedule a follow-up meeting.

The simple act of scheduling another meeting increases the likelihood that all participants will work on their part of the action plan. It's easy to focus on solving a problem for a short time (say, the length of a Planned Discussion), but then forget all about it. Knowing there will be a sustained effort to resolve the problem may bring the student a greater sense of accountability. Of course, the same is likely

Meet With Individual Students Regularly

Conducting planned discussions regularly with every student in your class is a great way to make each student feel important, and it gives you a chance to address each student's academic and behavioral issues before they balloon into major concerns. Many teachers think, "I don't have time to meet with individual students!" This is a legitimate concern. However, with only a few exceptions, teachers can create a daily window of opportunity to talk with students individually. Use the first 5 to 10 minutes of independent work periods to briefly meet with a few students one-to-one. Teachers of very young children (kindergarten and early-year first graders) or in potentially dangerous settings such as shop or chemistry, where extra vigilance is necessary for everyone's safety, may not be able to use this strategy.

Inform your class in advance that you will be meeting individually with students. Let them know that you want to get to know them and help every student be successful. Usually the meetings will not be about problems. They will just be a chance to talk with students about progress in class, their interests, or ways to make the class more relevant and interesting.

At the end of instruction and guided practice, before starting independent or cooperative group activities, give the class final directions: "If you have any questions about how to get started on this task, ask now, because for the next 5 minutes I will be at my desk talking with one or two students. Any questions?" If daily meetings with one or two students are standard practice, students won't even notice a Planned Discussion about a problem with one student.

This strategy allows you to set aside discrete times of the day when you can easily work in Planned Discussions. Keep a record of the students you meet with and ensure that you meet with all of your students at least once a semester (secondary) or once a month (elementary).

true for you, the teacher, and for the parents. Follow-up also ensures that student efforts are recognized and that the plan will be revised, if necessary. The follow-up meeting should take place a couple of days to a week after the initial meeting.

E. Conclude the meeting with words of encouragement. If appropriate, share a copy of the written record of the meeting with the student and parents.

STEP 3. Follow up with the student.

A. Encourage student efforts.

Recognize the student's efforts daily. It is not unusual to see immediate improvement following a discussion, followed by a loss of momentum. Your encouragement is important. The student hasn't yet realized the effect that seemingly small efforts today can have on her future endeavors. You may need to provide reminders about actions you agreed on at the meeting. Make a conscious effort to give the student feedback on successes, even the small steps that lead toward success.

B. Meet once a week with the student to discuss progress and adjust the action plan as needed.

Periodic meetings keep the momentum going. If the student's efforts are paying off, she deserves recognition. If behavior has improved but additional progress is needed, you can discuss ways to continue growing and learning. If the situation has not improved, discuss the option of more structured interventions.

C. Determine whether more structured interventions are required.

If you, the student, or the student's parents aren't seeing the progress you anticipated, it's time to consider more intensive intervention. You can maintain a positive focus by viewing this next step as a logical extension of the discussion-based problem-solving process, not as a failure.

D. Provide continued follow-up, support, and encouragement.

Whether or not the student is able to improve her behavior solely through Planned Discussion, follow-up discussions play an important role in keeping the student involved. If other interventions are needed, Planned Discussion will play a continuing role. If successful, the student needs to know that her efforts and successes are recognized. Without continued support, the student might return to old, established patterns of behavior. Though follow-up generally consists of short, informal discussions with the student, some discussions should be scheduled so they are not forgotten.

Task 1 Conclusion

Planned Discussion is a little like taking two aspirin when you have a headache. The strategy may not be powerful enough to change a student's behavior by itself, but it's worth a try and often works. It represents a good starting point—remember to always try the easiest thing first. The skill of using Planned Discussion is always useful because this strategy will be a subset of all subsequent interventions. Whenever you change an intervention to improve its efficacy, you need to talk with the student about those changes. One goal of Planned Discussion is to communicate that you are working *with* the student, as opposed to intervention being done *to* the student or even *for* the student.

Time is often the biggest barrier to implementing Planned Discussion, and finding the time will likely be your most important key to success. You might need to schedule discussions before school, during recess, or after school. With a colleague's consent, you might be able to schedule a discussion during another activity or class, such as music, PE, or library. When the concern is relatively simple, you might pull the student out of independent or small group work after you've provided instruction and the other students have begun work. Finding time is worth it, however. The time you spend on Planned Discussion will more often than not result in an early resolution to a brewing problem, saving everyone time, effort, and frustration.

TASK 2
Use Academic Assessment and Assistance

This intervention is about examining the relationship between academic competence and behavior problems. If you already know that the student is behind academically, plan to run parallel academic supports while working on designing behavioral interventions. If you're unsure whether the student is behind academically, investigate. Review current data, such as oral reading fluency norms.

> For more information about Academic Assessment and Assistance, see Sprick, R., & Garrison, M. (2008). *Interventions: Evidence-Based Behavioral Strategies for Individual Students* (2nd ed.; pp. 93–184). Eugene, OR: Pacific Northwest Publishing. This task corresponds to Intervention B in the *Interventions* book.

Too often teachers assume that misbehavior is willful—students are seeking attention or escape—when it is not. Consider the following example of a situation where, from the presenter's perspective, misbehavior might appear to be willful.

Imagine that you, along with 30 other teachers, are attending an inservice on motivating students. The presenter says, "For the next portion of the presentation, I want you to read the paper I'm handing out now, '28 Sure-Fire Solutions for Motivating Apathetic Students.' We'll have 5 minutes of silent reading time, and then you'll discuss the paper with your colleagues. So for the next 5 minutes, let's have no talking, no texting, no trips to the coffee pot, please. By the way, the paper is written in Japanese, but it's very good, so please do your best to read it."

Within 30 seconds, some of you would start talking to one another, some of you would pull out your phones and check your messages, and some of you would get up and grab a cup of coffee. Your behavior isn't directed at the presenter, and you're not trying to get attention. The presenter has given you a task that you have no hope of successfully completing or even starting, so you're going to find something else to do. That somewhat facetious example really summarizes the chicken-and-egg nature of academics and behavior issues.

In some cases, misbehavior is willful and related to academic deficits. We were working with the staff of a middle school on getting students to remember to bring their materials, which was a big concern among this staff. We helped the staff institute some simple schoolwide procedures: All teachers were to require that the students have the same material every day (rather than requiring textbooks on only some days), and all teachers were to conduct spot checks on random days and award bonus points to students who had their materials.

Those simple procedures worked and made a significant difference, but a few students continued to avoid bringing their materials to class. We discussed the situation with a colleague, who suggested that we investigate whether those resistant students had academic deficits. He used an unforgettable analogy to describe what those students might be thinking: "If I know you're going to hang me, I'm not likely to bring you the rope." Sometimes a seemingly simple behavior like remembering materials can be related to academic deficits.

In this task, we discuss mainly Academic Assessment—ascertaining whether a student's behavioral problem is related to academic deficits or is a strictly behavioral problem. Your district is probably already doing a lot of work with assessment of academic deficits and differentiating instruction to address those deficits. This early-stage intervention is designed to ensure that when a student exhibits behavior or motivation problems, you consider academic deficits and instructional interventions as part of the support the student may need to be successful.

STEP 1. Identify concerns and establish a focus.

A. Talk with staff members about this student.

Ask the student's other teachers about his behavior and academic performance.

B. Contact the student's parents or guardians.

Depending on school or district policy, parental permission may be required for Academic Assessment. Whether you do or do not need permission, however, share with the family your concerns, discuss your goals for improvement, and explain the measures you plan to take to investigate whether the student is capable of doing his schoolwork or whether some adjustments are needed.

STEP 2. Develop a plan for conducting an informal Academic Assessment.

We discuss four types of informal Academic Assessment procedures, although there are more. We suggest that you discuss the procedures we suggest and other assessment procedures with your school psychologist and content-area experts (math supervisors in your district, for example). The four procedures we present are:

- Analyze information from the Student Status Report.
- Analyze student work samples.
- Collect oral reading fluency data.
- Determine whether the student is capable of working independently.

A. *Analyze information from the Student Status Report.*

The Student Status Report (see Figure 4b on the next page) is a form that is routed to all of the student's teachers. Each teacher completes one column of the form. It takes each teacher only a few minutes, but the combined data from all teachers provides a great deal of useful information.

Each column can be labeled to represent a period (for secondary) or subject (for elementary). The teachers for each period or subject rate each Student Performance criterion on a 5-point scale, where 1 equals *never* and 5 equals *always*. To maintain student confidentiality, you can give each teacher a separate form and then consolidate the responses.

When you see all the responses on one page, it is relatively easy to answer important questions such as:

- Does the student have trouble in all or only some of his classes?
- Does the student have trouble in classes that involve reading, but less trouble in classes that involve, say, mathematics?
- What specific subjects cause difficulty?
- Does the student attend some classes regularly, but not others?
- Does the student seem to have a similar problem across different subjects (completing work, staying focused, following directions, organizing materials, and so on)?

The answers to these types of questions can help you analyze the nature of the student's behavior problem and develop some solutions to help the student.

B. *Analyze student work samples.*

Ask teachers to attach a sample of the student's work to the Student Status Report. If you are unfamiliar with the course content or the degree of competency the teacher expects from students, ask the teacher to include work samples by an excellent student and an average student for comparison.

Are there patterns in the errors the student makes? Does the student begin the assignment correctly but have trouble with the end? Does the student have trouble following directions? Work samples can provide information that may not be evident from standardized tests. For example, the student may read and comprehend well enough to pass multiple-choice reading tests but lack the organizational skills to summarize a passage in writing. The student may have the skills to research and write a report, but lack time management strategies for completing the work on schedule. A work sample may indicate that the student lacks basic skills. For example, he may perform well verbally but have trouble putting thoughts down on paper because of poor handwriting or typing skills.

Figure 4b *Student Status Report (F-11a) with sample summary of teacher responses*

Student Status Report, Version 1

Student __Aaron Mathison__   Grade/Class __8__

Staff member requesting information __Mr. Wagner__   Date __Nov. 15__

Please complete performance ratings for this student. This information will be used to develop an individualized plan of assistance and match the student with appropriate interventions.	Period or Subject Area						
	1	**2**	**3**	**4**	**5**	**6**	**7**
Key: 5 = Always *Note:* A rating of 3 or below 4 = Usually indicates a problem or concern 3 = Sometimes that warrants further follow-up. 2 = Rarely 1 = Never N/A = Not applicable	Math	Geography	PE	Lunch	English	Spanish	Physical Science
Student Performance							
Academic standing: List the student's current grade using the values assigned on the report card (letter grades, ✓/+/–, etc.).	B-	D-	A-	NA	F	C	B
Attends class regularly	5	5	5	NA	5	5	5
Punctual	5	5	5	NA	5	5	5
Cooperative	5	3	5	NA	2	4	5
Participates in class activities	4	3	5	NA	3	4	5
Stays on task	4	2	5	NA	2	4	4
Completes in-class assignments	5	2	5	NA	2	4	5
Completes homework	3	1	NA	NA	1	1	4
Quality of work is satisfactory	5	1	5	NA	1	5	5
Passes tests	5	3	5	NA	3	5	5

Student strengths (list at least three):

Math: Aaron is very good conceptually in math. He could be getting an A in math; however, he got a C last term because he didn't turn in his math notebook. All he had to do was keep his papers throughout the term.
Geography: Aaron participates well during class discussions.
PE: Aaron does well in PE. He cooperates and often helps other students.
Spanish: Aaron does well in Spanish. He participates and is cooperative.

List areas of concern:

Geography: Aaron needs to improve his classroom behavior, work on homework completion, and improve his test scores. English: Aaron has to work on his behavior so he can get his work done, both in class and at home. Cooperation is his biggest problem.
Spanish: The only reason he doesn't have a better grade is missing homework.
Physical Science: Aaron has a good conceptual understanding and participates in class. He could easily get an A if he does well on the next couple of tests.

Note: Please attach a representative sample of student work.

 This form can be printed from the Module F CD.

C. Collect oral reading fluency data.

You might already have oral reading fluency data from ongoing progress monitoring. If so, compare those data to your district-level norms. Is this student above or below the norms?

If you don't have oral reading fluency data, follow the instructions for oral reading fluency assessment procedures that we provide in the next few pages.

Although fluency alone is not sufficient for reading with understanding, it is clearly a necessary prerequisite for understanding, interpreting, and responding to print. Fluent readers quickly skim through text when material is familiar, and they read deeply when new, important, or difficult information is presented. Students who haven't developed into fluent readers are unable to adjust their reading strategies to the materials and the purpose of their reading. Thus, although fluency does not guarantee good comprehension, it certainly plays a critical role in facilitating timely completion of assignments.

Oral Reading Fluency Assessment Procedures

Oral reading fluency (ORF) assessment determines the number of words that students can read correctly in 1 minute (WCPM, or words-correct-per-minute, score). Assessments are administered to students individually.

Your school or district may already use or have access to a standardized ORF assessment tool that includes passages for various grade levels and directions for administering and scoring. The state of Florida, for example, offers Ongoing Progress Monitoring (OPM) tasks that measure reading fluency for grades 1–12. These are available at the Florida Assessments for Instruction in Reading website (hwww.fcrr.org/lookup). Other options include:

DIBELS. Dynamic Indicators of Basic Early Literacy Skills (DIBELS) is a set of standardized measures of early literacy development (grades K–6). Measures assess phonological awareness, alphabetic understanding, and fluency. For more information and to download DIBELS (6th ed.) assessment materials, visit dibels.uoregon.edu.

DIBELS Next materials are available for free download (you must register first) at: dibels.org/dibelsnext.html.

(continued)

AIMSweb (www.aimsweb.com), developed by Pearson Publishing, includes Standard Reading Assessment Passages (RAPs) for assessing ORF.

GORT-5 from PRO-ED (www.proedinc.com) is a norm-referenced measure of oral reading fluency and comprehension for ages 6–23.

CURRICULUM-BASED MEASUREMENT (CBM). If a standardized assessment is not available, you can use the curriculum-based measurement procedures that follow to collect ORF data.

Preparation

Select two passages from grade-level reading material (for example, a basal reading test or other reading material used in the class). The passages selected should:

- Each be approximately 250 words long
- Be unpracticed—the student hasn't read them yet
- Have a clear starting point
- Reflect the level of difficulty normally encountered in the class
- Use a minimum of difficult words, foreign words, and hard-to-pronounce names
- Contain minimal dialogue
- Be free of illustrations that might help the student interpret the content

Note: Scoring copies of ORF passages often have a cumulative word total in the right margin for ease of scoring. You can create scoring copies of your own passages with the Oral Reading Fluency Passage Generator at: www.interventioncentral.org/teacher-resources/oral-reading-fluency-passages-generator.

Materials

- Two copies of each passage (a reading copy for the student and a scoring copy)
- Stopwatch
- Pencil
- Clipboard

Procedure

1. Hand the student the student copy of the passage. Place the scoring copy on a clipboard, making sure the student is not able to see it.

2. Say to the student:

   When I say 'Start,' begin reading aloud at the top of this page. Read across the page. [Demonstrate by pointing.] Try to read each word. If you come to a word you don't know, I'll tell it to you. Be sure to do your best reading. Are there any questions?

   [Pause for questions]

   Start.

3. Start the stopwatch when the student says the first word in the passage (do not count the title).

4. Follow along on your copy of the passage, marking any words that are read incorrectly with a slash (/). See Scoring Guidelines below.

   If a student stops or struggles with a word for 3 seconds, tell the student the word and mark it as incorrect.

Scoring Guidelines

Mark the following as errors:

- Word that is skipped
  Note: If a student omits an entire line, make a horizontal line through the skipped text and note that the line was skipped. Do not count as an error and do not count the words in the total read.
- Word that is pronounced incorrectly (e.g., pronouncing "lead" as "led" in "This path will lead us to the parking lot," or misreading "seal" for "sill")
- Word substituted for another word
- Struggling or stopping for 3 seconds
- Words read in the wrong order count as two errors (e.g., reading "hopping and skipping" instead of "skipping and hopping")
- Words that are sounded out but not read as a whole

Do not count any of the following as errors:

- A word that is read correctly but repeated
- An error that is corrected by the student within 3 seconds
- A word inserted by the student that does not appear in the text
- A word mispronounced because of accent, dialect, or speech impairments
- A proper noun read with any reasonable phonetic pronunciation

(continued)

5. After 1 minute, say, "Stop." Place a vertical line after the last word read. Thank the student.

6. Repeat the assessment with the second passage.

Calculate WCPM

Count the total number of words ready by the student (WPM, or words-per-minute rate). Then count the total number of errors (slashes). To calculate WCPM, subtract the total number of errors from the number of words read in 1 minute. Calculate WCPM for each passage, then take the average of the two scores.

Interpreting

To interpret student performance scores, use the curriculum-based norms shown on the next page. These norms were derived in 2004 from thousands of students in grades 1 to 8. The sample included students from general education programs and students who were participating in compensatory, remedial, and special education programs.

The norms provide rough guidelines for determining adequate reading fluency. For example, a student who reads about 50 WCPM or better from beginning second-grade materials in the fall of second grade is making adequate progress. However, a third-grade student who reads about 50 WCPM from third-grade materials has fairly severe reading difficulties. Norms are not available for older students, but some liberty can be taken in extrapolating from existing norms. We can safely assume that by high school, students should read somewhere above 150 words per minute. (There is a point at which the rate of oral reading is no longer relevant. Due to rate of speech, some variance in acceptable oral reading rates above 150 words per minute is likely.) If in doubt, it may be useful to assess two or three capable students for comparison with the target student.

Note: Students scoring below the 50th percentile using the average scores of two unpracticed grade-level materials need a basic decoding and fluency program.

Procedure adapted with permission from *Curriculum-based measurement: Assessing special children,* M. R. Shinn (Ed.). Copyright 1989 by Guilford Press.

2005 Hasbrouck & Tindal Oral Reading Fluency Data

Grade	Percentile	Fall WCPM*	Winter WCPM*	Spring WCPM*
1	90		81	111
	70		47	82
	50		23	53
	25		12	28
	10		6	15
2	90	106	125	142
	75	79	100	117
	50	51	72	89
	25	25	42	61
	10	11	18	31
3	90	128	146	162
	75	99	120	137
	50	71	92	107
	25	44	62	78
	10	21	36	48
4	90	145	166	180
	75	119	139	152
	50	94	112	123
	25	68	87	98
	10	45	61	72
5	90	166	182	194
	75	139	156	168
	50	110	127	139
	25	85	99	109
	10	61	74	83
6	90	177	195	204
	75	153	167	177
	50	127	140	150
	25	98	111	122
	10	68	82	93
7	90	180	192	202
	75	156	165	177
	50	128	136	150
	25	102	109	123
	10	79	88	98
8	90	185	199	199
	75	161	173	177
	50	133	146	151
	25	106	115	124
	10	77	84	97

This table shows the oral reading fluency rates of students in grades 1 through 8 as determined by Hasbrouck and Tindal's data.

*WCPM = Words Correct Per Minute

Adapted with permission from Hasbrouck, J., & Tindal, G. (April, 2006) ORF norms: A valuable tool for reading teachers. *The Reading Teacher, 59*(7), 636–644.

Determine whether the student is capable of working independently.

There are two ways to investigate whether the student's academic difficulty is a *cannot* or a *will not* problem.

1. Work one-to-one with the student on an assignment.

   Sit beside the student and assist him as needed to complete an assignment. You might have the student redo an assignment that he did not complete satisfactorily earlier. Observe the student closely and ask him to clarify his understanding of expectations and strategies for working through the task. Keep the following questions in mind:

   - Does the student understand the instructions without further clarification from an adult?
   - Does the student possess the prerequisite skills necessary to complete the assignment (for example, handwriting, spelling, multiplication facts, ability to line up numbers correctly)?
   - Does the student have effective strategies for completing the assignment (for example, learning how to spell words, writing and solving equations, required knowledge to write an essay)?
   - Is the student able to stay on task for extended periods? (An intervention for teaching replacement behaviors or a structured reinforcement system might be needed.)

2. Offer a very high-value reward.

   Select an assignment that the student should be able to complete. Tell the student that if he completes the assignment correctly and within a reasonable amount of time, he will earn a reward. The reward should be something the student values highly—for example, free reading time, game time on the computer, time with a friend to play a game, a visit with the principal, and so on.

   If the student completes the assignment successfully, you know that he can do the work when he chooses to. The problem is motivation. If the student still cannot complete the assignment, you know that he lacks the skills to do so.

   You shouldn't use this technique often—it's best reserved for assessment purposes only.

STEP 3. Conduct the assessment.

Analyze the results and summarize student strengths and weaknesses using the Academic Assistance form (Form F-12a) shown in Figure 4c. Target specific areas in which assistance can be provided. A two-page version of the form is also available as Form F-12b on the Module F CD.

Figure 4c *Academic Assistance form (F-12a) with sample information*

Academic Assistance, Version 1 (One-page form)

Student __Aaron Mathison__   Grade/Class __8__   Teacher __Mrs. Thompson__   Date __Dec. 7__

A. Informal assessment information

  1. Oral Reading Fluency: __101__ words correct per minute

     Materials: __Geography text, The Red Pony__

  2. Strengths and weaknesses

	Subjects	Abilities	Behavior
Strengths	Math Physical Science Spanish	Verbal Strong conceptually Comprehension	Cooperation and participation in subjects he is doing well in.
Weaknesses	Geography English	Math Physical Science Spanish	No cooperation in classes he is not doing well in.

B. Remediation: _1) Reading fluency tutorial during homeroom: Corrective Reading Decoding B Pgm_

   2) Daily handwriting practice (at home, supervised by mom) with district-developed program

C. The Adaptation Process: Use the outline below as an optional framework for developing a plan for Academic Assistance.

  1. Identify assignments or activities that haven't been given yet.
  2. Anticipate problems that the student (and other students) may encounter.
  3. Design whole-class instruction to prevent anticipated problems.
  4. Consider making assignments more manageable by providing additional assistance.
  5. Consider alternative ways for the student to demonstrate knowledge or ability.
  6. Gradually fade the adaptations as the student gains competence.

D. The Adaptation Menu: Adaptation involves a never-ending variety of procedures. The following list of suggested strategies is not exhaustive. Discuss and brainstorm other possibilities.

  1. Focus assignments on essential course content and skills.
  2. Focus test items on essential course content and skills.
  3. Build cumulative review of essential objectives into subsequent units of instruction.
  4. Construct and use framed outlines.
  5. Design and use interactive graphic organizers.
  6. Identify and pre-teach essential vocabulary words.
  7. Highlight textbooks and printed materials.
  8. Transcribe or summarize highlighted text.
  9. Provide two-column study guides.
  10. Provide framed writing assignments.
  11. Teach the students to manage their homework.

E. Attach a summary of the Academic Assistance Plan.

F. Schedule a follow-up meeting. 12/8, 3:15---to review highlighting
                                 12/12, 3:15---to review the plan

 This form can be printed from the Module F CD.

STEP 4. Consider and plan for remediation options.

Students need tool skills, such as reading fluency, spelling skills, and handwriting skills, to function as independent learners. Adaptation strategies may be necessary to help students who lack these basic skills, but adaptation strategies alone will not provide students with the means to function independently. Some form of remediation is often required.

If tool skills are a problem, consider remediation for the student. Consult with a special education teacher or reading specialist. Sometimes remediation is appropriate as part of an Individualized Education Plan. However, when a student is not eligible for special education services, explore other possibilities, such as small group instruction in the classroom or a tutor. By discussing the possibilities with building or district specialists, it may be possible to set up programs that not only help the student to be successful through greater assistance and adaptation, but also provide the student with skills needed to become independent.

STEP 5. Consider adaptation options.

Identify assignments and activities that will be assigned in coming weeks, and anticipate problems that the target student may encounter. Whole class instruction can often prevent anticipated difficulties. For example, if several students do not take useful class notes, structured lessons on note-taking can increase the proficiency of all students while teaching lower-performing students to take adequate notes.

Consider making assignments more manageable by providing additional assistance or adjusting their length and complexity. Also consider alternative ways for the student to demonstrate knowledge or ability. For example, students who are visually impaired or reading disabled might require tape-recorded texts and oral exams. For students who are capable of learning a skill, adjust the way they demonstrate their knowledge and abilities only until remediation allows them to handle the regular assignment. Gradually fade the adaptations as the student gains competence.

Consider selecting or modifying strategies from the following menu of adaptations. Detailed information about each one appears in the *Interventions* book (Sprick & Garrison, 2008) and in other resources for differentiating instruction.

- Focus assignments on essential course content and skills.
- Focus test items on essential course content and skills.
- Build cumulative review of essential objectives into subsequent units of instruction.
- Construct and use framed outlines.

- Design and use interactive graphic organizers.
- Identify and pre-teach essential vocabulary words.
- Highlight textbooks and printed materials.
- Transcribe or summarize highlighted text.
- Provide two-column study guides.
- Provide framed writing assignments.
- Teach students to manage their homework.

STEP 6. Meet with staff to review the plan for academic assistance.

Review the Academic Assistance form you completed for the student, and review and discuss the adaptations you are considering. Then identify a manageable plan to help the student. You will also want to determine whether the plan is working, so identify at least two independent ways to evaluate the student's progress. Because academic success takes time, small improvements may go unnoticed unless you look for them. Evaluation might include subjective assessments by the teacher, student, and parent; monitoring work completion, grades, or office referrals; or comparing work samples.

Make sure all involved staff know their responsibilities, and schedule a follow-up meeting. This intervention usually benefits from a school community approach to helping the student. Plan to share data and discuss any ongoing concerns at the follow-up meeting.

STEP 7. Meet with the student to finalize the plan.

Review the problem and the goal. Discuss the plan that the staff drafted, and make revisions as necessary. Schedule a time to teach the strategies or skills. Also schedule follow-up meetings to discuss progress.

STEP 8. Implement the plan.

Provide the student with ongoing support and encouragement. Evaluate the effects of the intervention and revise and adjust as necessary.

More information about implementing Academic Assessment and Assistance is provided in *Interventions: Evidence-Based Behavioral Strategies for Individual Students* (2nd ed., Sprick & Garrison, 2008). Consider having the faculty conduct a book study. Have subgroups of faculty each study a section of Intervention B, then present the material to the rest of the faculty.

Task 2 Conclusion

Always consider whether a student's behavior might be related to academic deficits. Keep records of all assessments conducted for a student because those data will be useful within your tiered systems of support processes if you need to move to more intensive interventions.

Regardless of how supportive adults are, students must deal with their own sense of failure and frustration daily when they are unable to meet academic expectations. Some students respond with apathy. Some become irritated or angry. Some will do anything to avoid feeling incompetent, including misbehaving to distract from their academic problems. Though Academic Assessment and Assistance tends to be time and energy consuming, it gives students a chance to survive in and become competent members of the learning community.

TASK 3

Have students set goals

Research shows that Goal Setting is a surprisingly powerful intervention for both academic and behavioral problems. It can be very useful in the early stages of a behavioral or motivational problem. One of the strengths of setting goals is that when an adult tells a student, "You have so much potential. Let's tap into that and see how far you can go," the adult communicates high expectations and respect. You can dramatically change the trajectory of a student by helping her set some challenging yet attainable goals.

Students with behavior problems frequently lack a sense of direction and purpose. Though they often have the same long-range aspirations as "good" students, they might have difficulty doing what is necessary to develop the habits and skills required for success. They may know they should "try harder" and "be more responsible," but they often do not know how to take action to do so. As their perceived failures multiply, many of these students begin to view themselves as "bad" and incapable of success.

Students who experience repeated failure or lack positive guidance also often have difficulty setting realistic goals. They tend to select goals that are too easy, so they experience no pride in accomplishment. Or they select goals so challenging that they set themselves up for failure. These students often believe that their efforts are futile. This intervention can give them the direction and confidence they need to become more successful in school.

Goal Setting also has many positive side benefits. It increases both the clarity and specificity of the teacher's expectations, provides extra opportunities for the student to receive positive adult attention, and communicates (and fosters) high expectations.

Goal Setting helps students and adults identify goals that are specific, attainable, and worthy. When goals are clear and within reach, students can begin to take control of their actions. Adults can acknowledge accomplishments, and errors can be used to help students learn how to get back on track.

For more information about Goal Setting, see Sprick, R., & Garrison, M. (2008*). Interventions: Evidence-Based Behavioral Strategies for Individual Students* (2nd ed.; pp. 185–222). Eugene, OR: Pacific Northwest Publishing. This task corresponds to Intervention C in the *Interventions* book.

STEP 1. Develop a plan.

A. Review the problem and overall goals for the student.

Begin by identifying the student's strengths. By acknowledging a student's positive traits and skills, you can frame the goal discussion in terms of building on those qualities and avoid sounding overly critical.

Then determine the outcome you hope to achieve. If you want to reduce a problem behavior, think about replacement behaviors you could ask the student to work on. You might want to increase a particular behavior or trait. Think about how you will determine whether the student is making progress toward a goal. Can progress be measured objectively?

Poor examples of replacement behavior include:

- Improve classroom responsibility.
- Show respect for authority.
- Sit at your desk.

Better examples of replacement behaviors are:

- Hand in work by the end of the period without being asked.
- Talk in a calm voice to classmates, with no arguing.
- Sit in your chair for the entire class period unless you have permission to get up.

Review information gathered from previous interventions to help you determine whether the problem involves ability, motivation, or some other factor that might influence the goals you set with the student.

Decide whether to focus on short- or long-range goals or some combination of the two. Consider the age of the student. Long-range goals are more appropriate for older students. We discuss this type of goal setting a little later in this task.

Consider whether corrective consequences should be part of the plan. If consequences for rule violations are already in play, you probably want to continue with them as a standard part of your classroom management plan. You may also want to explore whether a different set of consequences would be more conducive to the goal-setting process. Tell the student in advance the corrective consequences you will implement if the target goal is not met so the student does not feel blindsided when consequences are assigned.

Decide whether rewards should be part of the plan. Generally, it's best not to include rewards as part of Goal Setting, at least initially. Wait and see whether positive feedback for achieving goals is enough to improve behavior. The student's motivation, morale, and outcome may very well improve from positive feedback alone. Structured reward systems are not bad and are sometimes necessary, but the danger is that the student comes to expect rewards and regresses to previous behavior patterns when the reward is faded.

Decide whether you will be directive (unilateral) or collaborative in negotiating goals with the student. As much as possible, make the student an integral part of the goal-setting process. Involving a student in negotiating goals makes the student feel like an active participant with an investment in the intervention process.

You may direct the conversation more actively in a couple of situations. First, when the student is a chronic attention-seeker, you will probably want to tell her how to get your and others' attention in more appropriate ways and set those replacement behaviors as goals. Second, for a passive student who rarely volunteers more than one-syllable responses, you will probably need to suggest goals and steer the student through the goal-setting process.

B. Select a goal-setting form.

Figure 4d on the next page shows a sample goal-setting form. You can find this and several other versions on the Module F CD (Forms F-14a–f). Goal Setting may involve short-range goals, long-range goals, or both. Goals may be behavioral, academic, or social. The form you select will depend on the age and sophistication of the student and the student's degree of readiness to improve. Feel free to modify the forms or design your own.

C. Determine who will meet with the student.

Invite parents to the goal-setting meeting. Parents or guardians should always be welcome to participate. Most parents appreciate the opportunity to be involved, and they can provide context regarding the student's prior school history, behavior at home, and family values and aspirations. Even when parents are not overly supportive, their participation can be important. For example, a parent who encourages his child to fight with others should hear that fighting is not tolerated in the school.

In the early stages of a minor problem, you can work with the student one-to-one on setting goals. The more serious the behavior, the more adults (counselor or administrator, for example) may be involved.

D. Set up a goal-setting conference.

Schedule a time to meet with the student and all adults who will be involved. Schedule it for a neutral time—that is, not right after a problem has occurred,

Figure 4d Goal Setting form (F-14a) with sample goal

Goal Setting, Version 1

Student Lizbeth Pedersen   Grade/Class   9   Teacher   Mr. Williams   Date   9/30

My personal goal is   to earn a 2.0 G.P.A. for the next grading period and to get along with others--including the teachers.

I can show that I am working on this goal by   1) Turning in all homework. 2) Studying for tests. 3) Not arguing with teachers. 4) Being friendly and acknowledging others.

Student signature   Lizbeth Pederson

· ·

I can help you reach this goal by   1) Getting you into the homework club. 2) Helping you set up a system for tracking your assignments and grades. 3) Helping you set up a system for studying for tests. 4) Setting up some sessions to practice dealing with anger-provoking situations.

Teacher/Mentor signature   Mr. Williams

 This form can be printed from the Module F CD.

when the student might feel angry, afraid, and defensive. The atmosphere needs to be as supportive and as upbeat as possible, and there should be enough time to explore options.

STEP 2. Meet with the student.

Introduce the concept of Goal Setting to the student. The student needs to understand that setting goals will help her take control. It isn't something that is being done to her, but is a process being done *with* her that can help her grow and mature.

A. Help the student establish long-range goals (optional).

Encourage an older student (seventh grade or above) to think about the kind of life she would like to have in the future. Many students have no idea of the cost and effort required to attain their vision. Discuss job options that capitalize on the student's interests, and help the student determine the qualifications for jobs that interest her. If the student has no aspirations, think about people the student might talk with about life goals—a community leader or local sports personality, for example.

Then identify some immediate actions the student can take to move toward her goal. In other words, work backward from the long-range goal to where the student is now to determine logical steps the student will need to take to reach the goal. If the job skills require a trade school or a college degree, what grades, extracurricular activities, and so on does the student need to attend the school? And working backward, how many credits does the student need to graduate from high school? How many credits does the student currently have? Does the student need help to pass particular classes? The conversation can naturally move into short-range goal setting: Determine what the student can do right now and in the near term to start taking conscious control of her immediate future and begin heading toward her long-range goals.

Fill out the Long-Range Goal Setting form (Form F-13 shown in Figure 4e on the next page) as you discuss goals with the student. Putting those thoughts into writing often makes them more real to the student, and she might think about her future more often and more seriously. You might revisit this form during future Planned Discussions.

With elementary and early middle school students, the discussion about long-range goals can be much more cursory. You might talk about what the student needs to accomplish to be successful in high school.

Some students will be unrealistic about their goals. In this case, acknowledge the goals and encourage the student to include other job possibilities. "You would like

Long-Range Goal Setting

Student <u>Lizbeth Pedersen</u> Grade/Class <u>9</u> Teacher <u>Mr. Williams</u> Date <u>9/30</u>

At the age of <u>22</u>, I hope to have or be doing the following.

Self-Sufficiency

I would like to support myself in a job that pays <u>about $40,000 per year.</u>

I would like a job where I work <u>outside a lot or play music. I would like to work in the woods.</u>

A job I might like to have is <u>working with the State Fish and Wildlife Commission.</u>

Personal Life

I hope that my family is <u>kind, caring, and generous. I would like to be married and hope to have one kid (with another one later on).</u>

I would like to spend time with people who are <u>friendly to others, considerate, and don't think only of themselves.</u>

During my free time, I would like to <u>ski, hike, and travel.</u>

 This form can be printed from the Module F CD.

to be a famous actor. Great! When we look at your short-range goals, we'll need to think about ways to get you in classes. Actors draw on a lot of real-life experiences to create t should be thinking about the kinds of experiences you can cho elp you. You should also think about other things you'd like to d ve major difficulties are often people who haven't given themselves many options. Think of other things you enjoy and the types of jobs that might be possible."

B. Brainstorm actions the student should avoid and actions the student should take to be more successful in school.

Ask the student to identify problems that are roadblocks to her success—hitting, fighting, poor grades, talking back, arguing, or putting others down, for example. Try to identify specific, observable behaviors. Then brainstorm specific actions the student can take to be more successful.

Actions to avoid	Actions to take
Hitting	Stop, think, get help
Calling names	Treat everyone with respect
Spitting	Respect school property

If the goal-setting conference included long-range Goal Setting, help the student determine behaviors that create roadblocks to achieving long-range goals and positive actions she can take to reach them (see T-charts below).

JOB GOAL

Actions to take	Actions to avoid
Work hard	Getting suspended
Pay attention	Fighting
Do my work	Smart-mouthing the teacher
Pass tests	Procrastinating
Earn a B average	Getting mad
Graduate from high school	
Go to college	

PERSONAL GOAL

Actions to take	Actions to avoid
Make friends	Picking fights
Listen	Thinking about just me
Think about others	Trying to get even
Be considerate of others	
Help people	
Go to college	

C. Help the student establish short-range goals.

Goals should be positively stated and attainable (see Table 4a). When a goal is stated negatively, the student cannot take pride or satisfaction in reaching it.

Table 4a   Examples of negative goals restated positively

Negatively stated goal	Positively stated goal
Don't hit other students	Play cooperatively with other students
Stop calling others names	Treat others with respect
Don't forget your materials	Come to class ready to work and learn
Stop acting helpless	Show more self-reliance
Stop pouting	Communicate responsibly

Use a Goal Setting form like the one that appears in Figure 4d to guide your discussion with the student.

D. Help the student identify specific actions she is willing to take to reach her short-range goals.

Review the list of actions to take and actions to avoid that you brainstormed earlier. Assist the student in selecting actions that are most likely to bring success.

E. Identify ways that adults can help the student reach her goals.

This step is important so that the student knows she is not alone. The adults at the meeting and the student should brainstorm a list of adult support activities. Then work with the student to pick items that would be the most helpful. For example:

- Give positive feedback when the student makes an effort to meet the goal.
- Call the student's parents on good days.
- Send home a daily report card.
- Let the student have lunch with the principal or a favorite teacher when things are going well.

F. If using rewards, a structured reinforcement system, or corrective consequences, make sure the student understands all of the contingencies.

If Goal Setting is initiated for a severe and chronic problem, a 180-degree turn-around is unlikely to result from this single intervention alone. In many cases, the student and adult should also clarify consequences for problem behavior. Avoid setting up harsh consequences because adults are often unwilling to implement them or do not implement them consistently.

Some goal-setting plans will also require structured reinforcement, but avoid these systems if the plan has a high probability of success without external rewards. They can take a lot of time and effort to establish and maintain, and they may decrease the likelihood that the student will continue to exhibit positive behavior as the reward is faded. In addition, if the student strives to achieve goals without a reinforcement system, it is easier for her to attribute success to her own commitment and efforts.

G. Set regular times to follow up and discuss progress.

Schedule the first follow-up meeting no later than 1 week after the initial conference and plan to meet regularly thereafter—perhaps once a week for a few minutes. If the problem is severe or the student is very young, brief once-a-day conferences may be necessary.

H. Review responsibilities and have all involved parties sign the Goal Setting form.

Rarely, a student refuses to sign the form. If this happens, ask the student what changes could be made so she would be willing to sign. If the student still refuses, don't turn the situation into a power struggle. Simply let the student know that the adults will carry out their end of the plan to help the student achieve her goals. If the student makes some progress, she may be willing to sign the form in a subsequent goal-setting session.

I. Conclude the goal-setting conference with words of encouragement.

STEP 3. Provide ongoing support and encouragement.

Like a sports coach, recognize progress—even if seemingly minute—and encourage the student to keep striving. With the student's permission, share her goals with other staff members who have contact with the student. For example, if the student has difficulty with peer relationships, playground supervisors should be informed of the student's goal-setting plan so they can recognize the student's efforts. "Rhonda, I noticed you were sharing the ball with Samantha today, even though you were the first to get it. I'm impressed!"

Also provide frequent positive feedback that links the goal behaviors to the broad label or trait. "Thank you for asking that question, Charlene. That was a great example of being independent and self-reliant."

When the student is not successful, correct calmly and avoid sounding disappointed or reproachful. This approach is particularly important when the student has been successful for a long period. Comments that convey disappointment ("Why did you do that? You were doing so well") foster the negative beliefs that the student might have in himself. Just state what the student did wrong and assign the consequence. As soon as the student is successful again, give positive feedback.

Over time, evaluate the impact of the intervention and make revisions and adjustments as necessary. Encourage the student to keep striving toward her goals. As the intervention is faded, continue to refer to the goal. If one or more goals have been attained, acknowledge the student's accomplishment and prompt her to set new goals. Reminding a student how far she has come is a great way to demonstrate your continued interest. Moreover, progress that is self-evident to you as a teacher may not be obvious or even apparent to the student. The student should know that her continued efforts are not taken for granted.

Task 3 Conclusion

Goal Setting is frequently overlooked when planning interventions for at-risk students, yet it offers these students opportunities to learn how to take control of their own actions. Many students fail to make the connection between their behavior and their experiences—how their daily actions help or hinder their ability to realize personal goals. Short-range Goal Setting shows students how they can set meaningful achievement targets and attain them. Setting long-range goals can help drifting students connect to their long-term aspirations and futures.

The first three interventions we describe in this presentation—Goal Setting, Planned Discussion, and Academic Assessment and Assistance—are relatively easy and don't take a lot of staff time to implement. But if those interventions don't work, the next step is to collect data and debrief with the student. Data collection is more time consuming and intrusive than the first three interventions.

TASK 4

Collect data and debrief

Data Collection and Debriefing has the potential to advance almost any student's behavioral goal. This intervention is appropriate for virtually any concern about a behavior that appears to be chronic. Whether to increase a positive behavior or decrease a negative behavior, a systematic approach to gathering data usually pays dividends. Even if no improvement results from this intervention alone, subsequent interventions will require ongoing collection of data to gauge their efficacy.

In the introduction to this presentation, we compared early-stage behavioral interventions with treating chronic headaches. The point at which you decide to see your doctor for your headaches is analogous to this stage—data collection—in the protocol of early-stage interventions. The headaches have not responded to simple remedies, so it's time to take your treatments to a higher level. The doctor will probably ask you to keep a log. For example, for each hour of the day, you write down whether you had a headache, the severity of the headache, what you were doing during that hour, what you ate, and so on. Over time, trends may emerge by frequency, time of day, date, diet, amount of sleep and stress, and so on. The data help inform possible treatment options and are used to assess the efficacy of every subsequent treatment. Data will continue to be collected and analyzed until you and the doctor find an effective treatment.

We recommend that Data Collection and Debriefing be an essential part of your district protocol for early-stage interventions. The previous interventions may or may not include Planned Discussion, Academic Assessment and Assistance, and Goal Setting, the first three interventions we explain in this presentation. You may prefer other interventions for the first two or three options. But Data Collection should be placed in the middle of a standard protocol. Not first—simpler, less time-consuming interventions should be attempted first. And not last—by now you know the problem is chronic (the first three interventions didn't work), and collecting data is the first step to dealing with a chronic behavioral problem.

For more information about Data Collection and Debriefing, see Sprick, R., & Garrison, M. (2008). *Interventions: Evidence-Based Behavioral Strategies for Individual Students* (2nd ed.; pp. 223–256). Eugene, OR: Pacific Northwest Publishing. This task corresponds to Intervention D in the *Interventions* book.

Gathering data often solves the problem all by itself.

Data Collection and Debriefing is a powerful intervention that often changes behavior by itself, without an accompanying behavioral intervention. People tend to do their best when being observed by someone important to them—a boss, girlfriend, teacher, or mentor, for example. You can probably think of examples in your own life. When is your home cleanest? If you're like most people, it's when you're expecting company.

Teachers can take advantage of this natural human tendency to put the best foot forward simply by recording the behavior of a student. The key technique in this intervention is to collect data in a manner conspicuous to the student, but subtle enough to be respectful of the student in front of his peers. The act of collecting data and debriefing with the student to discuss positive or negative trends may improve the situation, not because of any special intervention strategy such as a structured reward system, but simply because the student knows he is being observed and he responds as most humans respond to being observed—he tries to do better. This effect, though it can be frustrating to researchers because it can skew the results of a study, is a free bonus for teachers implementing an intervention with a child. You need not be concerned with why a student's behavior is getting better—just that it is!

> Three compelling examples of the power of Data Collection and Debriefing are included in the video version of this task. See the DVD for Module F, Presentation 4, Task 4.

Data will form the basis of all subsequent intervention planning.

If collecting data does not solve the problem by itself, it is still a necessary step that will assist in other interventions. Up to this point in our suggested protocol, systematic data collection hasn't been a requirement for intervening. If a problem can be solved easily, data aren't crucial to the success of the intervention or follow-up. This intervention represents a turning point. From this point on, data will drive your decisions about whether an intervention should be maintained, faded, or replaced with a different intervention. Data give collaborating teachers, administrators, and interventionists a common point of reference for looking at the issue constructively and making decisions about how to proceed.

Using data is the only way to determine objectively whether interventions are working.

Without data to evaluate efficacy, teachers have to rely on subjective perception, a notoriously cloudy barometer. Emotions, preconceptions, distractions, being busy with teaching—all of these diminish the usefulness of subjective impressions. In addition, sometimes progress is incremental and difficult for teachers to perceive. Data, especially when they are summarized visually on a chart, can tell the teacher that significant progress is taking place. Without a chart, a teacher might become discouraged and discontinue the intervention. With objective evidence of the student's progress, the teacher will continue working with the student.

Compelling Reasons to Use Data Collection and Debriefing

Just the act of collecting data and sharing them with the student can prompt dramatic improvement in behavior.

When improvement is incremental and difficult to perceive, data allow the teacher to see and measure progress.

When improvement isn't taking place, data can confirm that status and inform decisions about next steps—that is, more intensive interventions.

Before you begin

Collecting data requires that you identify an objective, observable, measurable problem. Imagine that you are concerned about a student's academic progress in relation to the rest of the class. Are you thinking about the student's work completion—a measurable behavior—or about the student's flagging motivation? Lack of motivation is not measurable. Until you define an objective clearly, you cannot proceed with Data Collection and Debriefing. Table 4b compares measurable behaviors to some common behavioral descriptors that need to be more narrowly defined before anything can be measured.

Table 4b *Examples of unmeasurable and measurable goals*

Unmeasurable (too broad)	Measurable
Bad attitude	Makes disrespectful comments
Unmotivated	Doesn't complete work
Off in his own world	Off task
Poor self-image	Makes negative statements about self
Attention deficit problems	Fidgets and makes tapping noises
Emotional problems	Displays episodes of intense anger

If you are having trouble narrowing your focus to an observable behavior that can be transformed into metrics or data, keep anecdotal notes for a few days and you'll begin to notice emerging patterns. Narrow your focus to one or two observable behaviors that you can monitor by counting the frequency, recording the duration, or grading on a rating scale. Pick the behavior you consider to be the most important and start keeping data on that behavior.

STEP 1. Choose an objective data collection method.

You already have some useful sources of data: your grade book, attendance record, tardiness record, and any records you already keep about behavior. For example, if your concern is work completion, your grade book can help you calculate the percentage of work completed week by week—just compare the number of assignments completed with the number you have given.

If your concern centers on something you do not have an existing data source for, consider using one of the following tools to collect data. All sample forms shown in this task, as well as additional related forms, are available on the Module F CD.

A. Weekly Misbehavior Recording Sheets

These forms can be used to track the frequency of rule violations and other misbehaviors for the entire class. It's easy to convert the information into useful data on a particular student. Figure 4f shows a Misbehavior Recording Sheet (Form F-16) designed for teachers who have the same group of students for the entire day, such as elementary or special education teachers. Figure 4g on p. 106 shows a form (Figure F-17) intended for a full week of data collection. It's suitable for secondary teachers who have students for only one class period (use one recording sheet for each class each week).

B. Basic frequency count

The most common type of behavioral data collected is a frequency count—simply the number of occurrences of a positive or negative behavior. There are many possible ways to count behaviors:

- Use a Behavior Counting Form such Form F-15 shown in Figure 4h (p. 107).
- Keep a tally on a card you keep in your pocket.
- Use a golf counter or hand tally counter.
- Put a handful of paper clips in your right pants pocket. Each time the student exhibits the behavior you are monitoring, move a paper clip to your left pants pocket.

Some interventionists recommend counting only the positive behavior you want to increase rather than the negative behavior you are trying to decrease. This strategy

Figure 4f *Misbehavior Recording Sheet (Daily by Student Name; F-16) with sample data for disruptions, off-task behavior, and talking*

Misbehavior Recording Sheet
Daily by Student Name

Date: __11/12__   Reminders: __Art museum field trip__

Name	1st Hour	2nd Hour	3rd Hour	4th Hour	5th Hour	Total
Anderson, Chantel				T		1
Baker, Ruben						0
Bell, Justin						0
Cabrezza, Melinda		T		T	T	3
Cummings, Teresa						0
Demalski, Lee			T			1
Diaz, Margo						0
Etienne, Jerry						0
Fujiyama, Kim						0
Grover, Matthew						0
Henry, Scott	DDT	DO		DT	T	8
Isaacson, Chris						0
Kaufman, Jamie						0
King, Mark						0
LaRouche, Janel				T		1
Morales, Marie Louisa				T		1
Narlin, Jenny						0
Neely, Jacob	D					1
Nguyen, Trang						0
Ogren, Todd	TT			T		3
Pallant, Jared						0
Piercy, Dawn				O		1
Reaes, Myra						0
Thomason, Rahsaan		T			T	2
Vandever, Aaron						0
Wong, Charlene						0
Yamamoto, Junko				O		1

Codes: D = Disruption
        O = Off task
        T = Talking

 This form can be printed from the Module F CD.

Figure 4g *Misbehavior Recording Sheet (Weekly by Student Name; F-17) with sample data for disruptions, off-task behavior, and talking*

Misbehavior Recording Sheet
Weekly by Student Name

Date: __Week of 11/3__   Reminders: __On Wed. remind about Fri. test__

Name	Friday	Monday	Tuesday	Wednesday	Thursday	Total
Anderson, Chantel				T		1
Baker, Ruben						0
Bell, Justin						0
Cabrezza, Melinda		T		T	T	3
Cummings, Teresa						0
Demalski, Lee			T			1
Diaz, Margo						0
Etienne, Jerry						0
Fujiyama, Kim						0
Grover, Matthew						0
Henry, Scott	DDT	DO		DT	T	8
Isaacson, Chris						0
Kaufman, Jamie				D		1
King, Mark						0
LaRouche, Janel				T		1
Morales, Marie Louisa				T		1
Narlin, Jenny						0
Neely, Jacob			O	O		2
Nguyen, Trang						0
Ogren, Todd	TTD	D	OO	T		7
Pallant, Jared						0
Piercy, Dawn			T	O	T	3
Reaes, Myra						0
Thomason, Rahsaan	TT		T	T	TT	6
Vandever, Aaron						0
Wong, Charlene						0
Yamamoto, Junko		T		OT		3

Codes: D = Disruption
       O = Off task
       T = Talking

 This form can be printed from the Module F CD.

Figure 4h   *Behavior Counting Form (F-15) with sample data*

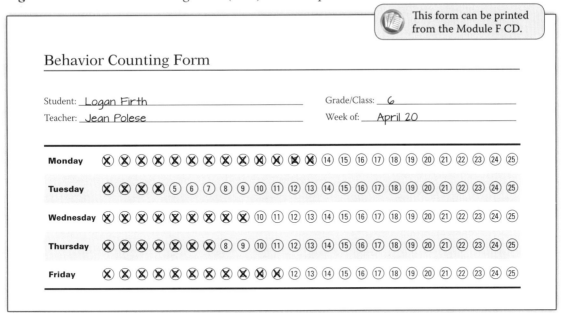

> This form can be printed from the Module F CD.

Behavior Counting Form

Student: __Logan Firth__   Grade/Class: __6__
Teacher: __Jean Polese__   Week of: __April 20__

Monday   Ⓧ Ⓧ Ⓧ Ⓧ Ⓧ Ⓧ Ⓧ Ⓧ Ⓧ Ⓧ Ⓧ Ⓧ Ⓧ ⑭ ⑮ ⑯ ⑰ ⑱ ⑲ ⑳ ㉑ ㉒ ㉓ ㉔ ㉕

Tuesday   Ⓧ Ⓧ Ⓧ Ⓧ ⑤ ⑥ ⑦ ⑧ ⑨ ⑩ ⑪ ⑫ ⑬ ⑭ ⑮ ⑯ ⑰ ⑱ ⑲ ⑳ ㉑ ㉒ ㉓ ㉔ ㉕

Wednesday Ⓧ Ⓧ Ⓧ Ⓧ Ⓧ Ⓧ Ⓧ Ⓧ Ⓧ ⑩ ⑪ ⑫ ⑬ ⑭ ⑮ ⑯ ⑰ ⑱ ⑲ ⑳ ㉑ ㉒ ㉓ ㉔ ㉕

Thursday Ⓧ Ⓧ Ⓧ Ⓧ Ⓧ Ⓧ Ⓧ ⑧ ⑨ ⑩ ⑪ ⑫ ⑬ ⑭ ⑮ ⑯ ⑰ ⑱ ⑲ ⑳ ㉑ ㉒ ㉓ ㉔ ㉕

Friday   Ⓧ Ⓧ Ⓧ Ⓧ Ⓧ Ⓧ Ⓧ Ⓧ Ⓧ Ⓧ Ⓧ ⑫ ⑬ ⑭ ⑮ ⑯ ⑰ ⑱ ⑲ ⑳ ㉑ ㉒ ㉓ ㉔ ㉕

won't always work and can potentially give you misleading data. For example, if your concern is the student's frequent disruptions in class, it is easier and more accurate to count and chart the frequency of disruptions than to try to count the absence of disruptions. In addition, opportunities to display the positive behavior might vary from day to day—the number of times the student raises his hand, for example, will depend on the format of the day's activities. Also, a student could increase his positive behaviors *and* his negative behaviors concurrently. If you collect data only on the positive, the negative increase is masked. If you want to track positive behaviors, we recommend that you consider tracking a negative behavior also. Counting both behaviors allows you to compute and display a percentage—appropriate hand raising vs. blurting out, for example.

C. Advanced frequency counts

You can fine-tune your frequency count by tallying behavior with different staff members, during different activities, or during different times of day. You can use codes to allow quick entry—*A* for a.m. and *P* for p.m., for example. Figure 4i shows an example of an advanced frequency count that also includes anecdotal notes and does not require a dedicated form.

D. Countoons/public posting

A *countoon* is basically a behavior counting form that includes cartoons to illustrate the behaviors being tracked. A countoon can be used to count positive behavior, negative behavior, or both. This method of recording data is most appropriate for younger students. The countoon will be publicly posted, so you need to make sure

Figure 4i   Sample advanced frequency count for bothersome behavior

Frequency count of Colin's bothersome behavior (4/3)

Type of activity and when:

Independent Work	Cooperative Groups	Transitions
AAAAAA AAAPP	PPPPP PPPPP	AAAAA PPP PPPPP
PPPPP PP		PPPP

NOTES:

8:40   Transition: As Colin is moving to join his cooperative group, he pokes Blaine in the arm, knocks Belinda's books off her desk, and pulls Maria's hair.

that it is OK with the student or students involved and you may want to consider counting only positive behaviors. Data reporting should never embarrass a child.

This strategy is appropriate for resource rooms and special education classrooms in which most, if not all, students have a behavioral or academic goal that is being recorded and charted—the countoon won't stand out as odd or appear to single out one student in these settings. Figure 4j shows a countoon for a student who makes frequent negative comments. The bottom half of this form (Form F-18) is a blank template for creating your own countoon.

E. Duration recording

When a behavior tends to last a long time, you may want to record duration—how many minutes the student engages in the behavior. Time the duration of the behavior with a stopwatch, wristwatch, or smartphone app, or by jotting down the time each occurrence begins and ends. With a stopwatch and some smartphone apps, don't reset the time to zero after each instance. Let the duration counts accumulate so that at the end of the day you have a total amount of time that the student engaged in the behavior. Divide the cumulative time by the number of behavioral episodes that occurred to get the average duration of the behavior for the day.

Examples of behavior on which you might collect duration data include off-task behavior, crying, and following directions (time between when a direction is given and when the student complies).

Figure 4j Countoon Behavior Counting Form (F-18) for a student who makes frequent negative comments

This form can be printed from the Module F CD.

Countoon Behavior Counting Form

Emilie Rausch — Name 3 — Grade/Class K. Klein — Teacher 3/16 — Date

F. Interval recording or scatterplot

Sometimes the behavior you want to understand is situational—it happens more in some situations or at particular times. Interval recording involves marking whether the behavior occurs during a particular time interval. A scatterplot is a fancy name for a data collection form that shows the interrelationship between two variables, such as the day of the week and a particular activity or time interval. The sample scatterplot shown in Figure 4k (Form F-19a) combines interval recording and frequency counts by recording a tally of the number of targeted behaviors that occur each day during each activity and transition. In this case, 2 weeks of observation show that Mondays are problematic and that reading, lining up, and hallway behaviors are problematic across all days. This detailed information has tremendous potential for aiding the design of a very targeted intervention plan.

Form F-19b (Figure 4l) on the Module F CD is a weekly interval chart/scatterplot that you can use to record the time of day behaviors occur.

G. Rating scale

You can rate the quality or intensity of a behavior on a simple scale. Though more subjective than the other methods discussed here, a rating scale can be made more objective by applying your judgment consistently over time and across activities. You could, for example, use three behaviors a student exhibits during different activities as a measure to build an overall picture of the student's behavioral pattern and identify possible points of intervention.

Figure 4k *Interval Chart/Scatterplot, Version 1 (F-19a) with sample data for the number of disrespectful comments that occur each day during each activity and transition*

Interval Chart/Scatterplot, Version 1

Student _Tristan Russell_   Grade/Class _5_   Teacher _Ms. Byers_   Date _October_

Behavior _Disrespectful comments_

Directions: Put a tally mark in the corresponding box each time the student engages in the targeted behavior.

		Week: 10/3					Week: 10/10					Week:					Week:				
		M	T	W	Th	F	M	T	W	Th	F	M	T	W	Th	F	M	T	W	Th	F
Activity	Opening	II					II														
	Reading	III	II	II	III	I	IIII	I	I	II	I										
	Writing/Spelling	II			I		I		I												
	Math																				
	Lunch	II	I				I				I										
	Science	I					I				I										
	Health	II				I	II		I												
	Recess	III		I			I				I										
	Social Studies	I																			
Transition	Entry	IIII					II	I													
	To/From ??	II	I	I			IIII														
	Lining up	III	I	I	I	II	IIII		I		I										
	Hallway	II		I	I	I	II		I	I	II										
	Cleanup	I					I														

 All forms can be printed from the Module F CD.

Figure 4l   Interval Chart/Scatterplot, Version 2 (F-19b)

Interval Chart/Scatterplot, Version 2

Student _____   Grade/Class _____   Teacher _____   Date _____

Goal _____

_____

Rating (+/−)	Monday	Tuesday	Wednesday	Thursday	Friday
8:00 – 8:30					
8:30 – 9:00					
9:00 – 9:30					
9:30 – 10:00					
10:00 – 10:30					
10:30 – 11:00					
11:00 – 11:30					
11:30 – Noon					
Noon – 12:30					
12:30 – 1:00					
1:00 – 1:30					
1:30 – 2:00					
2:00 – 2:30					
2:30 – 3:00					

Figure 4m shows a rating scale (Form F-20) in which a student receives a point for each of three behaviors that he exhibits appropriately during different activities. You can also rank behavior on a scale of 0 to 3. If the ratings have a specific descriptor, this type of scale is called an *anchored rating scale.* Figure 4n shows a sample Participation Evaluation Record (Form F-21) that uses an anchored rating scale to collect data on a student's participation in class.

STEP 2. Select a way to display the data.

How you display data may dictate the quality of your analysis and interpretation, and it will affect everyone's understanding of the data's meaning. Think about whether a table, line graph, bar graph, pie chart, or scatterplot will make trends and patterns apparent to you and the student.

Anecdotal notes have limited value as valid data. You can't chart anecdotal notes. You need numeric data that can be charted and analyzed for trends and patterns across time to determine objectively whether behavior is improving, staying the same, or getting worse.

Display changes across time so that when you meet with the student, you can illustrate the progress the student is making. You may want to use statistical techniques such as drawing the line of best fit, either by hand or automatically using a spreadsheet application such as Excel. Software allows you to automate charting and can help keep records of your data and generate meaningful statistics.

Ask yourself whether the data can show trends across time. This generally depends on the format in which the data were entered in the first place. Data collected on separate sheets of paper are of little use for conducting a cogent analysis. Consolidate the data in one place as a chart. Frequency counts, duration records, and rating scales should be summarized on a chart to help you and others make sense of their significance across time. On the other hand, interval recording and scatterplot forms steadily reveal more information as you enter your data; the relationships between the variables on the x and y axes become clearer as more data points are filled in. These forms may be fine without transferring the data to a separate chart, but by the time you have collected data for more than a week or two, you will probably need to display the trend on some kind of chart. For example, charting the number of intervals each day that the student was successful allows you to see progress over 2 or 3 months and perhaps correlate anomalies in the graph with events that occurred in class, at school, or in the student's life.

Figure 4m   Rating Scale (F-20) with sample data for three behaviors by subject

Rating Scale

> All forms can be printed from the Module F CD.

Student   Alita   Grade/Class   3

Teacher   Mr Johns   Period/Time   6

Subject

Monday (Behavior)	Reading	History	Lunch	Math	Music	Lang
Uses only appropriate language	① 0	① 0	① 0	① 0	① 0	① 0
Cooperates with others	① 0	1 ⓪	① 0	① 0	① 0	① 0
Problem-solves positively	① 0	1 ⓪	① 0	① 0	① 0	① 0

Figure 4n   Participation Evaluation Record (F-21) with anchored rating scale and sample data

Participation Evaluation Record

Student   Justin   Grade/Class   11

Teacher   Mr Mathison   Period/Time   12/6

Rating Scale:
0 = Did not participate verbally and did not take notes
1 = Participated verbally at least once but did not take notes
2 = Took notes but did not participate verbally
3 = Participated verbally at least once and took notes

Directions: For each subject, circle the number that best describes your level of participation.

Subject	Monday	Tuesday	Wednesday	Thursday	Friday
Science	0 ① 2 3	0 ① 2 3	0 1 ② 3	0 1 2 3	0 1 2 3
Health	⓪ 1 2 3	⓪ 1 2 3	0 1 2 3	0 1 2 3	0 1 2 3
English	0 1 ② 3	0 1 2 ③	0 1 2 3	0 1 2 3	0 1 2 3
Math	⓪ 1 2 3	0 ① 2 3	0 1 2 3	0 1 2 3	0 1 2 3
Art	⓪ 1 2 3	0 ① 2 3	0 1 2 3	0 1 2 3	0 1 2 3
History	0 ① 2 3	0 1 ② 3	0 1 2 3	0 1 2 3	0 1 2 3

STEP 3. Meet with the student.

Be sure to give the student's parents the option to attend the meeting.

A. *Explain the data that you plan to collect.*

Explain to the student that you will be collecting data not as a punishment, but to help both of you understand the significance of the problem and what everyone involved might do to improve the situation. Keep the discussion positive and encouraging.

Explain how you will communicate the data to the student as you are collecting them—neither your actions nor the data you collect should be secret. For example, if you are counting the frequency of disruptions, you might tell the student, "Ahmed, that's disruptive," when he is causing a disturbance, and then mark your tracking form. Both of these actions provide feedback that can help the student self-regulate future behavior. Be as overt as you reasonably can without causing embarrassment. This overtness is part of what might make the intervention work all by itself.

Thereafter, perhaps once a week, discuss the student's progress with him. Use a summary graph or chart to reinforce your shared understanding of the behavior and to monitor the student's progress in modifying his behavior.

B. *Meet regularly with the student to discuss the data and debrief.*

Plan to meet at least once a week to review the data, discuss trends, set improvement targets, celebrate progress, and so on. Invite the student's parents to join you for your regularly scheduled meetings.

Task 4 Conclusion

Data Collection and Debriefing represents a turning point in the nature and classification of the student's behavioral problem. You have already tried the simplest and least time-consuming interventions. The student's problem is chronic and possibly serious. Data Collection and Debriefing may help to solve the problem when it is used alone because of the natural human tendency to improve behavior when we are being observed. However, if this intervention is not sufficient by itself to improve the problem behavior, the data collected will serve as the foundation for subsequent intervention plans.

TASK 5

Maintain high ratios of positive to corrective interactions

Increasing positive interactions with students, coupled with maintaining high ratios of positive to corrective interactions, is a very powerful intervention strategy. It can take more time to design and implement this intervention compared with the four early-stage interventions we discussed in previous tasks, but it can yield very positive results. By reducing the frequency, duration, and intensity of the attention you pay to students' misbehavior and focusing more of your time and attention on responsible behaviors, you can rebalance your ratio of positive interactions (RPI)—the number of positive interactions to the number of corrective interactions—and try to make the ratio primarily positive.

Often a teacher is very positive with most of her students, providing at least three times as many positive interactions as corrective interactions, but there are one or two students with whom she has difficulty being positive. RPI can be a tough skill to acknowledge and master because teachers often fall into patterns of using more corrective than positive interactions with students. But when teachers have a clear understanding of what positive and corrective interactions are and learn a range of tried-and-true strategies to help them increase the positives, they can make real differences in the behavior of their difficult students.

Most students want and need adult attention. Therefore, they tend to engage in the behavior that gets them the most attention. Unfortunately, some students with chronic behavior problems have learned that the easiest and most reliable way to get attention is to misbehave. They have found that responsible behavior goes unnoticed, while behavior that annoys the teacher or disrupts the class results in riveted attention from the entire class, including the teacher, almost every time. Your tough, attention-seeking students operate on this logic (although probably not at a conscious level) both in and out of the classroom: *Work hard and behave appropriately, and the teacher or supervisor will ignore me. Screw up, and a teacher or supervisor will be there for me every 2 or 3 minutes.*

By rewarding *responsible* behavior with attention, you can shape behavior across time so the student is more likely to use appropriate behavior to get attention.

For more information about Increasing Positive Interactions, see *Foundations* Module C, Presentation 3, "Ratios of Positive Interactions" and/or Sprick, R., & Garrison, M. (2008). *Interventions: Evidence-Based Behavioral Strategies for Individual Students* (2nd ed.; pp. 257–304). Eugene, OR: Pacific Northwest Publishing. This task corresponds to Intervention E in the *Interventions* book.

Some students—the passive, quiet ones—may not misbehave to get attention, and they may not seek any attention at all. In these cases, the problem is not that the RPI is skewed to the negative, but rather that there are very few or even no interactions at all.

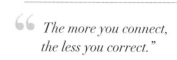

66 *The more you connect, the less you correct.*"

Increasing the amount of attention you give to these students' positive behavior may be a powerful intervention to increase their motivation as well as to demonstrate to other students that positive behavior is a better way to gain your attention and praise.

The research clearly shows that the more teachers connect with students by delivering positive interactions, the less they have to correct misbehavior. To reap the full benefits of the RPI intervention, you must first acknowledge and accept one fundamental concept: You cannot dislike the student on company time. Unburden yourself of any negative personal emotions you feel toward the student and begin relating to the student with a fresh approach. You do not even have to *like* the student—just recognize that liking or disliking should have nothing to do with the quality of care you provide. Quality of care dictates that, as a teacher and mentor, you build a positive relationship with the student. The student will read that improved attitude from your behavior. This, combined with higher RPI, will increase student motivation, responsible behavior, and self-esteem and give you more time to teach because you're spending less time correcting misbehavior.

What is a positive interaction?

When a student is engaged in positive behavior and you pay attention to the student, you've delivered a positive interaction. The attention can be **noncontingent**; that is, the student hasn't done anything to earn your attention. Noncontingent attention includes simple interactions such as greeting the student, smiling or nodding at the student, giving a high five or fist bump, shaking hands, and asking how her weekend was. The attention can also be **contingent**. Contingent attention is positive feedback in response to the student's appropriate academic work or behavior.

The key to recognizing a positive interaction is this: The student is following the expectations for appropriate behavior when the teacher gives attention, whether the attention is contingent or noncontingent, verbal or nonverbal.

What is a corrective interaction?

When a student is *not* following behavioral expectations and you pay attention to the student, you've delivered a corrective interaction. Corrections include reminders, assigning consequences, stating that the behavior is unacceptable, and gestures or looks that indicate disapproval of the student's behavior. For the purpose of documenting RPI, interactions with the student to correct *academic* errors are *not* corrective. An interaction to correct an academic error is positive because you are paying attention to the student while the student is engaged in positive behavior—in this case, participating in instruction.

Note: Some people argue that an academic correction is a corrective interaction unless some positive feedback is given at the same time. "Sam, the answer is the Fifth Amendment, not the Fourth Amendment. However, you are correct that the legal basis for the question is the Bill of Rights." For simplicity, we suggest counting academic corrections as positive as long as the student was behaving appropriately at the time. Be aware, however, that too many academic corrections without corresponding positive feedback on correct answers and other desirable academic skills could discourage the student.

Correctives are not wrong. We are not saying that you don't correct misbehavior when implementing this intervention. All students will engage in inappropriate behavior at some point. All humans err. Giving correctives is how we teach the student what the responsible behavior is. What we are saying is that by paying more attention to students when they are behaving appropriately, you will get fewer inappropriate behaviors.

> " *The student's behavior (not the teacher's behavior) at the time of the interaction defines it as either positive or corrective.* "

Here are some examples of positive and corrective interactions:

- Maria is on task, working at her table, when the teacher walks up to her and says, "Maria, that was a solid paper. Neatly written, with good spelling and a clear and concise summary paragraph." This is a positive interaction. The student is meeting behavioral expectations while the teacher delivers positive contingent attention.

- During silent independent work period, Maria is whispering to her tablemate when the teacher walks up and, to redirect her, says, "Maria, your work looks good. Get back to it, please." Although the teacher begins with positive words, this interaction is corrective. The student is *not* meeting behavioral expectations while the teacher delivers attention. Remember that the *timing* of the interaction defines it as positive or corrective.

- As Eric is walking down the hallway, the teacher says to him, "Hi, Eric. How did the basketball game go last night?" Eric is displaying appropriate hallway behavior, and the teacher delivered noncontingent attention. The interaction is positive.

- The teacher says, "Emma, please remember to raise your hand when you want to share an answer with the class." Emma had blurted out, so the interaction is corrective.

- The teacher says, "Hank, we're about to go to recess. Remember, I want you to walk slowly and use a Level 1 voice in line." Hank hasn't done anything wrong yet. The teacher is precorrecting—anticipating problems that might occur and reminding the student about the expectations for the next setting he will enter. It's a positive interaction.

- "Joe, do you need any help?" If Joe is working on his schoolwork when the teacher asks this question, the interaction is positive. If Joe is walking around the classroom instead of working on his assignment, the question is really a subtle verbal redirect and counts as a corrective interaction.

Think of RPI as a bank. Every positive interaction is a deposit into your relationship bank account for that student. Every corrective interaction is a withdrawal. If you make too many withdrawals, you'll overdraw your account and go bankrupt. Your goal is to get rich and so you continually make more deposits—at least three times more—into the bank than withdrawals. That way you will earn interest—more positive behavior from the student.

To practice identifying positive and corrective interactions, see the Counting RPI Exercises on the Module C Presentation 3 DVD.

STEP 1. Plan more positive interactions.

A. Review the problem and overall goal for the student.

Defining the nature and scope of the problem provides critical information for developing a successful intervention. If you have been collecting and analyzing data as described in the previous task, your goal is already clear. For example, Alisa is frequently disruptive, blurts out answers, and bothers other students during work times. The teacher is keeping a frequency count of Alisa's misbehaviors. The teacher's goal is for Alisa to reduce the frequency of her misbehaviors and increase her use of the replacement behaviors (the positive opposites of the target behaviors) that the teacher has described and taught to her.

If you have not been collecting data, consider doing so as part of your RPI implementation. Keep in mind that you are working toward a goal, and collecting data is a great way to determine whether you are making progress toward the goal.

B. Self-assess or have an observer monitor your RPI.

What is your current RPI with the target student? Many teachers are surprised to learn from their self-assessments that their ratios are skewed to the corrective. To evaluate yourself, keep a personal tally of positive and corrective interactions. Pick a 15- to 30-minute period when the student is likely to misbehave. You can simply carry an index card or a sticky note and mark a plus sign (+) when you deliver a positive interaction and a minus sign (–) when you deliver a corrective. Repeat this exercise two or three times over the next few days. You might search for an app that facilitates tally counts on your smartphone or tablet. You can also use one of the Ratios of Positive Interactions Monitoring Forms provided on the Module F CD. There are three versions (F-23a–c).

Calculate your ratio by reducing the positive to corrective fraction. For example, 20 positives to 10 correctives reduces to a 2:1 ratio. Five positives to 23 correctives reduces to 1:4.6. Remember, your goal is 3:1 or higher. If you conduct more than one observation, calculate the average ratio.

Also consider audio or video recording yourself teaching. Later in the day you can listen or watch the recording and tally your interactions. Audio recording is easy to set up, but somewhat limited because you will miss nonverbal interactions and you'll have to reconstruct from memory what the student was doing at the time of an interaction. Video recording is a great way to evaluate yourself, but make sure your school and district allow it. Video often captures interactions that go unnoticed by busy classroom teachers. After the initial novelty wears off and students are accustomed to a camera in the classroom, behavior tends to be natural. You can observe your body language, facial expressions, and the activity students are engaged in at the time of an interaction.

Possibly the best method of evaluating your RPI is to ask a trusted colleague to observe you work with the student and keep a tally. Just be sure this person has a thorough understanding of the definitions of positive and corrective interactions. Later, meet with the colleague privately to discuss the data.

C. Decide how you will respond to misbehavior.

It's important to have a game plan so that when you must respond to inappropriate behavior, you can do so in a very proactive, planned way that doesn't provide the student with a lot of emotional, reactive attention. Some students find such responses reinforcing, which is exactly what you want to avoid.

First, identify the student's negative behaviors, no matter how trivial. Then identify which of those behaviors are attention seeking in nature. Plan to completely ignore these behaviors. Planned ignoring can be a very powerful consequence because it deprives the student of the attention she desires.

To ignore misbehavior effectively, you must act as though you have not seen or heard the misbehavior. Stay calm and physically relaxed. A rigid body response or even shooting a meaningful look at the student might be reinforcing. And above all, you must be consistent! Ignore every instance of the behavior. If you don't, the student will learn that persistence pays—if she keeps blurting out, you will eventually react and she'll get what she wants: attention.

Develop a ladder of consequences. For the behaviors you plan to respond to (planned ignoring is not appropriate for them), select some mild consequences that you can implement quickly, easily, calmly, and consistently. Emotional responses can be reinforcing and undermine your delivery of consequences. When you must deliver a corrective, keep it unremarkable and nonintrusive—in a word, boring.

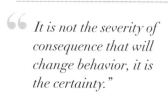

It is not the severity of consequence that will change behavior, it is the certainty."

TED KULONGOSKI, governor of Oregon, 2003–2011

For responding to the student's misbehavior, consider developing a consequence ladder. Develop a four-category system of nonprogressive, or fixed, consequences. Consider the various misbehaviors the student displays and then visualize four distinct categories.

If you've worked through Module D, *Responding to Misbehavior: An Instructional Approach*, you are familiar with the 3-level system of consequences that we recommend for schoolwide use. When a student is engaged in chronic misbehavior and is getting many Level 2 and Level 3 consequences, a behavior intervention plan is needed. This plan might include a customized consequence ladder for the target student that is more detailed than the 3-level system.

The first step of the ladder is misbehavior that receives no consequences at all, just reminders. In kindergarten, for instance, students sometimes simply forget that they are not supposed to shout out answers. There is no need to issue a consequence when a simple reminder will do. Planned ignoring fits into this category, too.

Misbehavior that receives a minor consequence falls on the second step of the ladder. For example, every time the student taps her pencil, she owes 15 seconds from recess. Sounds too simple to be effective? If you apply it consistently over time, this approach is very effective.

On the third step are more serious infractions—disrespect, bad language, and so on—that earn more serious consequences. Create a menu of consequences that the student knows about and understands. When the student commits a serious behavior, select one of the consequences from the menu. Examples of typical consequences for this category include time owed, timeout, detention, parental contact, and parent conference.

The fourth step is reserved for misbehavior that violates your school's code of conduct or involves physical or emotional violence. (This category is equivalent to Level 3 of the 3-level system described in Module D.) For these, and only these, you reserve the school's ultimate consequences—office referral and involvement of the principal or assistant principal. The four-category system allows some flexibility between classrooms in all categories except this one. Consequences for these severe misbehaviors should be consistently applied throughout the entire school.

Ensure that the student understands the system and knows what consequences apply to which behaviors.

Foundations Module D goes into great detail about developing levels of misbehavior and menus of consequences.

Detailed information about developing menus of mild, moderate, and severe consequences appears in *Foundations* Module D, Presentation 3; in *CHAMPS*; and in *Discipline in the Secondary Classroom*. Below are the consequences we suggest in Module D for the three levels. Consider them as you determine the menu of consequences for each step of your ladder.

Level 1 consequences (for mild to moderate misbehavior). See Form F-26 on the Module F CD for information about these corrective procedures.

- Nonverbal correction
- Gentle verbal reprimand
- Proximity correction
- Humor
- Frequency count
- Family contact
- Discussion
- Bumpy bunny timeout (Pre-K to second grade)
- Timeout at the student's desk (elementary)
- Timeout in a designated timeout area
- Timeout in another teacher's room
- Time owed
- Planned ignoring
- Restitution
- Positive practice

- Behavior Improvement Form
- Demerits
- Response cost/Loss of points
- Response cost lottery
- Loss of privilege
- Emotional reaction (used sparingly)
- Detention (classroom)
- Jot It Down strategy

Level 2 consequences (for moderate misbehavior)

- Notification to the office
- Detention (after school, lunchtime, Friday evening)
- Problem-solving room
- Timeout in another room
- Parental contact

Level 3 consequences (for severe misbehavior)

Office referral

D. Develop a plan to increase positive interactions

In addition to reducing the amount of attention the student gets for misbehavior, the success of this intervention depends on increasing your attention to responsible behavior. Adults must clearly demonstrate that students have a higher probability of getting adult attention when they behave than when they misbehave.

 Brainstorm a list of noncontingent positive interactions. For example:

- Say hello to the student by name as she enters the classroom.
- Deliver positive nonverbals, such as a wave, handshake, high five, fist bump, thumbs-up, shaka sign, OK sign, wink, or pat on the shoulder.
- Walk with the student when escorting the class to the cafeteria.
- Greet the student when she returns from lunch.
- Wish the student a happy vacation or good weekend.
- Say things such as, "I look forward to seeing you tomorrow."
- Talk about a shared interest.

We know from the research that noncontingent attention is highly effective and important for young students, low-achieving students, and students who come from low socioeconomic backgrounds. We are not suggesting that you become the student's best friend. You are still the adult, the professional educator. Your noncontingent attention simply tells that student that she is valued and important to you as a person and as a student.

Deliver noncontingent attention at dismissal or right before the bell rings, as you monitor independent work periods, during free time in class, and during classroom transition times. Noncontingent attention is very powerful when delivered outside the classroom. Plan to deliver *lots* of noncontingent attention—it's easy, quick, and powerful.

Plan to provide contingent positive feedback. Contingent positive feedback gives the student the attention she craves and information that describes what she was doing responsibly, which helps her learn what responsible behavior is. It is a very powerful tool to increase student motivation to behave appropriately.

Positive feedback should be specific. Briefly describe the behavior that prompted you to interact with the student. Tell the student what she did and possibly mention why it is important. "Maleka, thanks for waiting to be called on. Great example of following our guideline about cooperation."

Avoid falling into a pattern of nonspecific rote comments such as "terrific" and "nice job" (we call this the "good job" syndrome). Students may not even notice the attention because they're not getting usable information. They need to know how their specific actions translate into being responsible, on task, polite, and so on. Positive feedback is meaningful only when students are aware of what they did well.

Be sure the feedback is honest. Catch the student when she is legitimately demonstrating responsible or improved behavior. Also, link the positive feedback to the student's behavioral goals—if she is displaying a desired replacement behavior, make sure she knows that she is advancing toward her goal. It is especially crucial to provide frequent positive feedback when the student is learning a new skill (academic or behavioral) or when a skill is proving to be difficult.

How do you deliver positive feedback? Use your typical teaching voice. A general rule of thumb is to talk low and slow for corrections and use your normal volume and speed for positive feedback. Establish eye contact with the student. Use her name. Keep the interaction brief—no more than about 15 seconds.

> *They may forget what you said, but they'll never forget how you made them feel."*
>
> Attributed to many people, including Maya Angelou and Carl W. Buehner

Be businesslike and fairly neutral. Avoid gushing over the student, or you will risk embarrassing her.

Walk away as soon as you finish delivering the feedback. If you stay beside the student, she may think you want her to thank you for the feedback. For some students, that moment will be very awkward.

Sometimes tough students reject positive feedback. They might be embarrassed. Or they might feel they have to maintain their tough reputation, and getting positive feedback doesn't jibe with that reputation. If the student rejects your efforts to provide positive feedback, consider making the feedback more private. You might:

- Slip the student a note rather than verbalize the feedback.
- Pull the student aside for a brief conference at the back of the room.
- Catch the student when the bell rings and ask her to stay for a few seconds.
- Call the student at home.
- During class, give a prearranged signal that means, for example, "good self-control."

You might even allow the student to choose how and when to receive positive feedback. We know of a difficult middle-school student who chose to receive his positive feedback in this way: The teacher would establish eye contact with him, then touch her left earlobe. That action discreetly communicated to the student that he had done a good job on the preceding activity.

If the student still rejects your positive feedback, your relationship bank might be empty. We suggest that you back off on positive feedback and give more noncontingent attention for a couple of weeks. Fill up your bank, then gradually reintroduce the positive feedback.

Strategies to increase your RPI to at least 3:1

Give yourself a goal. Each time you correct the student, you owe her three positive interactions as soon as you can reasonably and honestly delivery them. Noncontingent attention will probably be the easiest way to meet your goal. This strategy not only increases your RPI, but it also communicates to the student that you don't hold a grudge, you're not angry at the student for misbehaving, and you still like the student (remember, you're a professional and you can't dislike the student on company time). In addition, the student will see that you do in fact recognize when she is behaving appropriately.

Use intermittent celebrations. In addition to positive feedback, provide a reward, celebration, or favorite activity when the student demonstrates a particularly important behavior or shows significant improvement. "Susan, today you've earned an extra 10 minutes of computer time." *Intermittent* is the key word—give the reward on some (not all) occasions when the student demonstrated desired behavior. The unpredictability of a small celebration or reward combined with positive feedback is very appealing to most students.

Note that rewards are not bribery. Bribery is defined as an inducement to do something illegal, unethical, or immoral. Offering a student a concrete reinforcer along with positive feedback is not encouraging anything illegal, unethical, or immoral.

Provide intermittent celebrations more often early in the intervention, then fade them as the student gets more competent with her ability to demonstrate replacement behaviors. The reward might be a small snack, inexpensive school supplies, additional free time, or anything that the student finds reinforcing. We know of a high school teacher who rewarded his math classes by performing a dance. When his students mastered a particularly difficult concept, they got to see their teacher do the Wally Wiggle. The students loved it.

A quick classroom task can also be used as an intermittent celebration. Students love to do jobs that give them attention, status, and a bit of authority. "Maya, can you help me copy and staple these papers? "Rudy, will you please make sure the whiteboard is erased at the end of the day."

Also note that a regular, daily school-based job can provide the student with much-needed attention and support. The book *Meaningful Work* gives ideas for over 100 school-based jobs that fulfill students' needs for attention, recognition, purpose, competence, and belonging. Meaningful Work can be especially powerful for students who struggle academically.

For information about implementing a program of school-based jobs, see Wise, B. J., Marcum, K., Haykin, M., Sprick, R. S., & Sprick, M. (2011). *Meaningful work: Changing student behavior with school jobs.* Eugene, OR: Pacific Northwest Publishing.

Use the Plan for Connecting and Motivating form. Consider using Plan for Connecting and Motivating (Form F-22a) shown in Figure 4o to help you plan these components of your RPI intervention:

- Noncontingent attention
- Positive feedback
- Consequences for misbehavior
- Strategies for increasing RPI
- Intermittent celebrations

Form F-22b on the CD is a copy of the Plan for Connecting and Motivating form that includes suggestions and reminders for each item. Writing down your intervention plan according to the structure of the form can really help you implement the plan successfully.

Consider involving other staff members in the plan. Inform other staff members who have contact with the student about the student's goals and ask them to watch for opportunities to deliver positive interactions. As the student experiences the support and recognition of other adults, the need for attention in the

Figure 4o   *Plan for Connecting and Motivating (F-22a) with sample plan*

Plan for Connecting and Motivating (p. 1 of 2)
What to Do When an Individual Student Is Not Motivated to Succeed in Your Class

Student __Sally__   Teacher __Mrs. Bradford__   Date __11/13__

Targeted Activities (activities in which the student is unmotivated and/or unsuccessful)	List the Student's Strengths	Replacement Behaviors
Coming to school regularly Completing assignments in class Completing homework	Gets along well with others Easily redirected Enjoys nonacademic activities	

1. List three strategies you will use to provide *noncontingent attention* to the student every day.

    a) I will smile at Sally and/or compliment her (e.g., "You look sharp this morning" or "My daughter has a pair of shoes like yours") every day as she enters the classroom.

    b) When I see Sally exhibiting appropriate behaviors when interacting with other students, I will establish eye contact and wink, smile, give a thumbs-up, etc.

    c) Every time Sally is absent, I will say to her on the day of her return something like, "I'm so glad you're back. It's just not the same without you here."

2. For which targeted activities will you provide *positive verbal feedback* to the student?

    a) Beginning an assignment on time

    b) Following a direction or responding to a redirection

    c) Turning in her homework

 All forms can be printed from the Module F CD.

Plan for Connecting and Motivating (p. 2 of 2)
What to Do When an Individual Student Is Not Motivated to Succeed in Your Class

3. What will you do if the student doesn't respond well to positive feedback?

   Try a different method of providing the feedback, such as writing her a private note.

4. Identify two strategies for increasing your ratio of positive interactions with the student and describe how and when you will use them.

   a) *I will make a point to greet Sally every morning when she enters the room and will tell her at dismissal that I'm looking forward to seeing her the next morning.*

   b) *I will provide both positive feedback and noncontingent attention when Sally is interacting appropriately with other students.*

5. Which intermittent celebration(s) will you use to reinforce the student for showing appropriate behaviors and/or progress on the targeted activities? How will you select the celebration and when will you deliver it?

   a) *I will have Sally use a prepared checklist to identify her top 5 choices for celebrations.*

   b) *I will randomly provide the celebrations once or twice a week when Sally comes to school and when she submits her homework.*

6. Track your RPI. Calculate your ratio by reducing the positive to corrective fraction. For example, 20 positives to 10 correctives equals a 2:1 ratio. Five positives to 23 correctives equals 1:4.6. Remember, your goal is 3:1 or higher.

Date	RPI		Date	RPI
_____	_____		_____	_____
_____	_____		_____	_____
_____	_____		_____	_____

classroom will be reduced. Let the staff members know that even simple noncontingent attention, such as greeting the student, making eye contact, and nodding, will be very helpful.

E. Continue to collect objective data to determine whether the intervention is helping the student's behavior improve

Because behavior is difficult to change, small improvements may go unnoticed unless you have established ways to measure progress. You have probably already worked through Task 4, Collect Data and Debrief, but if not, follow the instructions we provide for collecting meaningful data and continue to collect data throughout your intervention efforts.

Possible methods of monitoring student progress include direct observation, periodic frequency counts of the desired behavior, self-monitoring, grade book analysis, tracking work completion, and recording time on task. Evaluation systems will vary depending on the goal of the intervention, the sophistication of the student, and the time and personnel available to assist with monitoring.

STEP 2. Meet with the student.

Consider whether to include other adults in the meeting, such as parents or the school counselor. Always inform parents when you plan to implement an intervention with their child. Begin the meeting with a quick review of the problem and goal—specifically, what you are collecting data on and what improvements you hope the student will strive for.

Then help the student identify and rehearse specific actions she is willing to take to reach her goal. Though this intervention focuses heavily on teacher behavior, the student needs to know how to meet the expectations of the classroom. Have the student brainstorm actions she can take to reach her goal. Verbally rehearse what she will do to reach the goal. Model and have the student practice the replacement behavior.

Describe and discuss how you will respond to all of the student's misbehavior. If you developed a consequence ladder in Step 1C, help the student understand the behaviors that fall on each step of the ladder and the consequences at each step. If using planned ignoring, carefully explain which behaviors you will ignore and which behaviors you will give the student attention for. When the student is clear *and* you are consistent, the student is less likely to test the new rules and expectations by misbehaving.

Review the ways you and the student can engage in positive interactions. Set up a time to meet regularly with the student to discuss progress. With older students, you might meet once a week. With younger students, you might want to meet every 2 or 3 days, or even every day with a kindergarten student. Review the roles and responsibilities of all participants. Conclude the meeting with words of encouragement: "I really believe this plan will help you be more successful in my classroom and be happier at school."

STEP 3. Follow the plan.

We suggest that you begin this plan on a Monday or Tuesday. The plan requires that you change your behavior and be much more deliberate in your delivery of positive interactions, and you'll be able to ingrain that behavior better when you can practice it for 4 or 5 days in a row. For 2 or 3 weeks, focus on delivering lots of positive interactions and keeping the RPI high. At first, the student's behavior might not improve; in fact, it may worsen. Often students have learned that if they make a teacher miserable during the first couple days of a plan, the teacher will quit. Don't be that teacher. Stick with the plan and be relentless in boosting your RPI.

For a student, 2 weeks is a long time. We know from experience that students often begin modifying their behavior within 3 or 4 days of beginning the intervention. Teachers see a definite change in attitude. So after 2 weeks, the student will very likely be behaving much better.

We recommend that you discuss the plan with a colleague after a week or so. Talk about what is and is not working and consider tweaking any weak aspects of the plan.

If the student's behavior does not improve quickly, consider assessing your RPI, preferably by having a colleague observe you teach. Has your ratio improved? Are your positive interactions really positive? That is, are you interacting positively with the student when she is behaving appropriately? Review the definitions of positive and corrective interactions and practice identifying them using the Counting RPI Exercises on the Module C Presentation 3 DVD, if necessary. During your scheduled meeting with the student, review the expectations and goals. Consider monitoring your RPI every couple of days until you are consistently above a 3:1 ratio of positive to corrective interactions. But don't stop implementing the intervention! Once your ratios are consistently skewed to the positive, this intervention will work in almost all cases.

Task 5 Conclusion

Significant behavioral issues take time to change—sometimes months. This intervention modifies student behavior by improving your relationship with the student. This new, positive relationship and continuing high RPI will help you with any other interventions you implement with the student.

This is one intervention that you won't fade as you do most successful interventions. High RPI should become your routine with this student for the rest of the school year. In fact, your entire class can benefit from your honed skills with RPI.

TASK 6

Use a STOIC Function-Based Analysis and Intervention

STOIC analysis and intervention is intended to assist students with any chronic misbehaviors that have not responded positively to simple interventions. It may benefit a student whose behavioral problem has been resistant to other early-stage interventions. If you are considering this intervention, you have probably identified behaviors of concern, established goals, and collected data. If you have not completed these steps, consider doing so now. This intervention assumes that you have set goals and are collecting data. Use these data to analyze the efficacy of any procedures described in this task.

For more information about STOIC Analysis and Intervention, see Sprick, R., & Garrison, M. (2008). *Interventions: Evidence-Based Behavioral Strategies for Individual Students* (2nd ed.; pp. 305–334). Eugene, OR: Pacific Northwest Publishing. This task corresponds to Intervention F in the *Interventions* book.

This intervention requires more planning and forethought than previous interventions in this presentation because the problem is chronic and resistant to easy interventions. Function-based planning involves two processes:

1. Develop a hypothesis or a guess about why the behavior is happening (function-based thinking).

2. Design a multifaceted STOIC intervention based on that guess.

This intervention is *not* a formal functional behavior assessment (FBA). An FBA is usually conducted by a school psychologist or a certified behavior analyst, and it involves observing the student in multiple settings, doing a deep records search, and interviewing the student and the student's teachers and family. It's a complex, systematic, time-consuming process that is validated by research.

But the concept of function is not limited to FBAs. You can use it to think about any problem that persists despite early-stage interventions. Considering function just means you are asking two basic questions: What is the student getting from the behavior? What is the underlying reason for the behavior?

Consider three broad categories when thinking about function:

- Does the student lack the ability or awareness to exhibit the expected behavior?
- Is the student trying to get something?
- Is the student trying to avoid or escape something?

Asking these questions can help drive you toward interventions that address the function of the misbehavior for the student.

This process is driven by the STOIC Intervention Planning Form (F-24), shown in Figure 4p and included on the Module F CD. The STOIC acronym stands for Structure, Teach, Observe, Interact positively, and Correct fluently. We go through each variable a little later in this task. STOIC is also explained in great detail in Module A, Presentation 1, Task 2.

STEP 1. Review the information you have collected to date.

Review all the information you've collected on the student and summarize it on the STOIC Intervention Planning Form.

A. Planned Discussion: Review the Discussion Record form and any notes you took. When did the discussion take place? Did you conduct more than one? What were the goals and outcomes? Did you include the family in a Planned Discussion? When? What were the goals and outcomes?

B. Academic Assessment and Assistance: What is the student's oral reading fluency score? What do the Student Status Report and the Academic Assistance forms reveal about the student? What was the outcome of the assessment? Is the student able to do the work independently? What evidence supports or refutes that ability? What adaptations were made for the student?

C. Goal Setting: When did you meet with the student to set a goal? What were the goals and outcomes? Review the Goal Setting form and the Long-Range Goal Setting form.

D. Data Collection and Debriefing: List all the behaviors of concern that you've collected data on to this point. Let's say the focus so far has been on disruptions. Planned Discussion and Goal Setting didn't help and the student's academic ability does not seem to be a factor, so you moved on to Data Collection and conducted a frequency count on the incidents of disruption.

Review the charted data and consider whether you should continue to focus on disruptions or shift to other behaviors. Are disruptions still the major issue? Perhaps

STOIC Intervention Planning Form (p. 1 of 2)

Student <u>Eduardo</u>   Grade/Class <u>I</u>   Teacher <u>Ms. Phan</u>   Dates <u>10/20</u>

Step 1   Review the information you have collected to date.

A. Notes from Planned Discussions (dates, goals, outcomes):   9/26, follow-up on 10/2 and 10/8

Eddie is always apologetic about being out of his seat and off task, and promises to do better. He stays on task and in his seat for an hour or so after we talk, but then is back to getting up and wandering around.

B. Academic Assessment and Assistance: Oral reading fluency: <u>60</u>   words correct per minute

Despite being out of his seat so frequently, Eddie completes his work on time, and the quality is excellent.

C. Notes from Goal-Setting Activities (dates, goals, outcomes):

10/10 Set up a contract to reduce the number of times out of seat, but Eddie would forget and then get discouraged when he didn't meet the goal.

D. List all behaviors of concern from Data Collection and Debriefing:

Out of seat/off task: In the morning, he is out of his seat without permission 3-5 times during each subject. The number improves after lunch--he is out of seat only once or twice then. He also frequently goes off task while remaining in his seat--drawing on his notebook, playing with pencil and eraser, etc. This mainly happens during independent work--I have to give 2-4 reminders during each ind. work period.

Are these same behaviors to be the continued focus of intervention?   Yes

If no, what behavior will be the new focus, and what data will be collected to determine progress?

E. List your strategies for Increasing Positive Interactions and note how the student responds:

I've focused on increasing noncontingent attention, but probably not enough to offset the number of corrections Eddie receives.

F. Develop a hypothesis about the function of the problem behavior—what might be the reason the problem chronically occurs? Check any that may be applicable.

<u>X</u> Ability   ____ Awareness   ____ Attention from adults   ____ Attention from peers

____ Power or control   ____ Competing reinforcers   <u>X</u> Avoid work   ____ Avoid something

  All forms can be printed from the Module F CD.

STOIC Intervention Planning Form (p. 2 of 2)

Step 2   Develop an intervention that:
- Takes into account your hypothesis about the function of the misbehavior.
- Modifies some aspect of each STOIC variable.

This will ensure that you have a comprehensive plan tailored to help the student meet all of his or her needs in positive ways.

Structure
1) Try the idea of creating an "office" space so Eddie can move around without leaving his desk and disrupting the class. 2) Assign bonus assignment-something fun like a puzzle or word search, or maybe a book that he picks from the library--for Eddie to do when he completes independent work assignments. Think about providing a small reward for completing the bonus assignment. 3) Give Eddie morning tasks of running attendance list to the office and, later, picking up mail from the office.

Teach
expectations
See if Mr. Garza (counselor) can work with Eddie once a week on skills for staying focused.

Observe
& monitor
Continue to collect data on frequency of Eddie's off-task and out-of-seat behavior. Consider having Eddie self-monitor whether he is on or off task during independent work periods.

Interact
positively
Continue looking for opportunities for noncontingent attention. Also give positive feedback when Eddie stays in his office space, completes the bonus work, and does his assigned jobs.

Correct
fluently
Eddie will note on self-monitoring form every time he is out of his "office."

the student is exhibiting even higher-level misbehaviors such as tantruming. If you decide to change focus, what data will you collect to determine progress with that new behavior?

E. Increasing Positive Interactions: Summarize your strategies for increasing and maintaining at least three times as many positive as corrective interactions with the student. Consider whether you are truly delivering positive attention. Is the student always engaged in appropriate behavior when you give the attention? How does the student respond to the positive attention?

F. Hypothesis: Develop a hypothesis. Then review your summary and develop a hypothesis about the function of the behavior. Why is the problem occurring chronically? Why is it so resistant to simpler solutions? You're not diagnosing, you're just developing a guess. Consider these functions:

- Lack of ability
- Lack of awareness
- Seeking adult attention
- Seeking peer attention
- Seeking power and control
- Competing reinforcers
- Avoiding work or situations

Lack of ability. Some students act inappropriately because they're incapable of exhibiting the expected behavior or because they don't realize they're behaving badly. Lack of ability or awareness should always be considered and ruled out before proceeding with an intervention. Here are a few examples of students who lack the physiological or neurological ability to meet expectations.

- A paraplegic student violates the Walk in the Halls rule. The student is not trying to get or avoid something; he is physically unable to walk.

- A student with severe academic deficits does nothing during independent work periods. The student is not trying to avoid the work. She just knows she cannot complete the work and there's no point in trying.

- A student with Tourette syndrome cannot control his actions. Whenever the underlying condition is at least partly neurological or physiological, the intervening teacher must work closely with the student's physician to determine behaviors that might be reasonable to treat behaviorally and behaviors that should be tolerated and accommodated.

Consider a student who has been identified as having attention deficit/hyperactivity disorder (ADHD) and cannot stay seated. ADHD is a special case because some combination of modified expectations and accommodations may be the best course. Though the student who can't stay seated for long periods of time may have difficulty doing what comes easily to other students, it is not beyond that student's ability to learn how to sit still. It is perfectly reasonable to design a plan to try to help a student with ADHD practice and learn improved behavior. Some children with ADHD will overcome the difficulties associated with their condition, while others will continue to struggle and may benefit from some adjustment of expectations while they are learning new skills such as self-control and impulse control, staying still, and keeping their attention focused on a task. Teachers, while making some reasonable accommodations, can still hold high standards and firm behavioral expectations for their students with ADHD.

Intervention Strategies: If the behavior is outside the student's ability to control (Tourette syndrome, for example), merely create accommodations. If the behavior is within the student's ability to learn to control (ADHD tendencies, for example), interventions should involve making temporary accommodations while concurrently teaching replacement behaviors. With many students, do not expect immediate or complete behavior change.

Lack of awareness. Some students act inappropriately because they don't realize they're behaving badly. For example, imagine a fidgety student who constantly taps his pencil on the desk. The only time this student is not tapping his pencil is when his knee is bobbing up and down, which he does with equal unawareness. Only when he consciously thinks about keeping his hands and feet still is he completely quiet. He isn't irritating his teacher to get attention—in fact, he's completely unaware that his tapping and bobbing is having any effect at all on the teacher.

A student who raises her voice and gets very loud when she feels strongly about something may also have an awareness problem. Her pattern of speech may reflect the types of interactions that are common in her home, community, or circle of friends, or they may simply be a product of her temperament and physiological makeup. She may not realize that her behavior is perceived as rude or even threatening, and she may be genuinely confused when adults get angry with her or when teachers refer her for insubordination.

Intervention strategies: Interventions may involve accommodation, but should also involve signals or prompts, teaching replacement behavior, self-monitoring, positive reinforcement, or other strategies to help behavior improve over time. Providing a Koosh ball to a fidgety student is an example of an accommodation—giving the student something to do with his hands instead of the distracting behavior. You would concurrently implement some form of self-monitoring, positive reinforcement, or other strategy as a long-term intervention designed to change the behavior.

Seeking adult attention. Some students seek positive attention in inappropriate ways—an example is the student who chronically tattles on others. Another example is the student who constantly seeks reassurance or validation: "Look at my work!

Look what I did!" The student's motive is positive, but the method quickly becomes trying for the teacher.

Some students may be trying to get negative attention from the teacher—a scolding, a reprimand, a threat of disciplinary action. He may have had little success getting positive attention in the past. He may be struggling academically. He may be trying to impress his friends or appease his antagonizers. He may argue or be belligerent. Whatever the reason, consequences that are negative or aversive for most students may be serving as positive reinforcers for this student.

Intervention strategies: Interventions will involve planned ignoring and increasing the ratio of positive interactions—that is, delivering many more positive interactions than corrective interactions (see Task 5 for information about increasing RPI).

Seeking peer attention. The class clown is seeking laughter and social approval. The show-off wants to be seen as talented and popular. Conversely, some students want negative attention. They have found that they get attention from their peers only by annoying them, bullying them, or arguing with them.

Intervention strategies: Interventions will involve trying to increase the amount of attention the student receives from peers in prosocial ways, usually by teaching the student better social skills for interacting with peers and making friends. It may occasionally involve working directly with the peer group to reduce the amount of attention the student receives for acting out.

Seeking power and control. This is an extreme form of attention-getting behavior in which the student truly seems to want to get adults angry. Instead of being satisfied with any type of attention, the student actively tries to push the teacher's buttons. An emotional reaction from an adult is like fanning the flames of a fire and can be highly reinforcing to students who are deliberately trying to provoke such a response. (See Module D, Presentation 5, for information about emotional escalation and strategies for preventing it.)

Intervention strategies: The intervention will often involve giving the student more control by putting her in charge of some aspects of the classroom environment or of her own situation when she exhibits positive behaviors. At the same time, reduce any control (such as emotional reactions) that the student elicits from adults through misbehavior.

Competing reinforcers. This is a fancy name for a simple concept—the student would rather do something other than the assigned task or activity. An example is a very young child who, instead of doing her work, walks around the classroom or does other activities.

Intervention strategies: When a student is seeking different stimuli than the activity provides, the intervention will involve reducing access to outside reinforcers so that the reinforcers inherent in the desired activity are the best and most accessible ones available.

Avoiding work or situations. The student may use misbehavior to avoid or escape from something that makes her uncomfortable.

- *Overly difficult or overly simple work.* Assigned work may be beyond the student's ability. For example, suppose you set up a round-robin reading activity, with each student reading a paragraph in turn. A student who knows he is a poor reader might misbehave to escape having to read aloud in front of his friends. In other cases, a student might find the assignment extremely dull or simple and misbehave to avoid boredom more than the work itself.

  Intervention strategies: Adapt instruction to fit the student's academic abilities. If you know that a certain assignment will be too easy for the student, consider letting the student complete an alternative task instead. For example, if a student hasn't been completing boring work, try to create more interesting assignments while letting him know that occasionally he'll have to do the regular assignments. If the work is too difficult for the student, implement one of the adaptation strategies listed in Task 2: Academic Assessment and Assistance. If you have already implemented an academic intervention and the student is still unsuccessful, this would be a reasonable time to recommend a referral for special education assessment.

- *Uncomfortable situations.* Most students go to some lengths to avoid negative, harsh, or embarrassing situations. For example, knowing that the tough kids like to hang out in the restroom, a student might avoid going into the restroom during passing times to escape harassment. At some point during the day, that student will demand to be excused from class or will perhaps do something extremely negative to get thrown out of class so she can use the restroom while other students are not present.

  Some students avoid interactions with adults they find overly harsh, caustic, or critical. Even if the student isn't truly afraid of a teacher, the prospect of interacting with him may be too much to handle, so she searches for some escape, such as getting kicked out of class or chronic absenteeism.

  Intervention strategies: Try to restructure the student's environment so that exposure to the anxiety-producing stimulus is minimized. Also reduce the ways the student can easily escape unpleasant but necessary situations. For example, if the teacher is being overly harsh and critical, the teacher could be encouraged to work on increasing RPI.

STEP 2. Plan a STOIC intervention.

Develop an intervention plan that:

1. Takes into account your hypothesis about the function of the misbehavior.

2. Modifies some aspect of each of the STOIC variables.

If you can manipulate something in all five STOIC variables, the resulting behavioral plan will be much stronger than if you try to change only one variable. For example, some people are very good at teaching replacement behavior. It is a very powerful intervention with a great track record in the research literature, but it covers only the T of STOIC. If you put all your energy into teaching replacement behaviors, but don't consider altering any structural components that would make it easier for the student to be successful with the replacement behaviors you're teaching, your intervention will not be as strong as it could be.

Write your plan for each variable on the STOIC Intervention Planning Form. Decide in advance who will participate in the planning stages and complete the planning form. You may do this yourself and then present the form to the student and parents, or you may want to actively involve them in the planning process.

*S**tructure and organize the environment to set up the student for success.* Here are a few examples of structural variables you can manipulate.

Change assigned seating. The easiest modification of the physical environment is to change where a student sits. If the student always talks when seated with certain peers, move him away from them. If the student is highly distractible, consider moving her as far away as possible from high-traffic areas. If the student craves adult attention, move him closer to you so that he gets more attention while he is on task. Likewise, if the student is trying to attract peer attention, move her closer to you so that her peer interactions are easier to monitor.

Avoid placing the student in a corner, because teachers often miss the corners when they visually scan the classroom.

Change the work requirements. Modify the curriculum to fit the student's needs. If the student frequently fails to complete work, arrange for her to get feedback on the first part of an assignment: "Shannon, do the first five problems and then raise your hand. I'll come to you, correct those first five, and let you know whether you're on track." This is also a way for the student to reliably get positive adult attention. Curriculum can be modified in many ways to fit a student's needs and set up more success (see Task 2 for a list of adaptation strategies).

Change the schedule. Incorporate breaks into the class routine. If students are expected to remain seated during a 30-minute work period and several generally fail to comply, give the whole class a chance to stand up and stretch halfway through the period. If only one student struggles to get through the work period, give that student a legitimate excuse by asking her to run an errand or pass out some papers, thus permitting her to move around without having to misbehave to get relief. If the student works for 20 out of the 30 minutes, that's better than a 30-minute expectation that results in just 5 or 10 minutes of work from the student.

Change expectations or procedures. If you are flexible about when and how your expectations can be met, many students will appreciate and respond to the extra freedom. For a young student, you might place a masking-tape box on the floor around his desk and give him permission to stand and work when he wants, as long as he does not leave his "office." By changing this expectation, you have massively increased the number of opportunities to reinforce the student for meeting expectations. Even if the student is jumping up and down in his office, you can say, "Andrew, you're doing a good job showing self-control by staying in your office."

Assign a duty or responsibility. A job can be particularly helpful for a student who seeks power and control. If the student craves attention, assign her a job that provides a lot of attention—for example, trash-can duty, passing out papers, or cleaning computer keyboards. If the task provides just 2 minutes of positive time with an adult, it may be enough to substantially reduce the student's inappropriate attention-seeking behavior.

The book *Meaningful Work* (Wise et al., 2011) is full of ideas for school-based jobs for students.

Give the student viable choices. Sometimes students rebel when they believe they have no influence over their school experience. Giving these students a real sense of choice may help them see themselves as creators of their own experience and the authors of their own success. Offering a viable choice—some element of control—over situations that agitate or set off the student can have a calming effect.

This is *not* a viable choice: "You can either get your work done or you can stay in from recess." There's nothing wrong with saying it, but it is really a choice between doing exactly what the teacher expects or facing the consequence. A *viable* choice provides a range of options: "You can start with this assignment or that assignment. Before the end of the day, both have to be finished, but you can choose which one to do first."

Examples of viable choices include:

- Offer a choice of work locations.
- Allow the student to choose the order in which he completes a series of tasks.

- Set a self-initiated timeout. "You have my permission to go to the designated quiet area whenever you need to take a timeout. As long as you continue to get your work done, you can use that area any time you need to."

Teach expectations. Teach the student how to behave responsibly within the structure. Following are some ways to do this.

Re-teach classroom expectations. If several students are having trouble exhibiting your expectations for behavior in the classroom, you should probably re-teach the whole class. If everyone except Zac is doing well, however, re-teach your expectations to Zac. Explain to him one-to-one when he can talk, how he can get help, and any concept that seems to be unclear or unnecessary to him. Spending time re-teaching your expectations will save you time—potentially a lot of time— later on.

Teach the positive opposite of a problem behavior. Teaching the positive opposite means teaching the student how to practice a behavior that is incompatible with the problem behavior. For example, for a student who is unable to stay on task, teach specific skills for concentrating and staying focused. For a student who goes ballistic when you correct her work, teach a range of acceptable responses.

Teach a particular skill. A student might have difficulty focusing because he has never been taught how to focus. You can teach and show the student, in just a minute or two a day, how focused attention is something people can and do manage. The concept of being able to manage your attention—reminding yourself to get back to work, noticing when you're staring out the window, developing strategies to bring yourself back to what's happening right now—may be entirely foreign to some students, and consciously teaching the skill can make a difference in their behavior.

In Module D, Presentation 5, Task 3 we provide sample lessons for teaching students skills such as following directions, accepting compliments, accepting no for an answer, accepting corrections, and other skills. These lesson plans can be easily adapted for individual students. The one-to-one lessons can be taught by the teacher (if time permits), a school counselor, or even a skilled, sensitive paraprofessional under the supervision of a school counselor.

Teach social skills. Many matters of simple politeness, consideration, manners, and etiquette can be taught when a student appears to be lacking in one or more of these skills, such as how to accept a reprimand or compliment. Many districts have adopted social skills curricula such as *Second Step* by Committee For Children. When you are teaching social skills to all students, your target student might need just some remedial lessons that you or perhaps the school counselor can deliver.

***O**bserve and monitor the student's behavior.* Strategies to consider for this STOIC variable include:

Circulate frequently. Move unpredictably throughout the classroom and avoid spending time at your desk. Think about spending more time standing near the targeted student than you have in the past—just as a state trooper stations himself on a stretch of the highway where people are known to exceed the speed limit.

Increase frequency of visual scanning. Regardless of where you are, look at other areas of the classroom. Great teachers do not really have eyes in the back of their heads, they just seem to because they always know what is going on in all parts of the classroom. Try visually scanning areas close to the targeted student more frequently than other areas.

Collect data and debrief (Task 4). If you're considering a STOIC intervention, data collection is likely already involved, so continue with any data collection procedures and debrief the student regularly. Ask yourself if the data collection is working. Are you still focusing on exactly the same behaviors? Do you need to modify your focus? If you have not been systematically collecting data, begin doing so.

***I**nteract positively with the student.* Increase the frequency of noncontingent and contingent attention. Strategies for ongoing positive rapport with students are covered in Task 5, Maintain High Ratios of Positive to Corrective Interactions, and in Module D, Presentation 3, "Ratios of Positive Interactions (RPI)." If you are still concerned about the student after implementing strategies to increase RPI, redouble your efforts to greet the student frequently and cheerfully, offer assistance and encouragement often, and provide timely precorrections at critical points before the student veers off course. Praise the student for any progress you see in data on the student's goal behaviors. Praise any attempt you see the student make toward achieving the goal behaviors. If you are precorrecting, be sure to add plenty of direct, specific praise.

***C**orrect fluently—calmly, consistently, briefly, and immediately.* Plan responses so your reaction does not interrupt the flow of instruction. After thinking about the possible function of the student's misbehavior, take care to avoid reinforcing the misbehavior—your planned response should not feed into the behavior. For example, if the student's misbehavior serves to gain attention, keep your corrections brief and detached—you don't want to give the student any more attention than necessary while she is misbehaving.

Your chosen response should be something you will be willing to do each and every time the student exhibits the misbehavior. If the consequence is too harsh for mild to moderate misbehavior, you might not be able to follow through every time. Even if you decide to use gentle reprimands, use them every time. Getting angry after issuing five gentle reprimands not only fractures the consistency that characterizes fluent correction, but can also potentially teach or reinforce a host of unwelcome behaviors as the student learns that persistence is the trick to getting you riled up. See Module D, Presentation 3, Task 1 for a sample menu of corrective procedures for mild and moderate classroom misbehavior.

STEP 3. Meet with the student.

Discuss the intervention plan. Begin the meeting with a quick review of the problem, the goal, and any data collected to date. Then discuss the intervention plan. Explain any changes you plan to make in the student's routine, such as changes in structure, adaptations to curriculum, or correctional techniques. Provide brief explanations of what you plan to do with each of the STOIC variables. Focus more time and energy on the variables you identified as being most important according to your hypothesis regarding the function of the misbehavior. For example, if the student's problem is awareness, focus the meeting on teaching expectations and briefly explain other aspects of the plan. Model and rehearse any necessary skills or interactions and conclude the meeting with words of encouragement.

Follow up. Meet regularly with the student to discuss the data and debrief. Be sure to celebrate progress, and include the student's parents whenever possible.

Task 6 Conclusion

STOIC Function-Based Analysis and Intervention is designed to help you address the function of any chronic misbehavior. Any intervention plan has a much greater likelihood of success when it is designed to address the reason behind the misbehavior. When you are thinking about the function of a misbehavior, remember that you are not developing a diagnosis, merely a guess or hypothesis about why the behavior is occurring. If the function-based intervention is successful in changing the student's behavior, your hypothesis is probably correct. If the behavior does not change, your hypothesis may be incorrect.

This intervention appears at the end of this presentation about early-stage classroom interventions because it is the most complex of the six interventions. It takes more time to plan because you are manipulating the five STOIC variables: Structure, Teach, Observe, Interact positively, Correct fluently.

As we've said before, always try the easiest intervention first. If it works—great! You've been successful with the least burdensome, least intrusive, and least time-consuming strategy. If the student continues to misbehave, you need to try something that is a bit more detailed. If you've worked your way up to the STOIC intervention and the student is still misbehaving, then it is probably time to begin thinking about Tier 2 and Tier 3 problem-solving processes and personnel, which we discuss in subsequent presentations.

FIVE

Matching the Intensity of Your Resources to the Intensity of Student Needs

INTRODUCTION

Some students need only a safe, consistent, welcoming, and well-structured school to be successful. Many students need (and all students benefit from) well-managed classrooms with highly engaging and motivated teachers; these students need only universal behavior support to thrive. However, some students have a far greater level of need: *targeted support.* This support might be short term—for example, a student going through a temporary family upheaval may need some additional support during that time. A student experiencing significant but short-term peer problems may need support. A student who is facing temporary academic challenges for the first time might exhibit behavioral problems. Once those challenges are overcome, the students may no longer need the additional support.

Some students need long-term care—*ongoing targeted support.* A student with a significant problem such as oppositional defiant disorder or a student diagnosed with mild autism might need support throughout his or her school career.

And some students have *intensive* needs. These include students with chronic, severe neurological and cognitive disabilities and students with short-term but serious issues such as major depression with suicidal ideation.

In this presentation, we guide you through some systems-level thinking about the concept of targeted support. Specifically, in your school do you match the intensity of your resources to the intensity of student needs? Do you allocate your resources both efficiently and effectively? As you work toward being able to answer yes to these questions, you'll get closer to providing all students with what they need to be successful. No student should fall through the cracks of your behavioral and academic supports.

Should this issue of matching resources to student needs be the responsibility of the Foundations Team? Maybe not. If your school has a group that represents general education teachers and links to general education decision making or a group that ensures smooth operation of your tiered system of supports, perhaps one of those groups should examine the question of needs and resources. If you don't have such a group, the Foundations Team should probably take on this responsibility. At the very least, the Foundations Team should ensure that universal prevention and intervention is systematically integrated with all Tier 2 and Tier 3 efforts.

The process we refer to is not about *providing* support or services, or even about problem solving. Rather, it's about ensuring that the system meets the needs of students and staff and that your resources are allocated both efficiently and effectively. In other words, the Foundations Team does not develop intervention plans for Reiko or Kevin. Rather, it ensures that the school's tiered systems of support meet the needs of all students—even those who need additional support.

Task 1: Use Data to Identify Student Needs is about ensuring that the system (that means school and district staff, the protocols you follow, and the things you do to ensure that every student succeeds) is as aware of student needs as it can be. We discuss both universal screening for behavior and the concept of red-flag criteria. Red flags are data (data that you probably already have) that should signal the system when a child needs to be watched more carefully and might benefit from Tier 2 or Tier 3 supports. No student should fall through the cracks just because you weren't paying enough attention to the situation.

Task 2: Identify Support Personnel and Ready-to-Use Tier 2 Interventions discusses linking student needs to available resources and constructing a variety of policies and programs that can be immediately matched to individual students who are identified as needing additional support. For example, by establishing a check-and-connect program such as Connections, you can refer a student with inappropriate attention-seeking behavior to the program at any time during the year. A ready-to-use program like Connections is less time consuming and less intrusive for staff than implementing the collaborative problem-solving processes described in Presentation 6.

Task 3: Identify Tier 2 and Tier 3 Problem-Solving Processes and Support Personnel guides you through defining the resources, personnel, and problem-solving processes available in your school so that you can create a flowchart, or at least a conceptual understanding, of how students and staff can use the resources most efficiently and effectively. Usually the movement will be from universal supports to early-stage interventions to tiered systems of support, as necessary.

Here's an example of increasing levels of support: Let's say a sixth-grade student is chronically disruptive. The sixth-grade team modified the universal classroom management plan and implemented some early-stage interventions, but this didn't help. The next step should be for someone such as a counselor, administrator, or school psychologist to become an advocate for the student. The advocate reviews the student's data and considers whether the student needs resources beyond what the teachers have already provided. The advocate is also knowledgeable about resources available to students. In this case, the advocate might recommend that the student be enrolled in Connections, a check-and-connect program that is a ready-to-use Tier 2 intervention. Teachers monitor the student's behavior and give feedback to her after each class period.

If Connections doesn't work after a few weeks, the advocate would turn to more intensive intervention and problem-solving resources in the system. For example, he might suggest that the classroom teacher work through the 25-Minute Planning Process with another teacher or work through the Intervention Decision Guide: Teacher Interview with the school counselor or school psychologist. Both of these processes are tools for designing and implementing behavior improvement plans (see Presentation 6 for details). If these processes are not successful, the case may be referred to a multidisciplinary team that will consider special education placement.

TASK 1

Use data to identify student needs

The goal of this task is to ensure that student needs are identified as early as possible. The earlier you can begin an intervention with a student who needs one, the better. Imagine you're driving from Wichita, Kansas, to Florida, and a few miles outside of Wichita you make a wrong turn. It is far less time and energy consuming to correct yourself if you realize your mistake just a mile after the wrong turn than if you wait until you're in Portland, Maine. You can still get to Florida from Maine, but you'll use a lot more time and money doing so than if you had driven directly from Wichita to Florida.

This idea holds true with behavior intervention and even with a student at risk for depression. The sooner you can identify the problem and intervene to provide levels of support, the greater the probability that you can positively affect students. In this task, we provide information about two methods to help you identify students in need: universal screening and red flags.

Consider universal screening for behavior issues.

Why universal screening for behavior? Think about the universal screenings schools do for vision and hearing. Most schools check every student each year because students with undiagnosed hearing or vision impairments may be at risk for school failure and other life challenges. If impairments are not identified, the true cause of a failure might never be known. The screenings enable the school to identify students whose sight or hearing might be problematic and who should receive professional attention and diagnosis.

> How students behave influences how we teach, and how we teach influences how students behave. Teachers need information on behavioral patterns—externalizing, internalizing, and otherwise—so that this information can be used to inform instruction. (Lane, Menzies, Oakes, & Kalberg, 2012, p. 7)

Universal screening for behavior is similar to vision and hearing screenings. It's a proactive way to identify students whose behavior might be problematic and who should be evaluated to see whether they need Tier 2 or Tier 3 intervention. Between 9% and 13% of students have some kind of emotional-behavioral problems (Walker, Severson, & Feil, 2014). Schools generally don't do a good enough job of finding those students early enough, before behavioral patterns become so firmly established that they are less responsive to intervention. Left untreated, these students are certainly more likely to drop out of school and experience poor grades, troubled peer relationships, long-term unemployment, incarceration, substance abuse, and even suicide (Walker et al., 2014).

We use Systematic Screening for Behavior Disorders (SSBD) as the example throughout this task. SSBD is considered by many to be the gold standard of universal screeners for behavior (Lane et al., 2012). Developed by Drs. Hill Walker and Herb Severson, SSBD was first published in 1992, and online and print versions with updated norms came out in 2014. This program has been researched for more than three decades and has extensive comparative norms.

The information we present in this section is largely drawn from Walker, H. M., Severson, H. H., & Feil, E. G. (2014). *Systematic Screening for Behavior Disorders* (SSBD, 2nd ed.). Eugene, OR: Pacific Northwest Publishing.

Advantages of universal screening. First, teachers tend to refer only those students who severely disrupt the classroom or are atypical learners. Screening gives each student an equal chance to be screened and identified for serious behavioral adjustment problems that may lead to dropping out and damaged self-esteem, peer relations, and academic achievement.

Second, universal screeners such as SSBD can identify both externalizing and internalizing risk factors.

- *Externalizing behavior* is directed outward toward the social environment and involves behavioral excesses that are usually maladaptive and aversive to others (aggression, noncompliance). Intervention is usually necessary to decrease inappropriate behavior.

- *Internalizing behavior* is directed inward, away from the social environment. It often involves behavioral deficits and/or problems with self—lack of social skills, shyness, withdrawn behaviors, depression, or school phobia. Intervention is usually necessary to teach skills and increase appropriate prosocial behavior.

Finally, screening supports teachers. Lane et al. (2012, p. 8) write:

> Behavior screenings also provide support for teachers by eliminating the pressure of potentially missing a student who needs additional support . . . . Teachers are confronted with many demands over the course of a given school day and across the academic year. It is simply unrealistic (and creates too much pressure!) to expect teachers to be aware of all types of behavior concerns and then independently evaluate whether each student has each concern. A key benefit of behavior screening systems is that they protect and support students and teachers alike.

Limitations of universal screening. False negatives (overlooking a student who actually needs assistance) and false positives (incorrectly identifying a student as needing assistance) are possible outcomes of any screening process.

Because they are designed to be efficient, universal screening results provide only a snapshot of student behavior. More comprehensive assessment is often required to fully understand a student's behavioral needs.

In addition, unless linked to intervention, screening results have limited use. It is important for schools to carefully consider how to address the needs of students who will be identified when implementing a universal screening procedure.

Adopt and implement a universal behavioral screener.

If you determine that your school could benefit from using a universal screener for early detection of behavior issues, follow these steps to identify and implement one.

STEP 1. Choose a universal screener.

Note: Your school or district may have already made this decision.

A good system has the following characteristics:

- Cut scores (score at which students do or do not move on to Tier 2 or Tier 3 support) are reliable and valid. False negatives—overlooking a student who actually needs assistance—are minimized.

- It has demonstrated a high degree of reliability.

- It is feasible in terms of time, effort, and cost.

The screening options that follow are commercially or publicly available.

Systematic Screening for Behavior Disorders (SSBD; Walker et al., 2014): Examples and information in *Foundations* are based on this screener. The SSBD uses a two-stage process for screening and is designed to detect both externalizing and internalizing behavior patterns. In Stage 1, the classroom teacher identifies a small group of students who demonstrate the *most* risk for externalizing or internalizing problems. In Stage 2, the classroom teacher evaluates these students' behavior in more detail, using checklists and rating scales to verify or confirm their risk status. SSBD has been normed for use with students in pre-K through grade 9. This process requires only about an hour to screen an entire class. Paper and web-based versions are available from Pacific Northwest Publishing. The web-based version eliminates manual scoring and compiling.

BASC-2 Behavioral and Emotional Screening System (BASC-2 BESS; Kamphaus & Reynolds, 2007): This one-stage screener uses a multidimensional approach to conducting screening, using input from teachers, parents, and student self-reports. Three separate rating scales are included and can be used with students in preschool through Grade 12.

Student Risk Screening Scale (SRSS; Drummond, 1993): The SRSS is a one-stage universal screening tool for grades K–6. It is simple, reliable, and valid. Screening with SRSS takes about the same amount of time as with SSBD, but does not provide the detailed information needed to design individualized interventions.

Strengths and Difficulties Questionnaire (SDQ; Goodman, 1997): The SDQ is a one-stage screener for students ages 3–16. Teachers, parents, and students (age 11 and up) provide input.

State tools: Some states provide screening tools. Check with your state department of education.

STEP 2. Follow the directions for the screener used by your school or district. (To give you an idea of the process, we present implementation instructions for SSBD as an example.)

Note: Be sure to follow all applicable school and district policies in regard to parental notification, student opt-out, confidentiality, and other issues related to universal behavioral screening.

Who will conduct the screening?

In SSBD, classroom teachers are the primary source of screening information. For Stage 1 of the screening process, teachers nominate and rank order students on internalizing and externalizing behavior dimensions, calling attention to the students who are most likely to display behaviors associated with these two dimensions. In Stage 2, teachers complete the Critical Events Checklist and Combined Frequency Index for Adaptive and Maladaptive Behavior. (For pre-K and K students, teachers also complete the Aggressive Behavior Scale for externalizers and the Social Interaction Scale for internalizers.) Teachers are acknowledged to have the most extensive knowledge of the social, behavioral, and academic characteristics of their students.

One or two members of the Foundations Team should manage the administration of the screening and the collection and analysis of the data.

Which students will be screened?

The SSBD is designed for all students in pre-K through grade 9.

When will we screen?

Teachers should have at least 30 days to observe their students' typical classroom behavior before conducting the Stage 1 screening.

We recommend screening at least twice during the school year: in the fall and after winter break. Screening three times per year is even better—schedule screenings about six weeks after the school year begins, before winter break, and near the end of the school year.

Fall data: Use for implementing interventions right after the screening. The data can also be used to determine overall risk level and help identify teachers who may benefit from additional support because they have a high number of students in need of Tier 2 and 3 supports.

Winter data: Use for monitoring progress and making adjustments, as needed. Also be sure to screen any students new to the school.

Spring data: Use to establish year-end performance and direct next year's class placements.

ᙏ FOUNDATIONS RECOMMENDATION ᙅ

Conduct universal screening at least twice during the school year: in the fall and after winter break. Screening three times per year is even better— schedule screenings about six weeks after the school year begins, before winter break, and near the end of the school year.

How will we administer the screenings?

Stages 1 and 2 can be conducted during a 1- to 1.5-hour group meeting of teachers. One person who is versed in the screening procedure can give instructions to all teachers at once and ensure that they understand the definitions of externalizing and internalizing behaviors. Completing the screening process as a group can increase the reliability and consistency of the results and is also an efficient use of teacher time.

What is involved in a screening?

Figure 5a shows the screening process in flowchart form.

Stage 1: Teachers nominate and rank order the students in their classroom according to how closely their characteristic observed behavior patterns correspond to externalizing and internalizing behavioral profiles. The three highest ranked students from each category (externalizing and internalizing) go on to Stage 2 screening.

Stage 2: Teachers rate the six students identified in Stage 1 using more detailed measures. The scores determine whether students are considered as being at risk for externalizing or internalizing behavioral problems. At-risk students should be referred for further evaluation and possible intervention. Schools may elect to gather additional data or to move directly to implementing Tier 2 or Tier 3 support plans for the identified students.

Figure 5a *SSBD screening process*

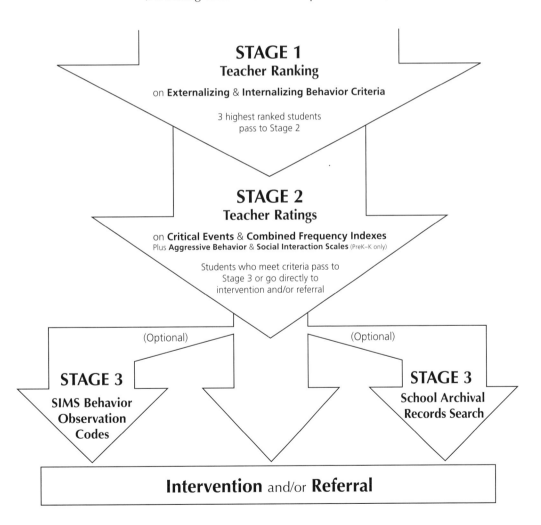

Universal Screening With SSBD
(Screening Time: ~45 minutes per classroom)

STAGE 1
Teacher Ranking
on **Externalizing** & **Internalizing Behavior Criteria**

3 highest ranked students
pass to Stage 2

STAGE 2
Teacher Ratings
on **Critical Events** & **Combined Frequency Indexes**
Plus **Aggressive Behavior** & **Social Interaction Scales** (PreK–K only)

Students who meet criteria pass to
Stage 3 or go directly to
intervention and/or referral

(Optional)   (Optional)

STAGE 3
SIMS Behavior
Observation
Codes

STAGE 3
School Archival
Records Search

Intervention and/or **Referral**

STEP 3. Interpret screening results.

Identify who will be responsible for compiling and using the universal screening data. If you are using a paper-based screener, someone will need to first score the completed protocols.

If more students are identified as needing Tier 2 interventions than you have staff and resources to accommodate, that is a good indication that your school should place much more emphasis on universal (Tier 1) intervention and prevention plans. Be sure that the Foundations Team thoroughly explores how schoolwide programs can help most of the identified students before you begin implementing Tier 2 interventions. Examples of schoolwide programs include policies to address tardiness, reward systems for respectful behavior, a training program for bus drivers, and modifications to cafeteria procedures. These types of schoolwide interventions can benefit every student and staff member and provide disciplinary consistency, and they are in the long run easier, cheaper, and less time consuming to implement and maintain than a large number of Tier 2 interventions.

One benefit of universal screening is that it can identify students in need of help early, before the misbehavior is ingrained and less responsive to intervention. Early-stage misbehavior can often be handled with simpler and less staff-intensive interventions than might be necessary later, when the misbehavior has become chronic. Take advantage of this window of opportunity to support students in the early stages of behavior problems.

If your school has few or no Tier 1 plans in place and many students are identified as at risk, plan to implement at least one Tier 1 intervention plan before proceeding with planning the Tier 2 interventions (see Step 4 below). Of course, some students will clearly need Tier 2 support immediately, and you should provide it in those cases.

STEP 4. Determine whether your initial focus should be primarily on universal prevention or targeted intervention.

If many students are identified as at risk, you might not have the resources to intervene with every one of those students at the Tier 2 or Tier 3 level. Instead, tailor your universal intervention procedures to address the behaviors that are most prevalent among the at-risk students. You can do this by analyzing the trends in critical events and adaptive and maladaptive behavior, then offering staff development opportunities that specifically address these trends.

For example, let's say that in School A, many students were rated low on "Expresses anger appropriately, e.g., reacts to situation without being violent or destructive" and "Complies with teacher requests and commands." Many students were rated high on "Behaves inappropriately in class when corrected, e.g., shouts back, defies the teacher, etc."

In School A, staff development could focus on providing teachers with strategies for teaching and reinforcing compliance and anger management.

In School B, many students were rated low on "Follows established classroom rules." Many students were rated high on "Tests or challenges teacher-imposed limits, e.g., classroom rules" and on "Creates a disturbance during class activities, e.g., is excessively noisy, bothers other students, out of seat, etc."

Staff development in School B could focus on general classroom management, including teaching expectations, establishing and enforcing rules, and using whole class or other group-based reward systems for meeting classroom expectations.

For individual students, prioritize your tiered levels of support. In SSBD, you can use percentile ranks from the Critical Events Index and Combined Frequency Index for Adaptive and Maladaptive Behavior to align level of support with severity of problems. Which students have the most urgent needs? (In SSBD, you use a student's raw score to determine the percentile rank for the student—that is, how a student at risk for externalizing behavior problems compares with other externalizers, and how an internalizer compares with other internalizers.)

In addition, analyzing the ratings for individual items on the SSBD Critical Events Index and Combined Frequency Index can help identify the behavioral content that should be included in an individualized intervention. For example, does the student need to learn:

- Anger management and self-control strategies?
- How to follow directions?
- Social skills for peer interactions?
- How to follow classroom rules and routines?
- Replacement attention-seeking behaviors?
- On-task and other work-related behaviors

In other words, the information derived from universal screening can be used to direct the focus of an individualized intervention so that it benefits the student as much as possible.

You will also need to identify who will be responsible for gathering additional information about behavioral issues and/or for creating, implementing, and monitoring the efficacy of the Tier 2 behavior support plan. This person may be a counselor, school psychologist, social worker, or behavior specialist, for example.

STEP 5. Report screening results to staff and others.

Be sure to consider confidentiality of individual students when sharing information.

Figure 5b is an example of how you might present the data visually. The data are from an elementary school of about 500 K–5 students. The number of students (and the percentage of students screened) who exceeded normative criteria for externalizing and internalizing behavior disorders decreased over a 3-year period. For example, during Winter 2007, 60 students were nominated as at risk in the externalizing category, while only 13 (6.81% of the total number of screened students) exceeded normative criteria in Stage Two. Two years later, that percentage dropped to 3.18%. Lane et al. (2012, pp. 38–39) reports:

> The faculty were encouraged by these data showing their primary prevention plan was sufficient for the majority of students (about 94%) in reducing and/or maintaining low behavioral risk, with particular benefits for students with internalizing patterns . . . . The team was encouraged by the continued decrease in the level of risk for internalizing behavior patterns. However, the team noted that the relatively stable number of students exceeding normative criteria for externalizing behavior patterns for be an area for improvement. In other words, the team chose to focus on secondary supports for students with externalizing behavior concerns and consider tertiary supports for the few students with the most intensive needs (behavioral and academic).

Consider red flags.

The concept of *red flags* is another approach to identifying students in need. Red flags are data (data that you probably already have) that should signal the system when a child needs to be watched more carefully and might benefit from Tier 2 or Tier 3 supports. No student should fall through the cracks just because you weren't paying enough attention to the situation. We suggest six red flags:

- Failing grades
- Chronic absenteeism
- One or more grade levels behind chronological peers
- Three or more office discipline referrals within a semester
- Six or more detentions
- Student, parent, and teacher requests

Failing grades. An example of a red flag for secondary schools is failing grades in two or more classes. We recommend that, at the end of the first quarter of freshman year, somebody identify students who have failed two or more classes. Why? Because

Figure 5b *SSBD results comparing the percentage of students nominated and exceeding normative criteria for both externalizing and internalizing behavior disorders over a 3-year period.*

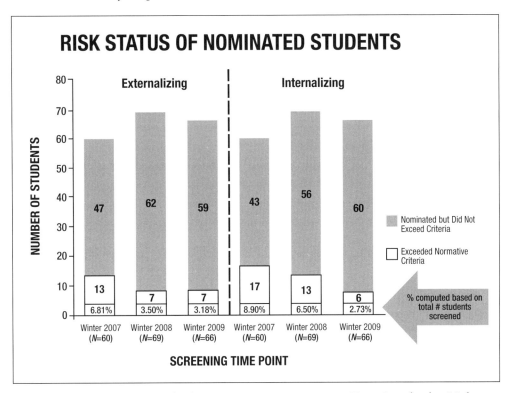

From *Systematic Screenings of Behavior to Support Instruction: From Preschool to High School* (p. 38), by K. L. Lane, H. M. Menzies, W. P. Oakes, and J. R. Kalberg, 2012, New York, NY: Guilford Press. Copyright 2012 by Guilford Press. Reprinted with permission.

by intervening early with these students, you can build a plan that will help them be successful in those classes in the second quarter.

Some schools have well-intentioned graduation coach programs—when a student is supposed to be a junior but is a year behind in credits, the school provides a graduation coach. But a student who has failed half of his classes during his first 2 years of high school will more than likely drop out. The graduation coach is entering the scene too late to do much good. When you instead intervene within the second 9 weeks of a student's freshman year, as soon as you see that this student is on a downward trajectory, the student's chances of making it to graduation are much higher. Remember the analogy we made at the beginning of this task? If you recognize and correct your wrong turn early, before you end up in Maine instead of Florida, your chances of reaching your destination are much higher.

Chronic absenteeism. Another red flag is chronic absenteeism, which we discussed extensively in Module C, Presentation 4. Any student who is absent more than 10% of school days should be flagged for additional attention. Don't wait until the end of the year to analyze attendance and absence rates. We recommend that someone analyze attendance data after the first month of school or 20 days of instruction. Students with two or more absences at that time are at or above the 10% absenteeism rate. Analyze attendance data to red-flag chronically absent students each month for the year to date.

One or more grade levels behind chronological peers. Students who are 1 year behind chronological peers have a high probability of dropping out of school. Roderick (1994) found that, of students who were retained once in kindergarten through eighth grade, more than 69% dropped out of high school. Students who are 2 years behind chronological peers are even more likely to drop out. Over 93% of students who were retained two or more times in kindergarten through eighth grade dropped out of school (Roderick, 1994).

There are significant developmental and social differences between a 15-year-old and a 17-year-old. Imagine being 17 and attending class with 15-year-olds. Many students would rather drop out than suffer that indignity. So any student who is a year or more behind chronological peers needs to be on somebody's radar screen for assessment: Is this student at risk for failure? Could this student benefit from Tier 2 support?

Three or more office discipline referrals within a semester. You might set the number at four or five, but we recommend three or more. If a student is sent to the office three times to see the principal or assistant principal and her behavior hasn't changed, that is a good indication that office disciplinary referral (ODR) by itself is probably not going to change her behavior. ODRs work when, after a student experiences one or two, she doesn't want to experience another and so changes her behavior. By the time a student is on the third ODR, the student's behavior is telling you that for her, ODR is no big deal.

We're not saying that teachers can't send students to the office more than three times. We're saying that three ODRs should flag the student as one who needs more attention. The counselor, behavior specialist, administrator, or whoever is designated to do so needs to begin constructing some Tier 2 supports for this student to reduce the probability that she will exhibit the behaviors that may result in another ODR.

Six or more detentions. We discussed the importance of tracking who is getting detention and how often in Module D, Presentation 3, Task 2. If a student has been in detention six times, you know that detention by itself will not work to change the student's behavior. Six detentions should flag the student so that the counselor or another qualified person begins to look for other strategies to try.

Our Texan colleagues have a colorful adage about this scenario: When the horse is dead, it's time to dismount. When a student has reached six detentions, the detention horse is dead. You need to construct some additional supports for the student.

Student, parent, and teacher requests. Ensure that students, parents, and teachers know how to request extra support and who they can talk with about behavior issues.

Consider universal prevention first.

With all of these red flags, be aware that if the criteria lead to too many students being flagged, you should probably deal with that particular issue with a universal prevention and intervention strategy. For example, if you overwhelm your resources because you flag so many freshmen for failing two or more classes in the first quarter of the freshman year, you need to do much more work on academic as well as behavioral universal prevention to reduce the number of students who are flagged.

All staff should know that when a student is flagged as at risk, he or she will be assigned an advocate. Ensure that staff know who in your school may serve as an advocate for students with higher needs. (In Task 2, we explain how to set up an Advocacy Program and the role of advocates in a tiered system of support.)

Set up a system to review data for red flags.

One way to ensure that someone looks for red flags regularly is to assign one or two red-flag categories to different people. For example:

- Failing grades ▶ school counselor
- Chronic absenteeism ▶ school psychologist
- One or more grade levels behind chronological peers ▶ school psychologist
- Three or more office discipline referrals within a semester ▶ administrator
- Six or more detentions ▶ administrator
- Student, parent, and teacher requests ▶ behavior specialist (Students, parents, and teachers should be notified that all requests go through this person.)

At about the same time that the Foundations Team conducts its quarterly review of data, the designated people analyze the data for red flags. The team Data/Evaluation Coordinator can ensure that the red-flag reviewers receive the appropriate data.

The red-flag reviewers report their findings to the administrator and to the chair of the Advocacy Program. At the next meeting of the advocates, newly flagged students are discussed. The chair should ensure that meeting agendas include a standing item to discuss flagged students.

CONCLUSION

Consider these two strategies—universal screening and red flags—to ensure that no student falls through the cracks and that you notice problems as early as possible. The sooner you can identify problems and intervene to provide levels of support, the greater the probability that you can positively affect students. Both of these strategies move the system to consider interventions beyond universal procedures for students who need them.

The administrator and interventionists should decide whether the staff will be involved in decisions regarding universal screening, red flags, and use of the resulting information to drive intervention planning. In most cases, these decisions will be district or building based and staff will not be involved.

Task 1 Action Steps & Evidence of Implementation

Action Steps	Evidence of Implementation
1. Consider universal screening. If you don't have a screening process: • Identify one or more team members who will investigate screeners and make recommendations. Include your school psychologist, school counselor, and others as appropriate in the search. • Concurrently explore whether this will be a building- or district-based decision. 2. Develop and implement a plan (specifying timelines and individuals responsible) for screening all students. • Ensure that all district and school policies in regard to parental notification, student opt-out, and confidentiality are followed. • Identify the program or software that will be used. • Identify who will conduct the screening. • Identify when the screening will be conducted. • Identify how screenings will be administered. • Interpret the screening results, with Tier 1 improvement priorities in mind. • Identify how the screening results will be reported to staff and other appropriate people. 3. Ensure that the screening results are archived on a secure server (ask the company that provided the software), or design and implement a plan for archiving the results.	Foundations Process: Universal Screening, Planning Calendar Final decisions about universal screening procedures should be filed in: Foundations Archive: Universal Screening Staff Handbook: Policies and Procedures in Place
4. Work through each item on the list of suggested red flags and discuss the following: • Does our school currently flag students as needing additional support based on this criterion? • If no, would such a flag benefit some students by ensuring earlier support? 5. Develop and implement a plan for adopting and implementing red flags.	Foundations Process: Red Flags Final decisions about red flags should be filed in: Foundations Archive: Red Flags Staff Handbook: Policies and Procedures in Place

TASK 2

Identify support personnel and ready-to-use Tier 2 interventions

Some schools do a great job of identifying student needs through universal screening or red flags, but they don't do anything with that information. Because of that gap, students' needs aren't being met. To ensure that this gap doesn't occur in your school, we recommend that you identify some staff members who can serve as *advocates* for identified students. The advocate's role is to watch the student more closely, consider whether the school is doing everything possible to meet the student's needs efficiently and effectively, and take any actions necessary to try to meet the student's needs.

We also present information on creating ready-to-use interventions that can serve as the first step of your Tier 2 intervention supports. With one or more ready-to-use interventions established in your school, an advocate can easily plug a student into the intervention and avoid more laborious problem-solving strategies.

We recommend that you invite staff who serve as interventionists in your school (counselor, school psychologist, social worker, and behavior specialist, for example) to join the Foundations Team in reviewing this task and working through the Action Steps. The administrator and the interventionists will make decisions about the role of interventionists and whether and how to use advocates for students who are identified as at risk by either universal screening or red flags.

Develop an Advocacy Program.

When a student is flagged or identified through universal screening as potentially at risk, the assumption is that this student may benefit from Tier 2 supports. One staff member needs to be assigned to investigate the problem and advocate for that student, the family, and the student's teachers until a successful intervention is found or it's determined that a different staff member should be the advocate. We use the term *advocate*, but if that term has other connotations in your system, use a different term. In some systems, *advocate* has legal overtones—people immediately think about an outside attorney who is suing the school and advocating for a student's needs. So choose a positive label, perhaps *school-based mentor* or *Tier 2 support person*.

Students, parents, and even teachers often don't know the range of support available in their schools or how to ask for assistance. The advocate should know the programs and personnel available and be able to link potentially at-risk students to the appropriate resources to ensure that they do not fall through the cracks of the system.

Advocate positions should probably be filled by the following professional-level people:

- Administrator
- Dean
- Nurse
- Social worker
- School resource officer
- School psychologist
- Counselor
- Parent liaison
- Behavior specialist

Teachers will probably not have enough time to serve as advocates unless they're on special assignment or they teach half time and spend their remaining time in a coaching or supervisory role. Advocates need to be willing to take a degree of ownership for making the system work for each student they are assigned.

An *advocate* is simply a school-based person whose role is to monitor the student, consider whether the school is doing everything possible to meet the student's needs efficiently and effectively, and take any actions necessary to ensure that the student's needs are met.

Early in the process, you don't necessarily have to ensure a perfect match between student and advocate. The key priority is that someone begins to examine the student's situation immediately and takes responsibility and ownership for ensuring that the school meets the student's needs. You might establish a rotation in which the dean is assigned a student, the nurse is assigned the next, the social worker is assigned the next, and so on. Later, if necessary, you can change advocates if someone else is better able to communicate and work with the student and family. For example, if a student's problem is chronic absenteeism that seems to be health related, the school nurse would probably be the most logical match.

Some advocates may have more assigned students than others, depending on their availability and positions in the school. For example, while a nurse might have only two or three students, a school counselor might have 10 or 12. The school psychologist may have no students if he or she is in the building only 1 or 2 days a week.

What does an advocate do?

The advocate informally evaluates the student's needs by reviewing her records, talking with her teachers, and talking with other advocates to get their perceptions of what action, if any, may be most beneficial for the student. The advocate explains to the student and family how the student was identified as someone who could potentially benefit from additional support and describes actions the school can take to help the student with her specific problem. The advocate also discusses with the teacher what he can do to help. Then the advocate can think about the ready-to-use interventions in the school that might benefit the student (we talk about those in the next section), place the student in one of these programs, and monitor and follow up with the student across weeks or months to assess whether the intervention is helping. Depending on the student's progress and the level of complexity and severity of the problem, the advocate might recommend moving immediately to a collaborative problem-solving process such as those we discuss in Presentation 6, thus bypassing the ready-to-use interventions. In some cases, the advocate might determine that even though the student was red-flagged as needing support, the student is successful and has no need for support at that time.

Identify existing ready-to-use Tier 2 interventions and possibly develop new interventions.

By *ready-to-use interventions*, we mean established interventions that are available to students at any time during the year. In others words, when a student has a need, the advocate doesn't have to assemble a problem-solving team to conduct an intensive behavior analysis and wait while an intervention is created for that student. The advocate can informally evaluate what seems to be driving the student's misbehavior and then try one or more of these ready-to-use interventions.

Concurrently with creating your system of advocates, identify the interventions available through the school and district as well as new interventions you might like to develop and establish as ready to use. Many of the programs we suggest below are explained in Module C, Presentation 6, so we don't go into a lot of detail here.

Special attention for targeted students (elementary and secondary levels). During a staff meeting, the advocate shows the staff a picture of the student, tells a little about the student's interests, and asks everyone to make overt efforts to greet, talk to, and praise the student. If many staff members consciously make the effort to engage the student, it is more likely that the student's needs for attention, acknowledgment, belonging, nurturing, and competence will be met. This may very well reduce the student's need to misbehave to get these needs met. The Falcon Fan Club (explained in Module C, Presentation 6) is another strategy for giving individual elementary students more attention.

Connections, or check-and-connect program (elementary and secondary levels). Students check in with a program coordinator each morning and receive a daily monitoring card, which they carry with them throughout the day. Teachers rate students for specific behaviors ("Follow directions," "Keep hands, feet, and objects to self," "Accept feedback without argument," for example) several times during the day.

Students then take the monitoring card home for parents to sign. The coordinator meets with students the next morning, provides feedback and reinforcement, and gives them a new monitoring card for the day. Later, the coordinator compiles the data and monitors the students' progress. Students may be enrolled in the program for a few weeks, a few months, or even a few years—until their ratings are consistently high enough that they can move to self-monitoring or graduate from the program.

Meaningful work (elementary level). Meaningful work is a very powerful program based on the idea that students thrive on feeling useful, needed, and important. Staff develop school-based jobs that can be assigned to students, and individual students are offered or apply for the positions. The program can be structured to meet the needs of individual students for acknowledgment, attention, belonging, competence, nurturing, purpose, recognition, and stimulation and change by engaging the students in meaningful jobs that contribute to the school. For example, a student who just needs to *move* for a while each day could spend 15 minutes each afternoon visiting all the classrooms and collecting empty coffee cups.

Leadership class (secondary level). Each semester, a for-credit elective class is taught by the school counselor (or another appropriate, available staff member) to a group of approximately 20 students. The class content includes communication skills, leadership skills, confidence-building activities, and so on. The students in the class complete two major projects: They plan and implement a community service project, and they organize a school dance. What makes this program different from most leadership classes is that staff members nominate students based on their lack of involvement in the school. The class is *not* for students who are already established as school leaders in some way.

Problem-solving task force (secondary level). This procedure is appropriate when there is a schoolwide problem, such as tardiness, vandalism, harassment, or increased numbers of students not completing work. The principal and the counselor convene a task force of students to evaluate the problem, propose solutions, implement a plan, and evaluate the plan's effectiveness. The goal of this procedure is to actively involve students in resolving school problems. Their participation can give them a sense of belonging and purpose and increase their pride in and willingness to take care of their school. An advocate who thinks that a student might benefit from helping to solve a problem in the school can get the student involved in the task force.

Mentorship (elementary and secondary levels). Adult volunteers are paired with individual students who would benefit from a friendly, nurturing, one-on-one relationship with an adult. Mentors meet with students on school grounds and during school hours at least once a week. Activities can include, but are not limited to, eating lunch together, playing a game, participating with the student in class activities or projects, or just taking a walk. Research strongly suggests that a connection with a caring adult can reduce a student's risk of health and life failure. Students who do not have nurturing home situations (and even some students who do) often benefit from a relationship with a caring adult who consistently meets with and shows an interest in them.

Structured recess (elementary). A PE teacher and several classified staff teach students how to play a few whole-group games such as ultimate Frisbee. During recess, selected students are required to pick one of three structured games that the whole group will play. Because all the selected students participate under adult supervision, there are very few of the extraneous negative behaviors that you often see on playgrounds. Students who need to build peer relationships or learn anger management can be plugged into structured play with adult supervision for a week or two, then move back to free play during recess.

Involve students in clubs (secondary level). Ensure that your school is providing a range of clubs, after-school activities, and other events that interest your students. If the advocate finds out that the student is interested in an activity—photography, for example—the advocate can tell the student about the club, introduce him to the staff member who advises the club, and help him with the process of joining.

All of the above programs can be established in your school so that an advocate just has to plug a student into the one that is most likely to help. For example, a high school's problem-solving task force might focus on a different problem every semester (graffiti, absenteeism, cliques, increasing school pride, a specific community service project). By knowing the upcoming focus, an advocate can consider whether any of his students might benefit from serving on the next task force.

If there is no ready-to-use intervention that fits the student's needs, the advocate needs to think about the process of building an individual intervention tailored to meet the specific needs of the student. Individual interventions are time consuming and a lot of work, so if a ready-to-use intervention will suffice, that's better. However, individual behavior improvement plans are sometimes necessary. We discuss this problem-solving process in Task 3 and throughout Presentation 6.

When does advocacy for a student end?

The student should continue to have an advocate until one of these three situations occur:

- The student no longer needs support because he is doing great.
- A different school-based professional becomes the advocate.
- The student is no longer enrolled in the school. If the student is moving to another school, the advocate should contact that new school and see if a new advocate can be assigned to watch over the student. Examples of

this situation include a fifth-grade student who is moving up to the middle school and a third-grade student who is moving across town to a different elementary school.

Meet regularly and keep clear, detailed records of all advocates and students.

Your Advocacy Program will function more effectively and efficiently with a leader or chair who can ensure that the group holds regular meetings and keeps detailed records. The records should include a list of all students who have been assigned advocates and who their advocates are. All the advocates should meet at least once a month and give brief reports about how each student is doing, including a quick review of any data they've collected. For students who aren't making progress, the group can discuss what the appropriate next steps might be.

Task 2 Action Steps & Evidence of Implementation

Action Steps	Evidence of Implementation
Discuss whether your school has an Advocacy Program. • If so, it is working for all students who are identified through universal screening or red flags? • If not, invite all support personnel (school counselor, school psychologist, social worker, and so on) to participate in exploring the concept and setting up a plan of action. • Agree on a different term if advocate does not fit your school's semantics. • Discuss how to structure the system so that no student who is flagged or identified through universal screening falls through the cracks. *Note:* This process may not require staff approval. The interventionists can collectively decide to use advocates for navigating Tier 2 and Tier 3 levels of support.	Foundations Process: Meeting Minutes, Current Priorities Foundations Archive: Interventions for Individual Students Foundations Archive: Support Available to Staff

TASK 3

Identify Tier 2 and Tier 3 problem-solving processes and support personnel

If simple advocacy and ready-to-use Tier 2 interventions—the topics of the previous task—do not seem sufficient for the intensity of need, or if ready-to-use interventions have been tried but did not work, the advocate for the student should work with the student, teacher, and family to determine next steps. You should establish a protocol or menu of problem-solving processes to consider in these situations.

What is a problem-solving process?

For social-emotional or behavior problems, problem solving involves the following steps: analyze the problem (including all data collected to date), develop an intervention plan, implement the plan, monitor the fidelity of implementation, and evaluate the efficacy of the plan.

Problem-solving processes consume much more time and resources than universal prevention, early-stage interventions, and ready-to-use interventions. Presentation 6 in this module outlines three specific processes for problem solving for the team to explore; this task is tied directly to Presentation 6.

Identify Tier 2 and Tier 3 interventionists and other members of problem-solving teams who deal with social-emotional and behavior problems.

Identify people within the school district or community who can help students with behavior problems that have been resistant to the easier solutions that we've talked about previously. These people are in roles that probably overlap those we suggest for advocates: nurse, social worker, school resource officer, school psychologist, counselor, behavior specialist. You might include community and district personnel, too, such as the county mental health psychologist, and any other professionals who can support the student directly or support the teacher-student relationship by designing a behavior improvement plan.

For clarity, we refer to the people in these Tier 2 and Tier 3 problem-solving roles as *interventionists*, but be aware that roles will likely overlap. For example, one person may serve as both an advocate for students and as a member of a multidisciplinary team that works on complex behavioral interventions.

Write job descriptions.

All interventionists should write a brief job description to clarify for the other interventionists and classroom teachers how their role fits within the process of supporting the needs of students and staff. The description should include services that are provided and when and how to access those services.

To be clear, the Foundations Team or MTSS team does not tell the school psychologist (for example) what to do. The school psychologist has a very defined role within the district and the school. The job description we suggest just serves to articulate the services the school psychologist offers so that all advocates and teachers are aware of and understand when, where, and how they can enlist the skills and expertise of the school psychologist in any given situation.

Each interventionist should look at Module E, Presentation 6, Task 2 and consider using a tool called the Intervention Decision Guide: Teacher Interview (IDG:TI). This tool guides the user through a discussion with the teacher to facilitate designing a function-based intervention. If the IDG:TI seems useful, it might be included in a job description: "If teachers are struggling with a student and early-stage interventions have not been sufficient, I can potentially collaborate with you through a structured interview process to develop a function-based intervention."

You should also identify any existing building- or district-based teams of interventionists that can engage in problem-solving processes. Ensure that they write job descriptions so that advocates and teachers know when and how to access their services. Task 3 in the next presentation outlines a multidisciplinary team process, and Task 1 describes a teacher-to-teacher problem-solving process—another option everyone should know about.

It boils down to this: All advocates and others in your system who are providing Tier 2 and Tier 3 support need to know who can assist them with problem solving. Who are the interventionists and teams available to help students with behavior problems? Advocates also need to know how best to help the student, family, and the teacher navigate the problem-solving process. Have you ever visited a government office, perhaps the Department of Motor Vehicles, and felt utterly lost and helpless because the signage was confusing, the lines were long and chaotic, and no one would help you figure out where to go? Try to avoid the bad structure that some DMVs model. An advocate should be able to choose from a menu of services, and if the first attempt doesn't work, have a clear idea of where to go next for help.

> *All advocates and others in your system who are providing Tier 2 and Tier 3 support need to know who can assist them with problem solving. Who are the professionals and teams available to help students with behavior problems?"*

Figure 5c shows a sample flowchart from an imaginary school that illustrates the services and personnel available to help students at every stage of need. Consider creating a flowchart like this example for your school. A similar flowchart is provided as Sample F-36 on the Module F CD.

Conduct case studies and analyze system failures.

Advocates can benefit from getting together periodically to conduct case studies and analyze whether their recommendations for students could have been improved. We also suggest that advocates periodically conduct a post hoc analysis of any system failure.

Good hospitals conduct a postmortem when a person dies under their care. The purpose of the postmortem is not to assign blame or to cover up mistakes; the purpose is to *learn* from mistakes. The doctors ask, "What could we have done better? Did we perform as well as we possible can? Are there any gaps in our system that we need to fix?"

So any time a student is expelled or drops out, and certainly any time a student commits a violent act, we suggest that the advocates meet to analyze, without blaming anyone, what happened. Could the system be structured more effectively? Do we have gaps in our system? Did we provide the best quality of care that we could? By addressing those questions, you might improve the outcomes for students in similar situations in the future.

Ensure that the intervention plan is implemented.

The advocates shepherd their students through the problem-solving process. They ensure that the process is as effective and efficient as possible and that all steps are completed:

1. Analyze the problem, including all data collected to date.

2. Develop an intervention plan.

3. Implement the plan.

4. Monitor the fidelity of implementation.

5. Evaluate the efficacy of the plan.

Let's look in more detail at Step 4: Monitor the fidelity of implementation. In 1998, researchers Wickstrom, Jones, LaFleur, and Witt analyzed several behavior intervention plans that were written through a problem-solving process. They asked the

Figure 5c *Flowchart for Tier 2 and Tier 3 behavioral interventions protocol at an imaginary school*

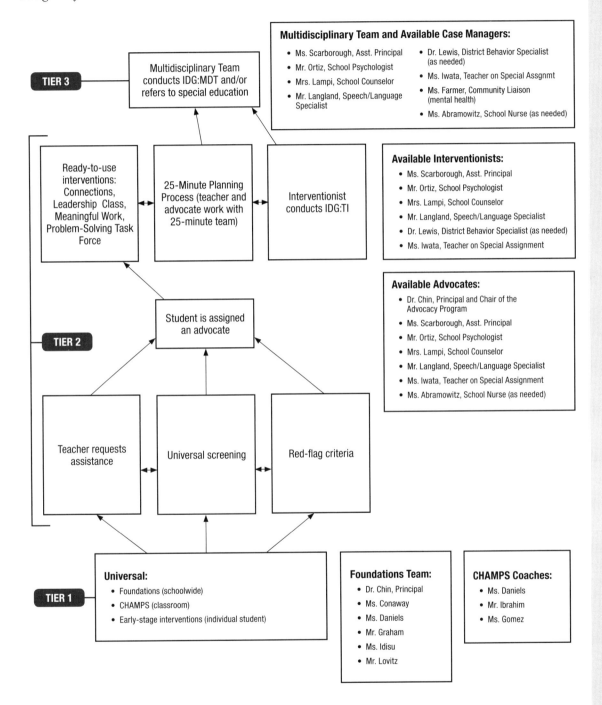

students' teachers whether they were implementing the plans. Almost half—46%—of the teachers admitted that they were *not* implementing the plans. The researchers also conducted direct observation, and found that only 4% of the behavioral intervention plans were being implemented with *fidelity*—that is, there was tangible evidence that the plan was being implemented. These statistics clearly indicate that it is not enough to write a behavior improvement plan—you also have to ensure that it is actually being implemented. All too often a plan ends up as just lifeless words buried in a file.

Why do implementation rates tend to be so low? If you search the Internet for "fidelity of implementation," you'll find lots of information. It's a fabulous area of study that educators are just learning more about. Following are some reasons that teachers do not implement behavioral intervention plans that have been written for their students.

Teachers have not been trained in behavioral intervention. We hope that the concept of early-stage intervention that we emphasize in *Foundations* improves teachers' understanding and use of behavioral interventions.

There's a gap in the efficient delivery of services. In some systems, when students are identified or teachers ask for help, months go by before help is available. When a teacher has had to live with the problem for 2 or 3 months, the teacher isn't looking for intervention help anymore. He just wants somebody else to take care of the problem.

The intervention design is not a collaborative process that involves both the teacher and the interventionist. In the next presentation, we discuss three processes that actively engage the teacher in designing an intervention plan that meets the needs of the student *and* fits the teacher's style. When teachers have more input into the plan, they will be more likely to implement it.

There's a lack of oversight. Nobody's monitoring the situation. But if you establish a system of advocates, you will have people monitoring student progress, talking with teachers, and asking how the plan is going, all with a positive, what's-best-for-the-student attitude. With more eyes on the situation, you increase the probability of implementation.

Task 3 Action Steps & Evidence of Implementation

Action Steps	Evidence of Implementation
1. Develop a list of professionals and teams who may be involved in some aspect of problem solving.	Foundations Archive: Interventions for Individual Students, Job Descriptions, Support Available to Staff
2. Have each person and team write a brief job description that includes information about when, where, and how to best use their services.	Staff Handbook: Staff Roles and Responsibilities, Available Support
3. Have the advocates work together to define and refine how to ensure that individual student needs are being met. They might develop a flowchart.	
4. Inform the staff about available support for students and how to access it.	
5. Seek recommendations and opinions from staff. However, clarifying roles and problem-solving processes should be the job of the interventionists.	

Problem-Solving Processes and Intervention Design

CONTENTS

Introduction

Task 1: Use the 25-Minute Planning Process
For the Foundations Team and possibly all faculty and interventionists

Task 2: Complete an Intervention Decision Guide—Teacher Interview (IDG:TI)
For the Foundations Team, the multidisciplinary team, and interventionists

Task 3: Complete an Intervention Decision Guide—Multidisciplinary Team Approach (IDG:MDT)
For the Foundations Team, the multidisciplinary team, and interventionists

DOCUMENTS*

- Flowchart for Tier 2 and Tier 3 behavioral interventions protocol (F-36)
- 25-Minute Planning Process (F-25)
- Corrective Procedures for Mild and Moderate Classroom Behavior (F-26)
- Intervention Decision Guide: Teacher Interview Worksheet (F-27)
- Intervention Decision Guide: Multidisciplinary Team Worksheet (F-28)

* All documents listed are available on the CD.

INTRODUCTION

In this presentation, we describe three problem-solving processes for analyzing the nature of the behavior problem, designing an intervention plan, and implementing the intervention.

Remember our slightly facetious definition of Multi-Tiered Systems of Support (MTSS) and Response to Intervention (RTI): Try the easiest, cheapest thing first, and hope it works. If it works—great! The behavior is no longer a problem. If it doesn't work, then you need to dig a little deeper into your menu of problem-solving processes.

Multidisciplinary team processes represent the opposite end of the scale—they are neither cheap nor easy. Your school and district probably already have processes for multidisciplinary teams to address really challenging situations. The most highly skilled professionals available design a multifaceted intervention plan that might even involve resources such as juvenile justice and county mental health. Before that process, another professional probably conducted a functional behavior assessment, which included observations in several areas, interviews with several staff members and the student, and a deep review of the student's records. It takes a lot of time and money to tap into the expertise of these highly skilled interventionists.

> Task 3 of this presentation addresses multidisciplinary team processes and can help you evaluate whether your team processes are as efficient and effective as possible.

So what lies between the easy and cheap end of the menu and the complex and expensive end? One concept within MTSS is that there should be several layers of relatively easy, quick, and cheap processes between universal prevention and multidisciplinary team processes. That's one of the reasons that *Foundations* emphasizes the importance of having a protocol of early-stage interventions that are planned and implemented by general education teachers. Think of general education teachers as somewhat similar to general practitioners or internists in medicine. When a problem can be solved at the level of the general practitioner, that's best for the patient and the health-care system. The expertise of specialists should be reserved for situations in which it's truly needed. Otherwise, the specialists become overburdened, expenses soar, and people wait long periods for services.

When the general practitioner is puzzled by a patient's problem, she talks with other general practitioners to gain their opinions and advice. That's the idea behind the 25-Minute Planning Process that we explain in Task 1. It's a teacher-to-teacher collaborative problem-solving process, and we recommend that you consider using it when teacher-developed early-stage interventions have not been successful.

For clarity, we refer to the people in Tier 2 and Tier 3 problem-solving roles as *interventionists*. Typically, the role of interventionist is filled by staff such as the school psychologist, counselor, school social worker, and behavior specialist, but an interventionist can be anyone with advanced training in behavioral issues and the time and motivation to collaborate with teachers on intervention plans. Roles may overlap. For example, one person may serve as both an advocate for students and as a member of a multidisciplinary team that works on complex behavioral interventions.

The next layer we recommend involves collaboration between the general education teacher and an interventionist to complete the Intervention Decision Guide: Teacher Interview (IDG:TI). This process is not as structured or time intensive as multi-disciplinary team problem solving, but it's more structured and time consuming than the 25-Minute Planning Process. It relies on training interventionists such as counselors, school psychologists, social workers, and behavior specialists in the concept of teacher interviews as part of a problem-solving process. Teachers know that when they need help with a problem that's been resistant to early-stage interventions and the 25-Minute Planning Process, they can talk to any of these trained interventionists. The IDG:TI is discussed in detail in Task 2. Likewise, an advocate for the student, as described in Presentation 5, can also request a 25-Minute Planning Process or suggest that the teacher and an interventionist conduct an IDG:TI, even if the teacher has not requested either process.

If a student's problems persist after these efforts, a multidisciplinary team approach is probably called for. Task 3 discusses this process and how to use a tool called the Intervention Decision Guide: Multidisciplinary Team (IDG:MDT) Worksheet.

Figure 6a shows a graphic illustration of the protocol for the Tier 2 and Tier 3 interventions we suggest in *Foundations*.

ℰ℧ FOUNDATIONS RECOMMENDATION ℘

Establish a formal protocol for using early-stage interventions and train all teachers to implement the protocol in the early stages of a behavior problem. When early-stage interventions do not work, use a teacher-to-teacher collaborative problem-solving process such as the 25-Minute Planning Process. If the misbehavior continues, use a teacher-with-interventionist problem-solving process such as the Intervention Decision Guide: Teacher Interview. If necessary, proceed to a multidisciplinary team approach.

Figure 6a *Flowchart for Tier 2 and Tier 3 behavioral interventions protocol (F-36)*

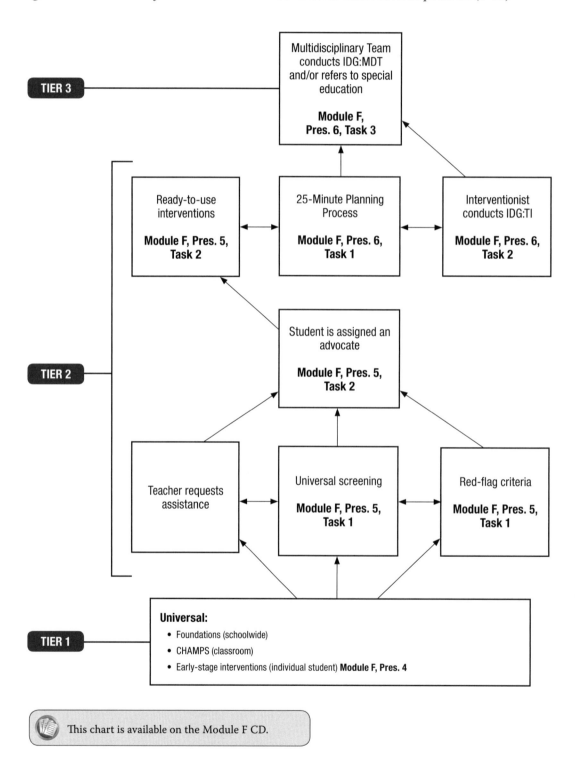

This chart is available on the Module F CD.

Module F: Establishing and Sustaining a Continuum of Behavior Support

Note: We consider early-stage interventions a bridge between universal prevention and targeted (Tier 2) support. When districts adopt a formal protocol for using early-stage interventions and train all teachers to implement that protocol in the early stages of a problem (as we recommend), the use of early-stage interventions becomes universal practice. As teachers progress through our suggested protocol, the interventions become more data driven and analytical about function, two hallmarks of Tier 2 support. Imagine a long bridge over a river—for example, the 4-mile-long Astoria-Megler Bridge that spans the Columbia River, linking the states of Oregon and Washington. There is an exact spot on that bridge that marks the official border between Oregon and Washington, but for all practical purposes, the entire 4-mile bridge is the border and connector between the two states. Early-stage interventions can arguably be called either universal or targeted, but the key point is that they constitute the bridge that links the two tiers.

Task 1: Use the 25-Minute Planning Process may be read or viewed by all teachers in the school and the Foundations Team. The team can then guide staff in setting up an organizational plan for when and how this process will be used.

Task 2: Complete an Intervention Decision Guide: Teacher Interview and **Task 3: Complete an Intervention Decision Guide: Multidisciplinary Team Approach** may be read or viewed by the Foundations Team, all members of your current multidisciplinary team, and any other clinicians, interventionists, and so on who can evaluate together whether and how these two processes might be used.

Note: More information about how to use the three collaborative problem-solving tools is available in the book *Behavioral Response to Intervention: Creating a Continuum of Problem-Solving and Support* by Randy Sprick, Mike Booher, and Mickey Garrison (2009), available through Pacific Northwest Publishing.

Keep Parents Informed

It is essential, both legally and ethically, to keep parents informed throughout the intervention process. Invite parents to be as involved as they want to be and view them as partners from the earliest stages of intervention planning.

Check with your district or central office to determine what type of parent/guardian consent is needed or recommended. Requirements can vary depending on the student's IEP status. Some families may be reluctant to participate or to have their child participate because of moral, religious, or other reasons. Ensure that all staff are sensitive to these concerns.

TASK 1

Use the 25-Minute Planning Process

The 25-Minute Planning Process involves teacher-to-teacher collaborative problem solving for chronic behavior problems. I (Randy) developed this procedure after observing several teacher teams struggle to come up with behavior improvement plans in an efficient manner. I was helping the state of Minnesota's cooperative service units in their effort to implement Teacher Assistance Teams, a teacher-to-teacher problem-solving approach developed by Chalfant and Pysh that was popular in the 1980s. The teachers had great success using this strategy for academic issues, but when they tried to implement it for behavior problems, they did not get positive results. I was asked to conduct some training and observe the groups as they worked on behavior issues. I realized the teachers tended to encounter at least one of three pitfalls when dealing with difficult behavior problems.

Problem admiring, not problem solving. Some teacher groups spent the entire meeting time talking about how difficult the problem was and complaining about the student and the family.

Reactive consequences rather than proactive procedures. Some teams worked past the problem-admiring stage and talked about what to do, but got stuck on the reactive—what can we do to make this kid behave? Although necessary, consequences alone are very unlikely to change a student's behavior because of their reactive nature. These teams spent most of their meeting time debating about what consequence to use.

Thirty minutes becomes 2 hours. Some teams spent just a little time complaining about the student and finding a consequence, then really got into some positive brainstorming. They discussed building relationships with the student, the structural and teaching elements of an intervention, and very positive, potentially very effective strategies. But their 30-minute meeting lasted 2 hours!

When 5 people each spend 2 hours developing an intervention, that amounts to an investment of 10 hours, so everyone really hopes the solution works. If it does work, great! But do teachers really have time to spend 2 hours planning every intervention? They are unlikely to go through the process again because that additional hour and a half should have been spent grading papers, preparing lessons, or relaxing with family. And if the intervention doesn't work, the staff might believe that the student's needs are beyond what they can provide. We suggest that for collaborative problem solving, teachers stick to a time limit. At the end of a meeting, it's OK if the perception is this: We came up with a solution. It's not perfect, but it's worth a try.

So, over time, the Minnesota state cooperative service units and I, along with the teachers we were training, jointly developed the 25-Minute Planning Process to help teachers be focused and efficient as they problem solve. It is a structured agenda for analyzing a problem, brainstorming solutions to the problem, selecting interventions from the list of brainstormed solutions, and defining who's going to do what—all in 25 minutes.

Organize to work through the process.

We suggest two ways to organize your staff for using the 25-Minute Planning Process. You may, of course, organize in any way that fits your building.

Grade-level teams. For example, all of the seventh-grade teachers meet, all of the eighth-grade teachers meet, and so on. This structure is especially powerful when you have scheduled early-release days every week or every other week for planning purposes. One week you can do grade-level curriculum planning and problem solving, and the next week you can work on behavior, climate, classroom management, and staffing one student. For 25 minutes of the planning time, all the seventh-grade faculty focus on the behavior problems of one seventh-grade student, all the eighth-grade faculty focus on one eighth-grade student, and so on. By using grade-level organization, every teacher participates, and every week or every other week one student from each grade gets the undivided attention of all grade-level staff for 25 minutes.

Representative team. If you don't have an early-release structure in place, asking every teacher to meet for 25 minutes each week to discuss an individual student may be too burdensome. Instead, you might organize a representative team that meets every week. In an elementary school, the team might consist of a primary-grade teacher, an intermediate-grade teacher, a special education teacher, a paraprofessional, and a counselor. The disadvantage of this approach is that few general education teachers are involved—only two in this particular example we gave. The advantage is that the process is less burdensome on all teachers. As compensation for their time, team members can be relieved of a school duty such as bus supervisory duty.

Teachers who would like help with a difficult student can ask to be added to the agenda. The teacher and the team work through the 25-Minute Planning Process. The student's advocate, who is responsible for ensuring that the student's needs are met, should also attend the meeting. This person probably has the deepest understanding of the student's background and issues that may affect the situation. (The concept of advocates is discussed in Presentation 5, Task 2.)

The advantage of grade-level teams is that potentially one student at each grade level is staffed each week. The advantage of the representative team approach is that the team members become well practiced in working with a wide range of grade levels and concerns. The disadvantage is that only one student in the school is staffed each week.

Assign team roles.

Whether you use grade-level teams or a representative team, ensure that team members are assigned roles.

Recorder. During the meeting, the recorder takes notes on the 25-Minute Planning Process Worksheet (Form F-25). Note that a fillable version of the worksheet is available on the Module F CD. You can open it in Adobe Reader, type directly onto it, and save your changes. After the meeting, the recorder distributes copies of the final worksheet to everyone involved.

Timekeeper. The goal is to complete the process in 25 minutes, so a timekeeper is essential. When the time limit for each step has been reached, the timekeeper alerts the group.

Leader. The leader should be an assertive person who can ensure that everyone stays on task and moves on to the next step when it's time.

Work through the 25-Minute Planning Process Worksheet.

Items in bold correspond to steps and tasks on the 25-Minute Planning Process Worksheet (Form F-25).

Prepare for the meeting by making copies of the worksheet (Form F-25) for each team member.

STEP 1. Background (5 minutes)

In this step, the student's teacher and anyone else with knowledge about the situation, such as the student's advocate, describe the presenting problem and other relevant background information for the rest of the team. Get the process started by reiterating the nature of proactive planning and describing Step 1. Team members should be encouraged to ask probing questions to gain a deeper understanding of the student's problems and abilities and what the teacher faces every day. Discuss in as much detail as possible the student's strengths and what has already been tried, with or without success.

If possible, have the teacher prepare for the meeting by discussing the situation with the student's advocate or perhaps the team leader for about 30 minutes. This way, the teacher has a chance to think about what she will say and identify the most important points of the case. The teacher will also have someone to support her and help her present the case to the team.

Figure 6b *25-Minute Planning Process Worksheet (F-25)*

25-Minute Planning Process Worksheet (p. 1 of 2)

Student _Charlie Metzger_ Age _10_ Grade _4_ Date _11/20_

Advocate _Ms. Trent_ Teacher(s) _Mr. Winfrey_

Other participants _Mr. Ingram, Ms. Zhang_ Starting Time _1:30_

Step 1: Background (5 minutes) Stop _1:35_

- Describe the presenting problem. Identify when, where, how often, how long, etc., the problem occurs.
  Charlie has difficulty working independently. She wanders aimlessly and bothers other students.

- Identify student's strengths.
  Social skills---she has lots of friends
  Academically---she is on or above grade level

- Identify strategies already tried.
  Keeping her from recess to finish independent work

Step 2: Problem/Goal/Data (4 minutes) Stop _1:38_

- Narrow the scope of the problem and identify a goal.
  Wandering around, off task. Goal---Learn to manage work time and space.

- Identify the data that will be used to track progress toward the goal.
  Self-monitoring system

Step 3: Corrective Consequences (2 minutes) Stop _1:40_

Determine whether irresponsible or inappropriate behavior will be corrected or ignored or whether a consequence will be implemented. Refer to Corrective Procedures for Mild and Moderate Classroom Behavior (F-26).

Ignored

Step 4: Responsible and Irresponsible Behavior (4 minutes) Stop _1:44_

Provide examples of responsible behavior and/or student strengths to encourage. Provide examples of irresponsible behavior to discourage.

Responsible Behavior	Irresponsible Behavior
Any quiet movement within her office space	Leaving "office" work space without permission
Raising her hand and asking permission to leave office space (sharpen pencil, turn in work, and so on)	Any loud noises, such as pounding her desk

---

 This form can be printed from the Module F CD.

25-Minute Planning Process Worksheet (p. 2 of 2)

Step 5: Proactive Strategies (4 minutes)   Stop ___1:47___

Brainstorm strategies to encourage responsible behavior. (Brainstorm, don't evaluate.) See the explanation of Step 5 in the book for menu of proactive strategies.

Use a point system that allows Charlie to earn points for special privileges.
Use a check-and-correct card that her parents have to sign every day.
Have Charlie set goals for her own behavior every day.
Try self-monitoring system in which Charlie observes and evaluates her own behavior hourly.
Have the school counselor work with her and teach her responsible behavior.
Use a question-card strategy.

Step 6: Proactive Plan (3 minutes)   Stop ___1:50___

Select a manageable set of proactive strategies to implement.

Self-monitoring of self-control behavior
Question-card strategy
Positive interactions---mother will read to Charlie before bedtime

Step 7: Final Details (4 minutes)   Stop ___1:54___

a. Evaluation: Identify at least two ways to determine whether the plan is working.

1. Mr. Winfrey will track positive interactions with Charlie
2. Charlie will complete self-monitoring form.

b. Support: Identify things other adults can do to assist the student and teacher. (Be specific—who, what, where, and when.)

Office staff and teachers can acknowledge Charlie in noncontingent ways. Mrs. Metzger will read to Charlie at home before bedtime.

c. Plan Summary: Identify each person's responsibilities and when actions will be taken. Identify who will discuss the plan with the student and when. Schedule follow-up.

Who	Responsibilities	Date(s)
Mr. Ingram	Give Mr. Winfrey self-monitoring booklet	
Ms. Trent	Teach Mr. Winfrey's class to ignore off-task behavior	Tuesday, 9 a.m.
Mr. Winfrey	Set up office space & self-monitoring sheet for Charlie	Monday, lunchtime
	Bulletin board project	Next Monday, after school
	Set up positive interaction monitoring system	

Discussion With the Student

Who _Ms. Trent and Mr. Winfrey_   Date __11/21__   Time _lunchtime_

Follow-Up Meeting

Who _Mrs. Metzger, Mr. Winfrey, Ms. Trent_   Date __12/9__   Time _3 p.m._

 This form can be printed from the Module F CD.

STEP 2. Problem/Goal/Data (4 minutes)

Narrow the scope of the problem and identify a goal. Determine which behaviors are most problematic or should be the focus of initial intervention efforts and prioritize them. If the student has hygiene problems, peer relation problems, anger management and self-control issues, academic deficits, and difficulty completing assigned tasks, you will not be able to correct all of those problems at once. A broad-based intervention plan that involves too many changes at once is likely to frustrate the student and teacher and yield fewer positive results. If you narrow the scope of the intervention to a focused plan that is truly manageable, you have the greatest possibility of success. If the student begins to experience success and increased confidence with a targeted intervention, other behaviors may naturally get better without the assistance of an intervention. Success breeds success. To identify priorities for the initial intervention, ask the following questions:

Which behavioral changes will help the student feel successful in the least amount of time? An intervention plan should initially target changes that have the highest probability of success in the least amount of time. Once the student begins to experience the sense of satisfaction that accompanies success, helping the student with other problems becomes progressively easier.

Which behavioral changes will help the teacher see improvements in the least amount of time? The second major consideration in identifying intervention priorities is to address problems that interfere with the teacher's ability to instruct or with other students' ability to learn. The more a problem interferes with the smooth operation of a class, the sooner the problem needs to be addressed. If a problem disrupts the natural flow of a classroom, the problem will likely escalate or generate other problems.

Keep Parents Informed

It is essential, both legally and ethically, to keep parents informed throughout the intervention process. Invite parents to be as involved as they want to be and view them as partners from the earliest stages of intervention planning.

Check with your district or central office to determine what type of parent/guardian consent is needed or recommended. Requirements can vary depending on the student's IEP status. Some families may be reluctant to participate or to have their child participate because of moral, religious, or other reasons. Ensure that all staff are sensitive to these concerns.

Identify a positively stated goal. Help the teacher decide whether the goal will be to reduce a misbehavior or increase a positive behavior. For example, a student who takes other students' things needs to learn to reduce the behavior, whereas the goal for a student who is painfully shy when interacting with adults may be to increase the behavior of interacting positively with adults.

State the goal in positive terms. "Learn to touch only your own things" is more positive than "Learn not to steal." "Learn to respect the property of others" is a worthwhile goal, but "Learn not to be destructive" is demeaning. The goal should also be specific and measurable. For example, "Behave respectfully" is too broad. "Respond to teacher instructions in a respectful tone of voice or with no verbal reply" is more appropriate.

Identify the data that will be used to track progress toward the goal. How will the success or failure of the intervention be evaluated? Although the student's and teacher's subjective perceptions will play a role and it is important not to overburden teachers with time-consuming data collection methods, it is also necessary to gather objective data through behavior counts, self-monitoring forms, observations, discipline referrals, truancy records, the teacher's grade book, rating forms, and other means.

Step 3. Corrective Consequences (2 minutes)

The team should quickly brainstorm possible consequences and then have the referring teacher select ones that can be implemented consistently. Simply have the teacher choose a reasonable consequence from your menu of possible consequences (verbal reprimand, timeout, time owed, planned ignoring, and so on) and move on. Remember that consequences may make a student behave, but they do not encourage the student to become responsible for his own behavior—that's what an effective intervention plan is designed to do. Team members should consider the hypothesized function of the misbehavior for the student (what is the student gaining or avoiding with the misbehavior?).

We discuss the benefits of developing menus of consequences for classroom misbehavior in Module D, Presentation 3. A menu of Corrective Procedures for Mild and Moderate Classroom Behavior (F-26) is available on the Module F CD.

Step 4. Responsible and Irresponsible Behavior (4 minutes)

In this step, team members look at the broad goal and clearly define positive behaviors that will lead to achievement of the goal and negative behaviors that will detract from it. A clear line between responsible and irresponsible behaviors will make it easier to teach expectations to students and easier for teachers to implement the plan and provide corrections and praise when appropriate. For example, if the student is working on being more respectful with adults, responsible behaviors might include saying hello when entering the classroom, using a respectful tone of voice, nodding when the teacher addresses the student, and answering patiently when the teacher asks a question. Irresponsible behaviors might include giving the teacher a dirty look, answering the teacher in a sarcastic tone, and mimicking the teacher.

Step 5. Proactive Strategies (4 minutes)

Brainstorm proactive strategies to teach and encourage responsible behavior. Come up with as many as possible in 4 minutes—at least 7 strategies and preferably around 14. Move through each suggestion quickly, without getting stuck on one possibility. Consider a broad range of options and be creative. Consider changing the student's schedule or placement in a room, ratios of interactions, self-monitoring systems, interventions that team members are familiar with, classroom management strategies, positive reinforcement, and so on. The recorder should write down every suggestion so that all possibilities will be available for future use even if they are not used in the initial plan.

As you gain experience working with different teachers and students, you'll develop a menu of proactive strategies that will help you move efficiently through this brainstorming step. Following is a sample menu of proactive strategies for the classroom. More information about these strategies is available in CHAMPS, *Teacher's Encyclopedia of Behavior Management* (2nd ed.; Sprick, 2012), and in *Foundations* where indicated. Plan to expand this menu with ideas you come up with during the 25-Minute Planning Process.

Sample menu of proactive strategies:

- Change desk location. (Mod. F, Pres. 4, Task 6)
- Modify schedule. (Mod. F, Pres. 4, Task 6)
- Explicitly teach and practice the expected behavior. (Mod. F, Pres. 4, Task 6)
- Allow student to work standing up.
- Create an "office space." (Mod. F, Pres. 4, Task 6)
- Modify assignments. (Mod. F, Pres. 4, Task 6)
- Break tasks into manageable units (e.g., when 25% of a task is completed, student can get it checked). (Mod. F, Pres. 4, Task 6)
- Allow student to select order of task completion or other choice/control. (Mod. F, Pres. 4, Task 6)
- Provide opportunities for breaks or self-imposed timeouts. (Mod. F, Pres. 4, Task 6)
- Provide tickets for good behavior (e.g., ten tickets for permission to get out of seat).
- Create a red flag/green flag feedback system (e.g., flip a two-sided sign to green when the student is on task, to red when the student is off task).
- Increase positive interactions. (Mod. D, Pres. 3; Mod. F, Pres. 4, Task 5)
- Set goals without rewards. (Mod. F, Pres. 4, Task 3)

- Set goals with structured reward systems. (Mod. F, Pres. 4, Task 3)
- Provide intermittent celebrations or rewards.
- Provide a mentor. (Mod. F, Pres. 5, Task 2; Mod. C, Pres. 6, Task 1)
- Use a mystery motivator.
- Use daily home notes.
- Assign a Meaningful Work job. (Mod. F, Pres. 4, Task 6; Mod. C, Pres. 6, Task 2)
- Enroll in Connections (check-and-connect program). (Mod. F, Pres. 5, Task 2; Mod. C, Pres. 6, Task 1)
- Have student self-monitor.
- Have student self-evaluate.
- Cue the student to self-correct (e.g., establish a verbal or physical prompt that signals the student to stop making noise and to mark a self-monitoring card).
- Precorrect (e.g., preview rules before an activity).
- Teach the student calming strategies (e.g., deep breathing).
- Assign structured recess (Mod. F, Pres. 5, Task 2).

Step 6. Proactive Plan (3 minutes)

From the list of strategies the team brainstormed in Step 5, have the teacher choose one to three strategies to implement. The teacher knows the student's tendencies and has to live with and carry out the plan, so the final decision about the intervention design should be his. Answer the teacher's questions and help flesh out the plan.

Step 7. Final Details (4 minutes)

In Step 7, the team lays out the final details so that the plan can be implemented successfully. These details include identifying ways team members can assist with implementation, determining whether other people inside or outside the school should be involved, and summarizing each person's roles and responsibilities. Help the teacher determine two ways to evaluate the efficacy of the plan. Possible sources of information include:

- Subjective perceptions on the part of teacher, parent, or student (Are things better, the same, or worse?)
- Rating scale by teacher
- Work products (assignments completed, grades, tests, quality of work)
- Self-monitoring forms completed by student
- Systematic observations
- Data from reinforcement system (points earned)

Team members might help the teacher by, for example, drafting a self-monitoring form, conducting observations, or teaching the student the expectations. Create a plan summary that clearly states who is going to do what and by when.

- Who will talk to the student? When?
- Who will teach and model positive behaviors to the student?
- When can the plan reasonably start?
- If parents aren't present, how and when will the plan be shared with them?
- Decide whether a substitute teacher will be asked to implement the plan on days the teacher is not present. If so, how will the plan be communicated to the substitute?
- Decide whether the plan needs to be shared with other staff members who work with the student.
- Give a written copy of the plan to the teacher and team members.

Schedule a follow-up meeting. If possible, the student's advocate or a member of the 25-Minute Planning Process team should check in with the teacher within a day or two of implementation. During the implementation phase, plans frequently need adjustment and fine-tuning. Occasionally, teachers need assistance implementing unfamiliar procedures.

Review previous staffings. Many schools that use this process schedule an extra 5 minutes at the end of the meeting to review staffings they conducted during previous meetings. They talk about how students and teachers are progressing with the interventions they developed, adding ongoing monitoring to the process.

The first time you work through the 25-Minute Planning Process, we recommend that you double the number of minutes allowed for each step so that the entire process takes about 50 minutes. This way, you can spend a few minutes reviewing and talking about what's supposed to happen during each step. On your second or third meeting, you'll be able to complete the worksheet in 25 minutes. We know of several school teams that are so practiced and skilled at this process that their meetings are sometimes as brief as 12 minutes.

As we said previously, this 25-Minute Planning Process is not perfect. You could create a more comprehensive plan by working with your colleagues for 2 or 3 hours—but you don't have 2 or 3 hours. Doing *something* is better than doing nothing. The process is efficient and fast, and with practice it gets easier and better.

Task 1 Action Steps & Evidence of Implementation

Action Steps	Evidence of Implementation
1. Foundations Team: Explore with the staff whether and how to use the 25-Minute Planning Process. (*Note:* Do this step after the Foundations Team has read Tasks 2 and 3, which summarize other collaborative problem-solving processes that you may incorporate into your school's continuum of behavior support.) 2. If staff are generally in favor of using the process, get input from them about whether to organize grade-level teams, one representative team, or some other team configuration. 3. Identify personnel who will serve as advocates. 4. Provide training to staff in how and when to use the 25-Minute Planning Process.	Foundations Process: Meeting Minutes, Current Priorities Final procedures should be included in: Foundations Archive: Support Available to Staff, Interventions for Individual Students Staff Handbook: Available Support

TASK 2

Complete an Intervention Decision Guide: Teacher Interview (IDG:TI)

Task 2 is about using a worksheet to guide interviews with teachers to assist them with designing behavioral interventions for students who have been resistant to early-stage interventions. This task may be of interest to the Foundations Team as you build your MTSS structure, but it will be especially useful to professionals with responsibility for assisting teachers with challenging students.

This teacher-with-interventionist problem-solving process can be used before or after a teacher-to-teacher problem-solving process, such as the 25-Minute Planning Process we explained in Task 1. As you read through the task, think about the design of your flowchart for helping teachers with behavioral interventions. Where would the IDG:TI be most useful? How does it fit with other problem-solving processes? (A sample flowchart, Figure 6a, appears in the Introduction to this presentation.)

> For clarity, we refer to the people in Tier 2 and Tier 3 problem-solving roles as *interventionists*. Typically, the role of interventionist is filled by staff such as the school psychologist, counselor, school social worker, and behavior specialist, but an interventionist may be anyone with advanced training in behavioral issues and the time and motivation to collaborate with teachers on intervention plans. Roles may overlap. For example, one person may serve as both an advocate for students and as a member of a multidisciplinary team that works on complex behavioral interventions.

Part of the rationale behind this process is embodied in the old adage "two heads are better than one." Anyone can, to some degree, be blind to a particular behavioral problem, the function of a problem, or possible solutions. When a teacher can collaborate with someone with a fresh outlook on the problem, the blinders often fall away. Two people working together can be more than the sum of their parts.

It's important that the teacher feel very comfortable with the interventionist who guides the interview. The teacher should be able to choose any interventionist in the school who knows how to use this process. If the chosen interventionist is not the student's school-based advocate, the teacher can decide whether the advocate should be present. For example, the teacher asks to work with the school counselor as the interventionist, but the school nurse is the student's advocate. The teacher can decide whether the nurse participates in the interview. In any case, the advocate should be informed that the interview will be taking place, and the interventionist should tell the advocate about any intervention plans that result from the interview process.

In the remainder of this task, we are addressing the interventionist.

To prepare for the interview, follow these suggestions:

- Give the teacher a copy of the IDG:TI Worksheet (Form F-27) in advance so he can become familiar with the questions you will ask. Make it clear that you don't expect the teacher to fill out the worksheet.

- Ask the teacher to bring any collected data to the meeting. Monitoring forms, scatterplot data, frequency graphs, and the like can be very useful for identifying trends in the student's behavior.

- Arrange a meeting area where you and the teacher can sit side by side at a table. A table can feel like a barrier when people sit on opposite sides of it. You want the teacher to see what you are writing on the worksheet so that the collaboration is not perceived as an evaluation (What is he writing about me?). It's also easier to share information when you are sitting next to each other.

- Create a sense of equity. Don't adopt an attitude that says, "I'm the expert, and this is what you should do." Create a sense that the two of you are just conversing and collaborating. The meeting should not resemble an interrogation!

If you are familiar with functional behavior assessment (FBA), you'll probably notice that the IDG:TI is essentially a quick and dirty, simple and easy FBA. It doesn't involve the observations in multiple areas, interviews, and records reviews of an FBA, but it does recognize that the teacher has a lot of knowledge about the situation because the teacher works with the student daily. The IDG:TI capitalizes on that knowledge and provides a protocol for function-based thinking that will guide the intervention design.

Figure 6c shows the Intervention Decision Guide: Teacher Interview Worksheet (F-27), which is provided on the Module F CD. Note that a fillable version is available—you can open it in Adobe Reader and type directly onto it. There are four stages to this process:

Stage 1: Background

Stage 2: Preparation

Stage 3: Intervention Design

Stage 4: Implementation

Intervention Decision Guide:
Teacher Interview Worksheet (p. 1 of 4)

Student <u>Jake Stillwell</u>   Age <u>10</u>   Grade <u>5</u>   Date <u>4/21</u>

Interventionist <u>Mrs. Bickman</u>   Teacher(s) <u>Ms. Thompson, Mr. Gill</u>

Other participants _____

Stage 1: Background

1. Reason for referral and description of problem:

   Jake plays pencil hockey at his desk & flicks rubber bands. He has severe anger problems and resorts to loud arguing with peers and teachers at a moment's notice. Jake doesn't have many friends and when he isn't exhibiting anger, he doesn't interact at all.

   Code Red: Is it an emergency situation? No

The behavior is a threat to physical safety.	➡ Intervention G: Managing Physically Dangerous Behavior*
The behavior is so disruptive the teacher cannot teach.	➡ Intervention H: Managing Severely Disruptive Behavior*

   *In *Interventions: Evidence-Based Behavioral Strategies for Individual Students* (2nd ed.), 2008

2. Are there situations that seem to set off the problem behavior?

   During independent work time, Jake gets restless and starts to bother other students. When his mom is sick, he becomes even more agitated.

3. Where do the problems tend to occur?

   Jake has problems in all school settings, but most are in the classroom because that's where he spends the most time.

4. When do the problems tend to occur?

   Times of day <u>More frequent in (but not limited) to morning</u>   Days of week <u>Doesn't seem to be a pattern</u>

5. How often do the problems occur? How long does the behavior last? How intense is the problem?

   The problems occur almost daily. The behavior lasts until a teacher intervenes.

6. Is the student psychologically and neurologically capable of controlling his or her behavior? Is there evidence to support this opinion?

   There's no medical paperwork to suggest Jake's problem is neurological, but his teachers think he may not be able to control himself at times. There is only observation of his abrupt outbursts of anger to support this opinion.

7. Is the student aware of the problem?

   Yes. Both teachers have discussed the problem with Jake, and he has expressed an understanding of learning to control the problem.

8. Does the student seem motivated to improve the behavior?

   Jake says he wants to make changes, but his teachers say they don't see any effort.

9. What is the function of the problem behavior? What seems to maintaining or reinforcing the misbehavior?

   ☒ Ability   ❏ Awareness   ❏ Adult attention   ❏ Peer attention

   ❏ Power or control   ❏ Escape or avoidance (task difficulty or discomfort)   ❏ Competing reinforcers   ☒ Other <u>venting frustration</u>

   Notes:

   Jake's behavior problems are escalating and becoming unmanageable.

 This form can be printed from the Module F CD.

Intervention Decision Guide:
Teacher Interview Worksheet (p. 2 of 4)

10. What are the student's strengths? (List at least three.)

    academically adequate, a hard worker, gets most of his work done, good baseball player

11. What is the teacher's goal or desired outcome?

    a) What would the teacher like to have happen?

    Jake stays on task during work time and manages his anger.

    b) What can't the teacher live with any longer?

    verbal hostility toward and harassment of other students

12. Identify methods for evaluating intervention effectiveness:

    frequency count of disruptions (in place)

    add rating scale (1-3) for self-control

13. Make notes on parental involvement:

    Contact date(s): 4/23

    Notes on the contact(s): Called mother. She can't participate because of poor health.

    What would the parents or guardians like to have happen?

    She supports whatever interventions are necessary to address Jake's behavior problems.

14. List other interventions tried and their results:

    Intervention D: Data Collection

    Are copies of this information available?   yes

    How successful were the interventions?

15. Note other information that the teacher is aware of (input from other adults who know the student—teachers, assistants, specialists, school counselors):

    Third-grade teacher suggests asking the custodian to serve as a mentor for Jake. Time spent with custodian could be positive reinforcer.

16. Review the student's records:

 This form can be printed from the Module F CD.

Figure 6c (continued)

Intervention Decision Guide:
Teacher Interview Worksheet (p. 3 of 4)

Stage 2: Preparation.

Possible interventions to consider:

Presenting Behavior	✓ if true	Intervention		Date implemented?	Effective? (+/−)
Several or many students in class misbehave.		Pre-intervention: Classroom Management*	Module F, Presentation 2		
The student may not know what is expected.		Intervention A: Planned Discussion*	Module F, Presentation 4		
The student may have an underlying academic problem.		Intervention B: Academic Assistance*	Module F, Presentation 4		
The student has difficulty with motivation and may not understand how to reach a goal.	X	Intervention C: Goal Setting*	Module F, Presentation 4		
The student's behavior appears to be chronic and resistant to simple intervention.	X	Intervention D: Data Collection & Debriefing*	Module F, Presentation 4		
The student gets a lot of attention from adults or peers for misbehavior or failure.	X	Intervention E: Increasing Positive Interactions*	Module F, Presentation 4		
The reason the behavior is occurring chronically needs to be analyzed and incorporated into the intervention plan.		Intervention F: STOIC Analysis & Intervention*	Module F, Presentation 4		
The student's escalating behavior is physically dangerous, or poses a threat to physical safety.		Intervention G: Managing Physically Dangerous Behavior*			
The behavior is so severe that the teacher cannot continue to teach.		Intervention H: Managing Severely Disruptive Behavior*			
The student is impulsive and has difficulty maintaining emotional control.		Intervention I: Managing the Cycle of Emotional Escalation*			
The student seems to be unaware of when he/she engages in inappropriate behavior.		Intervention J: Cueing & Precorrecting*			
The student has some motivation to change or learn new behaviors.	X	Intervention K: Self-Monitoring & Self-Evaluation*			
The student makes negative comments about him- or herself to others.	X	Intervention L: Positive Self-Talk & Attribution Training*			
The student does not know how to meet expectations.		Intervention M: Teaching Replacement Behavior*			
The student cannot or will not communicate verbally.		Intervention N: Functional Communication*			
The misbehavior is a firmly established part of the student's behavior.		Intervention O: Structured Reinforcement Systems*			
It is difficult to be consistent with the student because it is not always clear when the student has crossed the line between appropriate and inappropriate behavior. Consequences for misbehavior seem necessary, but do not seem to work.		Intervention P: Defining Limits & Establishing Consequences*			
The teacher feels anxious, worried, discouraged, or angry about one or more students.		Intervention Q: Relaxation & Stress Management*			
The student seems anxious, lethargic, or depressed.		Intervention R: Internalizing Problems & Mental Health*			

(Rows 2–7 grouped under TIER 1; rows 8–19 grouped under TIER 2.)

*In *Interventions: Evidence-Based Behavioral Strategies for Individual Students* (2nd ed.), 2008

Intervention Decision Guide:
Teacher Interview Worksheet (p. 4 of 4)

Stage 3: Intervention Design

1. Selected intervention(s):

   Goal-setting contract for self-control
   Increase positive feedback for on-task and self-controlled behavior
   Continue self-monitoring but add intermittent rewards

2. Summary of responsibilities for implementing the plan:

   Janelle will conduct the goal-setting meeting with the student and parents.
   Soraya (teacher) will develop a list of intermittent rewards and will strive for 5:1 ratio of positive to corrective interactions.

3. Summary of the final plan:

   By Monday, Janelle will arrange to meet with Jake and Mrs. Stillwell. Soraya will work immediately on increasing RPI and intermittent rewards. Janelle will observe 30 minutes per week to record Jake's on-task percentage and Soraya's RPI.

Stage 4: Implementation

1. Initial follow-up notes:

2. First follow-up meeting:

   Date:

   Purpose:

   Summary:

3. Second follow-up meeting:

   Date:

   Purpose:

   Summary:

 This form can be printed from the Module F CD.

Use the Intervention Decision Guide: Teacher Interview Worksheet to guide the discussion.

At the top of the worksheet, enter basic information about the student and the names of the interventionist and teacher. Be sure to include any information that may be needed later to demonstrate how this intervention interview fits as part of a comprehensive file—especially the date and the participants involved in the interview planning process.

> Items in bold correspond to steps and tasks on the IDG:TI Worksheet (Form F-27).

STAGE 1: Background

1. **Reason for referral and description of problem.**

   This step should be viewed as an opportunity to allow the teacher to explain any and every problem that is occurring with the student. Later you will narrow the intervention plan to address only the one or two behaviors of most concern, but initially you need to determine the breadth of the student's problems. To prompt the discussion, ask questions such as:

   - What does the student do?
   - What frustrates you?
   - Tell me more about what goes on every day.

   At this stage, try to achieve a balance between giving the teacher room to vent and discouraging unproductive cycling on the problem. The goals of Stage 1 are to ensure that the teacher has an opportunity to describe the full range of the problem and concerns about the student without getting mired in uncontrollable aspects of the problem. It is a challenging balance—you need to move things along while recognizing that if the teacher feels rushed or in any way bullied in the process, she is less likely to view you as an ally.

Keep Parents Informed

It is essential, both legally and ethically, to keep parents informed throughout the intervention process. Invite parents to be as involved as they want to be and view them as partners from the earliest stages of intervention planning.

Check with your district or central office to determine what type of parent/guardian consent is needed or recommended. Requirements can vary depending on the student's IEP status. Some families may be reluctant to participate or to have their child participate because of moral, religious, or other reasons. Ensure that all staff are sensitive to these concerns.

Rather than try to immediately identify and address the most critical problem, you will accomplish more in the early parts of the interview by being a good listener and acknowledging the range of problems that arise with the student. Active listening can set the stage for collaboration and goal setting and may also help you identify categories of problem behavior for a later stage of planning. Once the teacher has presented the full scope of the student's problems, let him or her know that eventually the two of you will need to determine the one or two major behaviors to address first with an intervention. Ask the teacher to reflect on which behaviors are of greatest concern as you continue working through the IDG:TI Worksheet. If the teacher begins to vent or repeat the same content about the problem, gently prompt the teacher to move on to the next step in gathering background information.

Code Red: Is it an emergency situation? Explicitly ask the teacher whether the student's behavior is currently or potentially physically dangerous or severely disruptive. If you don't ask this question directly, you might miss warning statements about such behavior and leave the teacher unprepared to handle a volatile situation. If the student's behavior is dangerous, skip simple intervention strategies and move directly to the protocol that your district has in place for handling severely disruptive and dangerous behavior. Physically dangerous and highly disruptive behaviors should be treated like a potential fire in the school—emergency procedures must be prepared and in place before the problem occurs. Teachers should have the same confidence in their ability to deal with dangerous behavior and severely disruptive students as they have in their ability to follow fire drill procedures.

If your district lacks policies for dealing with severely disruptive and dangerous behavior, see "Intervention G: Managing Physically Dangerous Behavior and Threats of Targeted Violence" and "Intervention H: Managing Severely Disruptive Behavior" in the book *Interventions: Evidence-Based Behavioral Strategies for Individual Students* (2nd ed.) by Randy Sprick and Mickey Garrison (2008). These protocols can help you develop emergency plans for dealing with out-of-control students.

Once temporary procedures have been put in place for defusing or responding to Code Red situations, continue with the IDG:TI to develop a long-term intervention plan that will help the student learn appropriate behavior.

Whether a student's behavior is severely disruptive or just a major annoyance is a judgment call that depends largely on the classroom teacher's skills and tolerance level. Because your district protocol (or Intervention H) may involve the removal of a severely disruptive student from the classroom, we recommend that you confirm the student's disruptive behavior by observing in the classroom or reviewing the student's records for complaints from parents or other students and reports of severely disruptive behavior in other settings. Be sure to involve the administrator in any decision about removing a student from the classroom.

2. **Are there situations that seem to set off the problem behavior?**

    Begin to focus the discussion on the student's main problems. Ask the teacher to consider whether these behaviors are set off by certain precipitating or escalating events. If the student fights with peers, what sort of interactions precipitate a fight? If the student is overtly defiant of authority, what events occur before the insubordinate acts? When you've identified specific triggers, you can focus the intervention on teaching the student to manage his behavior under those conditions or to avoid situations that result in problems. If the teacher can identify triggers—for example, the student has too much time to work on his own or the student spent the weekend at his dad's house—the teacher can begin to anticipate and help prevent problem behaviors.

    Ask the teacher to bring any collected data to the meeting. Monitoring forms, scatterplot data, frequency graphs, and the like can be very useful in identifying trends in the student's behavior.

    ---

3. **Where do the problems tend to occur?**

    Try to determine whether the student exhibits the problem behavior in multiple settings or whether the behavior is isolated to one location. Do problems occur only in the classroom? Does the student have difficulty in the halls or in special settings like the library, music room, playground, or cafeteria? Do the parents report similar problems at home? When problems are pervasive across all settings, the misbehavior may be firmly ingrained in the student's repertoire or the student may not have the expected behavior in his repertoire. On the other hand, if the problem occurs in only one or two settings, something specific about the setting may be contributing to the problem.

4. **When do the problems tend to occur?**

    Look at the data to see whether you can discern a pattern in the timing of the misbehavior. Do problems occur during certain times of the day? Are mornings better than afternoons? Do problems tend to occur more frequently on certain days? A pattern can help with intervention planning. For example, if a student has tantrums and angry outbursts more frequently on Mondays, weekends may be hard for the student. She may be tired. Her home situation may be particularly disruptive on weekends. The student may feel torn after custody visits. Given this situation, the interventionist can try to collaborate with parents to help reduce stress on weekends as well as identify school-based intervention strategies for Mondays. For example, you might give the student a chance to check in with the school counselor for a welcoming visit when the student arrives on Monday morning.

5. **How often do the problems occur? How long does the behavior last? How intense is the problem?**

   The frequency and duration of problems can also be critical information for planning interventions. When a young student throws tantrums once or twice a week, the problem may not be severe. However, when each tantrum lasts for 60 to 90 minutes, the student may need an intensive intervention plan. Also consider the intensity of the behavior: Is it sometimes more intense than other times? Has the teacher noticed any trends or patterns? If the problem involves not following directions, discuss the latency between when a direction is given and when the student complies. You or the teacher might collect data on a problem such as this if the teacher has not already done so.

6. **Is the student psychologically and neurologically capable of controlling his or her behavior? Is there evidence to support this opinion?**

   If a student has psychological or neurological impairments that make controlling behavior difficult or impossible, coordinate with the student's family physician, specialists within the district, or other professionals on accommodating the student in a way that allows her to experience success. For example, Tourette syndrome is a neurological disorder that will not respond to intervention. On the other hand, a student with Attention Deficit Hyperactivity Disorder (ADHD) is likely to be capable of making moderate behavioral changes. It is a disservice to the student to fail to offer interventions that will help her succeed.

7. **Is the student aware of the problem?**

   Unless there is a record of a planned discussion, goal-setting contract, or other indicator that someone has talked with the student about the problem, the student's awareness will be based on the teacher's subjective perception. Sometimes a teacher thinks that constant nagging is enough to convey behavioral expectations to the student, but the student still has no idea he is doing anything wrong. In other cases, the teacher has spoken to the student about the problem, but the student simply disagrees that the behavior needs to change.

   For example, the teacher may be concerned because a student is argumentative and insubordinate. In some cases, however, this behavior represents a cultural style difference between the teacher and the student. The student may not even know that the teacher finds the student's behavior argumentative and perhaps even frightening. Listen to the teacher's perception about whether the student is aware of the teacher's concern. But if the teacher declares, "She knows that behavior is unacceptable," some part of the intervention plan you are developing may need to involve directly teaching the student to become more aware of the behavior that concerns the teacher. In our example, one goal of the intervention may be for the student to learn to talk to the teacher in a quieter voice with less confrontational body language.

8. **Does the student seem motivated to improve the behavior?**

When a student has no motivation to change, the intervention selection process is affected because you must tailor the choice of intervention to the needs of the student. For example, "Intervention K: Self-Monitoring and Self-Evaluation" from the *Interventions* book is a powerful tool, but it is likely to be effective only when the student is motivated to do better.

Imagine a student who has no desire to complete work and no motivation to improve, yet is asked to self-monitor his completed assignments. Picture this student's great joy each day when he checks off "nothing accomplished today" on the form. In this case, self-monitoring may actually reinforce the student's poor participation. A student like this would benefit from an intervention tailored to increase his motivation, possibly through extrinsic positive reinforcement within a structured reinforcement system.

9. **What is the function of the problem behavior? What seems to be maintaining or reinforcing the student's misbehavior?**

Every behavior that occurs repeatedly serves some function for the student who exhibits the behavior—escaping, gaining attention or some other reinforcer, or venting frustration or anger, for example. Ask questions such as: What's in it for the student? Does the student control situations? Does the student handle frustration or anger by misbehaving? Does the student get out of doing work when she misbehaves?

For example, when a student consistently gets teacher attention for misbehavior, the student may enjoy the adult contact even though it is negative. When misbehavior consistently leads to removal from the classroom, the removal is probably satisfying to the student at some level. Perhaps the student struggles academically and hides deficiencies by getting kicked out of class, or maybe the student gains peer attention for his rebellious behavior. It is not always possible to determine the specific events or situations that reinforce and perpetuate the problem, and any ideas about the misbehavior's function will always be a guess or hypothesis. However, this discussion process may lead to useful insights that will assist in intervention planning.

Following is a list of possible functions that may be factors in the student's problem behaviors. Use this list to help the teacher develop a hypothesis about why the behavior is occurring.

Ability. Sometimes students do not have the neurological or physiological ability to behave the way the teacher would like. When this is the case, you cannot change the student's behavior with behavioral intervention. Instead, you must make accommodations for the behavior. Sometimes the problematic behavior occurs because the student lacks the information or skill to exhibit the appropriate behavior. Ability is the issue in this case, too, but behavioral intervention—particularly teaching replacement behaviors—holds great promise for helping the student learn new behaviors.

Awareness. We discussed awareness in Item 7. Help the teacher explore the possibility that the student is able to exhibit the positive behavior, but doesn't know that she is exhibiting it.

Adult attention. Some students are starved for adult attention. The form of the attention may not matter—both reprimands and compliments provide adult attention. Teachers often describe these students as needy, demanding, helpless, or aggravating, and may even say, "He drives me crazy."

Peer attention. A student may exhibit misbehavior to get attention or approval from peers.

Power or control. Sometimes a student's behavior serves to give the student a sense of control over some aspect of life. This could include negative behaviors such as arguing, insubordination, and overtly refusing to follow directions. It could also include passively negative behaviors such as just doing nothing.

This is a somewhat controversial issue in the behavioral field because many experts suggest that a hypothesis that differentiates power from other forms of attention does not imply differences in intervention. We have found that simple attention-seeking behavior often responds to an intervention in which the adults give less attention to misbehavior (ignoring) and more attention to positive behavior. If the student likes to exhibit behaviors that make adults frustrated and angry, however, we have found that when the behavior is ignored, the student is likely to accelerate the intensity of the behavior into something that cannot be ignored, such as hitting other students.

A more useful intervention in these cases may be to implement a consequence for the misbehavior as well as a proactive plan that gives the student a sense of importance and power, such as a highly visible school job (see information about Meaningful Work in Module C, Presentation 6). When the student gains a sense of power in positive ways, he has less need to exert power in negative ways.

Escape or avoidance (task difficulty or discomfort). This function may involve trying to get out of difficult, stressful, or uncomfortable situations. The most obvious example is the student who misbehaves to avoid work that is too diffi-cult. When escape is a possible function, the intervention will need to reduce the fear or stress of the situation the student is avoiding while concurrently teaching the student the skills needed to handle the situation.

Competing reinforcers. This function simply means that the student is not exhib-iting the desired behaviors because doing something else is more fun. For exam-ple, a kindergarten student may not do an assigned task, such as participating in centers, simply because he would rather be playing with puzzles. When this may be the case, the intervention will need to restrict access to the competing reinforcer (make it less accessible) while concurrently increasing the reinforcing aspects of the desired behavior through increased attention and possibly with a structured reinforcement system.

Other. Although the functions listed above are the most common, keep open to any and all possibilities. For example, the student may exhibit emotional out-bursts on Monday not because of what occurs in school on Mondays but rather to vent frustration and anger over things that occurred at home on the weekend. Or a student may misbehave at the end of the week and especially before vaca-tions because of anxiety about the upcoming separation from the security of school and a caring staff.

Remember that whatever you and the teacher come up with here is simply a hypothesis, not a diagnosis. As you move toward intervention selection, keep your hypothesis in mind and design an intervention that addresses the function, making it possible for the student to succeed and get her needs met in positive ways. If the intervention that you develop and implement is not successful, you may wish to revisit your hypothesis about the function as one part of the analysis about where to go next with the intervention plan. Maybe the intervention did not work because the student is not seeking attention but rather lacks the skill to exhibit the appropriate behavior. So the next intervention might put more emphasis on teaching replacement behavior.

10. **What are the student's strengths? (List at least three.)**

It's easy for the teacher of an at-risk student to become so frustrated by the every-day battle of interacting with and teaching the student that the teacher forgets that the student has positive qualities. The power of any intervention will be greatly increased by focusing on student strengths and the possibility of change rather than highlighting the frustration of working with such a student. Imagine a teacher who describes her eighth-grade student by saying, "He's a smart aleck. He's always making rude comments." Without hearing the student's strengths, you might move directly to a plan to reduce the frequency of this student's dis-ruptions. However, the teacher tells you that the student is academically capable, quite funny, and able to use his wit to make people either laugh or cry. With this information, you can include in the intervention ways for the student to use his strengths and power in positive ways. The problematic misbehavior may just go away, and the strength-based behaviors are more likely to take over more of the student's behavioral repertoire.

11. **What is the teacher's goal or desired outcome?**

This is a pivotal point in the intervention planning process. The focus shifts from what is known about the past to what the teacher wants in the future. Carefully guide the teacher toward developing a clear, reasonable, and achievable goal for the student's behavior.

Narrow the goal. If the intervention won't solve all of the student's problems and the teacher can pick only one or two major categories, what would he most like to change? If you are dealing with a student who has many problems, where are you going to start? It is important to identify objectives that will allow the student to focus on one or two areas of improvement. Remember that objectives should be ambitious but attainable.

By narrowing objectives and beginning with obtainable goals, you give troubled students a greater chance of success. Once the student experiences success, many secondary problems resolve themselves and positive momentum makes the other problems more amenable to future intervention efforts.

By listening to and writing down all the things the teacher says, you imply that you value his perceptions. Although the objectives may need to be adjusted later to ensure they are attainable, it is important to get the teacher's perspective on the most disruptive and impossible-to-live-with behaviors.

Other recommendations for selecting target behaviors include:

- Choose the most pivotal behaviors.
- Choose behaviors with more general usefulness over highly specific behaviors.
- Focus on building appropriate behaviors.
- Consider behaviors that will give the student increased access to naturally occurring reinforcers as well as behaviors that the student would like to improve.

Work for clarity. The goal of the intervention should be a specific observable behavior, such as "Help Mark learn to stay in his seat during class," rather than a general label or conclusion, such as "Stop Mark from being so fidgety." Encourage the teacher to use objective descriptions of the student's situation and avoid jargon and generalizations. By moving from subjective labels or conclusions to objective descriptions of the problem, logical objective goals are more likely to emerge. Table 6a shows some specific examples of each.

Table 6a   *Subjective vs. objective descriptions*

Conclusions	Objective Descriptions	Goal of Intervention
Sara is really lazy.	Sara has completed only one of eight assignments and has not turned in any homework.	Sara will complete in-class assignments and homework.
James is totally out of control at recess.	James runs through the games other students are playing. He pushes others, and he will not follow directions from the playground assistants.	James will follow directions from the playground assistants, and for 2 weeks during recess he will be assigned to a specific game that will be monitored closely by one of the assistants.
Mariah doesn't seem to have any confidence.	Mariah never talks with other students and talks with adults only when they initiate the contact.	Mariah will learn social skills that will result in her initiating interactions with both students and adults.

Prompt the teacher to use numbers to describe the severity of a problem. Numbers are objective and can help define the goal of the intervention. For example:

- Within 4 weeks, the student will be able to complete at least 80% of her classwork every day.
- The number of disruptive acts will be reduced by 50% within 2 weeks and by 80% within 2 months.
- The student will learn to stay calm and manage his anger without screaming, hitting, or engaging in aggressive acts. Each month, the number of disruptive incidents will be lower than in the previous month.

Stating the goal of the intervention in observable and measurable terms establishes criteria that you and the teacher can use to determine the success or failure of the intervention. If the goal can't be counted or measured somehow, it may be too broad or subjective, so guide the teacher in redefining her goal for the student's behavior.

12. Identify methods for evaluating intervention effectiveness.

This is where behavioral training comes into play. You will need to come up with a clear, definable, measurable goal and recommend a process for measuring intervention effectiveness. If the goal is not defined in terms of measurable and observable behaviors, go back to Item 11 and redefine the goal.

Identify at least one source of objective data to collect on the goal behavior or on each separate goal, if there is more than one. You may simply be able to continue or modify the monitoring procedures that are already in place, or you may need to develop a new system. To effectively monitor intervention plans and avoid misperceptions in the data, we recommend two independent means of evaluating progress. When selecting evaluation procedures, try not to overburden teachers. Objective data collection might include any of the following methods.

- Quality ratings (teacher rates behavior on a scale of specific criteria in a given period, such as hourly)
- Work products (percentage of assignments completed, test scores, grades, number of written words in a journal, and so on)
- Self-monitoring data (student tracks the frequency of his or her own behavior)
- Data from a reinforcement system (for example, number of points received, number of positive and negative markers)
- Frequency data (number of times student displays the behavior in a given period)
- Duration data (amount of time student engages in a behavior)
- Latency data (amount of time it takes for a behavior to begin after a stimulus occurs)
- Audio or video recordings (check with building and district administration about the policy for and legality of recording students)

Graphs visually depict trends and help teachers determine whether their subjective impressions match what is happening. When a student's behavior is especially stressful for a teacher, data may be needed to help the teacher recognize progress. If a teacher is feeling despair, burnout, and a sense that her efforts are not making a difference, visual information that depicts progress can encourage the teacher to continue her efforts.

ᏋᎧ FOUNDATIONS RECOMMENDATION ᏅᏂ

To effectively monitor intervention plans and avoid misperceptions in the data, use two independent means of evaluating progress.

---

13. **Make notes on parental involvement.**

By this point, parents should have been contacted and permission obtained for intervention planning. If this has not been done, contact the parents immediately before any further planning or action takes place. It is essential to try to bring parents in as partners in the earliest stages of the intervention process. Parents have a right, both legally and ethically, to know when their child is having a problem. Tell parents that the staff is concerned enough to initiate intervention planning and that interventions will likely be more effective with input from parents.

Review previous interactions with parents. How have parents reacted to indications that their child needs to change his or her behavior? What level of support did they show? Note any information provided by parents in previous contacts. Regardless of their current level of involvement, families should be brought into the process as much as possible. Children whose parents are involved consistently do better in school. You may be working with families who can't or won't function as partners, but they need to be invited nonetheless. Their wishes should be explored and their input valued.

14. **List other interventions tried and their results.**

List interventions that have been tried to date, how long they were implemented, and whether they were successful. As you move through this section, actively work to prevent teachers from feeling defensive or alienated. If no action has been taken yet, clarify to teachers that this is OK and that the information will help determine whether to start with one of your district's established early-stage interventions. If interventions have been attempted already, ask to look at records, contracts, and other data collected during the intervention. It may be useful to contact the student's previous teachers to find out whether they had success with any interventions. When designing an intervention, capitalize on anything that worked in the past and avoid interventions that have proven ineffective.

15. **Note other information that the teacher is aware of.**

Do you or the teacher know anything else that might be useful to consider? Ask the teacher if she has heard anything from other adults or students that should be looked into more thoroughly. Find out if the teacher has information about the student's medical history or involvement with outside agencies. It is important at this stage to consider all available information. As interventions are designed, implemented, redesigned, and reimplemented, any and all information about the student may prove to have value.

16. **Review the student's records.**

Consider the following when reviewing the student's records:

- *Medical history:* diagnosed illnesses or diseases, developmental issues, medications
- *Family history:* who lives with the student, siblings, education level and employment of parents/guardians, involvement of outside agencies

- *School history:* special education status, school changes and moves, absenteeism, retentions, academic grade averages
- *Test data:* standardized and state test results, psychological evaluations

Stage 1 will probably take 20 to 30 minutes.

STAGE 2: Preparation

The third page of the IDG:TI Worksheet lists 19 possible interventions to consider; your school or district may have its own list of protocols to choose from. An intervention is suggested for each Presenting Behavior listed in the first column. Note that the first, Classroom Management, is addressed in Foundations Module F, Presentation 2, and in related materials such as *CHAMPS: A Proactive and Positive Approach to Classroom Management* (Sprick, 2009) and *Discipline in the Secondary Classroom* (Sprick, 2013). Interventions A through F, the early-stage interventions, correspond to Tasks 1 through 6 of Module F, Presentation 4. All 19 interventions are available in *Interventions: Evidence-Based Behavioral Strategies for Individual Students* (2nd ed.; Sprick & Garrison, 2008). However, you don't necessarily have to get the book. By searching the Internet, you can find many tools to help you design all of these suggested interventions.

With the teacher, discuss each Presenting Behavior. If it is true for the student, check the Check If True column. If any of the interventions have already been tried, indicate the date and its effectiveness. If the intervention was successful or the teacher thinks it might be successful in combination with other interventions, check the Check If True column.

The first seven interventions are easy for classroom teachers to implement and should probably be tried before you consider more intensive interventions. Every teacher should be trained in these early-stage interventions. Some of them should have been attempted with the targeted student before the intervention planning meeting was called.

For example, if nine students in a classroom are all having the same problem, the teacher must first look at his classroom management and try a universal pre-intervention. If eight out of nine of the students respond well to the change, designing an individual intervention for the remaining student becomes a manageable task. If the teacher has already implemented other early-stage interventions without seeing progress by the student, he may consider using some of those interventions as part of the new behavior improvement plan. But they will probably be supplemental to more intensive, highly structured interventions that have not yet been implemented. If early-stage interventions have not been implemented, consider them during current planning because they represent some of the most powerful and easy-to-implement interventions.

The next 12 interventions on the IDG:TI, G through R, target more severe and ingrained problems. They are designed for students whose behavioral problems require more intensive intervention. Intervention specialists such as school psychologists, special education teachers, administrators, and anyone involved in an intervention planning team should be well versed in these Tier 2 interventions, but classroom teachers are not likely to be trained in these methods. These interventions will probably be implemented by or with the assistance of an interventionist, not by the classroom teacher alone. If your district uses any other approved interventions, you may wish to bring these to the table for consideration. You will also want to modify the IDG:TI to reflect your district's list of evidence-based interventions.

STAGE 3: Intervention Design

1. **Select the interventions to try first.**

   From the interventions with checkmarks in the Check If True column, choose one to three to implement. Selecting appropriate and effective interventions requires a thorough knowledge of all of the interventions. Interventionists should have training in all 19 interventions as well as in any other district-approved interventions. If you are not familiar with some of the interventions, take a day or two to become more familiar with them by reading through the corresponding chapter in *Interventions* or another comparable resource.

   Explain more about each possible intervention to the teacher: "If this is what you want to accomplish, let me tell you a little about each of the interventions that might help achieve the goal. We will work together to select the interventions that have the highest likelihood of success and are acceptable given your needs and time constraints."

   The teacher may also wish to look at the intervention more closely, either in the *Interventions* summary or by exploring the corresponding chapter. At this stage, give huge credence and decision-making power to the teacher. While you, as an interventionist, will guide the decisions, you are essentially saying to the teacher, "This is your intervention. I will help and guide you, but you will be living with it on a daily basis, so your input is essential."

   When selecting interventions to implement, determine whether the intervention is related to the identified goal or desired outcomes. Next, determine whether the intervention seems manageable for both the student and the teacher and whether it is appropriate to the situation and the student. Finally, try to balance the following, sometimes competing, variables:

   The amount of time and effort required from the teacher. Classroom teachers cannot implement an intervention that makes it impossible to meet the needs of other students or the normal responsibilities of teaching. The ability of teachers to implement intervention strategies will vary greatly. When considering an intervention, think about how intrusive the intervention will be (how much teacher time and effort it entails). If an intervention seems unwieldy or would put undue stress on the teacher, it would not be wise to use that intervention.

The degree of student responsibility and motivation. Select interventions that encourage the student to assume the greatest amount of responsibility for change, but make sure that these interventions provide enough support and structure for success.

Interventions with less support—requiring students to be more independent and responsible for change—take less time to set up, implement, monitor, and fade. Because students are required to take more responsibility, they are more likely to attribute success to their own abilities rather than feeling that adults made them change. These more independent interventions tend to be appropriate for relatively mild behaviors (ones that do not require a large change from the student), for more mature students, and for behaviors the student is motivated to change.

Other interventions provide high degrees of structure and support for ensuring student success. They tend to require more effort and support from teachers and other involved adults. More time is required to set up, implement, monitor, and fade the intervention. But because of the structure and support provided, there is a higher probability of success, especially with less mature or more troubled students. These interventions are appropriate when students have a long history of problem behavior and fairly severe problems that are likely to be resistant to change.

2. **Summarize the roles and responsibilities of everyone involved.**

   Summarize the plan in writing, listing each person's responsibilities. Good intentions and the best-laid plans are easily lost in the everyday bustle of school responsibilities, so you must clearly communicate that it is essential for each person to follow through on his or her part of the intervention plan. The danger is that if one person says he will take care of an aspect of the plan and then forgets, the intervention may fall through the cracks and not get started for a month or more. In the life of a troubled student, this month is a critical time, and the delay may lead to a loss of essential learning and progress.

   For example, the teacher decides that he needs to collect more data as part of the intervention. The interventionist says she will talk to a colleague who has developed several effective record-keeping forms and will obtain samples for the teacher to review. To ensure that no one forgets, the interventionist sets some deadlines, adds them to her smartphone reminder system, and ensures that the other involved parties know about the deadlines, too.

Oct. 18: Celia (interventionist/school counselor) talks with Ms. Garibaldi about sample forms (by 10/18 at the latest).

Oct. 19: Celia gives sample forms to Lyle (teacher).

Oct. 20: Lyle gives feedback to Celia. If needed, Celia copies or modifies one form.

Oct. 21: Lyle implements the new monitoring form.

3. **Finalize the intervention plan.**

Set times for follow-up meetings and observations, then tie up any other loose ends. Ask the teacher if you can check in after the first day or two of implementation to discuss progress and any unanticipated problems. Schedule follow-up meetings at weekly intervals to look at data and assess the intervention plan. Does it need to be modified, continued, or faded? Plan to continue the intervention process until the student is no longer having problems.

STAGE 4: Implementation

After the first day of implementation, conduct a quick checkup with the teacher to clarify procedures and help with any glitches, if necessary. Schedule any needed observations or assistance before the initial follow-up meeting that takes place a week after implementation begins.

In all subsequent follow-up meetings, work with the teacher to evaluate progress and make modifications to the plan, as needed. As a general rule, interventions should be scheduled to run at least 2 weeks. If the student is absent during part of that time, the intervention should continue for a longer period. In addition, follow-up must involve regular meetings with the teacher, the student, and the family to review the data being collected to determine if the situation is getting better, getting worse, or staying the same.

Briefly, guidelines for maintaining, modifying, and fading plans are as follows:

- Develop a new intervention plan if the student makes no progress or gets worse.
- Modify the plan to provide more support if progress is slow or comes to a halt.
- Maintain the intervention plan if the student is making good progress.
- Fade the intervention when there is a high probability that the student can maintain success.

Task 2 Action Steps & Evidence of Implementation

Action Steps	Evidence of Implementation
Foundations Team and interventionists: Discuss whether the IDG:TI will be useful in your school. (*Note:* Do this step after the Foundations Team has read Task 1 and Task 3, which summarize other collaborative problem-solving processes that you may incorporate into your school's continuum of behavior support.) If you decide to use it: • Determine whether it will be implemented before or after a teacher-to-teacher problem-solving process such as the 25-Minute Planning Process. • Determine whether the teacher can decide whether to use the 25-Minute Planning Process or the IDG:TI and when. • Identify personnel who will serve as advocates and interventionists. • Share with staff the decision to use IDG:TI and provide training in how and when to use it.	Foundations Process: Meeting Minutes, Current Priorities Final procedures should be included in: Foundations Archive: Support Available to Staff, Interventions for Individual Students Staff Handbook: Available Support

TASK 3

Complete an Intervention Decision Guide: Multidisciplinary Team Approach (IDG:MDT)

The IDG:MDT is designed to fit near the tip of the *Foundations* continuum triangle, after the 25-Minute Planning Process and the Intervention Decision Guide: Teacher Interview (IDG:TI) have been tried. Remember the bridge we described in the Introduction? We explained that early-stage interventions can be considered a bridge between universal prevention and targeted (Tier 2) support. As you move into a process that involves a multidisciplinary team, you are on another bridge, in this case one between Tier 2 and Tier 3 processes. Categorizing an intervention at this point, however, matters less than simply recognizing that a problem that has not responded to earlier, simpler, and less expensive problem-solving processes and interventions now requires expert advice from various professionals and lots of time to find and implement viable solutions.

This approach brings all your resources and expertise together to help students who continue to present behavioral problems. It collects the most information and is the most comprehensive collaborative problem-solving process that we present in *Foundations*. The IDG:MDT links a comprehensive intervention plan to the student's function for his or her misbehavior. The steps are similar to those in the 25-Minute Planning Process and the IDG:TI, but the IDG:MDT goes into greater detail, is more focused, and takes more time and effort.

For the IDG:MDT process to be effective and efficient, it is essential that Tier 2 interventions earlier on the continuum succeed in addressing most students with behavioral difficulties. Otherwise, the number of referrals to the IDG:MDT process can easily overwhelm the multidisciplinary team and make it very difficult for the team to be effective and efficient.

As in the other interventions we've discussed in this presentation, the student's classroom teacher should be viewed as an equal partner and active participant in the IDG:MDT process. The student's teacher should collaborate with the team in the development and implementation of any intervention plan. Establishing and nurturing a collaborative relationship with the classroom teacher enables the multidisciplinary team to provide crucial support needed for the teacher to faithfully implement the developed intervention plan.

Determine team membership.

Your school may already have a functioning multidisciplinary team. If it does not, we recommend establishing one. Such teams usually comprise school-based and itinerant staff members who represent different disciplines in the school and district, such as school counselor, school psychologist, school social worker, school nurse, special education personnel (for example, behavior specialist and speech/language specialist), curriculum specialist (for example, reading teacher and instructional coach), and administrator. Some teams include personnel from outside agencies. In some cases, a master general education teacher may also serve on the team.

All team members must be trained and experienced in behavioral consultation and the entire range of behavioral intervention strategies available in the district, including early-stage and highly structured interventions from *Interventions: Evidence-Based Behavioral Strategies for Individual Students* (2nd ed.; Sprick & Garrison, 2008). Team member should also be familiar with how to use *The Teacher's Encyclopedia of Behavior Management* (2nd ed.; Sprick, 2012) and resources like *The Tough Kid Tool Box* (Jenson, Rhode, & Reavis, 2009), as well as any other resources in team members' repertoires.

The ideal size of the multidisciplinary team is four to seven permanent members, with each member adding to the balance of expertise and experience. We recommend having no more than eight members. The team has the option of adding adjunct members for a referred student based on the student's unique needs and characteristics. For example, it would be appropriate to invite a speech/language specialist to join the team if the referred student has or is suspected of having a severe communication disorder.

Define and assign team roles.

Clearly defined team roles are another crucial factor in an effective and efficient multidisciplinary team process.

Team leader (or team coordinator). This should be a school-based person. The responsibilities of this role include receiving IDG:MDT referrals, developing the meeting agenda, assigning case managers, keeping the team focused on the agenda during meetings, keeping all participants engaged during meetings, and maintaining a file of completed forms and meeting notes for every student referred to the team. Some teams find it helpful to have coleaders. Splitting the leadership responsibilities between two members prevents one person from being overwhelmed. Having coleaders also allows one leader to conduct a meeting if the other leader happens to be a case manager for the student or cannot attend a meeting. The other key role for the coordinator or team leader is to make sure all members are actively involved, on task, and working together.

The Case Manager

The multidisciplinary team leader should assign a case manager to each student who is referred to the team. In many situations, the person who served as the interventionist or advocate earlier in the problem-solving process will naturally become the case manager. If greater knowledge and expertise is required, another person may take over the responsibilities of the advocate and function as the case manager.

Case manager is a well-established role from the mental health and medical fields that many schools have adopted for a role performed in special education. It is a team role like chair, recorder, timekeeper, and so on. The person's actual job title is seldom case manager, although some large districts have dedicated case managers. Instead, the role is assumed by a counselor, social worker, school psychologist, or special education staff member. The case manager's duties are to know all the background information and to serve as the direct contact person for teachers, parents, older students, and agencies.

The team should have at least three or four members who serve as case managers, who support and guide the referring teachers through the process and serve as liaisons between the teachers and the team. When assigning the case manager, consider factors such as the referring teacher's relationship with the person, the case manager's current caseload, and the age and presenting problems of the student.

We recommend that a student's case manager not lead meetings about that student. It's important to ensure an unbiased process to determine the student's needs, services, and possible classification in special education. The case manager needs to advocate for the student, parents, teachers, and school, which sometimes (in fact, often) results in dueling interests! It's best that the team leader not be seen as holding predetermined opinions about how to meet the student's needs.

Timekeeper. The responsibility of the person in this role is to use a watch, kitchen timer, or computer timer to remind team members how much time is left in a specific part of the meeting (brainstorming, for example). The timekeeper's role is critical in ensuring that the meeting proceeds efficiently from step to step.

Recorder. The recorder takes minutes on all parts of the team discussion and completes the team's official copy of the IDG:MDT Worksheet (Form F-28). Note that a fillable version of the worksheet is provided on the Module F CD. You can open it in Adobe Reader and type directly onto it. The recorder can also write down the list of brainstorming ideas during Stage 3, unless the team decides it will be more efficient to appoint another member to do this job.

Mediator. The mediator should have excellent interpersonal skills and be sensitive to people's feelings and emotions. This job entails ensuring that team members work together, support each other, and stay positive and proactive throughout the process.

Establish ground rules for meetings.

Establish expectations—ground rules—for the team's behavior during the process. Nothing is more discouraging to a team than meetings that chronically start late, end after the announced time, and become gripe sessions rather than productive problem-solving sessions.

> Best practice is to establish a set of ground rules (expectations) to guide team members' behavior so everyone is clear on what effective and efficient meetings look like and sound like.

Ground rules are especially important for the multidisciplinary team because people with specialized skill sets, knowledge, and expertise tend to talk a lot. Ground rules can help ensure that everyone collaborates, listens to each other, accepts and acknowledges different points of view, and stays positive. Ground rules can also give the teacher a sense that the group is truly focused on helping him or her find a way to help the student be more successful.

We suggest you develop ground rules as a team and review them often, especially at the start of the school year. Also post them in the meeting room. Set up the expectation that team members acknowledge behaviors that violate the rules. The team should revise the ground rules when needed.

Ground rules should cover the following topics:

- Attendance
- Punctuality
- Listening to each other
- Team members can disagree, but must be respectful
- Confidentiality
- Making the teacher feel welcome
- Making the teacher feel like an important contributor to the process
- Active participation by all team members

Note: Ground rules for meetings are also discussed in Module A, Presentation 2, Task 3.

Establish ground rules for brainstorming.

Problem solving often involves brainstorming as a critical piece of the process. We suggest you establish ground rules for brainstorming so that all team members feel they can contribute and are respectful of others. The recorder should include all suggestions in the meeting minutes so that all possibilities will be available for future use even if they are not used in the initial plan. Following are some sample ground rules for brainstorming:

- Establish a time limit for brainstorming (4 minutes, for example).

- Anything goes—don't hold back.

- Write down a summary statement or phrase for every strategy or idea.

- Record the ideas on chart paper, dry-erase board, or computer and LCD so everyone can see them.

- Any idea or strategy is acceptable.

- Piggybacking (that is, taking someone else's idea in a different direction) is encouraged.

- Members shouldn't look at the referring teacher when offering an idea (looking at the teacher can encourage the teacher to comment on the suggested strategy).

- Each team member should provide at least one strategy.

- Team members should not comment or ask questions about strategies until after the brainstorming.

- After 30 seconds of silence, read the list aloud to stimulate more ideas.

Consider these suggestions for effective and efficient meetings.

- Have comfortable chairs!

- Have the case manager sit next to the teacher. This will help convey the idea that the case manager is supporting the teacher and they are working together to present the student's case to the team and work toward a solution.

- Have a large table with plenty of space for writing.

- Ensure privacy—close the door.

- A wall clock will help everyone stick to time limits.

- Use a computer with a monitor that everyone can easily see. As the recorder fills in the IDG:MDT Worksheet, everyone can read it.

- Snacks and drinks can make the meeting seem less formal.

- Given the demanding schedules of its members, we recommend that the team establish a schedule of regular meetings for the semester or (preferably) for the entire school year. It is easier to cancel a meeting if there isn't a referred case than to try to find a convenient time to meet on short notice.

** & FOUNDATIONS RECOMMENDATION **

Establish a schedule of regular meetings for the semester or (preferably) for the entire school year. It is easier to cancel a meeting if there isn't a referred case than to try to find a convenient time to meet on short notice.

Establish guidelines for the IDG:MDT process.

The team should also establish broad guidelines for how long each stage of the IDG:MDT process should last, including setting a target date for when Stage 4 will be completed. If you don't clarify, for example, "We hope to be done with this entire multidisciplinary team process within 6 weeks," a case could drag out for 3 months or a whole semester and the teacher will feel like it never ended.

The IDG:MDT Worksheet (Form F-28 shown in Figure 6d) is divided into four stages. **The case manager and teacher complete Stage 1 before the team meets to discuss the subsequent stages.** The team should establish time parameters to keep the meetings relatively short, but focused and productive. For example:

First meeting, 15–20 minutes. Stage 2: Collect Other Essential Information. The team and referring teacher review the background of the case and set up a plan for observations, interviews, and records reviews.

Second meeting, 30 minutes. Stage 3: Intervention Design. Using all the information collected, the team and the referring teacher design the next intervention to be implemented.

Third meeting, 10–15 minutes. Stage 4: Follow-Up Meeting. The team and referring teacher determine whether the intervention should be modified, maintained, or faded, depending on the progress of the student.

Depending on the complexity of the case, you might be able to work through Stages 2 and 3 during one meeting. Another option is to have the case manager complete Stage 2 with the teacher, then share summaries of the collected data with the team during the Stage 3 meeting.

Figure 6d   *Intervention Decision Guide: Multidisciplinary Team Worksheet (F-28)*

Intervention Decision Guide:
Multidisciplinary Team Worksheet (p. 1 of 5)

Student _____ Age _____ Grade _____ Date _____

Referring teacher _____ Case manager _____

Other participants _____

Stage 1: Background From IDG: Teacher Interview (Form F-27)

1. Reason for referral and description of problem:

    Code Red: Are plans in place or needed? Y N If yes, describe the plans:

    | |
    | |
    | |
    | |

2. What goals (target behaviors to reduce and replacement behaviors to promote) have been previously established? Are they still the teacher's main priority? If not, what is?

3. What data have been collected on this goal?

4. Describe any academic or behavioral interventions implemented within the past 6 months. See the table of interventions to consider on p. 3 of the IDG: Teacher Interview (Form F-27).

    <u>Target behavior</u>   <u>Intervention</u>   <u>When</u>   <u>Outcomes (effectiveness & fidelity)</u>

5. What was the previous hypothesis regarding function? Did interventions confirm or contradict that hypothesis? (Or does lack of implementation fidelity keep this question open?)

6. How has the teacher corrected the student's misbehavior? Has this been effective?

7. Describe any proactive strategies used by the teacher. Have they been effective?

8. Should the existing goal be maintained? Y N If no, describe the new goal and decide if any additional data should be collected:

 This form can be printed from the Module F CD.

Intervention Decision Guide:
Multidisciplinary Team Worksheet (p. 2 of 5)

Stage 2: Collect Other Essential Information

Direct Observation

  1. Identify behaviors to observe:

  2. Set a schedule of observations for the classroom: Who? When (date and time)?

  3. Other settings in which to observe behavior: Where? When (date and time)?

School Staff to Interview

Identify other staff members who interact with the student regularly or who knew the student in previous years:

Who   Interviewed by   Questions to ask

Student Interview

  1. Who informed the student of the problem and the goal and when? If not done yet, who can interview the student and when?

  2. Is the student motivated to improve?

  3. Does the student have other goals or objectives?

  4. Other relevant information or questions to ask:

Parent/Guardian Interview

  1. Who informed the parents of the problem and the goal and when? If not done yet, who can interview the parents and when?

  2. Are the parents or guardians supportive of this goal? Do they have other goals or objectives?

  3. Other relevant questions to ask:

 This form can be printed from the Module F CD.

Intervention Decision Guide:
Multidisciplinary Team Worksheet (p. 3 of 5)

Pertinent Information from School Records Review

Student _____ School _____ Date _____

CONFIDENTIAL INFORMATION (To be kept in a secure location)	
Area	**Important Information and Notes**
Medical History	Any diagnosed illnesses or diseases? Y N If yes, disease and impact on student: Mother's age when child was born: _____ Significant birth and/or development history: History of medications? Y N If yes, which one(s) and any known side effects? Wears glasses? Y N Hearing loss? Y N
Family History	Who does the student live with? ❑ Birth parents ❑ Stepfamily ❑ Guardians ❑ Single-parent home ❑ Dual custody Sibling(s)? Y N Ages and genders: Education level and job: (mother) _____ (father) _____ Has a parent died? If yes, any details such as when, who, and how? Any seriously ill parent, grandparent, or sibling? If yes, describe the situation. Any agency involvement (mental health, DSS, private psychologist, etc.)?
School History	Is or was the student served by special education? Y N If so, which classification, how long, and what level of service? How many school changes/moves? _____ Where: History of absenteeism—few vs. excessive (more than 20 a year): Which years were excessive? Any retentions? Y N When? Summary of the history of report card grades: Identify strong and weak subjects from report cards: Describe any negative conduct ratings and comments from report cards:
Test Data	Summarize results from standardized and state accountability testing within the past 3 years: Has there been a psychological evaluation? Y N If yes, when given? Describe overall results:

Intervention Decision Guide:
Multidisciplinary Team Worksheet (p. 4 of 5) _____

Stage 3: Intervention Design

Date: _____   Members present: _____

_____

_____

1. Develop hypotheses: What is the function of the problem behavior? What seems to be maintaining or
    reinforcing the student's misbehavior?

❑ Ability	❑ Awareness	❑ Adult attention	❑ Peer attention
❑ Power or control	❑ Escape or avoidance (task difficulty or discomfort)	❑ Competing reinforcers	❑ Other _____ _____

2. Brainstorm possible interventions:

3. Design and describe a comprehensive intervention plan, including who will do what and when:

4. Select and describe at least two methods for evaluating the intervention plan during the first 2 weeks, including
    who will collect data and how:

5. Select a follow-up meeting date and time to discuss the intervention plan after 2 weeks:

6. Outcomes and recommendations (including the follow-up meeting) have been shared with:

    Classroom teacher? Y N   Date: _____   By whom: _____

    Parent/Student? Y N   Date: _____   By whom: _____

 This form can be printed from the Module F CD.

Figure 6d (continued)

Intervention Decision Guide:
Multidisciplinary Team Worksheet (p. 5 of 5) _____

Stage 4: Follow-Up Meeting

Date: _____   Members present: _____

_____

Data Collection

1. After 2 weeks, report all available data to the team (e.g., frequency counts from the teacher, self-monitoring forms from the student, and results of third-party observations).

2. Summary of the teacher's perception of how well the plan has addressed the target behavior:

Team Actions

1. Team recommendations:
   ❏ Continue implementation as is.
   ❏ Continue plan as is, but adjust actual implementation.
   ❏ Revise plan to address identified weaknesses.
   ❏ Amend the plan to address other target behaviors.
   ❏ Refer to special education.
   ❏ Begin to phase out plan due to successful intervention.
   ❏ Discontinue plan, as universal supports should be enough to maintain success.
   ❏ Other: _____

2. Brief explanation for the team's recommendation and who will be responsible for the follow-up:

3. Outcomes and recommendations (including the follow-up meeting) have been shared with:
   Classroom teacher? Y N   Date: _____   By whom: _____
   Parent/Student? Y N   Date: _____   By whom: _____

Keep Parents Informed

It is essential, both legally and ethically, to keep parents informed throughout the intervention process. Invite parents to be as involved as they want to be and view them as partners from the earliest stages of intervention planning.

Check with your district or central office to determine what type of parent/guardian consent is needed or recommended. Requirements can vary depending on the student's IEP status and whether the IDG:MDT is considered an evaluation for special education eligibility. Some families may be reluctant to participate or to have their child participate because of moral, religious, or other reasons. Ensure that all staff are sensitive to these concerns.

Case manager and teacher complete Stage 1 of the IDG:MDT Worksheet.

STAGE 1: Background from IDG:TI

Even if Stage 1 of the IDG:TI was completed earlier, it is still important that the case manager meet with the teacher (or teachers). This allows the case manager to update the information collected earlier and to start establishing a collaborative relationship with the teacher. We recommend that the Stage 1 meeting take place in the teacher's room when students are not there. Meeting in the teacher's room will increase the teacher's comfort level and allow easy access to records and work samples. This meeting will likely last 20 to 30 minutes.

> Items in bold correspond to steps and tasks on the IDG:MDT Worksheet (Form F-28).

The case manager should ask the teacher to collect data and have it available at the Stage 1 meeting. Student self-monitoring forms, frequency charts or tables, observations by other staff members, scatterplot data, anecdotal notes, and the like can be very useful to identify meaningful trends in the student's behavior.

The case manager should anticipate some venting from the teacher—this is natural and typical—and allow the teacher to vent and get those strong emotions out. Then the case manager should begin to move toward a discussion about how to help the student and teacher be more successful. The case manager should sit beside rather than across from the teacher, maintain eye contact, use a quiet, calm voice, nod her head to indicate agreement and support, and talk less and listen more. She should write minimal notes during the meeting and ensure that the teacher can see what she is writing.

First, the case manager should introduce the process by stating the goal: "Today we are meeting so we can support the student's behavioral needs by evaluating the information and data already collected and by working together to develop a comprehensive intervention plan." The teacher should receive a blank copy of the IDG:MDT Worksheet so that he can see what will be used to guide and document the process. The case manager should also describe:

- How the IDG:MDT process works

- The emphasis on collaboration between the teacher and the multidisciplinary team

- The importance of creating an intervention plan that the teacher selects and develops with guidance and help from the multidisciplinary team

- How the shared information will be considered confidential, including the IDG:MDT Worksheet

- The role of the parents during the IDG:MDT process (Have the parents been involved? When were they last contacted? How did the conversations with parents go?)

- How other staff members may be asked to assist

- Approximate timelines for completing the four stages of the IDG:MDT process

If an IDG:TI Worksheet (Form F-27) was completed earlier, be sure to have a copy available as you complete Stage 1 of the IDG:MDT Worksheet.

The IDG:MDT Worksheet provides a series of steps to follow so you can be focused and effective in the development and delivery of a comprehensive intervention plan to help the student and teacher.

1. **Reason for referral and description of the problem.**

   The case manager should review the teacher's reasons for referring the student and ask about the teacher's concerns, impressions, and frustrations. To understand what the teacher is saying and feeling, the case manager needs to talk less and listen more. This is likely to help the teacher believe that the case manager is interested in the teacher's perspective and feelings. Once the teacher's previous and current concerns are confirmed, the teacher needs to identify which behaviors are of the greatest concern at the current time.

Code Red: Are plans in place or needed? The case manager should determine if any emergency plans have been or need to be implemented to respond to dangerous behaviors by the student. If such plans were put in place, the case manager should have the teacher describe what was done and the outcomes. If emergency plans are needed, the case manager should immediately implement the district's protocol for such situations or employ the steps outlined in "Intervention G: Managing Physically Dangerous Behavior and Threats of Targeted Violence" or "Intervention H: Managing Severely Disruptive Behavior" from *Interventions: Evidence-Based Behavioral Strategies for Individual Students* (2nd ed.; Sprick & Garrison, 2008).

2. **What goals (target behaviors to reduce and replacement behaviors to promote) have been previously established? Are they still the teacher's main priority?**

   If the teacher needs to modify a goal, the case manager guides her in identifying a positive goal that states what is expected of the student (instead of what she doesn't want the student to do). For example, "Learning to be respectful" is perceived better by a student than "Learning to not talk back at the teacher." The goal should be stated in clear, observable terms. "Increase respect in the classroom" is not as strong or as specific as "Respond to teacher instructions in a respectful tone of voice or with no verbal reply." Effective goal statements include four parts:

   - Student
   - Target behavior
   - Time frame
   - Improvement metric

   Here are some sample goal statements:

   - Within 4 weeks, the student will complete at least 80% of her classwork.

   - The student will reduce the number of disruptive acts by 50% within 2 weeks and by 80% within 2 months.

   - The student will learn to stay calm and manage his anger without screaming, hitting, or engaging in aggressive acts. The number of disruptive incidents for the month (or week) will be less than for the previous month (or week).

3. **What data have been collected on this goal?**

   The case manager should ask the teacher about any objective data that have already been collected on the student's behavior, such as frequency counts, self-monitoring forms, duration data, latency data, quality ratings, and audio and video records.

4. **Describe any academic or behavioral interventions implemented within the past 6 months.**

The case manager should ask the teacher to describe the goals (target behaviors and replacement behaviors), intervention plans, when they were implemented and for how long, what data were collected to evaluate the plans, and what the outcomes were in terms of effectiveness and fidelity of implementation. Assuming that the intervention plans were not effective, the case manager can explicitly point out that some behavior problems require multiple plans and extra supports to be resolved, which will remove blame from the teacher. The case manager should obtain copies of any written plans or forms completed as part of these previous interventions.

5. **What was the previous hypothesis regarding the function of the student's target behaviors? Did interventions confirm or contradict that hypothesis?**

This hypothesis was generated either during the 25-Minute Planning Process or with the interventionist during the IDG:TI process. The hypothesis will likely fall into one of the following categories: ability, awareness, adult attention, peer attention, power or control, escape or avoidance (task difficulty or discomfort), competing reinforcers, or other. For detailed information about each function, see Task 2 of this presentation and Presentation 4, Task 6. The case manager and teacher should determine whether the previous interventions confirmed or contradicted the hypothesis.

It is also important to identify any variables that the teacher believes made it difficult for her to fully implement the previous interventions. For example, perhaps the consequences provided the student with too much attention, which reinforced the misbehavior. Identifying any key variables that affected the fidelity of the previous interventions will enable the case manager and teacher to ensure that similar variables are accounted for in future interventions.

6. **How has the teacher corrected the student's misbehavior? Has this been effective?**

The case manager should ask questions such as:

- What consequences were used (for example, verbal reprimand, time owed, timeout, points lost) and for what misbehavior?

- Was planned ignoring used for any misbehaviors? If yes, was it implemented consistently? What were the outcomes?

- How consistent was the teacher in delivering a consequence every time?

- How did the student respond to the consequences? Did she try to argue with the teacher and create power struggles? If so, what happened then?

- How effective were these consequences? Were any consequences more effective than others?

- Was there a time or day of the week when consequences seemed more effective? When or where were consequences less effective (for example, certain classrooms, the playground, hallways, and so on)?

- How often did the teacher refer the student to the office and for what behavior?

7. **Describe any proactive strategies used by the teacher. Have they been effective?**

The case manager should ask questions such as:

- Which positive strategies were used? Examples include noncontingent attention, positive feedback, intermittent celebrations (including tangible rewards, celebrations, and Meaningful Work), boosting the ratio of positive interactions to at least 3:1, and providing an incentive plan.

- Which positive strategies were most effective? Why did the teacher believe they were effective?

- What behaviors earned intermittent celebrations and incentives?

- How often did the student earn incentives? Which incentives appeared to be more powerful and effective with this student?

- Which positive strategies and incentives were not effective?

- Were any positive strategies or incentives delivered by the parents? If yes, what were they? How consistent were the parents? How effective were the home incentives?

8. **Should the existing goal be maintained?**

By the end of the Stage 1 meeting, the case manager and teacher will be in a good position to determine whether the existing goal (target behavior) should be maintained. If not, they should identify a new goal. The teacher should actively participate in selecting the goal and feel comfortable with it. The case manager and teacher should also decide if additional data need to be collected and how that might be done before proceeding to Stage 2.

All of the Stage 1 information should be recorded on the IDG:MDT Worksheet. Prepare copies for each team member for distribution at the Stage 2 meeting.

Note: Most schools have a multidisciplinary team process in place, so we do not provide a lot of detail about Stages 2, 3, and 4 in the following pages. For more detailed information on using the IDG:MDT Worksheet, see the book *Behavioral Response to Intervention: Creating a Continuum of Problem-Solving and Support* (Sprick, Booher, & Garrison, 2009).

Team meets to complete IDG:MDT Worksheet Stage 2: Collect Other Essential Information.

For Stage 2, the objectives are to collect additional data by conducting observations and interviews as well as by reviewing the student's school records. Begin the meeting by having the case manager and teacher summarize the collected information and data reported on the Stage 1 section of the IDG:MDT Worksheet.

Direct Observation. The team and teacher decide what direct observations are needed. Ask all observers to summarize their observations on one page or in a chart or table so that the data can be shared with the team at the Stage 3 meeting.

School Staff to Interview. Identify other staff members who interact with the student regularly or who knew the student in previous years. It can be especially helpful to talk with people who have or had positive relationships with the student or for whom the student behaves appropriately. This might be a school-based counselor or a social worker, for example. Determine who will conduct the interviews, when, and specific questions to ask.

Student Interview. Interviewing the student can yield important insights.

Parent/Guardian Interview. Ensure that information from this interview is kept confidential and shared only with staff members who have a legitimate reason to know.

For all interviews, ask each interviewer to summarize the information and share the essential highlights with the team at the Stage 3 meeting.

Pertinent Information From School Records Review. Page 3 of the IDG:MDT Worksheet serves as a one-page summary for recording relevant information from the student's records. The records review should probably be conducted by the case manager and the teacher. Ensure that this information is kept confidential. Only staff members with a legitimate reason should have access to the records review summary.

Team meets to complete IDG:MDT Worksheet Stage 3: Intervention Design.

Two or three days before the Stage 3 team meeting, share the first three pages of the IDG:MDT Worksheet with team members and ask them to review the information. Also remind team members that the information is confidential and that they should securely store the paper copies or electronic file. Spend the first 10 to 15 minutes of the meeting reviewing this information.

The main goal in Stage 3 is to design an in-depth intervention plan. It's important for the student's teacher to attend this meeting and actively participate in the development of the intervention. Team members confirm the goal, develop hypotheses about the function of the misbehavior for the student, and brainstorm consequences for the misbehavior as well as positive strategies to motivate the student to change his behavior. Also identify strategies the teacher might use when working with the student—for example, delivering precorrections and cues, boosting the ratios of positive interactions with the student, and assigning smaller chunks of academic work combined with helping the student with a few of the initial questions or problems.

The team and teacher then use those brainstormed ideas to design an intervention plan. The range of ideas might include early-stage interventions to highly structured interventions as well as ideas from the *Teacher's Encyclopedia of Behavior Management* (2nd ed.; Sprick, 2012) and *The Tough Kid Tool Box* (Jenson, Rhode, & Reavis, 2009). A top consideration is the amount of time and effort required of the teacher to implement the plan. Strategies that are too difficult to implement are unlikely to be successful.

Be sure to include specific strategies for the classroom and the school. Teams often identify actions that will occur outside of school, such as parent contact, agency contact, and referral to a physician. Those strategies can be very appropriate, but they should not be the only focus of the intervention plan. A significant portion of the plan should detail actions to take with that student in the classroom and in the school.

Document the logistical details of the plan, such as:

- Who will discuss the plan with the student? When?

- What parts of the plan will be discussed with the student?

- How much input should the student have?

- Who will teach, review, model, and role-play with the student the specific replacement behaviors needed to address the target behaviors?

- Who will assist the teacher in creating needed forms and materials?

- Who will assist the teacher in learning specific behavioral strategies, such as how to deliver fluent verbal redirects and how and when to use precorrections and cues?

- What is the start date for the plan? (The start date should be within the next 5 school days, preferably a Monday or Tuesday to ensure 4 or 5 sequential days of implementation.)

- Who will notify other staff members about the intervention plan, if appropriate, and determine whether they will participate in the plan in their settings?

- Will substitute teachers be expected to follow the plan? If so, how will they receive training?

- Who will inform the principal, assistant principals, counselors, and social workers?

- How and when will the plan be shared with parents (if they were not present at the meeting)?

- Should the student's class be told about the plan? How are students expected to behave in response to certain behaviors? (Inform the class when the target student is not in the classroom.)

Identify at least two different data collection methods you can use to evaluate the effectiveness of the intervention during the first 2 weeks, as well as who will collect the data. Then schedule a follow-up meeting 2 weeks after the start of the intervention plan when the team can review the data and assess and document the effectiveness of the intervention.

Team meets for Stage 4: Follow-Up Meeting.

During the brief Stage 4 meeting, the teacher and team discuss the collected data, how the plan is working, the teacher's impressions, and whether to continue, revise, or fade the plan.

Depending on the outcome, you might schedule additional brief follow-up meetings. Typically, teams meet one or two more times to revisit what has and hasn't been working with the student. In some cases, you might decide that you've gone as far as possible with the multidisciplinary team process and you need to look at other options, such as universal supports available in the school or even a referral to special education.

You can use copies of page 5 of the worksheet to document these additional meetings. Again, the worksheet is designed simply to provide you with a series of steps to follow so you can be focused and effective in the delivery of a comprehensive intervention plan to help the student and teacher.

Task 3 Action Steps & Evidence of Implementation

Action Steps	Evidence of Implementation
1. Foundations Team, with the administrator, other staff trained in intervention design, and appropriate district personnel: Discuss whether the IDG:MDT Worksheet will be useful in your school. (Note: Do this step after the Foundations Team has read Tasks 1 and 2, which summarize other collaborative problem-solving processes that you might incorporate into your school's continuum of behavior support.) 2. If you decide to implement the IDG:MDT: • Establish the order in which early-stage interventions, 25-Minute Planning Process, IDG:TI, and IDG:MDT are used. • Identify personnel who will serve as advocates, interventionists, and case managers. • Identify who will serve on the multidisciplinary team. • Determine criteria for referring a situation to the multidisciplinary team. • Consider creating a flowchart to visualize this process. 3. Share with staff the decision to use IDG:MDT, provide training in when to use it, and explain how to access the services.	Foundations Process: Meeting Minutes, Current Priorities Final procedures should be included in: Foundations Archive: Support Available to Staff, Interventions for Individual Students Staff Handbook: Available Support

Sustainability and District Support

DOCUMENTS*

- End-of-Year Game Plan (F-29)
- Common Area Observation Form (F-30)
- Data Summary Form (F-31)
- Talking Points for Implementation of Foundations and CHAMPS During and After Year 1 (F-32b)
- District-Based Foundations Team: Decisions and Tasks to Consider (F-33)
- CHAMPS and DSC Implementation Rubric (F-34)
- Classroom Management STOIC Checklist (F-35)

* All documents listed are available on the CD. Other documents not shown are available on the CD (see Appendix C for a complete list).

INTRODUCTION

This presentation is about supporting and sustaining your effective behavior support practices at the school and district levels. When your team has guided and unified the staff in the implementation of a vibrant mix of behavior support procedures, it would be unfortunate, even heartbreaking, if those procedures deteriorated so that 3 years from now your inviting climate has turned cold, some of your positive staff have fallen into negativity, or your consistency across staff has devolved into inconsistency.

In previous presentations we emphasized the importance of archiving all your work, both in-process and finalized: policies, procedures, lesson plans, job descriptions, data summaries, and so on. The main reason for documenting your in-process work is to preserve momentum, and archiving your final policies allows quick reference for continual renewal.

Documenting in-process work preserves momentum

Imagine this scenario: Your data show significantly more behavior incidents during the last 4 weeks of the school year than during other periods. (Note that problems during the last 4 weeks of school are sometimes masked when those 4 weeks occur in the last half of May and the first half of June because data are usually broken down by calendar month.) Your Foundations Team meets every other week in the spring, and you're trying to develop a proposal to adopt several procedures for inspiring and motivating students during those last 4 weeks. One of the meetings has to be canceled because several team members have obligations related to end-of-year testing.

By the time the next scheduled meeting occurs, 4 weeks have passed since the team last discussed the proposal. If the team has kept detailed meeting minutes and records of the data and information related to the proposal, you can probably pick up right where you left off. But if the team *doesn't* have detailed files of in-process work, you're likely to spend half or even three-fourths of your valuable meeting time trying to remember goals, what's been done so far, and what still needs to be done.

Archiving final policies and procedures allows quick reference for continual renewal.

Archiving your final policies, lesson plans, job descriptions, programs, and so on is important for two major reasons. First, it preserves and protects your cultural history from one year to the next across changes in staff. And second, it saves time.

Imagine this scenario: Behavior during end-of-day dismissal has become problematic during the middle of this school year. The Foundations Team reviews the archived information about dismissal procedures and decides to take a few extra measures to instill those procedures into the school culture. You redistribute to staff the 1-page summary of staff expectations for dismissal, and during the next staff meeting you briefly remind staff about supervisory expectations. You also modify the existing student lesson on dismissal, which was taught to sixth graders, by having an eighth-grade class turn it into a video lesson. You show the video to the entire student body during an assembly, and afterwards the principal issues a 1-minute reminder about safe behavior.

Because the summary of staff expectations and the student lesson on dismissal were archived and readily available, the plan for improving dismissal behavior was relatively easy and efficient to implement. But imagine if you had to re-create the student lesson plan and the guidance for staff about how to supervise—that would take many hours of the team's time.

So documenting and archiving the team's work are important tools for supporting and sustaining continuous improvement, but they are not the only tools we suggest. In Tasks 1 and 2, we discuss several other tools and processes that the Foundations Team can use at the building level to create long-term stability of the improvement process and ensure the smooth operation of your tiered systems of behavior support. In Tasks 3 and 4, we suggest some important processes to enhance district support and sustainability.

Why is district-level support and sustainability important?

Individual schools can do amazing and transformative work by implementing *Foundations* practices—that is, tiered systems of support for behavior. There's even more power to the work when the entire district is committed to infusing these approaches into school culture. *Safe & Civil Schools* trainers have had the privilege of working on implementations of *Foundations*, the classroom management approaches presented in *CHAMPS* and *Discipline in the Secondary Classroom* (DSC), and other interventions for individual students with large and small districts as well as urban and rural districts. When the superintendent conveys through words and actions that the social, emotional, and behavioral needs of students must be met and that this work contributes to the goal of academic excellence, and when central-office administrators are aligned with the superintendent's beliefs, the school principals become committed to improving behavior as part of their efforts to improve academics. The principals' attitude filters down to the teachers. When the teachers' association is involved and advocates for a continuum of behavioral support, great synergy and energy are created throughout the entire district about this work.

We refer to CHAMPS and DSC often throughout this presentation. We mean the classroom management approaches presented in the books *CHAMPS: A Proactive & Positive Approach to Classroom Management,* 2nd ed. (Sprick, 2009) and *Discipline in the Secondary Classroom,* 3rd ed. (DSC; Sprick, 2013) and the corresponding trainings offered by *Safe & Civil Schools.* CHAMPS is for grades K–8, and DSC is for grades 9–12.

When all schools in a district adopt a common approach and attitude toward helping students with behavior, it creates a sense of identity and pride throughout the district. Staff develop a common language that facilitates problem solving. Student misbehavior becomes not a threat, but a puzzle to be solved with the help and support of others who understand and speak the same language.

An example of a district that exemplifies top-down support for the *Foundations* approach is Wichita, Kansas. Our involvement with Wichita, a large urban district, began when the school board examined district data and realized they needed to make some major changes. They learned about the concept of Multi-Tiered Systems of Support (MTSS) and decided this was the approach they needed to improve both behavior—climate, safety, and discipline—and academics. With guidance from the state and others, they hired a new superintendent, John Allison, and charged him with the task of helping the district implement MTSS.

The school board, with John Allison, Denise Seguine, Neil Guthrie, and several other wonderful central-office administrators, constructed an improvement plan. *Safe & Civil Schools* was asked to oversee the behavior portion of that plan. During the first 2 years, half of the district's schools were trained in *Foundations* and behavior support, and half were trained in academic support. All of the schools received training in our classroom management models, CHAMPS (grades K–8) and DSC (grades 9–12). During the third and fourth years of the plan, the training was reversed. Schools that had been working mainly on academics began working mainly on behavior, and schools that had been working mainly on behavior began working on academics. All schools worked—and continue to work—on integrating behavior and academics. The result is that Wichita has become a district of problem solvers who speak a common language and have common goals. Schools are making a difference for students throughout the district.

We have had the privilege of working with other districts that achieve the level of support exemplified by Wichita, and it is always an awesome experience to witness the amount of positive change that can happen and the degree to which common language becomes part of the process. In many of these districts, all of the schools' faculty rooms feature STOIC posters to remind staff of the STOIC acronym and approach to behavior management. Most schools display CHAMPS posters throughout the building, and CHAMPS forms a common language among students.

So districts really need to actively foster continuous improvement and generational progress, creating and enhancing a cultural heritage at each individual school. Tasks 3 and 4 will be useful to district personnel and building-based administrators who have an interest in sustainability at the district level—that is, ensuring that all schools in the district, regardless of changes in building personnel, maintain a safe, consistent, and positive setting for all students.

All four of the tasks in this presentation include documents designed to help you carry them out. We encourage you to reproduce the applicable documents from the Module F CD and have them in front of you as you read or view each task.

Task 1: Develop Building-Based Sustainability, Part 1: Foundations Implementation Rubric and Checklists explains two tools that you can use to enhance sustainability by regularly evaluating the degree to which your school is implementing each *Foundations* module.

Task 2: Develop Building-Based Sustainability, Part 2: End-of-Year Game Plan describes a plan for collecting and analyzing data about your school's performance, addressing critical needs and decisions for the next school year, evaluating how the Foundations Team is functioning, and prioritizing your plans for next year's kickoff.

Task 3: Build District Support and Sustainability, Part 1 discusses two major actions districts should consider: establishing a district-based Foundations Team and developing talking points about *Foundations* to facilitate walk-through visits to school campuses

Task 4: Build District Support and Sustainability, Part 2 offers ideas for how the district can guide and lead school-based Foundations Teams in activities and orientations to enhance sustainability.

TASK 1

Develop building-based sustainability, part 1: Foundations Implementation Rubric and Checklists

This is the first of two tasks about building-based sustainability. In this task, we explain two tools you can use to enhance sustainability: the Foundations Implementation Rubric and the Foundations Implementation Checklist.

Complete the Foundations Implementation Rubric.

The rubric is a way for the Foundations Team to self-reflect on each major component of each *Foundations* module and rate the degree to which the school is actually implementing that component. We suggest that teams use it once or perhaps twice per year.

Each column on the rubric—Preparing, Getting Started, Moving Along, and In Place—represents a different implementation status (see Figure 7a). The text in each row describes what each status looks like for a particular *Foundations* presentation. For each presentation, the team should read the four descriptions from left to right and think about whether the statements are true for your school. If so, check the box. Each description assumes that the activities preceding it in the row have been attained, so stop working through the row when you reach a description that you cannot check off because you haven't implemented those tasks.

Thanks

We thank Carolyn Novelly, Kathleen Bowles, and their colleagues at Duval County Public Schools in Jacksonville, Florida, who have done a masterful job of implementing *Foundations* and CHAMPS for over 10 years as of this writing. They were the first to develop the concept of the rubric to help teams assess their level of implementation. Pete Davis of Long Beach, California, also contributed to this work by developing innovation configuration scales, which are similar in concept to a rubric but are more of a guide to reflective practice than an evaluation tool.

Based on their work and the work of several other districts, and with their permission, we developed a Foundations Implementation Rubric for each module in this third edition of the *Foundations*. We show the rubric for Modules A and B and the Foundations Rubric Summary in Figure 7a. The complete rubric (Form F-01) appears in Appendix A and on the Module F CD.

Figure 7a *Foundations Implementation Rubric and Summary, Modules A and B (pp. 1–2; F-01)*

School Name _____ Date _____

Foundations Implementation Rubric and Summary (p. 1 of 8)   *Module A*

Directions: In each row, check off each description that is true for your *Foundations* implementation. Then summarize your assessment on the Rubric Summary form. For Module B, evaluate each common area and schoolwide policy separately, and use the rows labeled Other for common areas and schoolwide policies that do not appear on the rubric by default. *Note:* Each block assumes that the activities in previous blocks in the row have been attained.

Presentation	Preparing (1)	Getting Started (2)	Moving Along (3)	In Place (4)
A1 Foundations: A Multi-Tiered System of Behavior Support	Staff are aware of the *Foundations* approach and basic beliefs, including that *Foundations* is a process for guiding the entire staff in the construction and implementation of a comprehensive approach to behavior support.	*Foundations* multi-tiered system of support (MTSS) processes are coordinated with academic MTSS (RTI) processes, and team organization has been determined (e.g., one MTSS Team with a behavior task force and an academic task force).	Staff have been introduced to the STOIC acronym and understand that student behavior and motivation can be continuously improved by manipulating the STOIC variables: Structure, Teach, Observe, Interact positively, and Correct fluently.	A preliminary plan has been developed for using the *Foundations* modules. For a school just beginning the process, the plan includes working through all the modules sequentially. For a school that has implemented aspects of positive behavior support, the team has self-assessed strengths, weaknesses, and needs using this rubric. **Evidence:** Foundations Implementation Rubric
A2 Team Processes	Foundations Team members have been identified. They directly represent specific faculty and staff groups, and they have assigned roles and responsibilities.	Foundations Team attends trainings, meets at school, and has established and maintains a Foundations Process Notebook and Foundations Archive.	Foundations Team members present regularly to faculty and communicate with the entire staff. They draft proposals and engage staff in the decision-making process regarding school climate, behavior, and discipline.	Foundations Team is known by all staff and is highly involved in all aspects of climate, safety, behavior, motivation, and student connectedness. **Evidence:** Staff members represented by Foundations Team members and presentations to staff are documented in the Foundations Process Notebook.
A3 The Improvement Cycle	Foundations Team is aware of the Improvement Cycle and keeps staff informed of team activities.	Foundations Team involves staff in setting priorities and in implementing improvements.	Foundations Team involves staff in using multiple data sources to establish a hierarchical list of priorities and adopt new policies. Team members seek input from staff regarding their satisfaction with the efficacy of recently adopted policies and procedures.	All staff actively participate in all aspects of the Improvement Cycle, such as setting priorities, developing revisions, adopting new policies and procedures, and implementation. Foundation Team presents to staff at least monthly. **Evidence:** Memos to staff and PowerPoint presentation files are documented in the Foundations Process Notebook.
A4 Data-Driven Processes	Administrators and Foundations Team review discipline data and establish baselines.	Common area observations and student, staff, and parent climate surveys are conducted yearly.	Discipline, climate survey, and common area observation data are reviewed and analyzed regularly.	Based on the data, school policies, procedures, and guidelines are reviewed and modified as needed (maintaining the Improvement Cycle).
A5 Developing Staff Engagement and Unity	Foundations Team regularly communicates with staff through staff meetings, scheduled professional development, memos, and so on.	Foundations Team members understand that they play a key role in staff unity. They periodically assess whether any factions of staff are disengaged and how they can develop greater staff engagement in the *Foundations* process.	A building-based administrator attends most *Foundations* trainings and plays an active role in team meetings and in assisting the team in unifying staff.	For districts with more than five or six schools, a district-based team meets at least once per quarter to keep the *Foundations* continuous improvement processes active in all schools. **Evidence:** Meeting minutes and staff presentations are documented in the Foundations Process Notebook.

If

School Name _____ Date _____

Foundations Implementation Rubric and Summary (p. 2 of 8)   *Module B*

Common Area	Preparing (1)	Getting Started (2)	Moving Along (3)	In Place (4)
Hallways	Common area observations are conducted and data from multiple sources are collected and analyzed.	Current structures and procedures have been evaluated and protected, modified, or eliminated.	Lesson plans have been developed, taught, practiced, and re-taught, when necessary.	Common area supervisory procedures are communicated to staff and monitored for implementation **Evidence:** Policies, procedures, and lessons are documented in the Foundations Archive and, as appropriate, in the Staff Handbook.
Restrooms	Common area observations are conducted and data from multiple sources are collected and analyzed.	Current structures and procedures have been evaluated and protected, modified, or eliminated.	Lesson plans have been developed, taught, practiced, and re-taught, when necessary.	Common area supervisory procedures are communicated to staff and monitored for implementation **Evidence:** Policies, procedures, and lessons are documented in the Foundations Archive and, as appropriate, in the Staff Handbook.
Cafeteria	Common area observations are conducted and data from multiple sources are collected and analyzed.	Current structures and procedures have been evaluated and protected, modified, or eliminated.	Lesson plans have been developed, taught, practiced, and re-taught, when necessary.	Common area supervisory procedures are communicated to staff and monitored for implementation **Evidence:** Policies, procedures, and lessons are documented in the Foundations Archive and, as appropriate, in the Staff Handbook.
Playground, Courtyard, or Commons	Common area observations are conducted and data from multiple sources are collected and analyzed.	Current structures and procedures have been evaluated and protected, modified, or eliminated.	Lesson plans have been developed, taught, practiced, and re-taught, when necessary.	Common area supervisory procedures are communicated to staff and monitored for implementation **Evidence:** Policies, procedures, and lessons are documented in the Foundations Archive and, as appropriate, in the Staff Handbook.
Arrival	Common area observations are conducted and data from multiple sources are collected and analyzed.	Current structures and procedures have been evaluated and protected, modified, or eliminated.	Lesson plans have been developed, taught, practiced, and re-taught, when necessary.	Common area supervisory procedures are communicated to staff and monitored for implementation **Evidence:** Policies, procedures, and lessons are documented in the Foundations Archive and, as appropriate, in the Staff Handbook.
Dismissal	Common area observations are conducted and data from multiple sources are collected and analyzed.	Current structures and procedures have been evaluated and protected, modified, or eliminated.	Lesson plans have been developed, taught, practiced, and re-taught, when necessary.	Common area supervisory procedures are communicated to staff and monitored for implementation **Evidence:** Policies, procedures, and lessons are documented in the Foundations Archive and, as appropriate, in the Staff Handbook.
Other: _____	Common area observations are conducted and data from multiple sources are collected and analyzed.	Current structures and procedures have been evaluated and protected, modified, or eliminated.	Lesson plans have been developed, taught, practiced, and re-taught, when necessary.	Common area supervisory procedures are communicated to staff and monitored for implementation **Evidence:** Policies, procedures, and lessons are documented in the Foundations Archive and, as appropriate, in the Staff Handbook.
Other: _____	Common area observations are conducted and data from multiple sources are collected and analyzed.	Current structures and procedures have been evaluated and protected, modified, or eliminated.	Lesson plans have been developed, taught, practiced, and re-taught, when necessary.	Common area supervisory procedures are communicated to staff and monitored for implementation **Evidence:** Policies, procedures, and lessons are documented in the Foundations Archive and, as appropriate, in the Staff Handbook.

If any items are rated as less than In Place or if it has been more than 3 years since you have done so, work through the Module B Implementation Checklist.

Date _____

Foundations Implementation Rubric and Summary (p. 8 of 8)

	Preparing (1)	Getting Started (2)	Moving Along (3)	In Place (4)
Module A Presentations				
A1. Foundations: A Multi-Tiered System of Behavior Support	X	X	X	X
A2. Team Processes	X	X	X	X
A3. The Improvement Cycle	X	X	X	X
A4. Data-Driven Processes	X	X	X	X
A5. Developing Staff Engagement and Unity	X	X		
Module B Presentations				
Hallways	X	X	X	X
Restrooms				
Cafeteria	X	X	X	X
Playground, Courtyard, or Commons				
Arrival				
Dismissal				
Dress Code				
Other:				
Other:				
Other:				
Other:				
Module C Presentations				
C2. Guidelines for Success	X	X	X	
C3. Ratios of Positive Interactions	X	X		
C4. Improving Attendance	X	X	X	
C5 & C6. School Connectedness and Programs and Strategies for Meeting Needs	X	X		
C7. Welcoming New Staff, Students, and Families	X	X	X	X
Module D Presentations				
D1. Proactive Procedures, Corrective Procedures, and Individual Interventions				
D2. Developing Three Levels of Misbehavior				
D3. Staff Responsibilities for Responding to Misbehavior				
D4. Administrator Responsibilities for Responding to Misbehavior				
D5. Preventing the Misbehavior That Leads to Referrals and Suspensions				
Module E Presentations				
E1. Ensuring a Safe Environment for Students				
E2. Attributes of Safe and Unsafe Schools				
E3. Teaching Conflict Resolution				
E4. Analyzing Bullying Behaviors, Policies, and School Needs				
E5. Schoolwide Bullying Prevention and Intervention				
Module F Presentations				
F2. Supporting Classroom Behavior: The Three-Legged Stool				
F3. Articulating Staff Beliefs and Solidifying Universal Procedures				
F4. Early-Stage Interventions for General Education Classrooms				
F5. Matching the Intensity of Your Resources to the Intensity of Your Needs				
F6. Problem-Solving Processes and Intervention Design				
F7. Sustainability and District Support				

 This form can be printed from the Module F CD.

After the Foundations Team works through every row, summarize the assessment on the Summary page (p. 8 of the form; see Figure 7a). If any items are rated as less than In Place, or if it has been more than 3 years since you last did so, work through the Implementation Checklist for that module. Of course, if you know that you need to begin work on a module or presentation, you can go directly to the corresponding content.

The Module B section of the rubric is a little different. We ask you to evaluate (separately) the common areas and schoolwide policies that you have implemented—that is, you've structured them for success and taught students the behavioral expectations. You can use the rows labeled Other for any common areas and schoolwide policies that do not appear on the rubric by default.

Figure 7a shows a summary form completed by an imaginary school in the spring of their second year of *Foundations* implementation. The Foundations Team has highlighted the boxes with checkmarks to create a horizontal bar graph, giving the evaluation an effective visual component. The school has done a great job on most of Module A, the common areas they've prioritized so far (hallways and cafeteria), and Welcoming New Staff, Students, and Families (C7). They need to work a bit more on staff engagement and unity (A5) and most of Module C, which they began in Year 2. Modules D, E, and F are blank because the school will work on them in future years.

Notice that the descriptions in the In Place column include a section about evidence, which suggests where to find objective evidence that the work described is truly in place. In earlier versions of the rubric, we didn't ask about evidence. The issue of evidence brings up a potential drawback to this self-reflective process. We've found that teams that study and work at implementing the *Foundations* process at a deep level tend to be hard on themselves when completing the rubric because they realize the detail and depth that is possible. Other teams that are doing an adequate job on *Foundations*, but not thinking through all the components as deeply as they might, tend to be less critical of themselves and check components on the rubric a bit carelessly.

So the evidence section serves to remind all types of teams—deep thinking and not-so-deep thinking—that when you have objective documentation that the described work is in place, you can check the In Place column in good conscience. If no documentation exists, think about whether the work has really been thoroughly completed.

When and how should you use the rubric? If you're just beginning *Foundations*, you might use the rubric toward the end of your first year of implementation. In Task 2, we suggest working through the rubric as one of several actions to consider as part of your end-of-year game plan.

After the first year, we recommend completing the rubric every spring. Consider also completing it in mid to late fall because it can guide your decisions about the work you want to do as well as the successes you can celebrate midyear.

For any items on the rubric that are not implemented—you have not yet started the content or it was so long ago that you need to start over—go directly to the corresponding module of *Foundations*. When implementation is low in a number of areas (all or parts of several modules), review data—survey results, observations of common areas, and incident reports—to prioritize potential improvements. If you are still not certain about what to implement first, consider beginning with Module A and working in order toward Module F. If you rate low on just a single item on the rubric, we suggest you go to the second tool we describe, the Foundations Implementation Checklist. While the rubric is a relatively quick snapshot of implementation, the checklist provides more details about what full implementation looks like. The checklist helps you identify what you have in place and where you might have gaps in either development or implementation.

Complete the Foundations Implementation Checklists.

The Foundations Implementation Checklists are essentially detailed versions of the rubric. They allow you to assess your progress in implementing the processes and objectives of each module. Like the rubric, each checklist suggests where to find evidence of implementation and effectiveness, which allows your team to hold itself accountable. Appendix B and the CD for each module include the checklist for that module, and all of the Foundations Implementation Checklists are included on the Module F CD.

The Foundations Implementation Rubric for Module A, Presentation 2 ("Team Processes"), for example, includes four brief assessment items. The Implementation Checklist (see Figure 7b) breaks down this topic into the following items:

1. The Foundations Team has been established by modifying an existing team or forming a new team. (Evidence in Foundations Process Notebook: Team Composition)

   - Team composition includes an administrator, classroom teachers, and others. (Evidence in Foundations Process Notebook: Team Composition)

   - The team formally represents the entire staff. Each team member knows the staff members he or she represents, and staff members know who represents them on the team. (Evidence in Foundations Process Notebook: Team Composition)

2. The team meets regularly for a minimum of 4 hours per quarter. (Evidence in Foundations Process Notebook: Meeting Minutes)

3. Team members have assigned roles. (Evidence in Foundations Process Notebook: Team Composition)

Module A Implementation Checklist (p. 1 of 29)

Implementation Actions	Completed Y/N	Evidence of Implementation	Evidence Y/N
Presentation 1: Foundations—A Multi-Tiered System of Behavior Support	✓		✓
1. Decisions have been made about how to integrate a multi-tiered approach to behavior (*Foundations/*PBIS) with a multi-tiered approach to academic and instructional improvement. You may use one team, two separate teams, or one large team with two separate task forces.	☐	Foundations Process: Team Composition*	☐
2. Information has has been presented to staff about *Foundations*, including, but not limited to, the following basic beliefs: • Punitive and corrective techniques are necessary, but have significant limitations; misbehavior is a teaching opportunity. • In common areas and with schoolwide policies, clear expectations and consistent enforcement are essential. • Staff behavior creates the climate of the school; a positive, welcoming, and inviting climate should be intentionally created and continuously maintained. • All students should have equal access to good instruction and behavior support, regardless of their skills or background. • All student behaviors necessary for success must be overtly and directly articulated and taught to mastery. "If you want it, teach it!" • Everyone (even students who make poor choices) should be treated with respect.	☐	Foundations Archive: Presentations/ Communications With Staff* *These notebooks are discussed in Presentation 2. Documentation of Presentation 1 tasks can be added to the notebooks when record-keeping procedures are established.	☐
Presentation 2: Team Processes			
1. The Foundations Team has been established by modifying an existing team or forming a new team. • Team composition includes an administrator, classroom teachers, and others. • The team formally represents the entire staff. Each team member knows the staff members he or she represents, and staff members know who represents them on the team. <div align="right">*(continued)*</div>	☐	Foundations Process: Team Composition	☐

 This form can be printed from the Module F CD.

Module A Implementation Checklist (p. 2 of 29)

Implementation Actions	Completed Y/N	Evidence of Implementation	Evidence Y/N
Presentation 2 (*continued*)	✓		✓
2. The team meets regularly for a minimum of 4 hours per quarter.	☐	Foundations Process: Meeting Minutes	☐
3. Team members have assigned roles, such as: • Chair or Cochair • Recorder • Data/Evaluation Coordinator • Materials Manager • Keeper of the List • Staff Liaison • Equity and Student Liaison • Family Engagement Coordinator	☐	Foundations Process: Team Composition	☐
4. The team creates processes for orienting new team members.	☐	Foundations Archive: New Staff Orientation	☐
5. At least once per month, the team communicates to staff about the *Foundations* implementation by (for example) sharing data, reminding staff about some aspect of implementation, sharing strategies, or celebrating successes.	☐	Foundations Process: Presentations/ Communications With Staff	☐
6. Record-keeping and archiving procedures have been established, including a Foundations Process Notebook, Foundations Archive, Staff Handbook, and Student and Parent Handbook. The Foundations Process Notebook is for working documents and includes at least the following (or similar) sections. • Team Composition • Planning Calendar • Meeting Minutes • Data Summaries • Current Priorities (with record of the data that led to the area or policy becoming a priority) • Safety • Guidelines for Success • Presentations/Communications With Staff • Communications With Parents • 3-Level System for Responding to Misbehavior • Foundations Implementation Rubric and Summary and Implementation Checklists	☐	See the four notebooks (listed for items 1–5 above).	☐

(*continued*)

 This form can be printed from the Module F CD.

4. The team creates processes for orienting new team members. (Evidence in Foundations Archive: New Staff Orientation)

5. At least once per month, the team communicates to staff about the Foundations implementation by (for example) sharing data, reminding staff about some aspect of implementation, sharing strategies, or celebrating successes. (Evidence in Foundations Process Notebook: Presentations/Communications With Staff)

6. Record-keeping and archiving procedures have been established, including a Foundations Process Notebook, Foundations Archive, Staff Handbook, and Student and Parent Handbook. (Evidence is the four notebooks)

7. The team has chosen a team name. (Evidence in Foundations Process Notebook: Team Composition, Meeting Minutes)

8. Team meeting ground rules have been established. (Evidence in Foundations Process Notebook: Meeting Minutes)

9. Annually, team members reflect on their roles as team members, perhaps by using the Are You an Effective Team Builder? self-assessment tool. (Evidence in Foundations Process Notebook: Meeting Minutes)

When and how should you use the checklists? As you near completion of any module, plan to use the implementation checklist for that module to ensure that you have fully implemented all of the recommendations. If you've decided not to follow some recommendations, just indicate on the checklist why your team or staff made the decision. If data show problems later, this record of what you implemented and what you chose not to implement could be helpful in deciding how to address the problem.

In addition to using the checklists as needed, plan to work through all *Foundations* checklists every 3 years or so. An apt analogy for the checklists is the 21-point inspection that a good mechanic performs on your car to catch any potential problems.

By working through the checklists, you can identify strengths to celebrate. Schools are sometimes so focused on identifying needed improvements that they forget to identify their successes, too! Remember to look for accomplishments and improvements in your data, and let staff, students, and parents know about them.

The checklists can also help you catch gaps in your implementation that you may be able to fill before a major problem emerges, much like a mechanic may notice that you need to replace some worn belts before they break and you are stranded on the highway.

If a checklist reveals weak implementation of a module, consider having the entire Foundations Team read or view the module's first presentation, which is always an introduction and preview. Then have groups of two or three team members read or view each of the module's remaining presentations so that each team member is responsible for no more than two presentations. At the next team meeting, discuss actions you might take to revise your policies and procedures or reinvigorate your staff to implement your current policies and procedures. Also discuss and determine the order in which you will tackle multiple priorities. In other words, you don't necessarily need to work through the whole module again step by step. You can just divide up the responsibility to review the material and identify strengths and weaknesses.

By using the Foundations Implementation Rubric at least annually (perhaps twice annually) and using the Foundations Implementation Checklists as you near completion of a module and every 3 years thereafter, you'll keep the *Foundations* energy alive and the process of continuous improvement in place so that your great school gets better and better every single year.

Task 1 Action Steps & Evidence of Implementation

Action Steps	Evidence of Implementation
1. Plan to complete the Foundations Implementation Rubric (Form F-01) at least annually.	Foundations Process: Foundations Implementation Rubric and Summary and Module Implementation Checklists, Planning Calendar
2. For any items on the rubric that are not implemented—you have not yet started the content or you need to start over—work through the corresponding *Foundations* module. If you rate low on just a single item on the rubric, complete the Foundations Implementation Checklist for that module.	Foundations Archive: Long-Term Planning Calendar
3. Plan to complete the Foundations Implementation Checklist as you near completion of any module. Complete all checklists every 3 years.	
4. If a checklist reveals weak implementation of a module, review the module and consider revising policies and procedures or motivating staff to implement current policies and procedures.	

TASK 2

Develop building-based sustainability, part 2: End-of-Year Game Plan

During the summer, some schools lose their momentum for implementing *Foundations*. The team exercise of completing the End-Of-Year Game Plan (Form F-29) in the spring can help maintain the momentum you worked so hard to create and help you prepare for a smooth start to the next school year.

Completing the End-of-Year Game Plan during a team meeting gives you an opportunity to analyze data about your school's performance, address the critical needs for and decisions about the next school year, evaluate how the Foundations Team is functioning, and prioritize your plans for next year's kickoff—that is, activities for teachers when they return to school (before the students report to school).

Seven main activities are covered in Task 2.

- Collect a range of data to evaluate the effectiveness of the *Foundations* program.
- Determine which implemented *Foundations* components are working well and can be celebrated with staff.
- Determine which implemented *Foundations* components need to be tweaked or revised.
- Determine which *Foundations* components (not yet implemented) need to be addressed during the next school year.
- Determine which *Foundations* components (common area policies, supervision skills, hallway or cafeteria signage, lesson plans for teaching expectations to students, essential classroom management skills, and so on) need to be taught or reviewed with the staff before students begin school.
- Decide who will present the new and review content at the start of the school year, how the content will be delivered most effectively, who will organize and copy the handouts, how much presentation time is needed, and so on. You want to maximize the delivery system so staff hear the information from a variety of people, both team and staff members.
- Finalize the appointment of new team members and determine their roles, establish team meeting ground rules, assign constituents for each team member, and develop a tentative meeting schedule.

Having all these items in place before the current school year ends will ensure that you begin the new year more confidently, with less confusion and chaos and with a clear sense of direction.

The End-of-Year Game Plan form (Figure 7c) guides the team through the meeting by suggesting specific data points to analyze and providing discussion topics. We suggest that you print the form (F-29) from the Module F CD and view it as you work through this task.

The first decisions to make concern the date when the team Data/Evaluation Coordinator and administrator will begin assembling data and the date when the Foundations Team will meet to work through the Game Plan form. Plan to hold the meeting about 4 weeks before the end of your school year. If the team has met regularly during the year, you may be able to complete the form in 1 to 2 hours. Some teams may need 2 or 3 hours, spread over two or three meetings. A couple of weeks before the meeting, the team Data/Evaluation Coordinator and the administrator should plan to assemble the data.

Consider how to conduct the meeting. The whole team might view the entire Task 2 video presentation and then reflect on what needs to be done. The team might view or read each major segment of the task, then stop and discuss. Or team members might read or view the task before the meeting so that they arrive at the meeting prepared to work through the form. We recommend that at the end of the first year of implementation, the entire team view the video presentation in order to understand the reasons for planning in the spring. After Year 1, different team members might review different parts of the task before the meeting, then provide a summary for the rest of the team at the beginning of the meeting.

You might also need to schedule an additional meeting if all the data aren't available, if the team decides that more data are needed, or you just aren't able to decide on everything during the initial meeting.

Assemble data for the end-of-year meeting.

Complete the first step prior to the end-of-year Foundations Team meeting,

> Items 1–4 correspond to the first page of the End-of-Year Game Plan.

1. The *Foundations* recommendation is to collect and analyze data every quarter. So for this end-of-year analysis, you'll probably use any available fourth-quarter data along with anything else that allows the team to reflect on the year as a whole. We suggest you use the following data:

   Incident referrals. By incident referral, we mean infractions that resulted in the student being sent to the office. You might use a different term, such as pupil behavior referral (PBR) or office disciplinary referral (ODR). Generate year-to-date reports by total numbers, grade, type of infraction, location, gender, race/ethnicity, and special education status.

Figure 7c *End-of-Year Game Plan (F-29)*

End-of-Year Game Plan (p. 1 of 15)

Select dates to work on the End-of-Year Game Plan.

_____ Date the Data/Evaluation Coordinator and administrator will begin assembling data.

_____ Date of team meeting to celebrate accomplishments and work through the fisrm (about 4 weeks before the end of the year).

Assemble data for the end-of-year meeting

1. Before the meeting, assemble the most recent data on the following:

   Incident referrals (i.e., infractions that resulted in the student being sent to the office): Generate year-to-date reports by total numbers, grade, type of infraction, location, gender, race/ethnicity, and special education status.

   Suspensions (out-of-school and in-school): Generate reports by total numbers, grade, gender, special education status, race/ethnicity, and frequent flyers (individual students with two or more suspensions).

   Detentions: Generate reports by total numbers, type, grade, gender, special education status, race/ethnicity, and frequent flyers (individual students who receive many detentions).

   Staff, student, and parent surveys (TRENDS Climate & Safety Survey reports, for example)
   - Even if you administered surveys in the fall or winter, the information is still useful. If you've addressed some survey items, discuss addressing the items that are next on the list.
   - See Section 1:C of this form for instructions for summarizing the data.

   Common area and schoolwide policy observations (from Foundations Common Area Observation forms, for example): Our general suggestion for observations is to conduct them a couple of times per year—once during the fall and once in midwinter to evaluate the efficacy of revised policies and procedures. If you can, also conduct end-of-year observations on one common area you revised during the year and one you are considering revising next year.

   Other data sources, such as:
   - Average daily attendance and absence rates
   - Tardiness rates
   - Expulsions and referrals to alternative education placements
   - Referrals to special education
   - Number of students referred to special education who did not qualify
   - Instances of vandalism and graffiti
   - Instances of other illegal activities

   - Injury reports (differentiate between playground injuries and other common area injuries)
   - Feedback from staff
   - Student focus groups
   - Social-emotional support (information from school social workers, counselors, and school psychologists)
   - Summary of students identified with red flags
   - Summary of universal screening

2. Complete a Data Summary form for the end-of-year data (the Data Summary form is available on the Module F CD and explained in Module A, Presentation 4, Task 1).

3. Complete a Data Summary form for comparable end-of-year data from the previous year (if you didn't do so last year).

4. Complete a Foundations Implementation Rubric or the Foundations Implementation Checklists for the modules you have implemented.

Steps 2, 3, and 4 can be completed by the team during the meeting.

 This form can be printed from the Module F CD.

Suspensions. Include both out-of-school (OSS) and in-school suspensions (ISS). Generate reports by total numbers, grade, gender, special education status, race/ethnicity, and frequent flyers (individual students with two or more suspensions).

Detentions. Some schools consider the number of detentions assigned as consequences for incident referrals. Generate reports by total numbers, type (lunch, after-school, Saturday school, and so on), grade, gender, special education status, race/ethnicity, and frequent flyers (individual students who receive many detentions).

Staff, student, and parent surveys (TRENDS Climate & Safety Survey reports, for example). Even if you administered surveys in the fall or winter, the information can help you determine whether you've addressed the concerns or perceptions that were judged to be of the highest priority. If you've addressed some survey items, discuss items that are next on the list. We suggest techniques for summarizing the data later in this task.

Common area and schoolwide policy observations (from *Foundations* Common Area Observation forms, for example.) Our general suggestion for observations is to conduct them a couple of times per year—once during the fall and once in midwinter to evaluate the efficacy of revised policies and procedures. If you can, also conduct end-of-year observations on one common area you've revised during the year and one you are considering revising next year.

Other data sources. These might include:

- Average daily attendance and absence rates
- Tardiness rates
- Expulsions and referrals to alternative education placements
- Referrals to special education
- Number of students referred to special education who did not qualify
- Instances of vandalism and graffiti
- Instances of other illegal activities
- Injury reports (differentiate between playground injuries and injuries in other common areas)
- Feedback from staff
- Student focus groups
- Social-emotional support (information from school social workers, counselors, and school psychologists)
- Summary of students identified with red flags
- Summary of universal screening

Items 2–4 below can be completed by the team at the meeting.

2. Complete a Data Summary form for the end-of-year data (the Data Summary form is available on the Module F CD (Form F-31) and explained in Module A, Presentation 4, Task 1).

3. Complete a Data Summary form for comparable end-of-year data from the previous year (if you didn't do so last year).

4. Complete the Foundations Implementation Rubric or the Foundations Implementation Checklists for the modules you have implemented.

Additional documents (available on the Module F CD) that are needed to complete the End-of-Year Game Plan form (F-29) include:

- Common Area Observation form (F-30)
- Data Summary form (F-31)
- Foundations Implementation Rubric (F-01) or Checklists (F-02)

Plan to bring the following items to the meeting:

- Foundations Archive (current policies)
- Foundations Process Notebook
- Staff Handbook (all team members should bring their copies)
- Student and Parent Handbook

Once data are assembled, the team will meet to work through the End-of-Year Game Plan form (F-29). The three main sections of the form are:

SECTION 1: Data

SECTION 2: Critical Team Issues and Decisions

SECTION 3: Plan Your *Foundations* Kickoff for the New School Year

In Section 1, the team will analyze and discuss the reports and Data Summary forms to identify:

- Which common areas and schoolwide policies are working well and should be protected and celebrated?
- Which common areas and schoolwide policies are working adequately, but could be improved or tweaked?
- Which common areas and schoolwide policies are not working and need to be substantially modified or completely redesigned?

Remember that safety issues are always top priorities.

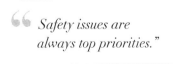

Safety issues are always top priorities."

In Section 2, the team will discuss some critical team issues and decide on team roles and responsibilities for the coming school year. In Section 3, the team will plan the *Foundations* kickoff for the new school year. The kickoff is an event held during the staff workdays before classes begin (typically in August). It is an opportunity to review the *Foundations* concepts with staff, bring them up to date on your accomplishments and goals, and celebrate the school's successes.

Plan to bring the school's Foundations Archive, the Foundations Process Notebook, and the Student and Parent Handbook. All team members should bring their copies of the Staff Handbook. File all the assembled data and the completed End-of-Year Game Plan form in your Foundations Process Notebook.

Complete the End-of-Year Game Plan.

This section corresponds to pp. 2–15 on the End-of-Year Game Plan.

SECTION 1: Data

We suggest that the team set time limits for discussion of each data source, such as 10 minutes for incident referrals, 10 minutes for observations, and so on. If you don't establish a structure for your meeting, you might spend 3 or 4 hours talking about the data and never move on to talking about actions to take to improve the school. Try to be focused and efficient as you share the information with the team and figure out what it means.

Be sure to bring copies of current policies to the meeting (they should be in the Foundations Archive) because you will be surprised by how often a problem pops up in the discussion and a team member says, "Well, doesn't the policy address that?" You should be able to check the policy immediately and proceed with the discussion.

If any staff members who are not on the team conducted observations, they should be invited to the meeting to share their results. They don't need to attend the entire meeting. Although they have probably provided a written summary, personal reports from common area observers are very powerful and worth scheduling.

The Data Summary form (Form F-31 on the Module F CD and explained in Module A, Presentation 4, Task 1) can be a valuable tool for recording notes and consolidating your analyses of the different data you review during the meeting. We suggest you complete one Data Summary form during the meeting for the current year and one for the previous year (if you didn't do so last year).

A. Incident Referrals.

Compare the number of year-to-date incident referrals for the current year with the number from the same period last year. If the difference is significant, discuss possible reasons. For example, if you have many new students at your school this year, an increase in office referrals might be logically attributed to the increase in the number of students. Another reason for a difference in numbers might be a new administrator who instituted new policies that more clearly articulate behavioral expectations, so students were sent to the office for behavior that would not have warranted a referral in previous years or, conversely, behaviors that previously resulted in office referral were dealt with by classroom teachers.

Determine which grade levels have the most office referrals. Discuss possible reasons that the top two grade levels have such high numbers of referrals, and discuss what you might do to address the trend among those cohorts of students next year. For example, you might need to increase supervision or tweak the student behavioral expectations.

If you can break down the data by type of infraction, location, gender, race/ethnicity, and special education classification, look for meaningful trends and patterns among these factors that might guide you in tweaking or revising policies or even just raising awareness among staff about potential issues as you prepare for next year. Remember to celebrate the improvements and successes that the data reveal, too!

B. Suspensions (Out-of-School and In-School) and Detentions

Compare the number of year-to-date suspensions for the current year with the number from the same period last year. If there are fewer this year, be sure to tell staff and celebrate. If there is no change or an increase, discuss possible reasons and what you might do next year to be more proactive in responding to the behaviors that resulted in suspension. Do the same analysis for detentions if you think the detention data will be relevant in addressing student behavior.

Analyze the grade levels with the most suspensions. For example, if last year's third-grade students had the most suspensions, how did they perform this year as fourth graders? Discuss the possible reasons for the high numbers of suspensions in the top two grade levels and discuss what the school might do to address the trend among those cohorts of students next year.

Look for trends and patterns in the data broken down by gender, race/ethnicity, and special education status. For example, are there any meaningful trends among African American males this year vs. last year? Are special education students disproportionately represented in the suspension data? How might the school need to respond to those trends?

With suspension data, we think it's wise to determine the number of frequent flyers—students who received two or more suspensions during the school year. In many schools where the total number of suspensions seems high, the data show that half or more of the suspensions are given to a relatively small number of students—perhaps 10 or 15. If that is the case in your school, discuss proactive measures you might take next year to intervene with these frequent flyers.

C. Staff, Student, and Parent Survey Results

You probably administered surveys back in the fall or winter, but the end of the year is a good time to review those results and discuss what you've done to address any identified issues. If you used the TRENDS Climate & Safety Surveys, you might evaluate the responses with the technique we describe below. Prepare these reports before the meeting.

In the TRENDS Surveys Rank Order Report, sort the Staff % Agree column from most to least. (Check "Exclude No Opinion responses from results" if you don't want to consider how many survey takers answered No Opinion.) Then click the Export Grid button to create a PDF. On the PDF, highlight the groups of Excellent, Effective, Adequate, and Inadequate responses:

Excellent:	≥90% agreement. "It ain't broke, so don't try to fix it!" Celebrate instead!
Effective:	70–89% agreement. Minor fine-tuning is needed, but it is a lower priority.
Adequate:	51–69% agreement. Improvements are needed but are not the highest priority if there are results in the inadequate range.
Inadequate:	≤50% agreement. Major problems exist and immediate improvements are needed.

A sample PDF is shown in Figure 7d. Distribute the marked-up PDF to the team at the meeting or project it for all to see.

Repeat the process with the Student % Agree column and Parent % Agree column.

Note: We do not recommend interpreting the Possible Problems survey results in the way we describe for the agree/disagree survey items. The problems range from relatively mild, such as inappropriate student language, to very serious, such as weapons. It is not reasonable to rank order such a wide range of possible problems.

Surveys are discussed in detail in Module A, Presentation 4, Task 2.

If you are using other surveys, determine your options for analysis and identify overall strengths and challenges as well as what has been done to address challenging areas. You might create a simple summary table that works for your

Figure 7d *Example of TRENDS Surveys Rank Order Report sorted by Staff % Agree. The four categories—Excellent, Effective, Adequate, and Inadequate—are highlighted.*

Buckeye Sec
Survey Interval: Fall 2012

No Opinion data omitted

Item	Question	Category	Staff % Agree	Student % Agree	Staff-Student Discrepancy	Parent % Agree	Staff-Parent Discrepancy
40	Students are glad to come to school most of the time. [Staff]	Students' Feelings About School	93.5	76.9	16.6	94.3	0.9
8	Students feel safe in the parking lot. [Staff]	Student Safety	92.9	81.0	11.9		
32	Students are taught the rules and expectations for behavior in the courtyard/common area(s). [Staff]	Rules, Expectations, and Procedures	92.7	89.2	3.5		
55	I have a clear understanding of when and how I am expected to motivate/encourage students to do their best. [Staff]	Staff Interactions and Perceptions	91.7				
30	Students are taught the rules and expectations for behavior in the hallways. [Staff]	Rules, Expectations, and Procedures	91.7	93.8	2.1		
24	Staff members treat students fairly. [Staff]	Staff–Student Interactions	91.7	72.6	19.0	96.8	5.1
42	Students are proud to be part of this school. [Staff]	Students' Feelings About School	91.5	84.4	7.1	96.9	5.4
39	For most classes, teachers do a good job of making sure students know how they can get help if they fall behind. [Staff]	Rules, Expectations, and Procedures	91.1	87.2	3.9	98.1	7.0
45	The staff does a good job of communicating with parents/families. [Staff]	Parent/Family Perceptions of School	89.4			95.5	6.2
35	Students are taught the rules and expectations for behavior in the bus loading/unloading areas. [Staff]	Rules, Expectations, and Procedures	87.8	89.0	1.1		
48	Staff members treat each other with respect. [Staff]	Staff Interactions and Perceptions	87.5	93.0	5.5		
27	Staff members let students know when they do things right. [Staff]	Staff–Student Interactions	87.5	80.4	7.1	97.5	10.0
12	It is easy for students to make friends. [Staff]	Student–Student Interactions	87.0	82.2	4.8	97.5	10.5
10	If a student knew that another student was involved in something illegal or dangerous to him/herself or to someone else, the student would let a staff member know (e.g., teacher, counselor, principal). [Staff]	Student Safety	87.0	76.0	10.9		
6	Students feel safe in the restrooms. [Staff]	Student Safety	85.4	85.7	0.3		
49	The school has a consistent approach to behavior management and discipline. [Staff]	Staff Interactions and Perceptions	82.6				
7	Students feel safe in the courtyard/common area(s). [Staff]	Student Safety	81.0	86.7	5.8		
47	Staff members do a good job of communicating with each other. [Staff]	Staff Interactions and Perceptions	80.9				
4	Students feel safe in the hallways. [Staff]	Student Safety	80.9	81.4	0.6		
52	The school's current approach to behavior and discipline is effective. [Staff]	Staff Interactions and Perceptions	80.0				
53	The school's current approach to behavior and discipline is effective. [Staff]	Staff Interactions and Perceptions	77.8				
33	Students are taught the rules and expectations for behavior in the restrooms. [Staff]	Rules, Expectations, and Procedures	77.3	82.6	5.3		
5	Students feel safe in the locker rooms/gym. [Staff]	Student Safety	76.3	82.3	6.0		
18	Students treat each other respectfully in the parking lot. [Staff]	Student–Student Interactions	72.7	76.1	3.4		
17	Students treat each other respectfully in the bus loading/unloading areas. [Staff]	Student–Student Interactions	71.1	70.5	0.5		
41	Students believe that the work they do at school is important. [Staff]	Students' Feelings About School	70.5	92.5	22.0	96.3	25.8
20	Students treat staff members respectfully. [Staff]	Staff-Student Interactions	67.4	68.4	1.0	88.9	21.5
19	Students treat each other respectfully in their classrooms. [Staff]	Student–Student Interactions	65.2	69.5	4.3		
13	Students treat each other respectfully in the cafeteria. [Staff]	Student–Student Interactions	62.2	61.3	0.9		
16	Students treat each other respectfully in the courtyard/common area(s). [Staff]	Student–Student Interactions	60.5	67.9	7.4		
15	Students treat each other respectfully in the locker room/gym. [Staff]	Student–Student Interactions	58.1	69.3	11.2		
14	Students treat each other respectfully in the hallways. [Staff]	Student–Student Interactions	43.5	50.8	7.3		
17	Students are taught the rules and expectations for behavior.[Parent]	Rules, Expectations, and Procedures				100.0	100.00
7	Students treat each other respectfully. [Parent]	Student–Student Interactions				83.8	83.8
4	Students generally feel safe at the school. [Parent]	Student Safety				98.8	98.8

90% and above = excellent

70%–89% = effective

51%–69% = adequate

50% and below = inadequate

Presentation 7: Sustainability and District Support

255

survey; see the sample shown in Table 7a. Write a question tag (a brief version of the survey question) and the % Agree in the appropriate row. For example, for the item "Students feel safe in the restrooms," write "Safe restroom 77%" in the EFFECTIVE row.

Table 7a *Survey data analysis table*

Percentage of Agreement	STAFF Surveys Percentage & Question Tag	STUDENT Surveys Percentage & Question Tag	PARENT Surveys Percentage & Question Tag
EXCELLENT ≥ 90% agreement			
EFFECTIVE 70–89% agreement			
ADEQUATE 51–69% agreement			
INADEQUATE ≤ 50% agreement			

Have the team discuss using these results to set priorities for what to work on and what to protect and celebrate. Even if you administered the surveys in the fall or winter, the information is still useful. If you've addressed some of the most pressing survey items, discuss addressing the next items on the list in the fall.

D. Common area and schoolwide policy observations (from Foundations Common Area Observation forms, for example)

Our general suggestion for observations is to conduct them a couple of times per year—once during the fall and once in midwinter to evaluate the efficacy of revised policies and procedures. These data are still useful for the End-of-Year Game Plan. But if possible, also conduct end-of-year observations and solicit staff and student feedback:

- Conduct two to four formal observations of a common area in which you implemented revised policies and procedures during the current year and one observation of a common area you are considering revising during the upcoming year. Follow the directions to complete the Common Area Observation form (the form is discussed in detail in Module A, Presentation 4, Task 3). Consider filming the common areas if the school and district allow it.

- Administrators and team members might also conduct informal observations of the common areas and schoolwide policies.

- Seek staff input via small group sessions or an email survey. Ask for three or four strengths and two or three challenges related to common areas and schoolwide policies. Ask questions such as how student behavior now compares with student behavior 1 or 2 years ago (before new policies were implemented) and how the policies and procedures could be improved.

- (Optional) Use a brief written classroom survey to seek input from students who will be returning in the fall. For example, ask whether students feel safe in each major common area, what makes them feel unsafe, and where they observe or experience disrespectful behavior.

E. Other data sources

Other potential data sources include:

- Average daily attendance and absence rates
- Tardiness rates
- Expulsions and referrals to alternative education placements
- Referrals to special education
- Numbers of students referred to special education who did not qualify
- Instances of vandalism and graffiti
- Instances of other illegal activities
- Injury reports (differentiate between playground injuries and other common area injuries)
- Feedback from staff
- Student focus groups
- Social-emotional support (information from school social workers, counselors, and school psychologists)
- Summary of students identified with red flags
- Summary of universal screening

Discuss these data and identify any concerns. *Remember that safety is always the top priority.*

F. Data Summary Forms

Complete a Data Summary form (Form F-31) for the end-of-year data (available on the Module F CD and explained in Module A, Presentation 4, Task 1).

Assemble comparable end-of-year data from the previous year and complete a Data Summary form for that year as well.

G. Decide on actions based on the data analysis

Once the Foundations Team has analyzed the data, it's time to figure out which policies and procedures are working well, which could benefit from re-teaching to staff or students, and which need to be revised.

Option 1: If the policies and procedures are working well, inform the staff and students. Continue to implement the policies and procedures for the remainder of the school year and next year as well. Plan to celebrate the school's success before the end of the school year and during the fall kickoff.

Option 2: The policies and procedures are working, but portions need to be re-taught to the staff or students (or both). Decide whether the re-teaching needs to take place before the end of the school year because of safety or other significant concerns. If so, determine how to re-teach the staff or student expectations soon after the meeting to improve the last 3 or 4 weeks of school. Keep the presentations brief—about 10 to 20 minutes. If cafeteria supervision needs to be re-taught, for example, just highlight the portions of the job expectations that need to be done differently to increase the chances that students will make better behavior choices. And be sure to tell staff what they are doing well along with what they need to improve.

If you decide that there is no compelling reason to re-teach expectations before the end of the school year, discuss how to re-teach next fall. The kickoff is a great opportunity to re-teach staff expectations. Plan to re-teach students as soon as possible after they report to school.

Option 3: If the team decides that a policy needs revising, determine:

- When to write the revisions. If only a few minor tweaks are needed, the team might work on those immediately and present them to the staff for adoption at the next opportunity. For more extensive revisions, you will probably need to schedule another team meeting.

- When to present the revised policy to staff for adoption. Plan for a 5–10 minute discussion with voting. Identify the percentage of support needed for adoption and the voting procedure you will use. Remember, staff need to approve any changes in policy before they are implemented.

Once a revised policy has been adopted, consider the following as you implement it:

- Decide if staff or students need to be taught the revised policies and procedures. Students need to be taught a revised policy when the behavioral expectations for students change. Plan to teach the new expectations as soon as possible next fall. Decide who will modify or write new lesson plans and who will teach the lessons.

- If the revisions affect staff logistics or supervisory assignments, figure out who will organize the new schedules or supervisory location assignments and ensure that they are shared with staff. Set a date for the new procedures to go into effect.

- Identify when to review policies and procedures during the upcoming school year (e.g., after winter and spring breaks, before and after state testing).

Note: See Module A, Presentation 3 for additional details on the Revise, Adopt, and Implement steps in the continuous Improvement Cycle.

H. Complete the Foundations Implementation Rubric and Implementation Checklists for the modules you have implemented.

Consider the big picture. Complete the rubric and checklists, which we discussed in Task 1 of this presentation. The rubric is a relatively quick broad assessment of your *Foundations* implementation. The checklists provide a more detailed assessment and give you the opportunity to identify gaps in your policies and procedures. We suggest that you complete the rubric at least annually during your End-of-Year Game Plan meeting (and perhaps also in mid to late fall). Use the appropriate checklist as you near completion of a particular module, and plan to work through all checklists every 3 years. Both of these tools will help you identify areas to work on improving next year.

We suggest that you focus on one or two *Foundations* priorities for improvement during the first semester of the new school year. Structure for success by limiting your workload. Identify items and support needed to accomplish your goals, such as additional training, materials, sample forms, and advocacy from the principal. Also identify what should be shared with the staff about the priorities for next year and what accomplishments from the current year can be celebrated.

I. What major changes will occur in the school next fall? How can you proactively address the changes in student and staff behavior that might result from the changes?

Consider any major changes that will occur in the school next fall—for example, major construction that affects arrival and dismissal procedures, a new principal or assistant principal, lots of new staff members, or attendance zone adjustments that send many new students to your school. Think about how to proactively address the changes in student (and staff) behavior that might result. If in the spring you plan strategies for handling these kinds of changes, you can communicate those strategies and expectations during the fall kickoff and increase the likelihood of a smooth start to the new school year.

SECTION 2: Critical Team Issues and Decisions

In Section 2 of the End-of-Year Game Plan form, team members assess the effectiveness and efficiency of the team during the school year. Consider the following questions and actions:

A. Has the Foundations Team been effective this year? Do you need more or fewer members? Do you need a more diverse membership?

B. Do you need to replace or add new members to the Foundations Team? If so, which grade or level needs to be represented, and how should staff members be approached and recruited? Do new members need any training in or orientation to *Foundations*? If so, how should the training be provided? (For example, they might view or read Modules A and B.)

C. When should new team members begin serving on the team? Consider having them join before the end of the current school year so they have support and time to become familiar with how the team functions.

D. What is your team name? Don't have one? Pick one! A unique team name can enhance your visibility and prominence in the school and emphasize the purpose of the team.

E. Review team roles and ensure that all roles are filled for the coming year. Ask for volunteers or nominations for any roles that need to be filled. Consider adding or eliminating roles, depending on your experiences with team meetings during the year.

In Module A, Presentation 2, Task 3 we discuss the following team roles:

- Chair (Cochairs)
- Recorder
- Data/Evaluation Coordinator
- Materials Manager
- Keeper of the List
- Staff Liaison
- Equity and Student Liaison
- Family Engagement Coordinator

F. Identify staff members represented by each team member.

Every staff member should have a direct representative on the team. We discuss team representation in Module A, Presentation 2, Task 1.

G. Review and renew your team's ground rules for meetings in the coming year. (Did your team have ground rules? If not, below are some sample ground rules to consider.)

   a. An established minimum number of members must be present.
   b. Meetings will start and end on time.
   c. No side conversations during the meeting.
   d. All team discussions and disagreements will be respectful.
   e. Before speaking, team members will paraphrase what the previous speaker said.
   f. A cochair will serve as the "on-task and on-time nag."
   g. Meeting minutes will identify specific tasks to be accomplished along with responsible staff and timelines.
   h. Decisions will be made by majority vote.
   i. The ground rules will be clarified and communicated to all team members.
   j. Minutes will be kept for all meetings and will be distributed to the team and all staff.

H. Determine a tentative Foundations Team meeting schedule for the next school year or at least for the first semester. We recommend a minimum of 4 hours per quarter. Schedule options include the following (we recommend the more frequent meeting options for new teams):

   • Meet weekly for 30 minutes before or after school.
   • Meet twice a month for 1 hour before or after school.
   • Meet once a month for a half day.
   • Schedule a combination of 30- to 60-minute regular meetings plus half-day meetings as needed to develop and revise policies and work on other *Foundations* initiatives.
   • Meet once a quarter for a full day (very experienced teams can consider this option).

SECTION 3: Plan Your *Foundations* Kickoff for the New School Year

During this time, decide what *Foundations* information needs to be shared with staff at the beginning of the next school year. Work with the principal to identify how much staff time is available before students report to school, and ensure that the kickoff is on the principal's schedule—there will likely be many activities competing for staff time and attention.

Also decide whether to plan and provide a separate orientation for new staff members so they understand the *Foundations* concepts and know their responsibilities for implementation and sustainability. If possible, provide this orientation before the general *Foundations* kickoff so that these new staff members have the background knowledge to fully participate in and benefit from the kickoff.

The kickoff might last 30 to 60 minutes, depending on what your team has shared about *Foundations* during previous years. Consider providing information on these topics:

A. Overview: Provide a brief overview of *Foundations* (program components, goals, beliefs, implemented policies, and so on) to give new and returning staff an understanding of the process and of the stage of *Foundations* your school is currently at (use the Foundations Implementation Rubric as a guide).

B. Review all previously implemented common area and schoolwide policies and the specific student and staff expectations for them. (Don't assume they will remember from last year!)

C. Describe how new common area and schoolwide policies will be implemented.

D. Teaching expectations: Share with the entire faculty how to teach all adopted common area and schoolwide policies to the students during the first week of school.

E. Supervisory skills: Teach or review effective supervision skills—Module B, Presentations 4 and 5 for supervisory staff and Presentation 6 for faculty. Decide how to conduct the training and who from the team will present.

F. Office referrals: Review the behavior infractions that should result in office referral and the procedures staff should follow, including how to complete incident referral forms.

G. Other topics: Are there any other *Foundations* topics to discuss or share at the kickoff? For example, the team might need to cover student incentives, staff buy-in activities, Guidelines for Success, or three levels of misbehavior.

Also cover the following topics, if applicable:

- If the staff has completed training in the classroom management model, the administrator should review the school's expectations for implementation. For example, are teachers expected to submit a classroom management plan to the principal?

- Describe any planned professional development activities tied to *Foundations* or classroom management.

- Describe any staff incentive activities to build staff support for and buy-in to *Foundations* and the classroom management model.

H. And finally, celebrate! Arrange to celebrate with the staff the behavioral and academic accomplishments of the school year that just ended.

Task 2 Action Steps & Evidence of Implementation

Action Steps	Evidence of Implementation
1. Establish a meeting date to work through the End-of-Year Game Plan (Form F-29).	Foundations Process: Planning Calendar
2. The Data/Evaluation Coordinator and/or administrator assembles information needed for the meeting.	Foundations Process: Data Summaries
3. At the team meeting, work through the End-of-Year Game Plan form. • Identify which common areas and schoolwide policies are working well and should be protected, celebrated, and renewed next year. • Identify which common areas and schoolwide policies are working adequately, but could be improved or tweaked. Revise those policies with staff input and proceed through the Adopt step. • Identify which common areas and schoolwide policies are not working and need to be substantially modified or completely redesigned. Work through the Improvement Cycle steps of Revise, Adopt, and Implement. • Identify any common area policies or schoolwide policies that need to be developed. Work through the Improvement Cycle steps of Revise, Adopt, and Implement. • Complete the Foundations Implementation Rubric or Foundations Implementation Checklists. • Examine how the Foundations Team is functioning and assign team roles and responsibilities for next year. • Plan your *Foundations* kickoff for the new school year.	Foundations Process: Meeting Minutes, Current Priorities, Foundations Implementation Rubric and Summary, Implementation Checklists, Team Composition

TASK 3

Build district support and sustainability, part 1

In Task 3, we suggest some general considerations about building and sustaining district support for *Foundations* as a districtwide behavior support system. We also discuss two major actions districts should consider:

- Establish a district-based Foundations Team.
- Establish talking points about *Foundations* to facilitate walk-through visits to school campuses

Build district-level support for *Foundations*.

District support plays a vital role in the success of *Foundations* in the schools. We've learned some valuable tips for district personnel from some of our most successful districts, and we share them with you below.

Talk the talk. From superintendents through administrators, teachers through non-certified personnel, everyone should use the common language of behavior support developed through *Foundations*.

Consider presenting information to the school board about *Foundations*, how schools are implementing it, and the successes schools are experiencing. Keeping the board informed will in turn keep the board supportive of these positive practices.

Celebrate progress. Congratulate staff and students on their accomplishments, and let them know that the district supports their efforts and is proud of them.

Make time for training and reenergizing. Even after staff have been trained initially, they will need periodic refreshers.

Integrate *Foundations* with other initiatives. Fresno Unified School District, for example, implemented *Foundations* with cohorts of 15 to 20 schools. When a cohort finished formal *Foundations* training, it worked on bullying prevention and restorative justice. The schools used the Foundations Team structure and made it clear that the restorative justice and bullying prevention program was not taking the place of *Foundations*; rather, it was an integrated component of *Foundations*.

Identify a district-level Foundations Champion. This person is responsible for keeping the focus on the process of continuous improvement that *Foundations* emphasizes, making decisions about next steps, and providing guidance and energy for *Foundations* implementations in the schools. If that person leaves the position, ensure that you find a replacement who is committed to *Foundations*. You want to avoid the "this too shall pass" phenomenon, wherein the district changes its behavior support initiative every few years depending on the current fad or the whim of whoever is in charge. *Foundations* can be—and has been by many districts—sustained across many, many years.

And plan to have some fun! Denise Seguine, the assistant superintendent of learning services at Wichita Public Schools, sent Randy this email:

> I had to share with you how widespread our implementation of CHAMPS is in Wichita Public Schools. This week at the district retirement and longevity recognition banquet, with approximately 500 people attending, the master of ceremonies "CHAMPed" the event. Attached is a picture of audience volunteers who held up posters, and below is the emcee's script. Of particular interest to me is how engaged the audience was in this, demonstrating their understanding of a districtwide initiative—even for plumbers, painters, and electricians! Thanks for the inspiration!

The photograph Denise sent is shown in Figure 7e. The volunteers holding the posters actually include Superintendent John Allison, Assistant Superintendent of Learning Services Denise Seguine, and other high-level central-office administrators. The master of ceremonies announced the CHAMPS expectations for the evening—for example:

> Conversation: Voices will be at Level 0 so that the names of our VIPs can be heard. I thought about making a joke about respecting our retirees' current hearing loss, but I've decided not to go there.

> Help: If one of our VIPs needs help standing up, please provide it.

Figure 7e   *Wichita Public Schools superintendent and other high-level administrators CHAMP a retirement banquet*

CHAMPing a retirement banquet is fun, clever entertainment, but it is also a powerful statement about how committed everyone is to CHAMPS as a districtwide classroom management approach.

Establish a district-based Foundations Team.

The purpose of forming a district-level Foundations Team is to increase the likelihood that the continuous improvement that is the essence of *Foundations* is sustained across years. In a small district, an individual, perhaps the superintendent or an assistant superintendent, might take on the role of Foundations Champion in place of a team. But for districts with a fairly large number of schools, we recommend establishing a district team.

❧ FOUNDATIONS RECOMMENDATION ☙

Establish a district-level Foundations Team to increase the likelihood that the continuous improvement that is the essence of **Foundations** *is sustained across years. In a small district, an individual, perhaps the superintendent or an assistant superintendent, might take on the role of Foundations Champion in place of a team.*

The team should include the following people:

- At least two building principals
- At least two teachers
- At least one central-office staff member. Include the person who is in charge of *Foundations* (probably the Foundations Champion) and a person whom the principals perceive as their immediate supervisor
- Someone from your department of special education or department of psychological services who is knowledgeable about integrating Tier 2 and Tier 3 interventions with universal procedures

The team should plan to meet at least quarterly. Following are some ideas that the team might promote and support throughout the district. The questions in bold correspond to those presented on District-Based Foundation Team: Decisions and Tasks to Consider (Form F-33 on the Module F CD). The form is shown in Figure 7f on the next two pages.

District-Based Foundations Team:
Decisions and Tasks to Consider (p. 1 of 2)

1. Will all schools be required to implement *Foundations*?

2. If so, will the district monitor *Foundations* progress during school walk-through visits with principals?

3. Will there be a nonevaluative site-visit team?

4. When and how will the district monitor building-based data on in-school and out-of-school suspensions, absenteeism, climate (your survey results), academic performance, injury reports, and so on?

5. How will this data be used to provide feedback to building-based administrators?

6. When and how will building- or district-based staff beliefs and Foundations Archives be integrated into hiring practices for new building administrators?

7. Has the district adopted a classroom management model?

   • Are there expectations for what administrators should look for in classroom walk-through visits? Have administrators been trained in how to implement classroom walk-through visits in their buildings?

   • Have the district- and building-based teams received guidance on the use of coaches for improving instruction and classroom management?

   • Have coaches been trained in nonevaluative coaching?

   • Does the district encourage each school to choose a staff member to act as facilitator for the classroom management model? (The facilitator encourages peer coaching, ongoing training, and self-reflective data collection and analysis.) Are facilitators given opportunities to meet with other facilitators to exchange ideas and support one another at least a half-day each year?

   • How will teachers new to the district receive training in the classroom management model?

   • How will implementation and efficacy of the model be evaluated?

8. Should the district establish a protocol regarding early-stage interventions for behavior?

   • When and how will teachers receive training in the early-stage interventions?

   • What record-keeping should be encouraged?

   • What record-keeping should be required?

   • Will interventionists (school psychologists, social workers, counselors, and so on) also receive training?

   • What should an interventionist do if a teacher has not implemented the protocol of early-stage interventions?

   • How will implementation and efficacy of the protocol and the interventions be evaluated?

 This form can be printed from the Module F CD.

District-Based Foundations Team:
Decisions and Tasks to Consider (p. 2 of 2)

9. How will the district integrate Tier 2 and Tier 3 interventions with Tier 1 procedures?

   • Will district-level universal screening take place?

   • Will the district establish a system of monitoring red flags such as chronic absenteeism, retention, in-school suspension, out-of-school suspension, detention, and any others?

10. Should the district provide recommendations on the use of problem-solving processes?

    Will the district provide definitions or recommendations about using the 25-Minute Planning Process, Intervention Decision Guide: Teacher Interview, and Intervention Decision Guide: Multidisciplinary Team approach?

11. Develop calendar reminders for building-based teams. Reminders should include, but not be limited to, the following items:

    • About 4 weeks into the school year, remind teams to evaluate their beginning-of-the-year procedures, including welcoming and orienting new staff members and students.

    • Remind teams to conduct universal screening in midfall and midspring (also in midwinter if screening three times per year).

    • Remind teams to conduct staff, student, and parent surveys annually at about the same time as universal screening. Note that in most districts, surveys will be administered in midfall, but midwinter or late spring is also appropriate, particularly when the data are used for setting priorities for the next school year.

    • During the last 4 to 6 weeks of school, remind teams to anticipate team membership changes for the next year and orient new team members.

    • Remind teams to complete the tasks associated with the End-of-Year Game Plan (Form F-29), including completing the Foundations Implementation Rubric and Implementation Checklists.

12. Should the district develop district-level staff beliefs or board policies that solidify your principles of behavior support?

 This form can be printed from the Module F CD.

District-Based Foundations Team: Decisions and Tasks to Consider (Form F-33)

1. **Will all schools be required to implement *Foundations*?**

2. **If so, will the district monitor *Foundations* progress during school walk-through visits with principals?**

    We recommend that you monitor progress during school walk-through visits, and we explain more about this idea later in this task. Duval County Public Schools in Florida brought the value of walk-throughs to our attention. Carolyn Novelly is a CHAMPS and *Foundations* trainer in that district, and when the assistant superintendents conduct their walk-through visits with the schools, they ask Carolyn to accompany them so they can learn what to look for regarding the implementation of *Foundations* and CHAMPS.

3. **Will there be a nonevaluative site-visit team?**

    In contrast to formal school walk-through visits, nonevaluative visits by team members from other schools along with district-based personnel (such as the district school psychologist) arc supportive and instructional in nature.

    The following idea comes from Bob Conlon, director of student support services at Fort Bend Independent School District in Texas. Laura Hamilton, one of the *Safe & Civil Schools* trainers, has worked a lot with Fort Bend. She conducted several site visits that the schools and the district found to be very beneficial. The district would have liked Laura to visit all 30+ of their *Foundations* schools, but that proved cost prohibitive. So Bob proposed the following idea to a group of key building- and district-based leaders who have a deep understanding of *Foundations*, CHAMPS, and DSC:

    > My proposal is that you all become *Foundations* site visitors. For 1 or 2 days per year, teams of two will conduct site visits in Fort Bend ISD schools. To get started, I ask you to attend a 1-hour session with Laura Hamilton at the end of the day on Tuesday, April 29. Then on the next day, April 30, each of you will be assigned a campus where you will observe Laura do a site visit. Each site visit typically lasts 60 to 90 minutes, so you will be away from your campus for that amount of time on the 30th. There are nine of you, so three will shadow Laura at each school.

After you observe Laura, you will be officially "knighted" as a *Foundations* site visitor. I will be at the training, too, so I will be Knight Number 10. Next year, you will spend one day during fall semester and one day during spring semester conducting site visits with another Knight. We hope each team can cover four campuses each day.

The required paperwork can be completed at the end of the site visit, before you leave the campus. Laura has a form that we can use.

If five teams of two Knights each visit four campuses a day for 2 days, that would add up to 40 site visits in a year. The benefits to you are that you will see great ideas in action at the schools you visit that you can take back to your own campus. And of course tremendous prestige comes with being one of the Knights of the Foundations Table— sorry, that's really bad, but it had to be said. Let me know if you would be interested.

There are many benefits to this plan for site visits. For example, good implementation ideas are spread from school to school. And when visitors are expected, school staff make efforts to demonstrate their best teaching and supervisory skills, not because of any evaluation aspect but because—to use an analogy— people's homes are usually cleanest right before guests arrive.

We thank Fort Bend ISD and Bob Conlon for their willingness to share this idea with us.

4. **When and how will the district monitor building-based data on in-school and out-of-school suspensions, absenteeism, climate (your survey results), academic performance, injury reports, and so on?**

5. **How will this data be used to provide feedback to building-based administrators?**

6. **When and how will building- or district-based staff beliefs and Foundations Archives be integrated into hiring practices for new building administrators?**

7. **Has the district adopted a classroom management model?**

   If no, review the benefits of a districtwide classroom management model outlined in Module F, Presentation 2.

   If yes, consider the following in relation to your adopted model.

- Are there expectations for what administrators should look for in classroom walk-through visits? Have administrators been trained in how to implement classroom walk-through visits in their buildings?

- Have the district- and building-based teams received guidance on the use of coaches for improving instruction and classroom management?

- Have coaches been trained in nonevaluative coaching?

- Does the district encourage each school to choose a staff member to act as facilitator for the classroom management model? (The facilitator encourages peer coaching, ongoing training, and self-reflective data collection and analysis.) Are facilitators given opportunities to meet with other facilitators to exchange ideas and support one another at least a half-day each year?

- How will teachers new to the district receive training in the classroom management model?

- How will implementation and efficacy of the model be evaluated?

8. **Should the district establish a protocol regarding early-stage interventions for behavior?**

   If you decide to establish a protocol for early-stage behavioral interventions (discussed in detail in Module F, Presentation 4), consider the following:

   - When and how will teachers receive training in the early-stage interventions?

   - What record-keeping should be encouraged?

   - What record-keeping should be required?

   - Will interventionists (school psychologists, social workers, counselors, and so on) also receive training?

   - What should an interventionist do if a teacher has not implemented the protocol of early-stage interventions?

   - How will implementation and efficacy of the protocol and the interventions be evaluated?

9. **How will the district integrate Tier 2 and Tier 3 interventions with Tier 1 procedures?**

   - Will district-level universal screening take place?

   - Will the district establish a system of monitoring red flags such as chronic absenteeism, retention, in-school suspension, out-of-school suspension, detention, and any others?

10. **Should the district provide recommendations on the use of problem-solving processes?**

   Will the district provide definitions or recommendations about using the 25-Minute Planning Process, Intervention Decision Guide: Teacher Interview, and Intervention Decision Guide: Multidisciplinary Team approach?

11. **Develop calendar reminders for building-based teams.**

   Reminders should include, but not be limited to, the following items:

   - About 4 weeks into the school year, remind teams to evaluate their beginning-of-the-year procedures, including welcoming and orienting new staff members and students.

   - Remind teams to conduct universal screening in midfall and midspring (also in midwinter if screening three times per year).

   - Remind teams to conduct staff, student, and parent surveys at about the same time as universal screening. Note that in most districts, surveys will be administered in midfall, but midwinter or late spring is also appropriate, particularly when the data are used for setting priorities for the next school year.

   - During the last 4 to 6 weeks of school, remind teams to anticipate team membership changes for the next year and orient new team members.

   - Remind teams to complete the tasks associated with the End-of-Year Game Plan form, including completing the Foundations Implementation Rubric and Implementation Checklists.

12. **Should the district develop district-level staff beliefs or board policies that solidify your principles of behavior support?**

   A district-based Foundations Team can guide the process for answering these kinds of questions. Without a district-based team, you might find that the *Foundations* initiative is a bit rudderless. With a team, it's clear who is responsible for making and following up on decisions, and building-based teams know who to contact for support and troubleshooting.

Develop talking points for school walk-through visits.

This section focuses on a part of sustainability that can be facilitated by key central-office administrators. This information is for those who are the direct supervisors of the building principals. When these people come on campus for a walk-through, the principal feels as though he or she is accountable for what happens in the school.

Figure 7g shows a document titled Talking Points for Implementation of Foundations and CHAMPS During and After Year 1, Bulleted (Form F-32b). This form can guide central-office personnel as they conduct school walk-through visits with principals. It suggests questions to ask about the implementation of *Foundations* and a classroom management model such as CHAMPS. A blank version (Form F-32a) is available on the Module F CD.

Principals should be introduced to the concept and purpose of the talking points document during a general meeting attended by all principals so that everyone knows in advance that no one is being singled out for a walk-through using these talking points. Clarify that the form represents a district-level process and is simply a component of the partnership between district administration and each campus. The purpose of the process is to ensure that each campus does in fact maintain continuous improvement in all aspects of positive behavior support.

Personnel conducting the walk-throughs should begin each visit by reiterating to the principals that this is not a "gotcha" process. Instead, the goal is to identify strengths to celebrate and areas to target for improvement in the safety, civility, culture, and climate of the school.

To end the visit, the person conducting the walk-through should:

- Thank the principal for his or her commitment.
- Summarize what the district office will do to provide support to the school.
- Ask whether the principal has any questions or information to add.
- Inform the principal if there will be a written report about the visit and that he or she can suggest changes to that report.
- Invite the principal to email or call if he or she thinks of any related issues or actions the district office can take to enhance the school's *Foundations* implementation.

No more than 4 weeks later, the district office should follow up with the principal to ask how improvement efforts are progressing and about the data the school is collecting to assess the progress. Repeat Question 1 about school climate. Has anything changed since the walk-through? Does recent data indicate a need to change priorities?

Readers who are very familiar with *Foundations* will realize that the form is essentially asking whether the school is following the Improvement Cycle. If a school is really committed to *Foundations*, the principal should know what the process is, what the priorities are, what the data say, and what progress is being made. Conducting walk-through visits with the Talking Points form lets principals know that a central-office administrator is supportive of continuous improvement and the *Foundations* processes and that the district is committed to keeping the dialogue about *Foundations*, CHAMPS, and DSC alive.

Talking Points for Implementation of Foundations and CHAMPS During and After Year 1, Bulleted (p. 1 of 2)

1. How would you describe the climate of your school from the perspective of safety, civility, and respect?

   - What evidence are you using to make that assessment?
   - What do parents and teachers say about any changes in the school's climate?

2. Is the Foundations Team functioning effectively and efficiently at your school?

   - Do you attend the team meetings?
   - How often has the team met this year?

3. Is your Foundations Team working on developing common area and schoolwide policies that reflect expectations for student and staff behavior? If yes, list the common areas (arrival, dismissal, lunch, hallways, restrooms, and so on) and schoolwide policies (dress code, appropriate language, following directions, ID badges, and so on). For each prioritized area and policy:

   - Will faculty input be sought before the final draft?
   - If the policy has already been taught to students and implemented, ask:
     - *What impact is the policy having on student and staff behavior?*
     - *Did staff members who supervise the common area receive any training or descriptions of how to use positive and proactive supervisory skills?*
     - *If so, did the training make any difference?*
     - *When did the Foundations Team last monitor or evaluate the policy?*

4. What are your school's behavioral or disciplinary strengths that can be celebrated?

   - How do you know?
   - Have you notified staff, students, parents, district office, and community about the good news?
   - If so, when and how?

5. Have your teachers implemented any of the strategies from the CHAMPS or DSC classroom management training?

   - Which strategies have you directly observed?
   - How many classrooms have you observed?
   - Do the teachers report improvements in student behavior?
   - How are you supporting, encouraging, and celebrating the teachers' CHAMPS or DSC classroom management efforts?

 This form can be printed from the Module F CD.

Talking Points for Implementation of Foundations and CHAMPS During and After Year 1, Bulleted (p. 2 of 2)

6. Tell me about your school's discipline data.

    - Have you conducted surveys (such as TRENDS Climate & Safety Surveys) of students, staff, and parents?
        —When did you administer them?
        —What strengths did the survey results reveal?
        —What challenges did the survey results reveal?
        —Were results shared with the faculty?

    - Have you analyzed data related to behavioral referrals to the office?
        —When were those data last analyzed?
        —What trends were found?
        —How do the results compare with the previous semester and year?
        —Were results shared with the faculty?

    - Have you analyzed data related to in-school and out-of-school suspensions?
        —When were those data last analyzed?
        —What trends were found?
        —How do the results compare with the previous semester and year?
        —Were results shared with the faculty?

7. What are your school's current priorities for improvement?

    - Why were those priorities selected?
    - For each priority, what outcomes are you are hoping to achieve?

To end the visit, the person conducting the walk-through should:
- Thank the principal for his or her commitment.
- Summarize what the district office will do to provide support to the school.
- Ask whether the principal has any questions or information to add.
- If there will be a written report about the visit, inform the principal and note that he or she can suggest changes to that report.
- Invite the principal to email or call if he or she thinks of any related issues or actions the district office can take to enhance the school's *Foundations* implementation.

Task 3 Action Steps

Note: Building-based teams should discuss whether to recommend this concept of a district-based Foundations Team to district-level leaders.

Identify the appropriate person or group who can decide whether and how to form a district-based Foundations Team. If appropriate, also:

- Discuss action steps for moving forward with establishing a district-level Foundations Team.
- Discuss ways to encourage the district to use the Talking Points document when conducting walk-throughs with building principals.

TASK 4

Build district support and sustainability, part 2

When the schools in your district have implemented most of the essential *Foundations* components (this usually occurs by the end of Year 2 or Year 3), the district should then take some responsibility for guiding and leading the teams in activities and orientations to enhance sustainability.

If there is no district leadership, we've found that Foundations Teams sometimes assume that no maintenance is necessary. They meet less frequently or not at all and stop thinking about the process of continuous monitoring via the Improvement Cycle that is at the heart of *Foundations*. It's vital that teams continue to sustain and support the schoolwide and common area policies and ensure that the Guidelines for Success and other *Foundations* climate initiatives are ingrained in the school culture, and to do so with energy, enthusiasm, and staff buy-in and support. Compared with the first couple of years of implementation, less team meeting time and effort are needed for the sustainability phase. District guidance and support can help ensure that teams make wise decisions to keep *Foundations* alive and well on their campus.

So, in this task, we present some ideas for how the district can support sustainability in the schools. The first section includes ideas for schoolwide Foundations implementations, and the second section offers corresponding ideas for the classroom management part of positive behavior support.

Consider district sustainability ideas for *Foundations*.

We suggest that the district-based Foundations Team and each school-based Foundations Team review the ideas below annually and select at least one or two to implement.

Foundations Implementation Rubric. Have school-based Foundations Teams complete the Foundations Implementation Rubric each year. Some teams may complete the rubric twice a year. For example, if they work through the rubric in October, when the school year has been underway for about six to eight weeks, the results can guide decisions about the work they want to do during the year as well as the successes to celebrate midyear. By completing the rubric in the spring, teams can evaluate what they've accomplished during the year and what needs tweaking for next year.

Foundations Implementation Checklists. Have school-based Foundations Teams use the Foundations Implementation Checklists as they near completion of any particular module. If the Foundations Implementation Rubric reveals any issues with implementation or sustainability, working through the corresponding checklist is a logical next step. Schools should plan to work through all the checklists every 3 years.

> The Foundations Implementation Rubric and Foundations Implementation Checklists are discussed in detail in Task 1 of this presentation.

Data collection and analysis. Set up the expectation that schools will collect and analyze data quarterly. School Foundations Teams should look at the number of incident referrals, suspensions (out-of-school and in-school), detentions, tardies to school, tardies to class, and absences (along with any other pertinent data, such as common area observations, graffiti, vandalism, and so on) and compare the data with those from previous quarters and previous years. Trends and patterns in the data can indicate problems that need attention and successes to celebrate.

> Data collection and analysis is discussed in detail in Module A, Presentations 3 (Task 1) and 4.

*E*xample From the Field

A middle school I was working with was in Year 5 of their *Foundations* implementation process, which had gone smoothly so far. During this year, the principal was out on maternity leave and there were two new assistant principals. The interim principal was a retired principal from the district. When they analyzed data for the first 9-week period of the year, they found that the number of incident referrals for the seventh grade was significantly higher than it had been during previous years. To figure out the reason for the increase, the Foundations Team talked to the interim principal and the assistant principals.

They discovered that someone had given the seventh graders an extra 5 minutes of lunch. Well, as all middle school staff know, it's almost always a huge mistake to give middle school students extra time with nothing to do. So, logically, the Foundations Team and administrators decided to reduce the seventh-grade lunch period so the students had less time to engage in inappropriate behavior. The quarterly data collection allowed this school to recognize a problem and take positive, proactive action early in the year so that the seventh graders' inappropriate behavior was nipped in the bud.   —M.B.

Surveys. Have schools administer surveys annually. Ideally, students, staff, and parents should complete surveys every year. If that schedule is not feasible, you might conduct staff surveys annually and student and parent surveys every other year.

We recommend that the district arrange for all schools to use TRENDS Climate and Safety Surveys. This allows district personnel to see annual trends for each school and provides opportunities to analyze district-level trends and patterns.

Surveys are discussed in detail in Module A, Presentation 4, Task 2.

Visits from the district Foundations Team. Arrange for 1-day site visits to schools by representatives of the district Foundations Team. These visits should be nonevaluative and supportive in nature. The team can observe common areas, interview selected staff and student members (picked randomly), and review schools' behavior data. Interviews can be particularly revealing. When students and staff are given the opportunity, they can be very honest and forthright about the positive and perceived negative aspects of the school.

If the district does not have a Foundations Team, the site-visit team might include the district Foundations Champion (a role we suggested in Task 3), Foundations Team chairs from other schools, principals, assistant principals, district office administrators, coaches, or other district personnel with knowledge of and experience with *Foundations*. As we've noted in other tasks, site visits prompt staff to exhibit their best teaching and supervisory skills and increase staff awareness of the quality of their work.

More information about site visits by district teams is available in Task 3 of this presentation.

School visits. Have school Foundations Team members visit other schools to observe exemplary *Foundations* implementations. The district might promote this idea by paying for substitute teachers. Whether it is hallway supervision, incentive programs, or programs to reduce tardiness (such as *START on Time!* [Sprick, 2003]), when a school is doing something well, other schools can benefit from observing those successful programs. Visiting team members come away energized and think, "We can do this, too."

Action calendar. Promote and develop a yearly calendar of recommended actions for school Foundations Teams and principals. Provide this to schools in May and again in August. Examples of items to include are quarterly data analyses, celebrations of accomplishments, and meetings to work through the End-of-Year Game Plan form. Reminding schools of the importance of these key actions can help ensure that teams don't lose sight of what they need to do to keep the *Foundations* process of continuous improvement going.

Documentation. Stress the importance of maintaining up-to-date documentation of common area and schoolwide policies in binders we call Foundations Archives. Staff Handbooks and Student and Parent Handbooks should also be kept up to date. By archiving the work of the Foundations Team, schools maintain the cultural traditions of the school, even across staff changes. For example, if a new principal enters the school, she should be able to find in the archive almost all of the information she needs about school policies and procedures, how students and staff are taught expectations, and how Guidelines for Success are integrated into the school culture.

We recommend that a member of every school Foundations Team formally review the Foundations Archive, Staff Handbook, and Student and Parent Handbook in the spring. Too often, outdated versions of the handbooks are automatically reprinted every summer. The team should ensure that the policies and procedures are updated in the master copies used to copy or print next year's handbooks.

Detailed information about archiving *Foundations* materials is in Module A, Presentation 2, Task 4.

Training. Offer district-level *Foundations* training opportunities. One or two schools in your district might have weaker implementations than most schools. Give those schools a chance to start over with the *Foundations* process by having district personnel provide support and training for school teams. The amount of time and training required will vary depending on the school team members' previous training and the implementation status of the modules.

Offer some optional sessions on selected *Foundations* topics for specific personnel. For example, offer training in staff supervisory skills for playground and cafeteria supervisors from all schools. Hold sessions for Foundations Teams and other interested personnel from all schools on topics such as schoolwide student incentives, reducing absenteeism, enhancing staff buy-in, reducing tardies, establishing red flags for early identification of at-risk students, and bullying prevention. Once a school has successfully addressed common areas, schoolwide policies, and classroom management, working on these kinds of topics can really enhance the initial *Foundations* implementation and keep the Foundations Team thinking about continuous improvement.

Other sessions you might offer include crisis team intervention, the impact of gangs on schools, and suicide intervention and prevention. Although these topics are not specifically addressed in *Foundations*, they are global topics that certainly have a place under the umbrella of schoolwide positive behavior supports.

Consider offering separate sessions for elementary and secondary school personnel. Often there are specific concerns unique to one or the other level, and staff will be more engaged when the entire session relates to their situation.

Visits from supervisors. Have district-level administrators who supervise principals conduct site visits that include talking points specific to the *Foundations* implementation. Walk-through visits like this can be very powerful for keeping *Foundations* a priority for principals.

> Detailed information about site visits using *Foundations* talking points is available in Task 3 of this presentation.

Orientation for new administrators. Provide a half-day *Foundations* orientation for new principals and assistant principals early during the summer break, especially if they are new to the district or were in a position or school that was not implementing *Foundations*, CHAMPS, and/or DSC. Someone from the district can provide an overview of *Foundations*, CHAMPS, and DSC, including information about the very important role of the principal and what school teams are doing so that new administrators don't begin the school year with no knowledge of what *Foundations* is. The school-based Foundations Teams can also meet with their new administrators to update them on the status of *Foundations* implementation in their specific schools. That first year will be much more positive for the new administrators when they have a solid base of knowledge in the *Foundations*, CHAMPS, and DSC processes.

Training for school Foundations Team chairs. Offer a half or full day of training for new Foundations Team chairs (and cochairs). These team leaders can benefit from information about how to work collaboratively with the principal (who is most likely a cochair), resources available from the district and how to access them, and how to work with various staff groups. The training might also include a review of the district's calendar of annual *Foundations* tasks, the game plan for administering staff and student surveys, and information about how and where to access discipline data from previous years. With this training, the new team chairs can hit the ground running when school starts.

Consider district sustainability ideas for classroom management.

We suggest that the district-based Foundations Team and each school-based Foundations Team review the ideas below annually and select at least one or two to implement.

We use *CHAMPS: A Proactive & Positive Approach to Classroom Management*, 2nd ed. (Sprick, 2009), for grades K–8 and *Discipline in the Secondary Classroom*, 3rd. ed. (DSC; Sprick, 2013), for grades 9–12 as our classroom management models in this section, but our suggestions can be adapted to almost any positive classroom management model.

CHAMPS and DSC Implementation Rubric. Set the expectation that schools complete the CHAMPS and DSC Implementation Rubric (Form F-34) twice a year (see Figure 7h). The principal, district- or school-level coaches, or the Foundations Team chair can lead a staff session where all faculty work through the rubric. Like the Foundations Implementation Rubric, the CHAMPS and DSC Implementation Rubric provides a fairly quick assessment of whether a teacher has all the major pieces of CHAMPS or DSC in place and helps them identify the areas they need to improve.

We suggest that faculty complete the CHAMPS and DSC Implementation Rubric a few weeks after school has started, after they have had time to establish their classroom routines and can use the rubric to think about what is working and what needs tweaking. They should complete the rubric again in late spring to evaluate how the year went and plan any needed modifications to their classroom management for the next school year.

Another tool that teachers might find useful is the Classroom Management STOIC Checklist for Teachers (Form F-35 on the Module F CD). See Figure 7j on pp. 288–291 at the end of this task.

Collect classroom management plans. Have the principals ask teachers to submit updated copies of their classroom management plans, along with CHAMPS or ACHIEVE behavioral expectations for key classroom activities and transitions (see CHAMPS Approach on p. 285). Each teacher should do this within the first 2 weeks of the school year.

Walk-throughs. Have principals conduct nonevaluative behavior walk-throughs in classrooms and provide feedback to teachers. The principal collects data on observable outcomes from effective classroom management, such as the number of opportunities to respond, number of disruptions, ratios of interactions, and time on task. Nonevaluative principal walk-throughs can be very powerful tools to facilitate motivating teachers to improve and be more aware of their disciplinary practices, and they emphasize to teachers that the principal is a collaborator in the process of effective classroom management. The book *Coaching Classroom Management* (Sprick, Knight, Reinke, Skyles, & Barnes, 2010) includes useful forms and directions on how to conduct behavior walk-throughs in Chapter 3.

Classroom data collection and coaching. Have the school instructional and behavior coaches or even some master teachers observe in classrooms and collect data. These opportunities should be considered collaborative, nonevaluative, and voluntary. The Basic Five tools in *Coaching Classroom Management* are very useful for these observations. The coaches should follow up with the teachers to share observation data and compare them with the book's benchmarks, offer suggestions for improvement, and assist the teachers in developing plans for working on identified challenges. We have seen some very positive effects from coaching sessions like this.

Figure 7h *CHAMPS and DSC Implementation Rubric (F-34)*

CHAMPS and DSC Implementation Rubric

Directions: In each row, check off each description that is true for your CHAMPS or DSC implementation. *Note:* Each block assumes that the activities in previous blocks have been attained. Add the total points to get a total score. Compare the score with past rubric scores to assess progress.

Topic	Preparing (1)	Getting Started (2)	Moving Along (3)	In Place (4)
Attention Signal	☐ I use an attention signal, but it doesn't have both visual and auditory parts or can be used only inside the classroom.	☐ I use and have taught an attention signal with both visual and auditory components.	☐ I use an attention signal daily, but some students don't respond consistently.	☐ All or almost all students respond consistently to the attention signal in and out of class.
Guidelines for Success (GFS)	☐ GFS are in rough draft form. I have not taught them to students.	☐ I have taught and posted the GFS. I refer to them during the class period.	☐ I have posted the GFS and review them with students one or more times weekly.	☐ When asked, students can identify and define at least one guideline.
Classroom Rules and Consequences for Rule Violations	☐ Three to five classroom rules that address the most frequent or irritating misbehavior and their corresponding consequences are in the planning stages.	☐ I have finalized and posted three to five classroom rules and their corresponding consequences, but I have not taught them to students.	☐ I have taught students the rules and consequences, but I don't reference the rules when correcting rule violations.	☐ I re-teach rules as needed, including after breaks in the school calendar, and I reference them when redirecting or correcting students.
Expectations for Classroom Activities (Independent Work, Tests, Cooperative Groups, Lecture)	☐ I have considered expectations for classroom activities, but I have not written them.	☐ I have written expectations in the CHAMPS or ACHIEVE plan, but I have not taught them to students.	☐ I sometimes teach or share the expectations with students before the activity.	☐ I review the expectations with students before each activity.
Expectations for Key Classroom Transitions	☐ I have considered expectations for classroom transitions, but I have not written them.	☐ I have written expectations in the CHAMPS or ACHIEVE plan, but I have not taught them to students.	☐ I sometimes teach or share the expectations with students before the transition.	☐ I review the expectations with students before each classroom transition.
Beginning and Ending Routines	☐ Planned routines aren't evident, or I communicate them only verbally.	☐ I have written my routines but review them infrequently.	☐ Routines are evident, and I implement them consistently.	☐ All or most students know and consistently follow the routines.
Understand Motivation	☐ I understand the power of influencing motivation by using extrinsic strategies to address *expectancy* and *value*.	☐ I sometimes use extrinsic strategies to address *expectancy* or *value* in academics and behavior.	☐ I sometimes use extrinsic strategies for both *expectancy* and *value* in academics and behavior.	☐ I always use extrinsic strategies to boost *expectancy* and *value* in academics and behavior.
Ratios of Positive Interactions (RPI)	☐ My RPI is less than or equal to 1:1 (positive to corrective interactions).	☐ My RPI is less than or equal to 2:1.	☐ My RPI with most but not all students is at least 3:1.	☐ My RPI is consistently at least 3:1 with all students.
Classwide Motivation System	☐ Problems with persistent misbehavior or apathy indicate the need to plan a classwide motivation system.	☐ I have implemented the system and have noted some improvements in student behavior.	☐ The system is effective in meeting my initial goals, and students are motivated by both positive feedback and rewards.	☐ The system is effective, and I have made the goals more demanding. I am moving toward intermittent rewards.
Corrective Procedures	☐ I am working on delivering appropriate mild to moderate corrective strategies for rule violations and early-stage misbehavior, but I am not consistent.	☐ I am consistent when correcting most students, but I sometimes refer minor misbehavior to the office out of frustration.	☐ I fluently deliver effective mild consequences for rule violations and early-stage misbehavior. I refer only severe misbehavior to the office.	☐ I fluently deliver effective mild consequences and implement effective strategies to address chronic misbehavior.
Classroom Management & Discipline Plan (CMDP)	☐ I am beginning to identify the details of my CMDP or Behavior Syllabus, which might be written but is not implemented.	☐ I have developed, written, and taught my CMDP or Behavior Syllabus.	☐ I use my CMDP or Behavior Syllabus daily.	☐ I use my CMDP or Behavior Syllabus daily and assess it regularly. I also share it with substitute teachers and other staff.
Total Points:	1 point for each checked box in this column. ___	2 points for each checked box in this column. ___	3 points for each checked box in this column. ___	4 points for each checked box in this column. ___

Total Score: Add the totals from the four columns. ___

© 2014 Pacific Northwest Publishing

This form can be printed from the Module F CD.

When the coaching is presented as an opportunity for professional growth, teachers don't feel as though they must do things differently because an evaluation said so, but because it's the right thing to do for the students.

Peer observation. Encourage principals to arrange for teachers to visit other classrooms to observe other teachers using CHAMPS or DSC skills, such as teaching CHAMPS or ACHIEVE expectations, handling dismissal, organizing independent work periods, or conducting classroom incentive programs. A new teacher who is struggling with a skill set can really benefit from observing a colleague who does the skill well. Reading about a technique in a book is one thing; seeing a master teacher use a technique fluently and effectively in the classroom provides another invaluable perspective.

Data analysis. Set the expectation that principals analyze incident referral, suspension, attendance, and tardy data quarterly, and consider the data from a classroom perspective.

- What percentage of incident referrals comes from classrooms? How does this number compare with previous years?

- What are the most frequent misbehaviors that result in office referrals from classrooms? What are the implications for staff training or refreshers on classroom management skills? For example, teachers might inadvertently promote insubordination and defiance because their corrections are not calm, immediate, brief, and respectful. Additional training on fluent correction techniques might be in order.

- Attendance and tardy data may reveal a need for classroom incentive programs.

If possible, principals should also look at data by time of day and grade levels. If certain times of day or grade levels have high numbers of incident referrals, principals should hold a staff discussion to share the data and discuss what support might be needed to address the problem through better classroom management—follow-up coaching or training, for example.

District-level professional development. Provide district-level professional development opportunities before the start of the school year.

Offer open-enrollment CHAMPS and DSC workshops for returning teachers who have never attended a training or who would like a refresher. Many participants in these workshops say they learned as much the second time as they did the first.

Offer training for paraprofessionals so they can better support the teachers' classroom management plans. Paraprofessionals are often overlooked for training, but we find that they are very receptive to opportunities for professional development.

CHAMPS Approach

In the CHAMPS approach, teachers define and teach behavioral expectations for each activity using the acronym CHAMPS:

C = Conversation	Under what circumstances can students talk to each other?
H = Help	How do students get their questions answered?
A = Activity	What is the expected end product of the activity or transition?
M = Movement	Under what circumstances can students move about during the activity or transition?
P = Participation	What does appropriate student work behavior during the activity look and sound like?
S = Soar to Success!	

For older students, the acronym ACHIEVE can be used:

A = Activity	What is the activity or transition?
C = Conversation	Under what circumstances can students talk to each other?
H = Help	How do students get their questions answered?
I = Integrity	What are the expectations regarding students doing their own work?
E = Effort	What does appropriate student work behavior during the activity look and sound like?
V = Value	How will participation in this activity be of value to the student?
E = Efficiency	What tips or suggestions can you give students for getting maximum benefit from the activity?

Safe & Civil Schools offers ParaPro training, which is a variation of CHAMPS. (See *ParaPro: Supporting the Instructional Process* [Sprick, Garrison, & Howard, 2000].)

Offer full CHAMPS or DSC training to new teachers, both teachers new to the district and new to teaching. We highly recommend this idea. We've heard very positive feedback from teachers who received this training—they felt more skillful and more prepared to handle the day-to-day responsibilities of being a classroom teacher. They will also be able to use the common language of CHAMPS and DSC to communicate with returning teachers and students immediately, as the school year begins.

You can schedule this training for 2 full days before school starts. Another schedule that works well is to cover the structural aspect of classroom management during 1 full day before the start of the school year, then schedule 2 half-day sessions during the first semester. A few weeks of teaching gives teachers time to try the skills, so during the half-day sessions they not only get some new CHAMPS or DSC content, but they can also discuss what works, what doesn't, and what they can do differently.

Offer interested schools the option of hosting whole-school CHAMPS or DSC training. The Foundations Team or the principal can facilitate this training and arrange for trainers to conduct a full workshop with the entire faculty.

School-level professional development. Recommend that principals and coaches schedule regular, brief staff professional development activities throughout the school year to ensure that classroom management concepts are reviewed regularly.

- Refer to the suggested schedules for collecting classroom data in CHAMPS (pp. 246–247) and DSC (p. 228). Figure 7i shows the CHAMPS schedule. Review the concepts behind the data collection tools, then have teachers use the tools in their classrooms.

- Review and identify classroom management in-service topics in the *Coaching Classroom Management* book that might benefit the staff.

- Consider using the DVD program *When Every Second Counts: Mini-Inservices for Handling Common Classroom Behavior Problems* (Sprick, 2008). It includes some fabulous video vignettes and an activity guide that covers common problems that should be addressed by any classroom management plan. The videos focus on secondary grades, but we have found that elementary teachers can adapt them to their level very easily.

Task 4 Action Steps

District-based Foundations Team or district Foundations Champion:

1. Review the suggestions in this task and select a few to implement. Selecting some different strategies each year will help to keep the process fresh.

2. Ask school-based Foundations Teams for ideas to promote and sustain *Foundations* and the district classroom management model.

3. Modify the strategies as needed and implement.

Figure 7i   *Suggested schedule for collecting classroom data (from CHAMPS)*

Week 3	Student Interviews or Quiz (Chapter 4, Task 3)
Week 4 or 5	CHAMPS Versus Daily Reality Rating Scale (Chapter 6, Tool 1)
2nd Month	Ratio of Interactions Monitoring Form (Chapter 6, Tool 2)
3rd Month (early)	Misbehavior(s) Recording Sheet (Chapter 6, Tool 3)
3rd Month (late)	Grade Book Analysis Worksheet (Chapter 6, Tool 4)
4th Month	On-Task Behavior Observation Sheet (Chapter 6, Tool 5)
January (early)	CHAMPS Versus Daily Reality Rating Scale (Chapter 6, Tool 1)
January (late)	Opportunities to Respond Observation Sheet (Chapter 6, Tool 6)
February (early)	Ratio of Interactions Monitoring Form (Chapter 6, Tool 2)
February (late)	On-Task Behavior Observation Sheet (Chapter 6, Tool 5)
March (early)	Grade Book Analysis Worksheet (Chapter 6, Tool 4)
April (after spring break)	CHAMPS Versus Daily Reality Rating Scale (Chapter 6, Tool 1)
Last Two Weeks	Family/Student Satisfaction Survey (Chapter 6, Tool 7)

Classroom Management STOIC Checklist (F-35)

Figure 7j   *Classroom Management STOIC Checklist (F-35)*

Classroom Management STOIC Checklist (p. 1 of 4)

STOIC Variables		Tasks from CHAMPS or DSC	Y	N	Comments/Notes/Evidence
Structure your classroom for success	Physical Arrangement	1. I have arranged the room so I can get from any part of the room to any other part relatively efficiently.			
	Schedule	2. My students and I can access all materials, work spaces, and the pencil sharpener without disturbing others.			
		3. My schedule provides the appropriate consistency, variety, and physical activity to meet the needs of my students and the academic content.			
	Attention Signal	4. I have chosen an attention signal that has both a visual and auditory component and can be used in all settings inside and outside the classroom.			
	Classroom Rules	5. I have identified three to five specific, observable, and positively stated classroom rules that do not have regular exceptions. I have aligned these rules with our schoolwide or classroom expectations (e.g., Guidelines for Success).			
		6. I have posted my classroom rules in my classroom.			
		7. I have identified my teacher responses to classroom rule violations.			
		8. I have identified procedures needed for my class to run smoothly.			
	Defining Clear Expectations	9. I have defined steps and clear expectations for all procedures.			
		10. I have identified and defined clear expectations for all instructional activities and classroom transitions (CHAMPS or ACHIEVE Plans).			

© 2014 Pacific Northwest Publishing

This form can be printed from the Module F CD.

Figure 7j (continued)

Classroom Management STOIC Checklist (p. 2 of 4)

STOIC Variables		Tasks from CHAMPS or DSC	Y	N	Comments/Notes/Evidence
Teach students how to be successful in your classroom	Lesson Plans	11. I have created lessons on my classroom rules and explicitly taught them to my class.			
		12. I have created lessons for my procedures, routines, and Guidelines for Success and explicitly taught them to the class.			
		13. I have created lessons for my major expectations for classroom activities (e.g., teacher-directed instruction, cooperative groups, independent seat work, etc.) and explicitly taught them to the class.			
	Teaching and Reviewing	14. I have created a schedule of when I will teach and review my attention signal, classroom rules, procedures, routines, and CHAMPS (or ACHIEVE) expectations.			
		15. I have taught (and reviewed when needed) until at least 90% of students routinely comply with my expectations every day.			
Observe student behavior	Active Supervision	16. I circulate and scan frequently as a means of observing and monitoring student behavior as it relates to my expectations.			
	Positive Supervision	17. I model friendly, respectful behavior while monitoring the classroom.			
	Collecting Data	18. I periodically collect data (e.g., CHAMPS vs. Daily Reality Rating Scale, Ratios of Positive Interactions Monitoring, etc.) to judge what is going well and what needs improvement in my classroom management plan.			

© 2014 Pacific Northwest Publishing

Figure 7j (continued)   *Classroom Management STOIC Checklist (F-35)*

Classroom Management STOIC Checklist (p. 3 of 4)

STOIC Variables		Tasks from CHAMPS or DSC	Y	N	Comments/Notes/Evidence
Interact Positively	Noncontingent Attention	19. I have a plan for when and how to interact with all of my students in a friendly manner (e.g., stand at the door every day to greet each student, speak to each student at lunch, etc.).			
		20. I interact frequently with every student in a welcoming manner (e.g., say hello, greet at door, use student's name, talk with students at every opportunity, etc.).			
	Positive Feedback	21. I frequently use effective positive feedback (i.e., specific, descriptive, accurate, contingent, immediate, age appropriate)			
		22. I have a plan for giving positive feedback as a way to establish at least 3:1 ratios of positive interactions with all of my students.			
	Intermittent Celebrations	23. I have a plan for using intermittent celebrations with individual students and the entire class.			
	Classwide Motivation Systems	24. I have a plan to use classwide motivation systems when needed.			
	Plan for Connecting and Motivating	25. I have a plan for connecting with and motivating individual students as needed to establish at least 3:1 ratios of positive interactions.			
	≥ 3:1 Ratios of Positive Interactions	26. I strive to interact more frequently with every student when he or she is engaged in appropriate behavior than when he or she is engaged in inappropriate behavior.			

© 2014 Pacific Northwest Publishing

This form can be printed from the Module F CD.

Figure 7j (continued)

Classroom Management STOIC Checklist (p. 4 of 4)

STOIC Variables		Tasks from CHAMPS or DSC	Y	N	Comments/Notes/Evidence
Correct Fluently	Respond Fluently	27. I correct student misbehavior consistently.			
		28. I correct student misbehavior calmly.			
		29. I correct student misbehavior immediately.			
		30. I correct student misbehavior briefly.			
		31. I correct student misbehavior respectfully by using appropriate tone of voice, nonverbal communication, personal space, etc.			
		32. I understand and use "either-or" and "when-then" requests for students who exhibit repeated noncompliance.			
		33. I understand how to recognize and avoid power struggles.			
		34. I understand and use graceful exits (e.g., take a personal timeout) when I find myself in a power struggle with a student.			
	Preplanned Responses	35. I have a menu of in-class teacher responses that can be applied to a variety of early-stage misbehavior not covered by my rules.			
		36. I have a plan for how to respond to different types of misbehavior fluently.			
		37. I develop and implement behavior intervention plans when necessary for a student who displays chronic misbehavior.			
		38. I understand teacher-managed vs. office-managed behavior as defined by my school.			
		39. I understand and follow the procedures for documenting minor misbehavior (teacher managed) in my classroom defined by my school.			
		40. I understand and follow the procedures for referring students to the office for major misbehaviors defined by my school.			

© 2014 Pacific Northwest Publishing

BIBLIOGRAPHY

Adams, C. (2011). Recess makes kids smarter. *Instructor, 120*(5), 55–59. Retrieved from http://www.scholastic.com/teachers/article/recess-makes-kids-smarter

Allensworth, E. M., & Easton, J. Q. (2007). *What matters for staying on track and graduating in Chicago public schools: A close look at course grades, failures, and attendance in the freshman year.* Retrieved from http://ccsr.uchicago.edu/sites/default/files/publications/07%20What%20Matters%20Final.pdf

American Lung Association, Epidemiology and Statistics Unit, Research and Health Education Division (2012). *Trends in asthma morbidity and mortality.* Retrieved from http://www.lung.org/finding-cures/our-research/trend-reports/asthma-trend-report.pdf

Anderson, G. E., Whipple, A. D., & Jimerson, S. R. (2002). *Grade retention: Achievement and mental health outcomes.* Bethesda, MD: National Association of School Psychologists. Retrieved from http://www.nasponline.org/communications/spawareness/Grade%20Retention.pdf

Applied Survey Research and Attendance Works (2011). *Attendance in early elementary grades: Associations with student characteristics, school readiness and third grade outcomes* (mini-report). Retrieved from http://www.attendanceworks.org/wordpress/wp-content/uploads/2010/04/ASR-Mini-Report-Attendance-Readiness-and-Third-Grade-Outcomes-7-8-11.pdf

Archer, A., & Gleason, M. (1990). *Skills for school success.* North Billerica, MA: Curriculum Associates.

Baker, M. L., Sigmon, N., & Nugent, M. E. (2001). *Truancy reduction: Keeping students in school* (Juvenile Justice Bulletin). Retrieved from U.S. Department of Justice, National Criminal Justice Reference Service website: http://www.ncjrs.gov/pdffiles1/ojjdp/188947.pdf

Balfanz, R., Bridgeland, J. M., Fox, J. H., DePaoli, J. L., Ingram, E. S., & Maushard, M. (2014). *Building a grad nation: Progress and challenge in ending the high school dropout epidemic.* Retrieved from http://diplomasnow.org/wp-content/uploads/2014/04/BGN-Report-2014_Full.pdf

Balfanz, R., & Byrnes, V. (2012). *Chronic absenteeism: Summarizing what we know from nationally available data.* Retrieved from Johns Hopkins University Center for

Social Organization of Schools website: http://new.every1graduates.org/wp-content/uploads/2012/05/FINALChronicAbsenteeismReport_May16.pdf

Balfanz, R., & Byrnes, V. (2013). *Meeting the challenge of combating chronic absenteeism: Impact of the NYC mayor's interagency task force on chronic absenteeism and school attendance and its implications for other cities.* Retrieved from Johns Hopkins School of Education website: http://new.every1graduates.org/wp-content/uploads/2013/11/NYM-Chronic-Absenteeism-Impact-Report.pdf

Becker, W. C., & Engelmann, S. (1971). *Teaching: A course in applied psychology.* Columbus, OH: Science Research Associates.

Brophy, J. E. (1980). *Teacher praise: A functional analysis.* East Lansing, MI: Institute for Research on Teaching.

Brophy, J. E. (1986). Teacher influences on student achievement. *American Psychologist, 4*(10), 1069–1077.

Brophy, J. (1987). Synthesis of research on strategies for motivating students to learn. *Educational Leadership, 45*(2), 40–48.

Bruner, C., Discher, A., & Chang, H. (2011). *Chronic elementary absenteeism: A problem hidden in plain sight.* Retrieved from http://www.attendanceworks.org/wordpress/wp-content/uploads/2010/04/ChronicAbsence.pdf

Cameron, J., & Pierce, W. D. (1994). Reinforcement, reward, and intrinsic motivation: A meta-analysis. *Review of Educational Research, 64*(3), 363–423.

Chang, H., & Romero, M. (2008). *Present, engaged, and accounted for: The critical importance of addressing chronic absence in the early grades.* New York, NY: National Center for Children in Poverty.

Collins, J. (2001). *Good to great: Why some companies make the leap . . . and others don't.* New York, NY: HarperCollins Publishers.

Colvin, G. (Writer/Producer). (1992). *Managing acting-out behavior: A staff development program* [video]. Longmont, CO: Sopris West.

Colvin, G., & Scott, T. E. (2015). *Managing the cycle of acting-out behavior in the classroom* (2nd ed.). Thousand Oaks, CA: Corwin.

Cooper, J. O., Heron, T. E., & Heward, W. L. (2007). *Applied behavior analysis* (2nd ed.). Upper Saddle River, NJ: Pearson.

Cotton, K. (1990). *Schoolwide and classroom discipline* (Close-Up #9). Portland, OR: Northwest Regional Educational Laboratory.

Donovan, M. S., & Cross, C. T. (Eds.) (2002). *Minority students in special education and gifted education.* Washington, DC: National Academy Press.

Emmer, E. T., & Evertson, C. M. (2012). *Classroom management for middle and high school teachers* (9th ed.). Upper Saddle River, NJ: Pearson.

Epstein, M., Atkins, M., Cullinan, D., Kutash, K., & Weaver, R. (2008). *Reducing Behavior Problems in the Elementary School Classroom: A Practice Guide* (NCEE #2008-012). Washington, DC: National Center for Education Evaluation and Regional Assistance, Institute of Education Sciences, U.S. Department of Education. Retrieved from http://ies.ed.gov/ncee/wwc/publications/practiceguides.

Esler, A., Godber, Y., & Christenson, S. (2008). Best practices in supporting school-family partnerships. In A. Thomas & J. Grimes (Eds.), *Best practices in school psychology V* (pp. 917–936). Bethesda, MD: National Association of School Psychologists.

Evertson, C. M., & Emmer, E. T. (2012). *Classroom management for elementary teachers* (9th ed.). Upper Saddle River, NJ: Pearson.

Fabelo, T., Thompson, M. D., Plotkin, M., Carmichael, D., Marchbanks, M. P. III, & Booth, E. A. (2011). *Breaking schools' rules: A statewide study of how school discipline relates to students' success and juvenile justice involvement.* Retrieved from http://csgjusticecenter.org/wp-content/uploads/2012/08/Breaking_Schools_Rules_Report_Final.pdf

Feather, N. T. (1982). Expectancy-value approaches: Present status and future directions. In N. T. Feather (Ed.), *Expectations and actions: Expectancy-value models in psychology.* Hillsdale NJ: Erlbaum.

Furlong, M., Felix, E. D., Sharkey, J. D., & Larson, J. (2005). Preventing school violence: A plan for safe and engaging schools. *Principal Leadership, 6*(1), 11–15. Retrieved from http://www.nasponline.org/resources/principals/Student%20Counseling%20Violence%20Prevention.pdf

Get Schooled and Hart Research (2012). *Skipping to nowhere: Students share their views about missing school.* Retrieved from https://getschooled.com/system/assets/assets/203/original/Hart_Research_report_final.pdf

Glossary of education reform for journalists, parents, and community members. Retrieved from http://edglossary.org/school-culture/

Gottfredson, D. C., Gottfredson, G. D., & Hybl, L. G. (1993). Managing adolescent behavior: A multiyear, multischool study. *American Educational Research Journal, 30*(1), 179–215.

Hasbrouck, J., & Tindal, G. (2005). Oral reading fluency: 90 years of measurement (Technical Report No. 33). Eugene, OR: University of Oregon, College of Education, Behavioral Research and Teaching.

Hasbrouck, J., & Tindal, G. A. (2006). Oral reading fluency norms: A valuable assessment tool for reading teachers. *The Reading Teacher, 59*(7), 636–644.

Hattie, J. (2008). *Visible learning: A synthesis of over 800 meta-analyses relating to achievement.* New York, NY: Routledge.

Hattie, J. (2011). *Visible learning for teachers: Maximizing impact on learning.* New York, NY: Routledge.

Walker, H. M., Block, A., Todis, B., & Severson, H. (in press). *School Archival Records Search (SARS).* Eugene, OR: Pacific Northwest Publishing.

Walker, H. M., & Severson, H. (in press). *SIMS Behavior Observation Codes.* Eugene, OR: Pacific Northwest Publishing.

Jensen, E. (2009). *Teaching with poverty in mind: What being poor does to kids' brains and what schools can do about it.* Alexandria, VA: Association for Supervision and Curriculum Development.

Jenson, W., Rhode, G., & Reavis, H. K. (2009). *The Tough Kid tool box.* Eugene, OR: Pacific Northwest Publishing.

Kerr, J., & Nelson, C. (2002). *Strategies for addressing behavior problems in the classroom* (4th ed.). Englewood Cliffs, NJ: Merrill/Prentice Hall.

Kerr, J., Price, M., Kotch, J., Willis, S., Fisher, M., & Silva, S. (2012). Does contact by a family nurse practitioner decrease early school absence? *Journal of School Nursing, 28,* 38–46.

Kim, C. Y., Losen, D. J., and Hewitt, D. T. (2010). *The school-to-prison pipeline: Structuring legal reform.* New York, NY: New York University Press.

Klem, A. M., & Connell, J. P. (2004). Relationships matter: Linking teacher support to student engagement and achievement. *Journal of School Health, 74*(7), 262–273.

Kounin, J. S. (1977). *Discipline and group management in classrooms.* Huntington, NY: Krieger Publishing.

Lane, K. L., Menzies, H. M., Oakes, W. P., & Kalberg, J. R. (2012). *Systematic screenings of behavior to support instruction: From preschool to high school.* New York, NY: Guilford Press.

Losen, D. J. (2011). *Discipline policies, successful schools, and racial justice.* Boulder, CO: National Education Policy Center. Retrieved from http://nepc.colorado.edu/ publication/discipline-policies

Losen, D. J., & Martinez, T. E. (2013). *Out of school & off track: The overuse of suspension in American middle and high schools.* Retrieved from http://civilrightsproject.ucla.edu/ resources/projects/center-for-civil-rights-remedies/school-to-prison-folder/federal-reports/out-of-school-and-off-track-the-overuse-of-suspensions-in-american-middle-and-high-schools/OutofSchool-OffTrack_UCLA_4-8.pdf

Maag, J. (2001). *Powerful struggles: Managing resistance, building rapport.* Longmont, CO: Sopris West.

Marzano, R. J., Marzano, J. S., & Pickering, D. J. (2003). *Classroom management that works: Research-based strategies for every teacher.* Alexandria, VA: Association for Supervision & Curriculum Development.

Maslow, A. H. (1962). Some basic propositions of a growth and self-actualization psychology. In A. W. Combs (Ed.), *Perceiving, behaving, becoming: A new focus for education* (pp. 34–49). Washington, D.C: Association for Supervision and Curriculum Development.

McNeely, C. A., Nonnemaker, J. A., & Blum, R. W. (2002). Promoting school connectedness: Evidence from the National Longitudinal Study of Adolescent Health. *Journal of School Health, 72*(4), 138–146.

National Association for Sport and Physical Education (2006). *Recess for elementary school children* (Position Statement). Retrieved from http://www.eric.ed.gov/PDFS/ ED541609.pdf

National Center for Education Statistics (2012). *Digest of Education Statistics* (NCES 2014-015). Retrieved from http://nces.ed.gov/programs/digest/d12/ and http://nces.ed.gov/ programs/digest/d12/tables/dt12_122.asp

O'Leary, K. D., & O'Leary, S. G. (1977). *Classroom management: The successful use of behavior modification* (2nd ed.). New York, NY: Pergamon Press.

O'Neill, R. E., Horner, R. H., Albin, R. W., Storey, K., & Sprague, J. R. (1996). *Functional assessment and program development for problem behavior: A practical handbook* (2nd ed.). Belmont, CA: Cengage.

Payne, C. (2008). *So much reform, so little change: The persistence of failure in urban schools.* Boston, MA: Harvard Education Press.

Purkey, W. W., & Novak, J. M. (2005). *Inviting school success: A self-concept approach to teaching, learning, and democratic practice in a connected world* (4th ed.). New York, NY: Wadsworth Publishing.

Ready, D. (2010). Socioeconomic disadvantage, school attendance, and early cognitive development: The differential effects of school exposure. *Sociology of Education, 83*(4), 271–289.

Rhode, G. R., Jenson, W. R., & Reavis, H. K. (2010). *The Tough Kid book: Practical classroom management strategies* (2nd ed.). Eugene, OR: Pacific Northwest Publishing.

Roderick, M. (1994). Grade retention and school dropout: Investigating the association. *American Educational Research Journal, 31*(4), 729–759.

Sheets, R. H., & Gay, G. (1996). Student perceptions of disciplinary conflicts in ethnically diverse classrooms. *NASSP Bulletin, 80*(580), 84–94.

Shinn, M.R. (Ed., 1989). *Curriculum-based measurement: Assessing special children* (pp. 239–240). New York, NY: Guilford Press.

Skiba, R. J., Horner, R. H., Chung, C.-G., Rausch, M. K., May, S. L., & Tobin, T. (2011). Race is not neutral: A national investigation of African American and Latino disproportionality in school discipline. *School Psychology Review, 40*(1), pp. 85–107.

Skiba, R. J., Michael, R. S., Nardo, A. C., & Peterson, R. L. (2002). The color of discipline: Sources of racial and gender disproportionality in school punishment. *Urban Review, 34*(4), 317–342.

Skiba, R., & Peterson, R. (2003). Teaching the social curriculum: School discipline as instruction. *Preventing School Failure, 47,* 66–73.

Sparks, S. D. (2010). Districts begin looking harder at absenteeism. *Education Week, 30*(6), 1, 12–13.

Spinks, S. (n.d.). Adolescent brains are works in progress. *Frontline.* Retrieved from http://www.pbs.org/wgbh/pages/frontline/shows/teenbrain/work/adolescent.html

Sprague, J. R., & Walker, H. M. (2005). *Safe and healthy schools: Practical prevention strategies.* New York, NY: Guilford Press.

Sprague, J. R., & Walker, H. M. (2010). Building safe and healthy schools to promote school
success: Critical issues, current challenges, and promising approaches. In M. R.
Shinn, H. M. Walker, & G. Stoner (Eds.), *Interventions for achievement and behavior
problems in a three-tier model including RTI* (pp. 225–258). Bethesda, MD: National
Association of School Psychologists.

Sprick, R. S. (1995). School-wide discipline and policies: An instructional classroom
management approach. In E. Kame'enui & C. B. Darch (Eds.), *Instructional classroom
management: A proactive approach to managing behavior* (pp. 234–267). White
Plains, NY: Longman Press.

Sprick, R. S. (2003). *START on time! Safe transitions and reduced tardiness in secondary
schools* (CD program). Eugene, OR: Pacific Northwest Publishing.

Sprick, R. (2008). *When every second counts: Mini-inservices for handling common classroom
behavior problems* [DVD]. Eugne, OR: Pacific Northwest Publishing.

Sprick, R. S. (2009a). *CHAMPS: A proactive and positive approach to classroom management*
(2nd ed.). Eugene, OR: Pacific Northwest Publishing.

Sprick, R. S. (2009b). *Stepping in: A substitute's guide to managing classroom behavior.* Eugene,
OR: Pacific Northwest Publishing.

Sprick, R. S. (2009c). *Structuring success for substitutes.* Eugene, OR: Pacific Northwest
Publishing.

Sprick, R. S. (2012). *Teacher's encyclopedia of behavior management: 100+ problems/500+
plans* (2nd ed.). Eugene, OR: Pacific Northwest Publishing.

Sprick, R. S. (2014). *Discipline in the secondary classroom: A positive approach to behavior
management* (3rd ed.). San Francisco: Jossey-Bass.

Sprick, R. S., & Garrison, M. (2000). *ParaPro: Supporting the instructional process.* Eugene,
OR: Pacific Northwest Publishing.

Sprick, R. S., & Garrison, M. (2008). *Interventions: Evidence-based behavior strategies for
individual students* (2nd ed.). Eugene, OR: Pacific Northwest Publishing.

Sprick, R. S., Howard, L., Wise, B. J., Marcum, K., & Haykin, M. (1998). *Administrator's desk
reference of behavior management.* Longmont, CO: Sopris West.

Sprick, R. S., Knight, J., Reinke, W., Skyles, T., & Barnes, L. (2010). *Coaching classroom
management: Strategies and tools for administrators and coaches* (2nd ed.). Eugene,
OR: Pacific Northwest Publishing.

Sprick, R. S., Swartz, L., & Glang, A. (2005). *On the playground: A guide to playground management* [CD program]. Eugene, OR: Pacific Northwest Publishing and Oregon Center for Applied Sciences.

Sprick, R. S., Swartz, L., & Schroeder, S. (2006). *In the driver's seat: A roadmap to managing student behavior on the bus* [CD and DVD program]. Eugene, OR: Pacific Northwest Publishing and Oregon Center for Applied Sciences.

Sugai, G., Horner, R. H., Dunlap, G., Hieneman, M., Lewis, T., Nelson, C. M., & Wilcox, B. (2000). Applying positive behavior support and functional behavioral assessment in schools. *Journal of Positive Behavioral Interventions, 2*, 131–143.

U.S. Department of Education. (2000). *Safeguarding our children: An action guide.* Retrieved from http://www2.ed.gov/admins/lead/safety/actguide/action_guide.pdf

U.S. Department of Health and Human Services, Centers for Disease Control and Prevention (2009). *Fostering school connectedness: Improving student health and academic achievement.* Retrieved from http://www.cdc.gov/healthyyouth/protective/pdf/connectedness_administrators.pdf

U.S. Department of Health and Human Services, Centers for Disease Control and Prevention. (2012). *Youth violence: Facts at a glance.* Retrieved from http://www.cdc.gov/violenceprevention/pdf/yv_datasheet_2012-a.pdf

U.S. Department of Health and Human Services, Centers for Disease Control and Prevention. (2013a). *Asthma and schools.* Retrieved from http://www.cdc.gov/healthyyouth/asthma/index.htm

U.S. Department of Health and Human Services, Centers for Disease Control and Prevention. (2013b). *State and program examples: Healthy youth.* Retrieved from http://www.cdc.gov/chronicdisease/states/examples/pdfs/healthy-youth.pdf

U.S. Department of Justice, Office of Justice Programs, Office of Juvenile Justice and Delinquency Prevention. (2006). *Statistical briefing book.* Retrieved from http://www.ojjdp.gov/ojstatbb/offenders/qa03301.asp

University of Utah, Utah Education Policy Center. (2012). *Research brief: Chronic absenteeism.* Retrieved from Utah Data Alliance website: http://www.utahdataalliance.org/downloads/ChronicAbsenteeismResearchBrief.pdf

Wald, J., & Losen, D. J. (2003). Defining and redirecting a school-to-prison pipeline. *New Directions for Youth Development, 99*, 9–15. doi:10.1002/yd.51

Walker, H. (1995). *The acting-out child: Coping with classroom disruption.* Longmont, CO: Sopris West.

Walker, H. M., Colvin, G., & Ramsey, E. (1995). *Antisocial behavior in school: Strategies and best practices.* Pacific Grove, CA: Brooks/Cole.

Walker, H., Ramsey, E., & Gresham, F. M. (2003–2004a). Heading off disruptive behavior: How early intervention can reduce defiant behavior—and win back teaching time. *American Educator, Winter,* 6–21, 45–46.

Walker, H., Ramsey, E., & Gresham, F. M. (2003–2004b). How disruptive students escalate hostility and disorder—and how teachers can avoid it. *American Educator, Winter,* 22–27, 47–48.

Walker, H. M., Ramsey, E., & Gresham, F. M. (2004). *Antisocial behavior in school: Evidence-based practices* (2nd ed.). Belmont, CA: Cengage Learning.

Walker, H. M., Severson, H. H., & Feil, E. F. (2014). *Systematic screening for behavior disorders* (2nd ed.). Eugene, OR: Pacific Northwest Publishing.

Walker, H., & Walker, J. (1991). *Coping with noncompliance in the classroom: A positive approach for teachers.* Austin, TX: Pro-Ed.

Wentzel, K. R., & Brophy, J. E. (2013). *Motivating Students to Learn* (4th ed.). New York, NY: Taylor & Francis.

Wickstrom, K. F., Jones, K. M., LaFleur, L. H., & Witt, J. C. (1998). An analysis of treatment integrity in school-based behavioral consultation. *School Psychology Quarterly, 13*(2), 141–154.

Wise, B. J., Marcum, K., Haykin, M., Sprick, R. S., & Sprick, M. (2011). *Meaningful work: Changing student behavior with school jobs.* Eugene, OR: Pacific Northwest Publishing.

Wright, A. (n.d.). Limbic system: Amgdala. In J. H. Byrne (Ed.). *Neuroscience online.* Retrieved from http://neuroscience.uth.tmc.edu/s4/chapter06.html

APPENDIX A
Foundations Implementation Rubric and Summary

The rubric is a relatively quick way for the Foundations Team to self-reflect on the implementation status of each of the modules. If you are just beginning *Foundations*, you might use this rubric toward the end of your first year of implementation. Thereafter, work through the rubric each year in the spring and consider using it in mid- to late fall to guide your work during the winter.

Each column—Preparing, Getting Started, Moving Along, and In Place—represents a different implementation status. The text in each row describes what that status looks like for each *Foundations* presentation. For each presentation, read the four descriptions from left to right. If the statements in the description are true, check the box. Each description assumes that the activities preceding it in the row have been attained. Stop working through the row when you reach a description that you cannot check off because you haven't implemented those tasks.

Notice that the descriptions for the In Place status include a section about evidence, which suggests where to find objective evidence that the described work is truly in place. If no documentation exists, think about whether the work has really been thoroughly completed. Throughout *Foundations*, we recommend archiving all your work so that policies and procedures are not forgotten or lost when staff changes occur.

When you've worked through every row, summarize your assessment on the Rubric Summary. If any items are rated as less than In Place, or if it has been more than 3 years since you have done so, work through the Implementation Checklist for that module. Of course, if you know that you need to begin work on a module or presentation, you can go directly to the corresponding content.

> Print the summary and rubric (Form F-01) from the Module F CD.

For Module B, evaluate (separately) the common areas and schoolwide policies that you have implemented—that is, you've structured them for success and taught students the behavioral expectations. Use the rows labeled Other for your school's common areas and schoolwide policies that do not appear on the rubric by default.

Figure A-1 shows a summary form completed by an imaginary school in the spring of their second year of *Foundations* implementation. They have highlighted the checkboxes to create a horizontal bar graph, giving the evaluation an effective visual component. They've done a great job on most of Module A, the common areas they've prioritized so far (hallways and cafeteria), and Welcoming New Staff, Students, and Families (C7). They need to work a bit more on staff engagement and unity (A5) and most of Module C, which they began in Year 2. Modules D, E, and F are blank because they plan to work on them in future years.

Figure A-1   *Sample Foundations Rubric Summary*

Date _____

Foundations Implementation Rubric and Summary (p. 8 of 8)

	Preparing (1)	Getting Started (2)	Moving Along (3)	In Place (4)
Module A Presentations				
A1. Foundations: A Multi-Tiered System of Behavior Support	X	X	X	X
A2. Team Processes	X	X	X	X
A3. The Improvement Cycle	X	X	X	X
A4. Data-Driven Processes	X	X	X	X
A5. Developing Staff Engagement and Unity	X	X		
Module B Presentations				
Hallways	X	X	X	X
Restrooms				
Cafeteria	X	X	X	X
Playground, Courtyard, or Commons				
Arrival				
Dismissal				
Dress Code				
Other:				
Other:				
Other:				
Other:				
Module C Presentations				
C2. Guidelines for Success	X	X	X	
C3. Ratios of Positive Interactions	X	X		
C4. Improving Attendance	X	X	X	
C5 & C6. School Connectedness and Programs and Strategies for Meeting Needs	X	X		
C7. Welcoming New Staff, Students, and Families	X	X	X	X
Module D Presentations				
D1. Proactive Procedures, Corrective Procedures, and Individual Interventions				
D2. Developing Three Levels of Misbehavior				
D3. Staff Responsibilities for Responding to Misbehavior				
D4. Administrator Responsibilities for Responding to Misbehavior				
D5. Preventing the Misbehavior That Leads to Referrals and Suspensions				
Module E Presentations				
E1. Ensuring a Safe Environment for Students				
E2. Attributes of Safe and Unsafe Schools				
E3. Teaching Conflict Resolution				
E4. Analyzing Bullying Behaviors, Policies, and School Needs				
E5. Schoolwide Bullying Prevention and Intervention				
Module F Presentations				
F2. Supporting Classroom Behavior: The Three-Legged Stool				
F3. Articulating Staff Beliefs and Solidifying Universal Procedures				
F4. Early-Stage Interventions for General Education Classrooms				
F5. Matching the Intensity of Your Resources to the Intensity of Your Needs				
F6. Problem-Solving Processes and Intervention Design				
F7. Sustainability and District Support				

Additional information about the rubric appears in Module F, Presentation 7, Task 1.

Thanks to Carolyn Novelly and Kathleen Bowles of Duval County Public Schools in Florida. We modeled the Foundations Implementation Rubric on a wonderful document they developed called the School Climate/Conditions for Learning Checklist. Thanks also to Pete Davis of Long Beach, California, for sharing samples of rubrics and innovation configuration scales.

School Name _____   Date _____

Foundations Implementation Rubric and Summary (p. 1 of 8)   *Module A*

Directions: In each row, check off each description that is true for your *Foundations* implementation. Then summarize your assessment on the Rubric Summary form. For Module B, evaluate each common area and schoolwide policy separately, and use the rows labeled Other for common areas and schoolwide policies that do not appear on the rubric by default. *Note:* Each block assumes that the activities in previous blocks in the row have been attained.

Presentation	Preparing (1)	Getting Started (2)	Moving Along (3)	In Place (4)
A1 Foundations: A Multi-Tiered System of Behavior Support	Staff are aware of the *Foundations* approach and basic beliefs, including that *Foundations* is a process for guiding the entire staff in the construction and implementation of a comprehensive approach to behavior support.	*Foundations* multi-tiered system of support (MTSS) processes are coordinated with academic MTSS (RTI) processes, and team organization has been determined (e.g., one MTSS Team with a behavior task force and an academic task force).	Staff have been introduced to the STOIC acronym and understand that student behavior and motivation can be continuously improved by manipulating the STOIC variables: Structure, Teach, Observe, Interact positively, and Correct fluently.	A preliminary plan has been developed for using the *Foundations* modules. For a school just beginning the process, the plan includes working through all the modules sequentially. For a school that has implemented aspects of positive behavior support, the team has self-assessed strengths, weaknesses, and needs using this rubric. **Evidence:** Foundations Implementation Rubric
A2 Team Processes	Foundations Team members have been identified. They directly represent specific faculty and staff groups, and they have assigned roles and responsibilities.	Foundations Team attends trainings, meets at school, and has established and maintains a Foundations Process Notebook and Foundations Archive.	Foundations Team members present regularly to faculty and communicate with the entire staff. They draft proposals and engage staff in the decision-making process regarding school climate, behavior, and discipline.	Foundations Team is known by all staff and is highly involved in all aspects of climate, safety, behavior, motivation, and student connectedness. **Evidence:** Staff members represented by Foundations Team members and presentations to staff are documented in the Foundations Process Notebook.
A3 The Improvement Cycle	Foundations Team is aware of the Improvement Cycle and keeps staff informed of team activities.	Foundations Team involves staff in setting priorities and in implementing improvements.	Foundations Team involves staff in using multiple data sources to establish a hierarchical list of priorities and adopt new policies. Team members seek input from staff regarding their satisfaction with the efficacy of recently adopted policies and procedures.	All staff actively participate in all aspects of the Improvement Cycle, such as setting priorities, developing revisions, adopting new policies and procedures, and implementation. Foundation Team presents to staff at least monthly. **Evidence:** Memos to staff and PowerPoint presentation files are documented in the Foundations Process Notebook.
A4 Data-Driven Processes	Administrators and Foundations Team review discipline data and establish baselines.	Common area observations and student, staff, and parent climate surveys are conducted yearly.	Discipline, climate survey, and common area observation data are reviewed and analyzed regularly.	Based on the data, school policies, procedures, and guidelines are reviewed and modified as needed (maintaining the Improvement Cycle).
A5 Developing Staff Engagement and Unity	Foundations Team regularly communicates with staff through staff meetings, scheduled professional development, memos, and so on.	Foundations Team members understand that they play a key role in staff unity. They periodically assess whether any factions of staff are disengaged and how they can develop greater staff engagement in the *Foundations* process.	A building-based administrator attends most *Foundations* trainings and plays an active role in team meetings and in assisting the team in unifying staff.	For districts with more than five or six schools, a district-based team meets at least once per quarter to keep the *Foundations* continuous improvement processes active in all schools. **Evidence:** Meeting minutes and staff presentations are documented in the Foundations Process Notebook.

If any items are rated as less than In Place or if it has been more than 3 years since you have done so, work through the Module A Implementation Checklist.

School Name _____   Date _____

Foundations Implementation Rubric and Summary (p. 2 of 8)

Common Area	Preparing (1)	Getting Started (2)	Moving Along (3)	In Place (4)
Hallways	☐ Common area observations are conducted and data from multiple sources are collected and analyzed.	☐ Current structures and procedures have been evaluated and protected, modified, or eliminated.	☐ Lesson plans have been developed, taught, practiced, and re-taught, when necessary.	☐ Common area supervisory procedures are communicated to staff and monitored for implementation. **Evidence:** Policies, procedures, and lessons are documented in the Foundations Archive and, as appropriate, in the Staff Handbook.
Restrooms	☐ Common area observations are conducted and data from multiple sources are collected and analyzed.	☐ Current structures and procedures have been evaluated and protected, modified, or eliminated.	☐ Lesson plans have been developed, taught, practiced, and re-taught, when necessary.	☐ Common area supervisory procedures are communicated to staff and monitored for implementation. **Evidence:** Policies, procedures, and lessons are documented in the Foundations Archive and, as appropriate, in the Staff Handbook.
Cafeteria	☐ Common area observations are conducted and data from multiple sources are collected and analyzed.	☐ Current structures and procedures have been evaluated and protected, modified, or eliminated.	☐ Lesson plans have been developed, taught, practiced, and re-taught, when necessary.	☐ Common area supervisory procedures are communicated to staff and monitored for implementation. **Evidence:** Policies, procedures, and lessons are documented in the Foundations Archive and, as appropriate, in the Staff Handbook.
Playground, Courtyard, or Commons	☐ Common area observations are conducted and data from multiple sources are collected and analyzed.	☐ Current structures and procedures have been evaluated and protected, modified, or eliminated.	☐ Lesson plans have been developed, taught, practiced, and re-taught, when necessary.	☐ Common area supervisory procedures are communicated to staff and monitored for implementation. **Evidence:** Policies, procedures, and lessons are documented in the Foundations Archive and, as appropriate, in the Staff Handbook.
Arrival	☐ Common area observations are conducted and data from multiple sources are collected and analyzed.	☐ Current structures and procedures have been evaluated and protected, modified, or eliminated.	☐ Lesson plans have been developed, taught, practiced, and re-taught, when necessary.	☐ Common area supervisory procedures are communicated to staff and monitored for implementation. **Evidence:** Policies, procedures, and lessons are documented in the Foundations Archive and, as appropriate, in the Staff Handbook.
Dismissal	☐ Common area observations are conducted and data from multiple sources are collected and analyzed.	☐ Current structures and procedures have been evaluated and protected, modified, or eliminated.	☐ Lesson plans have been developed, taught, practiced, and re-taught, when necessary.	☐ Common area supervisory procedures are communicated to staff and monitored for implementation. **Evidence:** Policies, procedures, and lessons are documented in the Foundations Archive and, as appropriate, in the Staff Handbook.
Other: _____	☐ Common area observations are conducted and data from multiple sources are collected and analyzed.	☐ Current structures and procedures have been evaluated and protected, modified, or eliminated.	☐ Lesson plans have been developed, taught, practiced, and re-taught, when necessary.	☐ Common area supervisory procedures are communicated to staff and monitored for implementation. **Evidence:** Policies, procedures, and lessons are documented in the Foundations Archive and, as appropriate, in the Staff Handbook.
Other: _____	☐ Common area observations are conducted and data from multiple sources are collected and analyzed.	☐ Current structures and procedures have been evaluated and protected, modified, or eliminated.	☐ Lesson plans have been developed, taught, practiced, and re-taught, when necessary.	☐ Common area supervisory procedures are communicated to staff and monitored for implementation. **Evidence:** Policies, procedures, and lessons are documented in the Foundations Archive and, as appropriate, in the Staff Handbook.

If any items are rated as less than In Place or if it has been more than 3 years since you have done so, work through the Module B Implementation Checklist.

Foundations Implementation Rubric and Summary (p. 3 of 8)

Schoolwide Policy	Preparing (1)	Getting Started (2)	Moving Along (3)	In Place (4)
Dress Code	☐ Foundations Team has discussed the clarity and consistency of the current schoolwide policy.	☐ Data from multiple sources about the efficacy of the policy have been gathered and analyzed.	☐ The policy has been analyzed for clarity, efficacy, and consistency of enforcement.	☐ Schoolwide policies, lessons, and procedures have been written and are reviewed as needed with staff, students, and parents. **Evidence:** Policies, lessons, and procedures are documented in the Foundations Archive and, as appropriate, in the Staff Handbook.
Other: ____	☐ Foundations Team has discussed the clarity and consistency of the current schoolwide policy.	☐ Data from multiple sources about the efficacy of the policy have been gathered and analyzed.	☐ The policy has been analyzed for clarity, efficacy, and consistency of enforcement.	☐ Schoolwide policies, lessons, and procedures have been written and are reviewed as needed with staff, students, and parents. **Evidence:** Policies, lessons, and procedures are documented in the Foundations Archive and, as appropriate, in the Staff Handbook.
Other: ____	☐ Foundations Team has discussed the clarity and consistency of the current schoolwide policy.	☐ Data from multiple sources about the efficacy of the policy have been gathered and analyzed.	☐ The policy has been analyzed for clarity, efficacy, and consistency of enforcement.	☐ Schoolwide policies, lessons, and procedures have been written and are reviewed as needed with staff, students, and parents. **Evidence:** Policies, lessons, and procedures are documented in the Foundations Archive and, as appropriate, in the Staff Handbook.
Other: ____	☐ Foundations Team has discussed the clarity and consistency of the current schoolwide policy.	☐ Data from multiple sources about the efficacy of the policy have been gathered and analyzed.	☐ The policy has been analyzed for clarity, efficacy, and consistency of enforcement.	☐ Schoolwide policies, lessons, and procedures have been written and are reviewed as needed with staff, students, and parents. **Evidence:** Policies, lessons, and procedures are documented in the Foundations Archive and, as appropriate, in the Staff Handbook.
Other: ____	☐ Foundations Team has discussed the clarity and consistency of the current schoolwide policy.	☐ Data from multiple sources about the efficacy of the policy have been gathered and analyzed.	☐ The policy has been analyzed for clarity, efficacy, and consistency of enforcement.	☐ Schoolwide policies, lessons, and procedures have been written and are reviewed as needed with staff, students, and parents. **Evidence:** Policies, lessons, and procedures are documented in the Foundations Archive and, as appropriate, in the Staff Handbook.
Other: ____	☐ Foundations Team has discussed the clarity and consistency of the current schoolwide policy.	☐ Data from multiple sources about the efficacy of the policy have been gathered and analyzed.	☐ The policy has been analyzed for clarity, efficacy, and consistency of enforcement.	☐ Schoolwide policies, lessons, and procedures have been written and are reviewed as needed with staff, students, and parents. **Evidence:** Policies, lessons, and procedures are documented in the Foundations Archive and, as appropriate, in the Staff Handbook.
Other: ____	☐ Foundations Team has discussed the clarity and consistency of the current schoolwide policy.	☐ Data from multiple sources about the efficacy of the policy have been gathered and analyzed.	☐ The policy has been analyzed for clarity, efficacy, and consistency of enforcement.	☐ Schoolwide policies, lessons, and procedures have been written and are reviewed as needed with staff, students, and parents. **Evidence:** Policies, lessons, and procedures are documented in the Foundations Archive and, as appropriate, in the Staff Handbook.
Other: ____	☐ Foundations Team has discussed the clarity and consistency of the current schoolwide policy.	☐ Data from multiple sources about the efficacy of the policy have been gathered and analyzed.	☐ The policy has been analyzed for clarity, efficacy, and consistency of enforcement.	☐ Schoolwide policies, lessons, and procedures have been written and are reviewed as needed with staff, students, and parents. **Evidence:** Policies, lessons, and procedures are documented in the Foundations Archive and, as appropriate, in the Staff Handbook.

If any items are rated as less than In Place or if it has been more than 3 years since you have done so, work through the Module B Implementation Checklist.

School Name _____ Date _____

Foundations Implementation Rubric and Summary (p. 4 of 8)

Presentation	Preparing (1)	Getting Started (2)	Moving Along (3)	In Place (4)
C2 Guidelines for Success (GFS)	☐ All staff understand what Guidelines for Success (GFS) are and why they are important.	☐ Foundations Team has drafted proposals and engaged all stakeholders in the decision-making process of developing GFS.	☐ GFS have been finalized and posted and are reviewed regularly.	☐ GFS are embedded into the culture and are part of the common language of the school. **Evidence:** Procedures for teaching and motivating students about GFS are documented in the Foundations Archive, Staff Handbook, and Student and Parent Handbook.
C3 Ratios of Positive Interactions	☐ Staff have been taught the concept of 3:1 ratios of positive interactions and the importance of creating a positive climate and improving student behavior.	☐ Staff have been taught how to monitor ratios of positive interactions and are encouraged to evaluate their interactions with students.	☐ Administrator plans for teachers to observe and calculate other teachers' classroom ratios of interactions; the teachers involved meet to discuss outcomes.	☐ Observation data show that most staff at most times strive to interact with students at least three times more often when students are behaving responsibly than when they are misbehaving. **Evidence:** Procedures for teaching and motivating staff are documented in the Foundations Archive and Staff Handbook.
C4 Improving Attendance	☐ Average daily attendance is monitored to view long-term trends and patterns. Faculty and staff have been made aware of the importance of encouraging regular attendance by all students.	☐ All students with chronic absenteeism (absent 10% or more of school days) are identified at least quarterly; Foundations Team determines whether universal intervention is warranted.	☐ Each student with chronic absenteeism is identified and assigned one school-based support person who monitors whether additional support is needed. Foundations Team has analyzed attendance data and analyzed policies for clarity and efficacy.	☐ Every student with chronic absenteeism that has been resistant to universal and Tier 2 supports becomes the focus of a multidisciplinary team effort. **Evidence:** Data on average daily attendance and chronic absenteeism as well as efforts to improve attendance (e.g., parent newsletters) are documented in the Foundations Process Notebook.
C5 & C6 School Connectedness and Programs and Strategies for Meeting Needs	☐ Foundations Team has analyzed the degree to which current programs and practices meet the needs of all students (outstanding, average, and at risk).	☐ Foundations Team has developed proposals for programs and practices that might help meet unmet needs of students (e.g., the average student's need for purpose and belonging).	☐ Faculty and staff have implemented programs and practices designed to meet basic needs of all students (e.g., Mentorship, Student of the Week, Meaningful Work).	☐ Programs to meet students' basic needs are in place and analyzed at least once per year to determine their effectiveness and assess whether the needs of any student groups are not being met. **Evidence:** Analysis is documented in the Foundations Process Notebook, and programs and practices for meeting needs are documented in the Foundations Archive.
C7 Welcoming New Staff, Students, and Families	☐ Foundations Team has reviewed the welcoming aspects of the school, such as signage, website, and phone and front office procedures, and has suggested improvements.	☐ Foundations Team has analyzed procedures and suggested improvements for welcoming and orienting new students and families at the beginning of the school year. (New students include those in a new grade-level cohort (e.g., ninth graders in high school) and students who are not part of that cohort.)	☐ Foundations Team has analyzed procedures and suggested improvements for welcoming new students and families who arrive during the school year. Improvements might include written information about rules, procedures, GFS, and so on.	☐ Foundations Team has analyzed procedures and suggested improvements for welcoming new staff members, both professional and nonprofessional, at the beginning of the year. New staff members are oriented to essential procedures and the culture and climate defined by the school's behavior support procedures. **Evidence:** All policies and procedures for welcoming and orienting staff, students, and families are documented in the Foundations Archive.

If any items are rated as less than In Place or if it has been more than 3 years since you have done so, work through the Module C Implementation Checklist.

Foundations Implementation Rubric and Summary (p. 5 of 8)

Presentation	Preparing (1)	Getting Started (2)	Moving Along (3)	In Place (4)
D1 Proactive Procedures, Corrective Procedures, and Individual Interventions	☐ Foundations Team is aware of data and staff opinions about consistency in correcting misbehavior, including clarity of staff roles in discipline compared with administrative roles.	☐ Staff understand the potential limitations of office referral as a corrective procedure and avoid using it whenever possible.	☐ Staff have been made aware of the limited benefits and potential drawbacks (including disparate impact) of out-of-school suspension (OSS) as a corrective consequence.	☐ Staff avoid pressuring administrators to use OSS. Staff perceptions of consistency and administrative support for disciplinary actions are documented in staff survey results. **Evidence:** Discussions on these topics are documented in the Foundations Process Notebook.
D2 Developing Three Levels of Misbehavior	☐ Staff are aware of the concept of three levels of misbehavior: Level 1 (mild), Level 2 (moderate), and Level 3 (severe) misbehavior.	☐ Annually, staff discuss and agree on what behavior *must* be sent to the administrator, what can be sent to the administrator, and what should be handled in the setting in which the infraction occurred (3-level system for responding to misbehavior).	☐ A referral form that reflects the agreed-upon definition of Level 3 misbehavior has been developed. A notification form that reflects the agreed-upon definition of Level 2 misbehavior has been developed. (Alternatively, both Level 2 and Level 3 may be on one form.) Accurate data are kept and analyzed quarterly for all Level 2 and Level 3 misbehaviors and consequences.	☐ Data are collected on the implementation of the 3-level system for responding to misbehavior and on staff and administrator satisfaction with the system. **Evidence:** All aspects of the policy are documented in the Foundations Archive and Staff Handbook.
D3 Staff Responsibilities for Responding to Misbehavior	☐ Staff have generated and administrators have approved a menu of corrective consequences for use in common areas.	☐ Staff have generated and administrators have approved a menu of corrective consequences for use in classrooms.	☐ Staff have been trained in how to use Level 2 notifications as a process for moving toward collaborative planning for severe or chronic behavior problems.	☐ Staff have been trained in writing objective and appropriate office referrals for Level 3 misbehavior. **Evidence:** Menus and procedures are documented in the Foundations Archive and Staff Handbook.
D4 Administrator Responsibilities for Responding to Misbehavior	☐ Procedures have been developed for responding to Level 2 notifications to ensure that the reporting staff member receives timely feedback and that administrators and support staff take appropriate actions.	☐ Office procedures for dealing with students sent to the office have been analyzed and streamlined. Students do not get too much attention from office staff or staff members who visit the office	☐ Administrators are familiar with the game plan for dealing with Level 3 incidents. The game plan includes a menu of alternative consequences to out-of-school suspension.	☐ If the school has an ISS program, that program has been analyzed and revised as needed to ensure that it is highly structured and includes an instructional component. **Evidence:** All procedures for Level 2 and Level 3 infractions are documented in the Foundations Archive.
D5 Preventing the Misbehavior That Leads to Referrals and Suspensions	☐ Foundations Team has examined data on Level 2 and Level 3 infractions to determine what misbehaviors get students into trouble.	☐ Foundations Team has reviewed the lessons in Module D (how to interact appropriately with adults) and discussed whether they might reduce misbehaviors that get students into trouble.	☐ To avoid duplication, the Foundations Team has compared the Module D lessons with other social skills or social-emotional curricula currently in use. Staff have agreed on a plan for when and how to teach expected behaviors to all students.	☐ Foundations Team has discussed whether re-teaching the Module D lessons (or similar) in ISS or detention settings would be beneficial; if so, the team has planned when and how to re-teach. **Evidence:** Lesson plans and teaching logistics and schedule are documented in the Foundations Archive.

If any items are rated as less than In Place or if it has been more than 3 years since you have done so, work through the Module D Implementation Checklist.

Foundations Implementation Rubric and Summary (p. 6 of 8)

Presentation	Preparing (1)	Getting Started (2)	Moving Along (3)	In Place (4)
E1 Ensuring a Safe Environment for Students	☐ Team members are aware of their responsibilities for overseeing school safety efforts. The team coordinates with other teams or task forces that may be doing similar work and avoids duplicating other efforts.	☐ Foundations Team has viewed or read Module E and has compared that content with the school's current efforts toward safety, managing conflict, and bullying prevention. The team has developed a proposal for closing any gaps in the current efforts.	☐ Foundations Team has made staff aware of the importance of a comprehensive view of safety that includes preparing for outside attackers as well as the more common occurrences of playground injuries, student fights, bullying, and so on.	☐ Foundations Team has assessed problems with safety, conflict, and bullying within the last 3 years. If problems exist, a plan for using or adapting information from this module and integrating them with current curriculum or procedures has been completed. **Evidence:** Data analyses are documented in the Foundations Process Notebook, and final policies and procedures are documented in the Foundations Archive.
E2 Attributes of Safe and Unsafe Schools	☐ Team members and other staff directly involved with safety concerns have viewed or read Presentation 2 and have completed (individually) the form Understanding the Attributes of Safe and Unsafe Schools.	☐ Foundations Team has compiled individual responses to Understanding Attributes of Safe and Unsafe Schools and correlated those data with safety assessments completed in the last 3 years. Information about strengths and concerns has been shared with staff, and priorities have been set.	☐ Foundations Team and other staff involved with safety concerns have completed the form Assessing Emergency Preparedness, evaluated current plans for natural disasters and man-made emergencies, revised any weak procedures, including training on policies regarding seclusion and restraint.	☐ Foundations Team has completed the form Lessons to Increase Safety and Belonging, reviewed the Module E sample lessons, and evaluated whether current problems and policies address all features of the sample lessons. If there are gaps, a plan to teach some or all of the *Foundations* lessons is established. **Evidence:** Lesson plans and procedures are documented in the Foundations Archive.
E3 Teaching Conflict Resolution	☐ Foundations Team has assessed whether the school has a conflict resolution strategy that students and staff use when necessary. If so, document the effective procedures in the Foundations Archive (and skip the rest of this row).	☐ Foundations Team has reviewed the concepts and lessons in the Stop-Think-Plan (STP) approach and has prepared an implementation plan for staff.	☐ With staff input, lessons have been revised, an implementation plan has been established, and a process is in place for training all staff in how to encourage students to use the conflict-resolution strategy.	☐ Foundations Team has established a process for evaluating the effectiveness of STP by analyzing multiple data sources. The policy and lessons are revised and staff are retrained when necessary, and successes are celebrated. **Evidence:** Data analyses are documented in the Foundations Process Notebook, and lessons and teaching procedures are documented in the Foundations Archive.
E4 Analyzing Bullying Behavior, Policies, and School Needs	☐ Foundations Team is aware of the content of this presentation and can compare it with current policies and procedures related to bullying.	☐ Foundations Team has completed the form School-Based Analysis of Bullying Data and has identified whether new or revised procedures need to be implemented to enhance the current use of data related to bullying.	☐ Foundations Team has completed the form School-Based Analysis of Bullying Policies and has identified whether new or revised policies need to be implemented to enhance current policies related to bullying.	☐ Quarterly, the Foundations Team reviews data related to bullying. Annually, the team uses those data to answer each of the questions in the form STOIC Analysis for Universal Prevention of Bullying (or an equivalent process), and improvement priorities are established. **Evidence:** Data analyses are documented in the Foundations Process Notebook.
E5 Schoolwide Bullying Prevention and Intervention	☐ Foundations Team has completed the form Staff Training in Preventing and Responding to Bullying and has developed and implemented a plan to fill in any identified gaps in current practices.	☐ Foundations Team has completed the form Student Training in Preventing and Responding to Bullying. As part of a previously adopted bullying curriculum or through the *Foundations* lessons, students are taught about bullying prevention.	☐ Foundations Team has completed the form Family Training in Preventing and Responding to Bullying and has developed an implementation plan to fill in any identified gaps in current practices.	☐ Foundations Team has completed the form Active Engagement for the Prevention of Bullying and has developed an implementation plan to fill in any gaps in current practices. Bullying issues are a regular part of the team's work and are integrated into staff development efforts. **Evidence:** Ongoing discussions are documented in the Foundations Process Notebook. Established programs to enhance student engagement are documented in the Foundations Archive.

If any items are rated as less than In Place or if it has been more than 3 years since you have done so, work through the Module E Implementation Checklist.

Foundations Implementation Rubric and Summary (p. 7 of 8)

Presentation	Preparing (1)	Getting Started (2)	Moving Along (3)	In Place (4)
F2 Supporting Classroom Behavior: The Three-Legged Stool	A research-based model for classroom management has been adopted at the building or district level. All teachers have access to training, and teachers new to the building or district receive the same training.	School and district personnel are identified as resources for teachers who would like observations, feedback, and coaching. An effort is made to actively market the benefits of coaching support.	The administrator has communicated clear outcomes and goals of effective classroom management: • 90% engagement • 95% respectful interactions • 95% of behavior matches posted expectations	The model creates a common language among teachers, support staff, coaches, and administrators for problem solving and intervention. Data are collected and analyzed to evaluate classroom management efforts. **Evidence:** Information on the model, administrative walk-through visits, and coaching supports is included in the Foundations Archive and Staff Handbook.
F3 Articulating Staff Beliefs and Solidifying Universal Procedures	Foundations Team has reviewed sample staff beliefs about behavior management.	In faculty and staff meetings, faculty and staff have examined and discussed sample staff beliefs about behavior management.	All staff have developed and adopted a set of written staff beliefs regarding discipline and behavior, and ensured that it aligned with the school's mission statement.	To solidify the culture of the school and to guide the ongoing development of school policies and procedures, staff beliefs are reviewed, discussed, and revised as needed at least annually. **Evidence:** Staff beliefs and the review process are documented in the Foundations Archive and Staff Handbook.
F4 Early-Stage Interventions for General Education Classrooms	Foundations Team and support staff (counselor, school psychologist, and so on) understand the concept of early-stage intervention.	Foundations Team, support staff, and principal (or district administrators) agree on the interventions that should be included in the early-stage protocol.	All teachers and support staff have been trained on the interventions in the school or district early-stage protocol, including how and why to keep records of each intervention.	Data Collection and Debriefing (or an equivalent) is adopted as a required intervention for most chronic behavioral problems. Data must be charted before assistance is requested from support staff or problem-solving teams. **Evidence:** Expectations about when and how to get assistance are included in the Foundations Archive and Staff Handbook.
F5 Matching the Intensity of Your Resources to the Intensity of Your Needs	Foundations Team and support staff (counselor, psychologist, and so on) have identified a set of red-flag criteria and (if possible) have conducted universal screening to identify students who may need individual behavior support.	Foundations Team, support staff, and principal (or district administrators) agree on who can serve as advocates for students who need additional support.	The advocates meet regularly to discuss progress and case studies to ensure that each student's needs are being met. Patterns of need are communicated to the Foundations Team so prevention efforts can be implemented.	All support staff and problem-solving teams have written brief job descriptions that outline the services they can provide. The documents are shared with staff to inform them about available resources. **Evidence:** Suggestions for accessing these services are in the Foundations Archive and Staff Handbook.
F6 Problem-Solving Processes and Intervention Design	Foundations Team understands that it will not conduct staffings (team-based problem solving) on individual students, but the team should examine current processes for supporting students and staff.	Foundations Team and support staff (counselor, school psychologist, and so on) have discussed the range of problem-solving support (individuals and teams) currently available to students and staff.	Foundations Team and support staff have discussed the problem-solving processes suggested in *Foundations* (e.g., the 25-Minute Planning Process), and have determined whether the processes would strengthen current practices.	A flowchart or description of how the school meets the needs of students and staff has been created. It clarifies how the intensity of student needs matches the intensity of both problem-solving processes and intervention design and implementation. **Evidence:** This information is documented in the Foundations Archive and summarized in the Staff Handbook.
F7 Sustainability and District Support	Foundations Team archives data, in-process work, and all completed policies and procedures, and builds on this work each year.	Foundations Team orients new staff and re-energizes returning staff about all policies and procedures, and emphasizes unity and consistency.	Foundations Team uses the rubric annually and the Implementation Checklists as individual modules near completion and every 3 years thereafter. The team uses this information to guide staff in setting improvement priorities.	In larger districts (more than four schools), a district-based team works on sustainability. The team reminds schools about important milestones (e.g., surveys, year-end tasks, etc.) and ongoing staff development opportunities on behavior support. **Evidence:** This information can be found in district communications (e.g., emails) to schools and agenda items for principals' meetings.

If any items are rated as less than In Place or if it has been more than 3 years since you have done so, work through the Module F Implementation Checklist.

Foundations Implementation Rubric and Summary (p. 8 of 8)

	Preparing (1)	Getting Started (2)	Moving Along (3)	In Place (4)
Module A Presentations				
A1. Foundations: A Multi-Tiered System of Behavior Support				
A2. Team Processes				
A3. The Improvement Cycle				
A4. Data-Driven Processes				
A5. Developing Staff Engagement and Unity				
Module B Presentations				
Hallways				
Restrooms				
Cafeteria				
Playground, Courtyard, or Commons				
Arrival				
Dismissal				
Dress Code				
Other:				
Other:				
Other:				
Other:				
Module C Presentations				
C2. Guidelines for Success				
C3. Ratios of Positive Interactions				
C4. Improving Attendance				
C5 & C6. School Connectedness and Programs and Strategies for Meeting Needs				
C7. Welcoming New Staff, Students, and Families				
Module D Presentations				
D1. Proactive Procedures, Corrective Procedures, and Individual Interventions				
D2. Developing Three Levels of Misbehavior				
D3. Staff Responsibilities for Responding to Misbehavior				
D4. Administrator Responsibilities for Responding to Misbehavior				
D5. Preventing the Misbehavior That Leads to Referrals and Suspensions				
Module E Presentations				
E1. Ensuring a Safe Environment for Students				
E2. Attributes of Safe and Unsafe Schools				
E3. Teaching Conflict Resolution				
E4. Analyzing Bullying Behaviors, Policies, and School Needs				
E5. Schoolwide Bullying Prevention and Intervention				
Module F Presentations				
F2. Supporting Classroom Behavior: The Three-Legged Stool				
F3. Articulating Staff Beliefs and Solidifying Universal Procedures				
F4. Early-Stage Interventions for General Education Classrooms				
F5. Matching the Intensity of Your Resources to the Intensity of Your Needs				
F6. Problem-Solving Processes and Intervention Design				
F7. Sustainability and District Support				

APPENDIX B
Implementation Checklists

Implementation Checklists are detailed checklists of the processes and objectives in each *Foundations* module. The Module F checklist (Form F-02, pp. 316–344) includes checklists from all modules and and can be printed from the Module F CD.

As you near completion on the module, use the Implementation Checklist to ensure that you have fully implemented all recommendations. If you've decided not to follow some recommendations—you've adapted the procedures for your school—indicate the reason on the checklist. If data show problems later, this record of what you implemented and what you chose not to implement could be helpful in deciding what to do to address the problem.

In addition to using the checklists as needed, plan to work through all *Foundations* checklists every 3 years or so. See the sample schedule below. Additional information about Implementation Checklists appears in Module F, Presentation 7, Task 1.

Sample Long-Term Schedule: Improvement Priorities, Data Review & Monitoring

Year 1	Work on:
	• Modules A and B (continuous improvement process, common areas and schoolwide policies)
	• Cafeteria
	• Guidelines for Success
	In late spring, work through the Foundations Implementation Rubric for Modules A, B (cafeteria), and C2 (Guidelines for Success).
	Use the Modules A and B Implementation Checklists to assess status as you near completion of those modules.
Year 2	Work on:
	• Module C (inviting climate)
	• Hallways
	In the fall, evaluate cafeteria data.
	In late spring, work through the Foundations Implementation Rubric for Modules A, B (cafeteria and hallways), and C.
	Use the Module C Implementation Checklist to assess status as you near completion of Module C.

Year 3	Work on:
	• Module D (responding to misbehavior)
	• Playground
	In the fall, evaluate hallway data.
	In late spring, work through the Foundations Implementation Rubric for Modules A, B (cafeteria, hallways, and playground), C, and D.
	Use the Module D Implementation Checklist to assess status as you near completion of Module D.
Year 4	Work on:
	• Module E (safety, conflict, bullying prevention)
	• Arrival and dismissal
	In the fall, evaluate playground data.
	In late spring, work through the Foundations Implementation Rubric for Modules A, B (cafeteria, hallways, arrival and dismissal), C, D, and E.
	Use the Module E Implementation Checklist to assess status as you near completion of Module E.
	Monitor Year 1 priorities:
	• Module A Implementation Checklist
	• Module B Implementation Checklist for cafeteria
	• Module C Implementation Checklist for Guidelines for Success (C2 only)
Year 5	Work on:
	• Module F (classroom management and sustaining *Foundations*)
	• Assemblies
	• Guest teachers
	In the fall, evaluate arrival and dismissal data.
	In late spring, work through the Foundations Implementation Rubric for Modules A, B (playground, arrival and dismissal, assemblies, guest teachers), C, D, E, and F.
	Use the Module F Implementation Checklist to assess status as you near completion of Module F.
	Monitor Year 2 priorities:
	• Module B Implementation Checklist for hallways
	• Module C Implementation Checklist

Year 6	In the fall, evaluate assemblies and guest teacher data.
	Work through the Foundations Implementation Rubric for all modules.
	Monitor Year 3 priorities:
	• Module B Implementation Checklist for playground • Module D Implementation Checklist
Year 7	In the fall, work through the Foundations Implementation Rubric for all modules and all common areas and schoolwide policies.
	Monitor Year 4 priorities:
	• Module A Implementation Checklist • Module B Implementation Checklist for arrival, dismissal, and cafeteria • Module C Implementation Checklist for Guidelines for Success (C2 only) • Module E Implementation Checklist
Year 8	In the fall, work through the Foundations Implementation Rubric for all modules and all common areas and schoolwide policies.
	Monitor Year 5 priorities:
	• Module B Implementation Checklist for assemblies, guest teachers, and hallways • Module B Implementation Checklist for hallways • Module C Implementation Checklist • Module F Implementation Checklist
Year 9	In the fall, work through the Foundations Implementation Rubric for all modules and all common areas and schoolwide policies.
	Monitor Year 6 priorities:
	• Module B Implementation Checklist for playground • Module D Implementation Checklist

Module A Implementation Checklist

Implementation Actions	Completed Y/N	Evidence of Implementation	Evidence Y/N
Presentation 1: Foundations—A Multi-Tiered System of Behavior Support	✓		✓
1. Decisions have been made about how to integrate a multi-tiered approach to behavior (*Foundations*/PBIS) with a multi-tiered approach to academic and instructional improvement. You may use one team, two separate teams, or one large team with two separate task forces.	☐	Foundations Process: Team Composition*	☐
2. Information has has been presented to staff about *Foundations*, including, but not limited to, the following basic beliefs: • Punitive and corrective techniques are necessary, but have significant limitations; misbehavior is a teaching opportunity. • In common areas and with schoolwide policies, clear expectations and consistent enforcement are essential. • Staff behavior creates the climate of the school; a positive, welcoming, and inviting climate should be intentionally created and continuously maintained. • All students should have equal access to good instruction and behavior support, regardless of their skills or background. • All student behaviors necessary for success must be overtly and directly articulated and taught to mastery. "If you want it, teach it!" • Everyone (even students who make poor choices) should be treated with respect.	☐	Foundations Archive: Presentations/ Communications With Staff* *These notebooks are discussed in Presentation 2. Documentation of Presentation 1 tasks can be added to the notebooks when record-keeping procedures are established.	☐
Presentation 2: Team Processes			
1. The Foundations Team has been established by modifying an existing team or forming a new team. • Team composition includes an administrator, classroom teachers, and others. • The team formally represents the entire staff. Each team member knows the staff members he or she represents, and staff members know who represents them on the team. *(continued)*	☐	Foundations Process: Team Composition	☐

Module A Implementation Checklist

Implementation Actions	Completed Y/N	Evidence of Implementation	Evidence Y/N
Presentation 2 (*continued*)	✓		✓
2. The team meets regularly for a minimum of 4 hours per quarter.	☐	Foundations Process: Meeting Minutes	☐
3. Team members have assigned roles, such as: • Chair or Cochair • Recorder • Data/Evaluation Coordinator • Materials Manager • Keeper of the List • Staff Liaison • Equity and Student Liaison • Family Engagement Coordinator	☐	Foundations Process: Team Composition	☐
4. The team creates processes for orienting new team members.	☐	Foundations Archive: New Staff Orientation	☐
5. At least once per month, the team communicates to staff about the *Foundations* implementation by (for example) sharing data, reminding staff about some aspect of implementation, sharing strategies, or celebrating successes.	☐	Foundations Process: Presentations/ Communications With Staff	☐
6. Record-keeping and archiving procedures have been established, including a Foundations Process Notebook, Foundations Archive, Staff Handbook, and Student and Parent Handbook. The Foundations Process Notebook is for working documents and includes at least the following (or similar) sections. • Team Composition • Planning Calendar • Meeting Minutes • Data Summaries • Current Priorities (with record of the data that led to the area or policy becoming a priority) • Safety • Guidelines for Success • Presentations/Communications With Staff • Communications With Parents • 3-Level System for Responding to Misbehavior • Foundations Implementation Rubric and Summary and Implementation Checklists (*continued*)	☐	See the four notebooks (listed for items 1–5 above).	☐

Implementation Actions	Completed Y/N	Evidence of Implementation	Evidence Y/N
Presentation 2 (*continued*)	✓		✓
The Foundations Archive is for finalized documents and includes at least the following (or similar) sections: • Long-Term Planning Calendar • Guidelines for Success • 3-Level System for Responding to Misbehavior • Job Descriptions for Common Area Supervisors • Schoolwide Policies • Common Area Policies and Procedures • Safety Policies • Lesson Plans for Teaching Common Area and Schoolwide Policy Expectations • Lesson Plans for Teaching Safety Expectations • Lesson Plans for Teaching Guidelines for Success • Lesson Plans for Teaching Expectations for Interacting With Adults			
7. The team has chosen a team name.	☐	Foundations Process: Team Composition, Meeting Minutes	☐
8. Team meeting ground rules have been established, such as: • An established minimum number of members must be present. • Meetings will start and end on time. • No side conversations during the meeting. • All team discussions and disagreements will be respectful. • Before speaking, team members will paraphrase what the speaker before them said. • A cochair will serve as the on-task and on-time "nag." • Meeting minutes will identify specific tasks to be accomplished with responsible staff and timelines; these tasks will be highlighted. • Meetings will follow an agreed-upon agenda.	☐	Foundations Process: Meeting Minutes	☐
9. Annually, team members reflect on their roles as team members, perhaps by using the Are You an Effective Team Builder? self-assessment tool.	☐	Foundations Process: Meeting Minutes	☐

Module A Implementation Checklist (p. 4 of 29)

Implementation Actions	Completed Y/N	Evidence of Implementation	Evidence Y/N
Presentation 3: The Improvement Cycle	✓		✓
1. The team annually **reviews** multiple data sources about climate, discipline, and safety (some data sources are reviewed more frequently).	☐	Foundations Process: Data Summaries	☐
2. The team presents summaries of the data for staff (and for students and parents, as appropriate).	☐	Foundations Process: Presentations/ Communications With Staff presentations	☐
3. At least once per semester, the staff **prioritizes** one to three problem areas or concerns for improvement.	☐	Foundations Process: Current Priorities	☐
4. The team (or a special task force) develops a comprehensive proposal to **revise** policies and procedures to address the prioritized problem or concern and presents the proposal to staff for feedback.	☐	Foundations Process: Current Priorities	☐
5. The staff **adopts** or rejects the proposal using a consensus-based process such as the Five Levels of Satisfaction Voting System. • If the proposal is rejected, the team or task force reworks it and presents it to staff again (as many as two revision cycles). • If the staff rejects the initial and two revised proposals, the principal determines the final policy or procedure.	☐	Foundations Process: Meeting Minutes	☐
6. When a policy or procedure is finalized, all staff are provided guidance in how to **implement** it.	☐	Foundations Process: Presentations/ Communications With Staff	☐
7. The team and building-based administrators monitor the fidelity of implementation and efficacy of the policy, making adjustments as needed.	☐	Foundations Process: Current Priorities	☐

Implementation Actions	Completed Y/N	Evidence of Implementation	Evidence Y/N
Presentation 4: Data-Driven Processes	✓ ☐		✓ ☐
1. A plan for data review is in place and includes the range of data sources to be used, the frequency of review, due dates, and responsible team members. The following data sources have been considered:		Foundations Process: Planning Calendar, Meeting Minutes, Data Summaries	

- Anonymous surveys of staff, students, and parents to assess their perceptions of school safety, climate, connectedness, bullying, and so on (administered at least annually).
- Formal observations of both student and staff behavior in common areas (conducted in winter and spring).
- Trends and patterns of incident reports, including both office referrals and Level 2 Notifications (explained in Module D; review at least quarterly).
- Data to assess the *Foundations* suggestions about 90% Thresholds (review at least annually).
    - Every family helps children attend at least 90% of school days, on time and ready to learn.
    - Every administrator ensures that at least 90% of school minutes (minus lunch) are instructional.
    - Every teacher uses at least 90% of instructional time for instructional activities.
    - At least 90% of students are engaged during every instructional activity.
    - Every student is engaged at least 90% of instructional minutes.
- Other pre-existing data sources (review at least annually and some, such as chronic absenteeism, at least monthly). Sources include:
    - Average daily attendance and absence rates
    - Tardiness rates
    - Suspensions, expulsions, and referrals to alternative education placements
    - Referrals to special education
    - Number of students referred to special education who did not qualify
    - Instances of vandalism and graffiti
    - Instances of other illegal activities
    - Injury reports
    - Feedback from staff

(continued)

Implementation Actions	Completed Y/N	Evidence of Implementation	Evidence Y/N
Presentation 4 (*continued*)	✓		✓

1. (*continued*)
   ◦ Focus groups
   ◦ Social-emotional support (information from counselors, social workers, school psychologists)
   ◦ Red flags
   ◦ Summaries of universal screening			

2. The team collects, analyzes, and presents summaries and findings to staff at least quarterly.	☐	Foundations Process: Presentations/ Communications With Staff	☐
3. The staff uses these data summaries to identify a manageable number of priorities for improvement.	☐	Foundations Process: Meeting Minutes, Current Priorities	☐
4. The team uses data to assess the implementation of revised policies and procedures. Is behavior in prioritized common areas and related to schoolwide policies improving?	☐	Foundations Process: Data Summaries, Current Priorities	☐
Presentation 5: Developing Staff Engagement and Unity			

1. At least quarterly, the team discusses activities, programs, and strategies for motivating staff and increasing the degree to which staff buy in to and actively implement and support policies and procedures that support student behavior.
   • If some staff members are reluctant to buy into *Foundations*, the team discusses ways to encourage and include those staff.
   • The team discussses rituals and incentives for motivating staff, and they implement any that are appropriate.
	☐	Foundations Process: Meeting Minutes	☐

2. The principal and assistant principals have reviewed the content in Task 2, reflected on the leadership suggestions, and identified the skills that seem most useful to facilitate continuous improvement efforts in your school.	☐	Interview with administrators	☐

Date of Discussion: _____

Annually, the Foundations Team as a group should evaluate the three items below.

Implementation Actions	Completed Y/N	Evidence of Implementation	Evidence Y/N
1. All staff have been involved in completing a list of the school's common areas (settings and situations) and schoolwide policies.	✓ ☐	Foundations Process: Current Priorities	✓ ☐
2. All staff have been involved in ranking the common areas and schoolwide policies from most to least urgent and deciding which area or policy (and how many) to work on.	☐	Foundations Process: Current Priorities	☐
3. Each year, multiple data sources (surveys, observations, incident referrals, and injury reports) are used to assess strengths and concerns about each common area and schoolwide policy. Areas of concern are identified to eventually become priorities for improvement.	☐	Foundations Process: Data Summaries	☐

The following checklist is an abbreviated version of the Revision Checklist and STOIC Worksheet (Form B-06). You do not need to work through the STOIC portion of the checklist for each common area or schoolwide policy each year. It is most useful for common areas and schoolwide policies that have been targeted as a priority for improvement. For example, as you are preparing to present a revision proposal to the staff for adoption, the checklist can help you evaluate whether you have addressed all essential issues. For areas and policies that you've already revised, we recommend you work through this checklist as a team every 3 years (anytime during the year) to determine whether the policies and procedures are still working well, need tweaking, or need to become a priority for improvement (for example, when observations show major safety issues).

Over time, every common area and schoolwide policy should be analyzed and revised as needed, and the procedures documented in the Foundations Process Notebook

Common Area or Schoolwide Policy: _____

Implementation Actions (Using STOIC Framework)	Completed Y/N	Evidence of Implementation	Evidence Y/N
1. (S) Structure	✓ ☐	Foundations Process: Current Priorities	✓ ☐
A. Considerations for improving the structural and organizational features of the prioritized common area or schoolwide policy have been considered, including (but not limited to) whether and how the following might be contributing to student behavior problems: • Physical setting and materials • Entry and exit procedures • Scheduling • Overcrowding • Procedures		*When policies are final, file them in the Foundations Archive:*	
B. Current behavioral expectations for the prioritized common area or schoolwide policy have been evaluated and revised as needed to ensure that the expectations are: • Clear • Age appropriate • Sufficiently detailed • Reasonable and humane (for example, students are not expected to do nothing) • Known by all supervising staff members and other adults who might be in the setting or situation	☐	Foundations Archive: Schoolwide Policies, Common Area Policies and Procedures	☐
C. Elementary schools have determined whether schoolwide policies for behavior with specialists are needed.	☐	Foundations Archive: Schoolwide Policies	☐
D. Current supervision arrangements for the prioritized common area or schoolwide policy have been evaluated and, if needed, revised to ensure that the following measures are in place: • There are enough supervisors. • The supervision schedule is adequate. • Supervisors are strategically placed throughout the setting or situation. • Supervisors circulate unpredictably throughout the setting or situation. • Emergency communication procedures are established for supervisors to use. • Supervisors are trained in established emergency communication procedures. *(continued)*	☐	Foundations Archive: Schoolwide Policies	☐

Implementation Actions (Using STOIC Framework)	Completed Y/N	Evidence of Implementation	Evidence Y/N
(*continued*) **(S) Structure** E. Develop job descriptions for supervisors of particularly complex settings, such as playgrounds and cafeterias.	✓ ☐	Foundations Archive: Job Descriptions for Common Area Supervisors	✓ ☐
2. (T) Teach expectations. One or more lessons have been developed to teach students the expectations for behavior in the prioritized common area and related to the schoolwide policy. An implementation plan for the lessons has been developed and includes: • Who will teach the lessons • A schedule for teaching the lesson(s) to students and communicating essential information to parents (e.g., dress code) • A plan for when and how lessons will be re-taught	☐	Foundations Archive: Lesson Plans for Teaching Common Area and Schoolwide Policy Expectations	☐
3. (O) Observe and supervise. Staff who have supervisory responsibilities for the prioritized common areas and schoolwide policies have been trained in active supervision. If there is a job description, staff have been trained in all the details.	☐	Foundations Process: Presentations/Communications With Staff Foundations Archive: Job Descriptions for Common Area Supervisors	☐
4. (I) Interact positively with students. Staff who have supervisory responsibilities understand and follow through on: • Using noncontingent interactions such as greetings. • Using age-appropriate positive feedback. • Maintaining 3:1 ratios of positive interactions.	☐	Staff Handbook: Roles and Responsibilities	☐
5. (C) Correct fluently. Staff who have supervisory responsibilities understand and follow through on correcting misbehavior: • Consistently • Calmly • Immediately • Briefly • Respectfully	☐	Staff Handbook: Roles and Responsibilities	☐

Implementation Actions	Completed Y/N	Evidence of Implementation	Evidence Y/N
Presentation 1: Constructing and Maintaining a Positive Climate	✓		✓
1. The team has presented to or reviewed with all staff the concept of and the role staff members play in consciously constructing a positive, inviting school climate.	☐	Foundations Process: Presentations/ Communications With Staff	☐
2. The team has presented to or reviewed with all staff how an inviting climate affects school connectedness, which in turn affects academic achievement, dropout rates, the health choices students make, and more.	☐	Foundations Process: Presentations/ Communications With Staff	☐
Presentation 2: Guidelines for Success			
1. During initial development, the team has determined whether the school already has something comparable to Guidelines for Success (GFS), such as schoolwide goals or a pledge, and whether it is used by staff throughout the school, taught to students, and communicated to families. If yes, skip development tasks 2 and 3 below.	☐	Foundations Process: Guidelines for Success	☐
2. When developing the school's GFS, the team or task force presented the concept and usefulness of GFS to the entire staff.	☐	Foundations Process: Presentations/ Communications With Staff	☐
3. When developing the school's GFS, the team or task force gathered suggestions from staff, students, and families on both the content of and the name for the GFS, and the team or task force designed a development process that actively involved the staff and created a sense of value and ownership among staff.	☐	Foundations Process: Guidelines for Success	☐
4. GFS (or equivalent) are highly visible throughout the school, in all classrooms, in communications with parents, and in staff and student handbooks.	☐	Observable; Staff Handbook; Student and Parent Handbook; Foundations Process: Communications With Parents	☐
5. GFS are relaunched and directly taught to students at the beginning of each new school year.	☐	Foundations Archive: Lesson Plans for Teaching GFS	☐
6. A GFS implementation calendar is developed to ensure that GFS are woven into the fabric of school life and used as the hub of all behavior management and motivation practices.	☐	Foundations Process: Planning Calendar	☐

Implementation Actions	Completed Y/N	Evidence of Implementation	Evidence Y/N
Presentation 3: Ratios of Positive Interactions	✓		✓
1. The team has presented to or reviewed with all staff the concept of ratios of positive interactions (RPI) and the differences between and definitions of attention to positive behavior (positives) and attention to corrective behavior (correctives).	☐	FoundationsProcess: Presentations/ Communications With Staff	☐
2. Staff have received training and understand the potential negative impact of ratios skewed to correctives—specifically, that some students learn that it is easier to get adult attention by breaking rules than by following rules. Conversely, staff understand that a ratio skewed at least 3 to 1 toward the positive can be a powerful tool in setting a positive climate and encouraging responsible behavior.	☐	Foundations Process: Presentations/ Communications With Staff	☐
3. Staff have received training in how to identify and count both positives and correctives.	☐	Foundations Process: Presentations/ Communications With Staff	☐
4. At least once per year, staff use the Ratios of Positive Interactions Monitoring Form (Reproducible Form C-03a, b, and c) to monitor and analyze their RPI with students during the most challenging 30 minutes of the school day.	☐	Interviews With Staff	☐
5. Annually, staff use the document Strategies for Increasing Positive Interactions (Reproducible Form C-04) and place reminders in their planning calendars to consciously work on keeping the positives at a very high level.	☐	Interviews With Staff	☐
6. Staff are encouraged (perhaps even required) to observe a colleague and count RPI.	☐	Interviews With Staff	☐
7. Whenever a student exhibits chronic motivation or behavior problems, staff consider the RPI concepts and establish a plan to modify some aspect of their current interactions with that student.	☐	Interviews With Staff	☐
8. The team involves staff in developing a plan for giving respectful, attention-grabbing reminders about RPI to staff.	☐	Foundations Process: Meeting Minutes, Planning Calendar	☐

Implementation Actions	Completed Y/N	Evidence of Implementation	Evidence Y/N
Presentation 4: Improving Attendance	✓		✓
1. The Foundations Team has developed information about the importance of attendance and presents it to staff, students, and families regularly throughout the school year.	☐	Foundations Process: Presentations/ Communications With Staff, Communications With Parents	☐
2. The team has reviewed the current attendance policy and revised it as needed to increase clarity and to address any absenteeism concerns.	☐	Foundations Process: Attendance Initiatives	☐
3. The team (or attendance task force) meets regularly (at least once a month) to review attendance data, identify schoolwide trends and priorities, and link individual students who meet red flag criteria with individual support systems.	☐	Foundations Process: Meeting Minutes	☐
4. The team (or attendance task force) has identified and implemented schoolwide strategies (as described in Module C, Presentation 4) to address the trends and causes of absenteeism suggested by attendance data.	☐	Foundations Archive: Attendance Initiatives	☐
5. Each student with chronic absenteeism has been assigned one school-based support person who monitors whether additional support is needed. When a student has been resistant to universal and Tier 2 supports, the student becomes the focus of a multidisciplinary team effort.	☐	Foundations Process: Attendance Initiatives	☐
6. The team has a plan to provide a comprehensive review of the importance of attendance with staff, students, and parents every 3 years (or more frequently).	☐	Foundations Archive: Long-Term Planning Calendar	☐

Implementation Actions	Completed Y/N	Evidence of Implementation	Evidence Y/N
Presentation 5: School Connectedness—Meeting Basic Human Needs and Presentation 6: Programs and Strategies for Meeting Needs	✓		✓
1. The Foundations Team has discussed whether the proposed list of eight basic needs or an alternative construct will work best as a vehicle to make the school a great place for all students.	☐	Foundations Process: Meeting Minutes, Students' Basic Needs	☐
2. The team has generated a list of the school's current positive programs and practices, and that list has been analyzed for the basic needs the various programs might address.	☐	Foundations Process: Students' Basic Needs	☐
3. Each team member has completed the Analysis of Student Needs Worksheet (Reproducible Form C-07), and the team has compiled the data and analyzed them for patterns of unmet needs. The team plans to conduct this analysis every 3 years (or more frequently).	☐	Foundations Process: Students' Basic Needs	☐
4. The team (particularly at the secondary level) has considered asking the staff to identify students who have no involvement in school activities and no or few staff members they can converse with.	☐	Foundations Process: Students' Basic Needs	☐
5. The team has discussed ways to modify existing programs and practices to get nonconnected students involved in school activities.	☐	Foundations Process: Meeting Minutes, Student's Basic Needs	☐
6. The team has reviewed the programs and practices described in Module C, Presentation 6 to determine whether new programs or practices might be developed to meet the needs of students whose needs are not currently being met.	☐	Foundations Process: Meeting Minutes, Student's Basic Needs	☐

Implementation Actions	Completed Y/N	Evidence of Implementation	Evidence Y/N
Presentation 7: Making a Good First Impression—Welcoming New Staff, Students, and Families	✓		✓
1. The team has analyzed the physical building (especially signage), website, and office staff skills (both in person and on the phone) to assess how welcoming and helpful the school is to visitors and new arrivals. Problems and gaps have been addressed. The team plans to conduct this analysis every 3 years (or more frequently).	☐	Foundations Process: Meeting Minutes	☐
2. *Elementary level:* The team has collected data from focus groups or surveys of a new cohort of parents (e.g., entering kindergarten students) to learn what the school can do to improve the orientation and acculturation of entering students and families.	☐	Foundations Process: Data Summaries	☐
3. *Secondary level:* The team has collected data from focus groups or surveys of a new cohort of students (e.g., entering sixth graders or ninth graders) to learn about what the school can do to improve the orientation and acculturation of entering students.	☐	Foundations Process: Data Summaries	☐
4. The team analyzes how well the school welcomes new cohorts, students entering at the beginning of the year who are not part of the cohort, and students entering midyear. Extra thought is given to recent immigrants. Adjustments are made so that the school is as supportive and welcoming as possible to these students.	☐	Foundations Archive: New Student Orientation	☐
5. The team analyzes how well the school welcomes and acculturates new staff members. Additional thought goes into the needs of first-year teachers and new noncertified staff. Adjustments are made so that the school is as supportive and welcoming as possible for these staff members.	☐	Foundations Archive: New Staff Orientation	☐

Implementation Actions	Completed Y/N	Evidence of Implementation	Evidence Y/N
Presentation 1: The Relationship Between Proactive Procedures, Corrective Procedures, and Individual Student Behavior Improvement Plans	✓		✓
1. Data are collected (e.g., from staff surveys) and staff have discussed concepts relating to consistency in correcting student misbehavior.	☐	Foundations Process: Presentations/ Communications With Staff	☐
2. Staff have discussed and identified their perceptions of their roles in correcting misbehavior in relation to the principal's (or assistant principal's) role.	☐	Foundations Process: Presentations/ Communications With Staff	☐
3. Staff understand the potential limitations of office referrals. At the elementary level, staff understand the potential inconsistencies of a progressive discipline system (in which students must be removed from class after the third or fourth infraction) and modify the system so it is fair and consistent.	☐	Foundations Process: Presentations/ Communications With Staff	☐
4. Staff are aware of the limited benefits of and potential drawbacks to out-of-school suspension (OSS) as a corrective consequence.	☐	Foundations Process: Presentations/ Communications With Staff	☐
5. Staff are aware of and can have honest discussions about national data on the disparate impact of OSS on minority students and students with disabilities.	☐	Foundations Process: Presentations/ Communications With Staff	☐
6. Staff avoid pressuring administrators to use OSS.	☐	Interview with administrator	☐
Presentation 2: Developing Three Levels of Misbehavior			
1. The Foundations Team has communicated to staff the *Foundations* concept of three levels of misbehavior: Level 1 (mild), Level 2 (moderate), and Level 3 (severe). Staff understand that the levels are defined more by the staff member's response to the misbehavior than by the misbehavior itself.	☐	Foundations Process: Presentations/ Communications With Staff	☐
2. The Foundations Team has solicited information from the administrator about the types of misbehaviors that currently result in office referrals.	☐	Foundations Process: 3-Level System for Responding to Misbehavior	☐
3. Administrators have defined the specific behaviors that *must* be considered Level 3 (e.g., weapons). *(continued)*	☐	Foundations Archive: 3-Level System for Responding to Misbehavior	☐

Implementation Actions	Completed Y/N	Evidence of Implementation	Evidence Y/N
Presentation 2 (*continued*)	✓		✓
4. Staff have reached consensus on the types of behaviors that *must* be referred to the office as Level 3 and those that *may* be referred.	☐	Foundations Archive and Staff Handbook: 3-Level System for Responding to Misbehavior	☐
5. Staff understand that Level 2 notifications provide a way to get support for the staff member and to keep administrators and support staff informed about students with severe or chronic behaviors who may need additional support.	☐	Foundations Process: Presentations/ Communications With Staff	☐
6. A referral form or forms and a data system have been developed to facilitate efficient and clear communication and data collection.	☐	Foundations Process: Presentations/ Communications With Staff	☐
Presentation 3: Staff Responsibilities for Responding to Misbehavior			
1. Staff have reached consensus on menus of corrective actions for Level 1 mild misbehaviors for both classrooms and common areas.	☐	Foundations Archive and Staff Handbook: 3-Level System for Responding to Misbehavior	☐
2. Staff have reached consensus on staff procedures for Level 2 moderate misbehaviors for both classrooms and common areas.	☐	Foundations Archive and Staff Handbook: 3-Level System for Responding to Misbehavior	☐
3. Administrators have developed procedures for responding to Level 2 moderate notifications that support the staff member who wrote the notification.	☐	Foundations Archive: 3-Level System for Responding to Misbehavior	☐
4. Staff have reached consensus on a menu of corrective actions for Level 2 moderate misbehavior that includes all Level 1 corrections and all schoolwide consequences that do not require administrator involvement.	☐	Foundations Archive and Staff Handbook: 3-Level System for Responding to Misbehavior	☐
5. Staff have reached consensus on Level 2 notification procedures, such as whether to contact parents and whether to have students sign the form.	☐	Foundations Archive and Staff Handbook: 3-Level System for Responding to Misbehavior	☐
6. Staff have been given information about writing effective referrals, with an emphasis on correct grammar and spelling and on use of objective descriptions rather than labels or emotional language.	☐	Foundations Process: Presentations/ Communications With Staff	☐

Implementation Actions	Completed Y/N	Evidence of Implementation	Evidence Y/N
Presentation 4: Administrator Responsibilities for Responding to Misbehavior	✓		✓
1. Decisions have been made about who will process Level 2 notifications.	☐	Foundations Archive: 3-Level System for Responding to Misbehavior	☐
2. Staff, administrator, and support-staff procedures have been coordinated to ensure that students who receive notifications get the support they need to be successful.	☐	Foundations Archive: 3-Level System for Responding to Misbehavior	☐
3. Data collection procedures for Level 2 notifications have been developed so trends and patterns of notifications can drive school improvement.	☐	Foundations Archive: 3-Level System for Responding to Misbehavior	☐
4. Administrators have developed detailed procedures for managing Level 3 office referrals, including the following: • "Who Is Responsible" list • Game plan for dealing with referred students • Menu of corrective consequences that includes alternatives to out-of-school suspension • Sequence of steps for returning students to their regular schedules	☐	Interview with administrator Foundations Archive: 3-Level System for Responding to Misbehavior	☐
5. Current office procedures have been analyzed and streamlined, if needed, to address the following questions: • How will office staff supervise referred students throughout the entire process? • What will office staff do if the administrator is unavailable when referred students arrive at the office? • Where will referred students wait for the administrator? • What should referred students do while waiting for the administrator? • How should office personnel interact with referred students?	☐	Foundations Archive: Common Area Policies and Procedures Staff Handbook: Staff Roles and Responsibilities	☐
(continued)			

Implementation Actions	Completed Y/N	Evidence of Implementation	Evidence Y/N
Presentation 4 (*continued*)	✓		✓
6. If the school has an in-school-suspension process, that process has been analyzed and streamlined, if needed, to address the following questions: • What conditions are necessary to effectively implement an ISS program? • What skills do staff need? • Who will develop the program and document the program policies and procedures in writing? • How will the program's efficacy be evaluated, and who will evaluate it?	☐	Foundations Archive: 3-Level System for Responding to Misbehavior	☐
Presentation 5: Preventing the Misbehavior That Leads to Referrals and Suspensions			
1. The Foundations Team has analyzed whether students would benefit from lessons on how to interact appropriately with adults. Would these skills reduce the behaviors that lead to referrals and suspensions (e.g., refusal to follow reasonable directions from staff)?	☐	Foundations Process: Meeting Minutes, Presentations/ Communications With Staff	☐
2. The Foundations Team has reviewed the sample lessons in *Foundations* and has compared them with student skill deficits and social skills or social-emotional curricula currently in use to determine whether the lessons might benefit some or all students.	☐	Foundations Process: Meeting Minutes Foundations Archive: Lesson Plans for Teaching Expectations for Interacting With Adults	☐
3. If appropriate, a process has been established for finalizing lesson content, and a timeline has been set for lesson delivery.	☐	Foundations Archive: Lesson Plans for Teaching Expectations for Interacting With Adults	☐

Implementation Actions	Completed Y/N	Evidence of Implementation	Evidence Y/N
Presentation 1: Keeping Students Safe From Physical and Emotional Harm	✓		✓
1. The Foundations Team (or a subset of the team) has viewed or read Presentation 2 on safety, completed the Presentation 2 portion of this Implementation Checklist, and, if needed, established a plan of action.	☐	Foundations Process: Safety	☐
2. The team (or a subset of the team) has viewed or read Presentation 3 on conflict resolution, completed the Presentation 3 portion of this Implementation Checklist, and, if needed, established a plan of action.	☐	Foundations Process: Safety	☐
3. The team (or a subset of the team) has viewed or read Presentations 4 and 5 on reducing bullying, completed the Presentations 4 and 5 portions of this Implementation Checklist, and, if needed, established a plan of action.	☐	Foundations Process: Safety	☐
Presentation 2: Attributes of Safe and Unsafe Schools			
1. The Foundations Team or safety task force has completed the Attributes of Safe and Unsafe Schools form (Form E-03), then as a group discussed and reached a consensus score for each item. Consensus scores have been recorded and used to establish priorities for improving safety in the school.	☐	Foundations Process: Safety	☐
2. The team or task force has identified any other staff members or groups working on school safety and has coordinated with those people or groups to ensure that efforts are not duplicated. The team or task force has also determined whether any school safety assessments were conducted in the last 3 years.	☐	Foundations Process: Safety	☐
3. The team or task force has completed Assessing Emergency Preparedness (Form E-04) and, if needed, established priorities for improvement.	☐	Foundations Process: Safety	☐
4. All possible emergency situations (natural disaster, man-made, medical, and student behavior) that need written response plans have been identified, and all plans are complete and current. *(continued)*	☐	Foundations Archive: Safety Policies	☐

Implementation Actions	Completed Y/N	Evidence of Implementation	Evidence Y/N
Presentation 2 (*continued*)	✓		✓
5. A system is in place to ensure that all emergency plans are reviewed and updated annually.	☐	Foundations Process: Planning Calendar	☐
6. The team or task force has completed the Evaluation Form: Lessons to Increase Connectedness and Safety (E-05) and used that information to establish priorities for improving safety in the school.	☐	Foundations Process: Safety	☐
7. The team or task force has developed and implemented a plan for informing students and parents annually about all important safety considerations, including but not limited to student lessons.	☐	Foundations Archive: Safety Policies Student and Parent Handbk: Policies and Procedures	☐
8. The team or task force has reviewed the sample lessons in Presentation 2 and developed a plan to use those lessons (with modifications as needed), implement other published curricula, or create new lessons. A plan for initial delivery and subsequent review has been developed and implemented.	☐	Foundations Archive: Lesson Plans for Teaching Safety Expectations Foundations Process: Planning Calendar	☐
Presentation 3: Teaching Conflict Resolution			
1. The Foundations Team (with the administrator) has reviewed the tasks and sample conflict resolution lessons and has determined (or guided the staff through determining) whether to implement STP. If not, the team has clarified the reason why (e.g., the school already has a conflict resolution strategy that students and staff actively use, or conflict resolution is not currently a priority).	☐	Foundations Process: Safety	☐
2. If the school will adopt STP, the team has completed the following implementation steps: • Ensure that staff, especially teachers, are aware of STP's major steps. • Design schoolwide lessons and implement them. • Determine how supervisors will be trained and implement that plan. • Work through possible areas of staff resistance to implementing STP. • Decide on schoolwide procedures for teaching students about dispersing from a conflict. *(continued)*	☐	Foundations Process: Safety, Presentations/ Communications With Staff Foundations Archive: Lesson Plans for Teaching Safety Expectations, Safety Policies Staff Handbook: Policies and Procedures Student and Parent Handbook: Policies and Procedures	☐

Implementation Actions	Completed Y/N	Evidence of Implementation	Evidence Y/N
Presentation 3 (*continued*) • Inform staff of the content of any extension lessons. • Establish feedback loops so that information about actual conflicts goes to the people who teach the lessons. • Decide how to involve parents. • Develop a plan to get students to generalize the STP strategy. • Evaluate the effectiveness of the STP implementation and make adjustments as needed. • Develop emergency procedures so that if STP fails, all staff know what to do. • Develop long-range procedures for dealing with students who chronically fight or exhibit aggressive behavior, including re-teaching of STP processes	✓		✓
3. The team has developed and implemented a plan for sharing conflict resolution information and strategies with parents, including presentations at a PTA meeting or Back to School Night, website content, newsletters, email blasts, and video examples posted online.	☐	Foundations Process: Planning Calendar, Communications W/ Parents Foundations Archive: Lesson Plans for Teaching Safety Expectations	☐
Presentation 4: Analyzing Bullying Behavior, Policies, and School Needs			
1. The Foundations Team (with the administrator) has viewed or read the tasks in Presentations 4 and 5 and determined (or guided the staff through determining) whether the tasks and suggested actions will be implemented. If not, the team has clarified the reason why (e.g., the school already has an approach to bullying prevention and intervention that accomplishes the suggested actions).	☐	Foundations Process: Meeting Minutes, Presentations/ Communications With Staff	☐
2. The team or bullying prevention task force has completed School-Based Analysis of Bullying Data (Form E-06). Based on that information, any gaps or weaknesses in current data collection policies and procedures have been identified and addressed.	☐	Foundations Process: Meeting Minutes Foundations Archive: Bullying Prevention	☐

Implementation Actions	Completed Y/N	Evidence of Implementation	Evidence Y/N
Presentation 4 (*continued*)	✓		✓
3. The team or task force has completed School-Based Analysis of Bullying Policies (Form E-09). Based on that information, any gaps or weaknesses in current policies and procedures have been identified and addressed. The completed policies ensure that all staff, students, and families have the information they need to prevent bullying and respond effectively when it occurs.	☐	Foundations Process: Meeting Minutes, Presentations/ Communications With Staff, Communications With Parents Final policies will be placed in the Foundations Archive: Schoolwide Policies, Bullying Prevention	☐
4. The team (or task force) analyzes all data related to bullying at least annually and answers the questions on STOIC Analysis for Universal Prevention of Bullying (Form E-10). If needed, additional data are collected (e.g., to determine why a particular location is a hot spot for bullying), and a plan is developed and implemented to address concerns.	☐	Foundations Process: Data Summaries, Current Priorities	☐
Presentation 5: Schoolwide Bullying Prevention and Intervention			
1. The Foundations Team or bullying prevention task force has completed Staff Training in Preventing and Responding to Bullying (Form E-11). Based on that information, any gaps or weaknesses in current staff training have been identified and addressed.	☐	Foundations Process: Presentations/ Communications to Stafff	☐
2. The team or task force has completed Student Training in Preventing and Responding to Bullying (Form E-12). Based on that information, any gaps or weaknesses in current student training have been identified and addressed.	☐	Foundations Archive: Lesson Plans for Bullying Prevention	☐
3. The team or task force has completed Family Training in Preventing and Responding to Bullying (Form E-13). Based on that information, any gaps or weaknesses in communicating with and training families have been identified and addressed. Scripts for staff that facilitate conversations with families of students who were involved in bullying incidents have been developed.	☐	Foundations Process: Communications With Parents Foundations Archive: Bullying Prevention	☐

(*continued*)

Implementation Actions	Completed Y/N	Evidence of Implementation	Evidence Y/N
Presentation 5 (*continued*)	✓ ☐		✓ ☐
4. The team or task force has completed Active Engagement for the Prevention of Bullying (Form E-14). Based on that information, any gaps or weaknesses in current engagement practices have been identified and addressed, especially related to students who are victimized by and students who engage in bullying behavior.		Foundations Archive: Students' Basic Needs, Bullying Prevention	

Implementation Actions	Completed Y/N	Evidence of Implementation	Evidence Y/N
Presentation 1: The Vision of a Continuum of Behavior Support	✓		✓
1. The Foundations Team has reviewed Presentation 2 within the last 3 years and is prepared to support and enhance three components: (a) a building- or district-based plan to support a classroom management model, (b) clarity from building-based administrators on what they will monitor when visiting classrooms (e.g., posted expectations, student on-task behavior, respectful behavior from and between staff and students, and whether student behavior meets posted expectations), and (c) nonevaluative coaching support for teachers who want assistance with classroom management and student behavior.	☐	Foundations Process: Meeting Minutes	☐
2. The Foundations Team has developed (or reviewed, if already developed) a written statement that summarizes staff beliefs about student behavior and staff responsibility to support responsible student behavior. These beliefs are communicated to all new staff and briefly reviewed with all returning staff each year.	☐	Foundations Process: Meeting Minutes Staff Handbook: Staff Beliefs	☐
3. The Foundations Team and building- and district-based interventionists have reviewed Presentation 4 and determined whether and how to develop, adopt, and annually review with staff a protocol of early-stage interventions. All teachers review this protocol annually and receive training. All school-based interventionists are trained to encourage and require implementation of these early-stage strategies before moving to more structured and intensive problem-solving and intervention processes.	☐	Foundations Process: Meeting Minutes Staff Handbook: Early-Stage Interventions	☐
4. Within the last 3 years, the Foundations Team and all school-based interventionists have reviewed Presentations 5 and 6 and evaluated the school's Multi-Tiered System of Support (MTSS), including problem-solving processes and the continuum of intervention support for students. These processes are fully integrated with academic MTSS or Response to Intervention (RTI). Based on that review and evaluation process, adjustments are made as needed.	☐	Foundations Process: Meeting Minutes	☐
5. The Foundations Team and, if applicable, a district-based team have reviewed Presentation 7 within the last 3 years and have developed or revised a plan for long-term implementation and sustainability of effective behavior support and continuous improvement.	☐	Foundations Process: Meeting Minutes, Planning Calendar	☐

Implementation Actions	Completed Y/N	Evidence of Implementation	Evidence Y/N
Presentation 2: Supporting Classroom Behavior—The Three-Legged Stool	✓		✓
1. The Foundations Team has discussed whether the school or district has an adopted classroom management model. If so, the team has evaluated whether: • All teachers new to the school or district receive training. • All returning staff members get a refresher course. • Staff discuss the model strategies when problem solving. • There are multiple opportunities for reviewing, applying, and extending the model. If the answer to any of the above items is no, the team has discussed actions and goals. If the school or district has not adopted a classroom management model, the Foundations Team has discussed whether the school could benefit from one, and, if so, actions they might take to move the school or district toward adopting one.	☐	Foundations Process: Meeting Minutes File information about the adopted model in: • Foundations Archive: Classroom Management Model • Staff Handbook: Classroom Management Model	☐
2. The Foundations Team has determined whether building-based administrators will observe for the three student behaviors described in Task 2 (academic engagement, respectful interactions, and following classroom expectations). The team also has considered whether and how these observations fit within teacher evaluation practices. The Foundations Team and building-based administrators have communicated with staff about these expectations—specifically what administrators will observe for during walk-through visits to classrooms.	☐	Foundations Process: Meeting Minutes, Presentations/ Communication With Staff	☐
3. The Foundations Team, building administrators, instructional coaches, and lead teachers have developed a plan for using designated coaches, peer coaching, and a building-based facilitator to ensure that teachers get support and feedback to create continuous improvement in classroom management.	☐	Foundations Process: Meeting Minutes, Classroom Management Model	☐

Implementation Actions	Completed Y/N	Evidence of Implementation	Evidence Y/N
Presentation 3: Articulating Staff Beliefs and Solidifying Universal Procedures	✓		✓
1. The Foundations Team has developed a process and timeline for involving the staff in developing a statement of staff beliefs.	☐	Foundations Process: Meeting Minutes, Staff Beliefs	☐
2. School staff have developed a statement of staff beliefs about behavior support practices.	☐	Include final adopted statement of staff beliefs in: • Foundations Archive: Mission Statement/Staff Beliefs/Team Purpose • Staff Handbook: Staff Beliefs • Student and Parent Handbook: Staff Beliefs	☐
3. Staff beliefs are celebrated, highly visible, and reviewed each year.	☐	Foundations Process: Planning Calendar	☐
4. The Foundations Team and the administrator have identified and implemented ideas for using the statement of staff beliefs in administrative reviews and coaching. They have implemented school rituals and traditions that incorporate the statement of staff beliefs.	☐	Foundations Process: Staff Beliefs	☐
Presentation 4: Early-Stage Interventions for General Education Classrooms			
1. The Foundations Team, support staff, and principal (or district administrators) have agreed on the interventions to include in the early-stage protocol.	☐	Foundations Process: Meeting Minutes	☐
2. All teachers and support staff have been trained on interventions in the early-stage protocol, including how and why to keep records of each intervention. Data Collection and Debriefing (or an equivalent) is a required intervention for most chronic behavior problems. Data must be charted before assistance is requested from support staff or problem-solving teams.	☐	Foundations Process: Presentations/Communications With Staff File final protocol, training plan and materials, and expectations for documentation in: • Foundations Archive: Interventions for Individual Students • Staff Handbook: Early-Stage Interventions	☐

Implementation Actions	Completed Y/N	Evidence of Implementation	Evidence Y/N
Presentation 5: Matching the Intensity of Your Resources to the Intensity of Student Needs	✓		✓
1. Universal screening to identify students at risk for internalizing and externalizing disorders is conducted one to three times each year. Results are used to match students' needs to available support resources. Screening results are archived on a secure server or other secure location.	☐	Foundations Archive: Support Available to Staff, Interventions for Individual Students	☐
2. Red-flag criteria such as office referrals, chronic absenteeism, and failing grades have been established and are used to identify students at risk of behavior problems or school failure. This information is used to match students' needs to available support resources.	☐	Foundations Archive: Support Available to Staff, Interventions for Individual Students	☐
3. All students identified as at risk, through either screening or red flags, are paired with a school-based professional staff member who serves as an advocate for matching student needs to school and community resources. Advocates meet regularly to discuss cases and evaluate student progress and possible intervention support.	☐	Foundations Archive: Support Available to Staff, Interventions for Individual Students	☐
4. A list of professionals (interventionists) and teams who may be involved in some aspect of problem solving has been created. Each person and team has written a brief job description that includes information about when, where, and how to best use the services.	☐	Foundations Archive: Support Available to Staff, Interventions for Individual Students, Job Descriptions	☐
5. Staff know when and how to work with interventionists and teams to ensure that student needs are met (e.g. when and how to access the school psychologist or school counselor).	☐	Foundations Process: Presentations/ Communications to Staff Staff Handbook: Staff Roles and Responsibilities, Available Support	☐

Implementation Actions	Completed Y/N	Evidence of Implementation	Evidence Y/N
Presentation 6: Problem-Solving Processes and Intervention Design	✓		✓
1. The Foundations Team has explored with the staff whether and how to use the 25-Minute Planning Process (or similar teacher-to-teacher problem-solving resource). If staff are in favor of using the process, a decision has been made to organize grade-level teams, one representative team, or some other team configuration. The 25-minute meetings occur regularly.	☐	Foundations Process: Meeting Minutes, Current Priorities File final procedures in Foundations Archive: Support Available to Staff, Interventions for Individual Students Staff Handbook: Available Support	☐
2. The Foundations Team and interventionists have discussed whether the Intervention Decision Guide: Teacher Interview (IDG:TI) or similar will be useful. If so, the team has determined: • Whether it will be implemented before or after a teacher-to-teacher problem-solving process such as the 25-Minute Planning Process. • Whether the teacher can decide whether to use the 25-Minute Planning Process or the IDG:TI and when. • Personnel who will serve as advocates and interventionists. Staff have been notified about the decision to use IDG:TI and have received training in how and when to use it.	☐	Foundations Process: Meeting Minutes, Current Priorities File final procedures in Foundations Archive: Support Available to Staff, Interventions for Individual Students Staff Handbook: Available Support	☐
3. Foundations Team, the administrator, interventionists, and appropriate district personnel have discussed whether the Intervention Decision Guide: Multidisciplinary Team (IDG:MDT) will be useful. If so, they have: • Established the order in which early-stage interventions, 25-Minute Planning Process, IDG:TI, and IDG:MDT are used. • Identified personnel who will serve as advocates, interventionists, and case managers.	☐	Foundations Archive: Support Available to Staff Staff Handbook: Available Support	☐

Implementation Actions	Completed Y/N	Evidence of Implementation	Evidence Y/N
Presentation 6 (*continued*) • Identified who will serve on the multidisciplinary team. Determined criteria for rerferring a situation to the multidisciplinary team. • (Optional) Created a flowchart to visualize this process. • Shared with staff the decision to use IDG:MDT, provided training in when to use it, and explained how to access the services.	✓		✓
Presentation 7: Sustainability and District Support			
1. On completing each *Foundations* module, the Foundations Team works through that module's Implementation Checklist. In addition, each checklist is completed at least every 3 years to assess the effectiveness of procedures and implementation. The Foundations Team completes the Foundations Implementation Rubric and Rubric Summary (Form F-01) annually. For any items on the rubric that are not being implemented, a plan for working through the corresponding module of *Foundations* has been established. If a checklist reveals weak implementation, the team reviews that module and considers revising policies and procedures or motivating staff to implement current policies and procedures.	☐	Foundations Process: Foundations Implementation Rubric and Summary and Module Implementation Checklists, Planning Calendar Foundations Archive: Long-Term Planning Calendar	☐
2. At the end of each school year, the Foundations Team uses the End-of-Year Game Plan (Form F-29) to assess work to date and plan for renewed implementation at the beginning of the new year. This can be done in conjunction with working through the Foundations Implementation Rubric:	☐	Foundations Process: Meeting Minutes, Presentations/ Communications With Staff, Planning Calendar	☐
3. Key district staff have considered forming a district team to coordinate efforts with other district initiatives, set districtwide priorities, and ensure implementation of Foundations in all district schools.	☐		
4. The district-based Foundations Team has discussed ways to encourage the district to use the Talking Points document (F-32a) with principals when conducting school walk-through visits.	☐		

APPENDIX C
Guide to Module F
Reproducible Forms and Samples

The CD provided with this book contains many materials to help you implement *Foundations*. A thumbnail of the first page of each form or sample appears in this appendix. Most forms can be completed electronically. See the Using the CD file for more information about using fillable forms. Unless otherwise noted, all files are in PDF format.

Folders included on the CD are:

- Forms (F-01 through F-35)
  ◦ Fillable Forms
  ◦ Print Forms
  ◦ Word Form
- Samples (F-36 and F-37)
- PowerPoint Presentations (F1 through F7)
  ◦ F1 Vision.pptx
  ◦ F2 Classroom Behavior.pptx
  ◦ F3 Staff Beliefs.pptx
  ◦ F4 Early-Stage Interventions.pptx
  ◦ F5 Match Resources to Needs.pptx
  ◦ F6 Problem-Solving Processes.pptx
  ◦ F7 Sustainability.pptx

Forms
(F-01 to F-35)

F-01 *Foundations Implementation Rubric and Summary (8 pages)*

F-02 *Implementation Checklist (29 pages)*

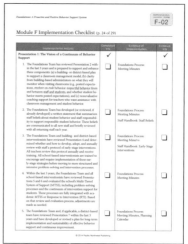

Form F-03 *CHAMPS Implementation Requirements, Grades K–8*

Form F-04 *DSC Implementation Requirements, Grades 9–12*

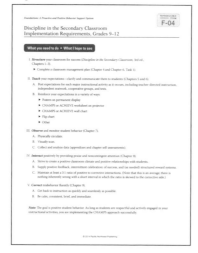

F-05 *Creating a Statement of Staff Beliefs: Authors' Response to Question 1*

F-06 *Creating a Statement of Staff Beliefs: Authors' Response to Question 2 (2 pages)*

F-05 *Creating a Statement of Staff Beliefs: Authors' Response to Question 3 (2 pages)*

F-08 *Clarify Staff Beliefs: Alternative Development Plan (3 pages)*

346

Module F: Establishing and Sustaining a Continuum of Behavior Support

F-09 *Staff Beliefs Nomination Form (Word format)*

F-10 *Discussion Record*

F-11a *Student Status Report, Version 1*

F-11b *Student Status Report, Version 2*

F-12a *Academic Assistance, Version 1 (One-page form)*

F-12b *Academic Assistance, Version 2 (Two-page form)*

F-13 *Long-Range Goal Setting*

F-14a *Goal Setting, Version 1*

F-14b *Goal Setting, Version 2*

F-14c *Goal Setting, Version 3*

F-14d *Goal Setting, Version 4*

F-14e *Goal Setting, Version 5*

F-14f *Goal Setting, Version 6 (2 pages)*

F-15 *Behavior Counting Form*

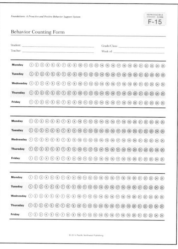

F-16 *Misbehavior Recording Sheet, Daily by Student Name*

F-17 *Misbehavior Recording Sheet, Weekly by Student Name*

F-18 *Countoon Behavior Counting Form*

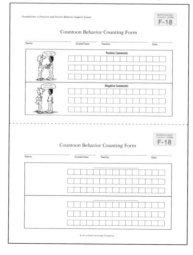

F-19a *Interval Chart/Scatterplot, Version 1*

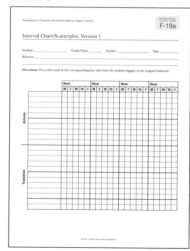

_F-19b_ _Interval Chart/Scatterplot,_
Version 2

_F-19c_ _Interval Chart/Scatterplot,_
Version 3

_F-19d_ _Interval Chart/Scatterplot,_
Version 4

_F-20_ _Rating Scale_

_F-21_ _Participation Evaluation Record_

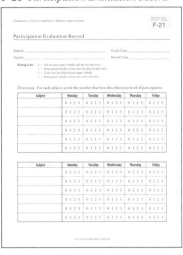

_F-22a_ _Plan for Connecting and_
Motivating (2 pages)

_F-22b_ _Plan for Connecting and_
Motivating With Bullet Points (2 pages)

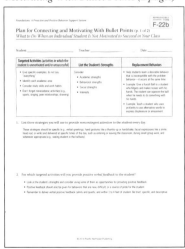

_F-23a_ _Ratios of Positive Interactions_
Monitoring Form, During a Particular
Time of Day

_F-23b_ _Ratios of Positive Interactions_
Monitoring Form, With a Particular
Student

F-23c *Ratios of Positive Interactions Monitoring Form, For a Particular Behavior*

F-24 *STOIC Intervention Planning Form (2 pages)*

F-25 *25-Minute Planning Process Worksheet (2 pages)*

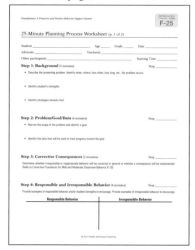

F-26 *Corrective Procedures for Mild and Moderate Classroom Behavior (4 pages)*

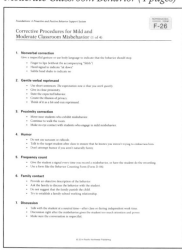

F-27 *Intervention Decision Guide: Teacher Interview Worksheet (4 pages)*

F-28 *Intervention Decision Guide: Multidisciplinary Team Worksheet (5 pages)*

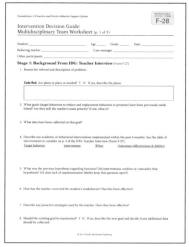

F-29 *End-of-Year Game Plan (15 pages)*

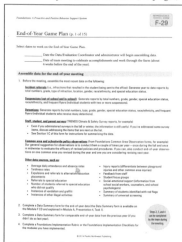

F-30 *Common Area Observation (4 pages)*

F-31 *Data Summary Form (4 pages)*

F-32a *Talking Points for Implementation of Foundations and CHAMPS During and After Year 1*

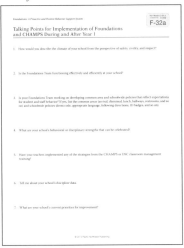

F-32b *Talking Points for Implementation of Foundations and CHAMPS During and After Year 1, Bulleted (2 pages)*

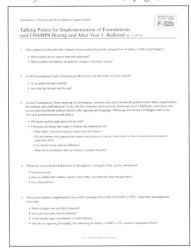

F-33 *District-Based Foundations Team: Decisions and Tasks to Consider (2 pages)*

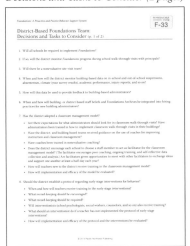

F-34 *CHAMPS and DSC Implementation Rubric*

F-35 *Classroom Management STOIC Checklist (4 pages)*

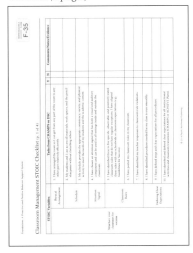

Samples
(F-36 and F-37)

F-36 *Flowchart for Tier 2 and Tier 3 Behavior Interventions Protocol*

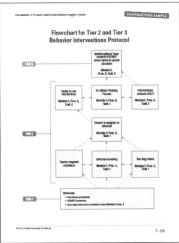

F-37 *Statements of Staff Beliefs from Four Schools (2 pages)*

PowerPoint Presentations
(F1 to F7)